DISPUTE RESOLUTION

DISPUTE RESOLUTION

CARL BAUDENBACHER (ED.)

www.germanlawpublishers.com
International Law Edition

ISBN 978-3-941389-03-8

The Deutsche Nationalbibliothek lists this publication in the Deutsche Nationalbibliografie; detailed bibliographic data are available on the Internet at http://dnb.d-nb.de.

© 2009 German Law Publishers, Stuttgart

All rights reserved. No part of this publication may be reproduced, translated, stored in a retrieval system or transmitted, in any form or by any means, electronic, mechanical, photo-copying, recording or otherwise, without prior permission of the publisher.

Typesetting: GreenTomato GmbH, Stuttgart
Printing and binding: Druckhaus »Thomas Müntzer«, Neustädter Straße 1–4, 99947 Bad Langensalza

Preface

In October 2008, the International Dispute Settlement Conference, which was held for the third time in the last few years, was generously hosted by the City of St. Gallen, which followed in the steps of Austin, TX and Salzburg. Renowned experts from all over the world, attended the International Dispute Settlement Conference to discuss and debate the newest developments in the field of dispute resolution.

Dispute resolution touches upon key aspects of law, politics and business, which alludes to its practical significance and its high grade of interdisciplinarity, a feature that we, at the University of St. Gallen, hold very dear. There are even plans under way to set up a center for international dispute resolution.

The editor of this book is deeply indebted to the speakers and moderators. Without their contributions and personal support the International Dispute Settlement Conference as well as this publication would not have been possible.

The conference did justice to the numerous aspects of dispute resolution by inviting speakers with different professional backgrounds and integrating plural opinions in honest but friendly discussions. After a warm welcome by ERNST MOHR the conference was opened by DIDIER PFIRTER, who spoke about diplomatic conflict resolution. Under the panel topic "Diplomacy v. arbitration and adjudication", SVEN NORBERG first dealt with disputes in intergovernmental economic relations. NICOLAOS LAVRANOS delivered his view on misguided judicial deference by the ECJ and ECrtHR. The focus is concluded with the contribution by PATRICIA HANSEN that provides perspectives on diplomacy, arbitration and adjudication from the United States and Latin America. DIANA PANKE, PAUL MAHONEY and RETO MALACRIDA gave insightful presentations on the topic of "Effect, non-compliance and enforcement of judgments of international/supranational courts". JACQUELINE RIFFAULT-SILK concluded the first day with her keynote speech on the relation of international/supranational and national law under special consideration of competition law. At the beginning of the second day I had the pleasure of delivering my keynote speech on dialogue between high courts. This was followed by the contributions of MARK VILLIGER, PHILIPPE VLAEMMINCK and HJALTE RASMUSSEN on the topic of "Proportionality and the margin of appreciation: National standards v. harmonization by international courts". Later ALAN RAU, CHRISTOPH SCHREUER, THOMAS COTTIER and myself examined the topic of "arbitration and adjudication". The conference concluded with the expertise of JACQUES BOURGEOIS, who shed light on the question of whether the WTO dispute settlement system was embedded in public international law.

Finally, I want to thank those who assisted in the planning, organization and coordination of the International Dispute Settlement Conference, namely BENJAMIN RHYNER, PHILIPP SPEITLER, CHRISTIAN MAYER, FELIPE PÉREZ POSE and FRANK BREMER. In particular, I would like to mention SIMON PLANZER, who was in charge of preparing this conference, not only with regard to organisation, he was also heavily involved in the substance of the conference. Additionally, I would also like to express my warmest thanks to FELIPE PÉREZ POSE and WIKTORIA FURRER for the valuable help in the editing and preparation of this book.

St. Gallen / Luxemburg, June 2009 *Carl Baudenbacher*

Table of Contents

Preface	V
Authors	XI
Moderators	XIII
Welcome ERNST MOHR	15
Keynote	19
Diplomatic Conflict Resolution DIDIER PFIRTER	21
Discussion	25
Focus: Diplomacy v. Arbitration and Adjudication	37
Introduction RUTH MACKENZIE	39
Disputes in Intergovernmental Economic Relations of a Traditional Character and in those with Supranational Mechanisms, Respectively SVEN NORBERG	43
On Misguided Judicial Deference by the ECJ and ECrtHR NIKOLAOS LAVRANOS	53
Perspectives on Diplomacy, Arbitration and Adjudication from the United States and Latin America PATRICIA HANSEN	65
Discussion	73

Focus: Effect, Non-Compliance and Enforcement of Judgments of International/Supranational Courts   79

Introduction   81
ULRICH HALTERN

The European Court of Justice as an Instance of High Legalisation:
What Have We Learned on the Prospects to Foster Compliance with EU Law?   83
DIANA PANKE

The European Court of Human Rights as a Case-Study   95
PAUL MAHONEY

Legal Consequences of Non-Compliance with Dispute Settlement Decisions:
The Case of the WTO as a "Benefits-Centred" Organization   119
RETO MALACRIDA

Discussion   143

Keynote   151

The Relation of International / Supranational and National Law:
The Case of Competition Law   153
JACQUELINE RIFFAULT-SILK

Discussion   169

Keynote   173

Some Considerations on the Dialogue between High Courts   175
CARL BAUDENBACHER

Discussion   191

Focus: Proportionality and the Margin of Appreciation: National Standards v. Harmonization by International Courts   201

Introduction   203
CARL BAUDENBACHER

Proportionality and the Margin of Appreciation:
National Standard Harmonization by International Courts   207
MARK VILLIGER

Discretionary Power of States in the ECJ & EFTA Court: The Difficult Case of Gambling Services PHILIPPE VLAEMMINCK	215
Why Deprive the European Judges their National Brethren of their Treaty-Given Competence to Perform Proportionality-Review? HJALTE RASMUSSEN	223
Discussion	233

Focus: Arbitration and Adjudication — 243

Introduction GABRIELLE KAUFMANN-KOHLER	245
Underlying Tensions in the Field of Arbitration ALAN RAU	247
Investment Arbitration CHRISTOPH SCHREUER	257
Arbitration in Public International Disputes CARL BAUDENBACHER / FRANK BREMER	265
The WTO Dispute Settlement System: From Arbitration to a World Court System THOMAS COTTIER	299
Discussion	303

Keynote — 309

The World Trade Organization Dispute Settlement System: Embedded In Public International Law? JACQUES BOURGEOIS / RAVI SOOPRAMANIEN	311
Discussion	357

Authors

PROF. DR. Carl Baudenbacher, President of the EFTA Court, Professor of Law and Director of the Institute of European and International Business Law EUR-HSG, University of St. Gallen

DR. JACQUES BOURGEOIS, Advocaat, Wilmer, Cutler, Pickering, Hale & Dorr LLP (Brussels), Professor at the College of Europe (Bruges)

ASS. IUR. FRANK BREMER, LL.M. (Liverpool), Research Associate at the Institute of European and International Business Law, University of St. Gallen

PROF. DR. THOMAS COTTIER, Professor at the University of Berne, Panelist in various dispute settlements in WTO/GATT, Director of the Institute of European and International Economic Law, Director of the World Trade Institute and of the MILE programme (Master of International Law and Economics), Dean of the Faculty of Law of the University of Berne

PROF. PATRICIA HANSEN, JD, MPA, AB, J. Waddy Bullion Professor of Law at the University of Texas School of Law, Austin, Director of the dual degree programme in Law and Latin American Studies

DR. NIKOLAOS LAVRANOS, LL.M., Max Weber Fellow, European University Institute, Florence

PAUL MAHONEY, President of the European Civil Service Tribunal (Luxembourg), former Registrar of the European Court of Human Rights (Strasbourg)

DR. RETO MALACRIDA, Counsellor, WTO Legal Affairs Division

DR. DR. H.C. SVEN NORBERG, Senior Advisor KREAB Strategic Communication Counsellors, Brussels, Former Director in DG Competition of the EC Commission, Former Judge of the EFTA Court

DR. DIANA PANKE, Lecturer in European Politics, School of Politics and International Relations, University College Dublin

HIS EXCELLENCY DR. DIDIER PFIRTER, Ambassador at Large for Special Assignments (including Middle East and Columbia), former Special Envoy of Federal

Council for the issue of the Emblems of the Geneva Conventions, former Legal Advisor of the UN Secretary General's Good Offices on Cyprus ("Annan Plan")

PROF. DR. HJALTE RASMUSSEN, Professor at the University of Copenhagen, Honorary Jean Monnet Professor of European Law

PROF. ALAN RAU, Burg Family Professor of Law at the University of Texas School of Law, Austin, Panelist on the Commercial and International Panels of the American Arbitration Association

JACQUELINE RIFFAULT-SILK, Judge at the French Cour de Cassation, Paris

RAVI SOOPRAMANIEN, Barrister, LL.B., King's College London (Hons); LL.M., London School of Economics (with Distinction); M.I.L.E., World Trade Institute (*Summa Cum Laude*)

PROF. DR. CHRISTOPH SCHREUER, Professor at the University of Vienna

PROF. DR. MARK VILLIGER, Judge at the European Court of Human Rights in respect of the Principality of Liechtenstein, "Titularprofessor" at the University of Zurich

PHILIPPE VLAEMMINCK, Attorney at Law, Head of the Law office Vlaemminck & Partners, Brussels

Moderators

PROF. DR. CARL BAUDENBACHER, President of the EFTA Court, Professor of Law and Director of the Institute of European and International Business Law EUR-HSG, University of St. Gallen

PROF. DR. ULRICH HALTERN, Professor and Chair at Leibniz University of Hannover, Director of the Hannover Institute for National and Transnational Integration Studies

PROF. DR. GABRIELLE KAUFMANN-KOHLER, Professor at the University of Geneva, Director of the Geneva Master in International Dispute Settlement, Attorney at law and Partner with Levy Kaufmann-Kohler, Geneva, Honorary President and former Chair of ASA, Member of ICCA, the ICC Court of International Arbitration and of the Board of the AAA

RUTH MACKENZIE, BSc, LL.M., UCL, London, Deputy Director and Principal Research Fellow, Centre for International Courts and Tribunals, University College London

Welcome

ERNST MOHR[1]

Distinguished speakers, Dear participants, Dear Carl, I am delighted to welcome you at this year's International Dispute Settlement Conference in St. Gallen. The University of St. Gallen proudly presents you in the next two days a conference with outstanding speakers and moderators. The conference will deal with burning topics which await proposals for solutions. The conference will also offer you, dear speakers and participants, the opportunity to meet and exchange views in an enjoyable setting. I am glad that we can use for that purpose the facilities of the Canton of St. Gallen while our university campus is under heavy reconstruction.

Prof. Baudenbacher has chaired this conference in the last few years, first in Austin, Texas and then in Salzburg. This year, St. Gallen is proudly hosting the conference. It aims at bringing together leading experts from the field of dispute settlement and an international body of participants. We have participants originating from not just numerous countries but also several continents, including Asia as well as Northern and Latin America. The same goes for the speakers and panel chairs with present and former judges from international and national courts, professors from Europe and the US, and other distinguished experts.

The University of St. Gallen was founded 1898 in the heydays of the Swiss textile industry, to train the young in what was then the most advanced global industry. Quite naturally it developed into an international university with a strong focus on management, economics, law and international relations. By now, more than 6000 students from over 80 nations are enrolled.

As a Swiss cantonal university we are a public university. But as such we earn more than 50% of our income from sources outside the public sector, which is due to our strong links with the world of practice. Our alumni network has 18'000 members interconnecting via more than 50 alumni clubs worldwide.

As an international university under cantonal ownership, strengthening our roots in and links with the region is essential. I am therefore glad that the conference can take place in St. Gallen and in the beautiful surroundings of its abbey precinct hosting one of the world's oldest and most precious medieval libraries.

Thank you Carl for making this possible.

---

1 Rector of the University of St. Gallen.

In this futuristic hall, built by the Spanish architect Santiago Calatrava, we are next to the former wine cellar of the old abbey. That brings us right back to the topic of the conference. Dispute settlement, especially economically sound dispute settlement has a very long tradition in our region, it may even have been invented here.

During the so-called Appenzell wars, lasting over the first quarter of the 15th century, between the prince abbot and his recalcitrant peasants from the surrounding mountains, the abbatical troops once killed some 40 mercenaries having come from a region which is now known as the Canton of Schwyz, in support of the recalcitrant peasants, troops which actually were notorious in looting for prey.

Their captain ordered to bury them on a nearby cemetery, which resulted in fierce opposition from the village people, because the notorious troops from the Canton of Schwyz had been under papal excommunication.

The village people feared that the funeral would lead to a desecration of their cemetery. This dispute got fiercer when the captain threatened to burn down their church if they opposed the funeral.

But the village priest then settled the dispute by calming down his people with the economic argument that it will be much cheaper to consecrate the cemetery a second time compared to building up a new church.

Ladies and gentlemen, you can now imagine that economically sound dispute settlement looks back on a long tradition in this part of the world and I am glad that it is back once again in St. Gallen. And I am looking forward that you all will come again in the years to come.

It is now my pleasure to present you our first keynote speaker: His Excellency, Ambassador Dr. Didier Pfirter.

Didier Pfirter has been Ambassador at Large for Special Assignments, including conflicts in the Middle East and in Columbia. Formerly, he was the Special Envoy of the Swiss government for the issue of the Emblems of the Geneva Conventions. Those negotiations about a new emblem of the International Red Cross, alongside the Red Cross and the Red Crescent, resulted in December 2005 in the creation of the Red Crystal.

Ambassador Pfirter was also involved in the negotiations for the so-called "Annan Plan" on the conflict in Cyprus.

By the way, Kofi Annan has visited the University of St. Gallen in December 2007 on the occasion of receiving the Freedom Price of the Max Schmidheiny Foundation.

Ambassador Pfirter just recently took up his new position as the ambassador of Switzerland to Columbia. He has consequently acquired a rich experience in dispute settlement and I am keen to hear what he will tell us in his keynote speech on diplomatic conflict resolution.

I wish you all an inspiring and productive conference and a pleasant stay in St. Gallen. I now give the floor to his Excellency, Ambassador Dr. Didier Pfirter.

Keynote

Diplomatic Conflict Resolution

DIDIER PFIRTER[1]

Indeed I feel most honoured to have been invited to give the keynote address to this illustrious gathering. As a lawyer by training and a diplomat by vocation, the subject of this conference is of great interest to me. In search of ways to resolve conflicts I studied law and specialised in International and Comparative Constitutional Law. And aiming to convince rather than fight or impose, I then became a diplomat. I would however hold that the boundary between the different forms of conflict resolution is much more fluid than one might at first sight think.

Diplomatic conflict resolution can hardly be successful without a good dose of pressure and thus imposition. While arbitration and adjudication can hardly be imposed if they are not based on convincing arguments at least in the international sphere. Diplomatic conflict resolution can include arbitration. In the 19th Century the Swiss Federal Council was for instance asked to fix the border between Brazil and British Guiana and between Colombia and Venezuela. Courts can find themselves to some extent in a mediating role, so the International Court of Justice in the North Sea Continental Shelf Case of the Federal Republic of Germany against the kingdoms of Denmark and the Netherlands in 1969. And diplomatically mandated adjudicating commissions, like the UN Boundary Commission for Ethiopia and Eritrea, established by the Algiers cease-fire agreement in 2000, can find themselves in the uncomfortable position of being bound by their mandate, like a court by the law, to take a decision – in this case over the little town of Badme – which they themselves do not find necessarily the most appropriate and wise under the circumstances and which may well fuel the conflict rather than resolve it.

While courts and arbiters tend to apportion right and wrong, diplomatic mediators must seek to convince both parties to obtain their agreement. In doing so they must be guided by the law, they must also often deviate from a strict implementation of legal principles if one of the parties is strong enough or circumstances otherwise make it seem appropriate. This can give diplomatic mediators clear advantages over judges and arbiters in the real world, but it also exposes them to sometimes aggressive criticism and painful agonising over the right thing to do. How many lives should be put at risk to uphold legal principles? And how far can one go in giving in to might for the sake of saving lives?

---

1   Ambassador at Large for Special Assignments (including Middle East and Columbia), former Special Envoy of Federal Council for the issue of the Emblems of the Geneva Conventions, former Legal Advisor of the UN Secretary General's Good Offices on Cyprus ("Annan Plan").

The archetype of diplomatic conflict resolution is, of course, the pure facilitation or mediation. Its success naturally depends on numerous circumstances extraneous to the facilitation or mediation, but also on the mediator's skills. She or he must firstly gain the trust of the parties. Only then can she or he tackle the substance of the conflict. Profound knowledge of the facts and their history is a prerequisite in this endeavour, but equally if not more important are psychological skills and namely a great capacity for empathy. The reality of conflicts consists of shades of grey. The more one dives into it, the more one realises that there is little black and white. The press and the political discourse tend to obfuscate this. Conflicts are usually complex situations, where much more wrong has been done by and to both sides than can possibly be redressed through any solution. Solutions therefore tend to be bitter pills, unsatisfactory to both parties if they are to be somewhat balanced. A mediator or even a mere facilitator can therefore, in my opinion, only succeed if she or he is capable of putting her or himself in the shoes of the people on both sides of the divide, of feeling their pain, their anguish and most treasured aspirations; all of which are usually nurtured by a complex and often bitter history perceived through glasses much tainted by legend, glorification, vilification and manipulation. It is of little avail to stick to the dry historic facts as they are not what shape the thinking of the parties. One must therefore be able to see the conflict with the eyes of the parties, as they have come to see it, based on their actual or imagined collective experience.

The comparison that comes to mind when I try to assess the required empathic capacity is that of an actor, who can only do a convincing job if she or he can truly identify with the role she or he has to impersonate. This must however, in my opinion, not go as far as to adopt the position of the parties in one's discourse with them. Though many mediators do precisely this, and are often temporarily successful with this tactic. The mediator should instead strive to reconcile the positions also on the emotional level, and ideally succeed in presenting a consolidated view of all aspects of the conflict which both sides can identify with. This is, especially in the beginning, certainly the harder way as parties tend to hear much more loudly the aspects of this consolidated vision that represent the view of the other side. In the long run, I consider it to be a more successful approach, however, than that of double-talk, which is bound to eventually blow up in one's face.

The second quality that I consider crucial for a diplomatic mediator or facilitator is creativity. If conflicts were easy to resolve, one would not need mediators. When one tries to tackle old and entrenched conflicts, one is walking a mine field. It starts with terminology. Innocent words become red rags capable of causing mortal offence and the inadvertent use of the wrong term can prematurely end a mediator's tenure. Many things have already been tried and rejected by either side, if not by both. The German language with its ease for creating new terminology is thus a useful mother tongue for a would-be mediator, even if mediations nowadays are mostly conducted in the language of Shakespeare.

As indispensable as these requirements may be, they will not be enough to convince a horse to drink if it is not thirsty. And combat horses have an amazing faculty for not being thirsty. And they are most rarely thirsty at the same time as their adversary. In Cyprus the conventional mediator's wisdom was that there had never been two leaders at the negotiating table who actually wanted to solve the conflict. There were occasionally such leaders on both sides, but they were never lucky to face an equally willing counterpart. Often enough the mediator seems to be the only "thirsty" person at the table. *"Now Mr. No will talk to Mr. Never"*, a Turkish Cypriot opposition leader once commented a change in leadership on the Greek Cypriot side. Though he failed to say who was who in his eyes. Chances look good that for the first time in almost 50 years there are now two thirsty leaders on the island.

If a diplomatic mediator has no means to increase the thirst of the parties to the conflict resolution, her or his chances of ultimate success are minimal. Such is the situation of small state mediators like Switzerland. Having no means of pressure certainly increases the credibility of the mediator and makes her or him an ideal choice if both parties are truly longing for a solution. Even where this is not the case, an uninterested mediator can make an important contribution to building some trust between the parties and to narrowing the gap. If ultimate success will more often than not elude them, they nonetheless play a crucial role in defusing explosive situations and preparing the ground for solutions.

Some diplomatic mediators are however in a position of turning up the heat under the parties to increase their thirst for solving the conflict. This is obviously the case of regional or global powers. It is also, depending on the circumstances, the case of regional or global multilateral actors such as OSCE, AU or the United Nations. Under specific circumstances it can even be the case of small states. As depository of the Geneva Conventions, Switzerland plays a special role in the development of international humanitarian law and this position can considerably enhance its capacity to resolve conflicts in that field if it acts in close cooperation with other interested nations.

In the course of my career, I have been in almost all possible positions in which a diplomatic mediator or facilitator can be; a fly on the wall as legal advisor and number two of the United Nations Secretary General's Good Offices for Cyprus and later a virtual arbiter in the same capacity when the United Nations had been requested by the parties, under some pressure from the United States and the EU, to complete a plan that would be submitted to referendum if the parties could not agree by a certain date. Working for the Swiss government, I had an inverted experience and keenly felt the difference between first acting on behalf of the depository of the Geneva Conventions in solving the issue of the emblems recognised by those conventions and later as the special envoy of Switzerland for the different conflicts in the Middle East. It is not obvious to me which position is preferable, from a personal point of view. Less clout may bring frustration, but also more freedom and room for creativity. More clout comes with obvious importance which may soothe the ego, but also with the burden of a huge responsibility which is not easy to bear.

It is in these latter positions that one can imagine how judges and arbiters must feel.

Discussion

CARL BAUDENBACHER
Thank you very much, Ambassador Pfirter, for this wonderful first speech. I might add that there is a community now building up, particularly in the United States but also in Europe, dealing with what is usually referred to as judicialisation of international law. This community consists of more or less the same faces and whenever they talk about the topic, they always start with diplomacy and then they go on and say, *"but you know the key development is something else"*. The key development is judicialisation. More and more international courts, more and more judges become active and the diplomats are successively moving to the background. That is why we felt that it would make sense to have as a first keynote speaker a diplomat and we are particularly grateful that someone of your standing and with your experience has agreed to speak at our conference. I am convinced that your relatively short remarks have made it clear that the picture is much broader than just international courts. So I would like to open up for discussion.

BERNHARD EHRENZELLER
You gave a very interesting explanation of the possibilities of mediation in the diplomatic world and especially of the role of Switzerland in that kind of dispute settlement. But in these months, in the last few years perhaps, there were some problems regarding the notoriety of Switzerland as a mediator. The public seemed to have some doubts about whether Switzerland as a mediator has really been neutral. Could you perhaps comment on that?

A judge is independent, however, a mediator after months and months of mediation possibly gets closer to one party than to the other. Considering the means of mediation – official, unofficial and informal –, the question comes up, if mediation is really the right way to resolve some conflicts.

DIDIER PFIRTER
Are you referring to any specific conflict, are you referring to Columbia? It is what I said at some point in my address that if you try to have a balanced view and to see both sides' pain and legitimate aspirations and to express them in a consolidated discourse, the parties inevitably will tend to hear what they do not like much more loudly than what they like. This is precisely the drawback of being in a neutral position. As a matter of fact, Columbia has never accused Switzerland of not being neutral; it has accused us of being too neutral. These were the words of the Columbian High Commissioner for Peace. In the view of the Columbian government, there is a conflict between a

democratically elected legitimate government and a criminal gang of drug dealers and hijackers and it is not appropriate for a self-respecting state with a long democratic tradition like Switzerland to be neutral between two such parties. What they failed to understand, I think, is that it is one thing where Switzerland stands as a state in the international community, where our place clearly has to be with the democratically elected government of Columbia and there can be no doubt that the current Columbian government and the current Columbian President enjoy overwhelming support of the Columbian population. It is something else if you are officially mandated by the government of Columbia to play a role in resolving aspects of the conflict, that there in this particular specific role you must be neutral. You cannot say *"we are on the side of the government but now we are going to try and solve the conflict between the government and the guerrillas"*. And this is a situation in which one finds oneself often. We also found ourselves in the same dilemma with the UN in Cyprus.

I would contest, however, what you said, that the more you are involved the more sympathetic you tend to become towards one side. My experience has rather been the opposite. It has been that when you start working with a conflict and you have necessarily partial knowledge, you are much influenced by the press and political discourse; you tend to have more sympathies towards one side. And the more you get to hear details and hear people out and see how they view things, what they went through, the more you can see that the truth is not black and white, but very complex and that from the subjective point of view of the parties they are both right.

NIKOLAOS LAVRANOS
My name is Nikos Lavranos. The name sounds Greek but I am not asking the question as a Greek with regard to Cyprus, let me state that clearly. I liked what you said, and I truly hope that there will be a quick solution to this problem, since, as an EC law expert, I find it very strange that one part of Cyprus is a member of the UN and the other part is somehow in a black hole. But to come back to the question, in regard to the proliferation of courts and tribunals and so forth – especially in the context of the Cyprus dispute – it appears to me, that there is also a proliferation of diplomats, of missions, of mediators and of all sorts of different parties. Can that be a problem in terms of overlap? And if so, can that kind of proliferation be an obstacle to a solution? In other words, would it not be better if only one mediator would try to get the job done?

DIDIER PFIRTER
I fully agree with you. It can be a problem. Parties tend to forum shop, of course, if they have a choice. And they tend to blackmail the would-be mediator by saying, *"well, if you are not doing it the way I like, there are others who are waiting"*. I do not think it was a problem in Cyprus, certainly not during the time I was involved. Many countries have special envoys for Cyprus. I did not have the impression that, save for probably two, they played much of a role. The UN was very much in the driving seat, I must say that Alvaro De Soto played his hand very well in this regard. Of course, in order to be in the driving seat when you do not really hold the cards, or certainly not all of

them, you have to closely work with those who do hold the cards in order to earn not only the trust of the parties, but also of those interested powers so that they let you be in the driving seat; which does not mean that we got instructions from those powers as has often been said and written by people who were not involved and who have not spoken to those who were involved. I can firmly assess here that all the decisions that were ever taken, regarding how things evolved and what was to be proposed in Cyprus were taken by the UN. Not one decision, in the positive sense, was imposed on the UN by any power which said you have to do this. There were a couple of situations where we did not do things that we might have otherwise done because we were advised not to do these things. So there was sort of a veto power if you want, of course never formalised, but there was never any manipulation or imposition of actions by outside powers on the UN.

And in my opinion, this model which Alvaro Del Soto has developed in his successful mediation in El Salvador, where he closely worked with the interested states, is a very promising one. One has to maintain a single shop, or one stop line if a mediation is to be successful and at the same time one cannot ignore the others if one wants them to grant you this status.

CARL BAUDENBACHER
May I just, before giving the floor to other people, add something, Ambassador? Even while you spoke previously, I was amazed by how many panels there seem to be between adjudication and diplomacy and now it turns out that there is more. Now, regarding the proliferation of courts and proliferation of diplomats, you said that there is also the parallel of a potential forum shopping, that the parties pick the forum which they think is most favourable to them. But on the other side, is there not also a development in progress in that mediators are offering themselves in order to attract parties? If I am not mistaken, the Swiss Foreign Minister has been accused by conservative politicians in this country of being too pro-active in offering Switzerland's services. That is something an international court can hardly do. But still, in the area of international courts, there are mechanisms by which you try to attract cases. Would you like to comment on this?

DIDIER PFIRTER
In the field in which I have worked we have never approached unwilling parties. For instance one new track that we started in the last two years was Lebanon. It was at the request of all the Lebanese parties. Unfortunately, to some extent, there are fewer would-be mediating states nowadays than before, during the Cold War. You have Sweden, you have Austria and Finland, who have become EU Member States and therefore members of a powerful group of nations which is rarely neutral – not even if it wanted to be; once you are too powerful you cannot really be neutral because your opinion carries so much weight. And at the same time, some of the divisions are growing deeper and it is for a country like Switzerland not only an opportunity to place itself in the international arena and make the best of its situation of not being a member of

the EU or NATO or other powerful groups, I would argue it is actually a responsibility. Other countries who are members of the EU carry their responsibilities in other ways. And being in the situation in which we are, we have to play a complimentary role and we have to try and build bridges. This is not – as some people tend to think, also in Switzerland – contrary to what others may do through the projection of power, through sanctions etc., it is complementary because sanctions are imposed and power is used or menaced in order to get people to change their positions and eventually acquiesce to a mediator's solution. But for this to happen you also need someone to build the bridges that these people eventually will have to cross, when sanctions or the use of power will have done their work.

DIANA PANKE

I have a rather personal question for Ambassador Pfirter. I would be interested in how you personally evaluate the effectiveness of diplomatic mediation vis-à-vis judicialised, legalised dispute settlement when it comes to the implementation phase. I myself, as political scientist, when thinking about parties, I think about unitary actors. Very often you have a government facing domestic veto players, in particular in conflicts where the government's abilities to act and implement things might be limited. And while diplomatic mediation might be extremely creative in finding a particular solution to a conflict, judicialised dispute settlement, legalised dispute settlement might have a big advantage in the implementation phase, because an authoritative judgement differentially empowers a government vis-à-vis domestic veto players. I was just interested in whether you see that the same way.

DIDIER PFIRTER

The main thing I would see in this context is that implementation is a phase in conflict resolution which is traditionally not given enough attention. Many good solutions have not been implemented because people concentrated so much on the substance of the solution and so little on how it will be implemented. So it is certainly a very important, crucial aspect.

There may be an advantage for judicial solutions in this field, because they tend to be clearer and more rigid, so that there can be less discussion. There is a vice among some mediators in that they think there is virtue in being ambiguous. I think it is the mother of all sins for a mediator. I am glad to have learned from Alvaro Del Soto that it is better to have painful truth and clarity before a solution is adopted, than start a new conflict the day after in haggling over what this ambiguity actually means. There may be an advantage in judicial solutions in that they can afford more easily to be absolutely clear.

ERICH SCHANZE

In your rich presentation you referred to creativity. And I just wonder whether you could possibly return to that notion. Is creativity more important than professional ideology? And what exactly do you mean by creativity? What is the relation between creativity and normativity in terms of the regularities you referred to in your speech? I got the impression, that the disputes that were effectively settled, mostly contained references to known cases and events. For instance, I worked with a person in the context of the Law of the Sea Conference who simply knew hundreds of stories and he used to settle conflicts in this very aggressive battlefield, simply by alluding to his extremely rich knowledge about past normativity. I wonder how you draw the line between normativity and creativity?

DIDIER PFIRTER
I do not think there is any antagony between the two concepts. In my opinion, a solution must be absolutely clear and unambiguous. The creativity comes in formulating things in such a way that they can be accepted by the parties, because they build up very antagonistic, very absolute positions and they build them up publicly so that they can tell you, *"well, I cannot possibly accept that, you know I have publicly told my people that never ever, only over my dead body"*. And then somehow you have to overcome this in order to come to what, as you say, may seem to be the obvious solution.

I would describe this in a way as squaring the circle; I think, in Switzerland we have developed a skill at this. We had a brief civil war between federalists and confederalists in the middle of the 19th Century. And the federalists who won were wise enough to build a clearly, purely federalist state, but to give as much trimmings and decorations to the confederalists so that they could eventually live with it. So they called the federation a confederation. They said that the Cantons were sovereign within the limits of the Constitution which precisely said that they were not sovereign. And many things like this.

We tried to do some of these things in Cyprus. A federation was out by the Turkish Cypriots. On the other hand, sovereignty for the constituent states was in and it was out for the Greek Cypriots. Eventually, we invented the word "sovereignly". Now the constituent states would sovereignly exercise their powers within the federal Constitution. Some people then argued that this was a word that did not exist and did not mean anything. We were lucky enough to find that Shakespeare had already used it and therefore it did very well exist and must mean something. These are the sort of things to which I allude. I think it is more in the way you present things but not only. For instance, there are clear dilemmas. You have a situation like in Cyprus where you have less than 20% Turkish Cypriots, you have more than 80% Greek Cypriots, where you have a history that the Turkish Cypriots had veto power on certain issues and none on others. On those latter issues the Greek Cypriots used to completely ignore the Turkish, going as far as adopting the Greek national anthem as the Cypriot national anthem. And then you try to find a way which on the one hand makes it necessary for the Greek Cypriots to take into account the view of the Turkish Cypriots and on the other hand also takes into account that there are four times more Greek than Turkish Cypriots and does avoid deadlocks. And there you do need a certain amount of creativity to come up with solutions that try to bridge this obvious dilemma.

ANNE VAN AAKEN

I have a question concerning the training in mediation. You talked about personal skills, which in my opinion are very important. I guess there is a lot of training on the job. But you also talked about the requirement of psychological skills. Now we know that for example national judges are getting more and more trained in mediation. Germany, for instance, has a whole mediation programme, which might lead to more legitimacy for this dispute settlement method. However, I am not sure about that. Could you comment on that?

Now mediation, as far as I know, is rather under-theorised. We do not really know how those things work. There is, however, quite a useful theory that very much comes back to what Ernst Mohr said, namely behavioural economics, which is a joint undertaking of psychologists and economists. And they are very much focused on looking for what kind of biases individuals have. As a reference point they take the rational individual. They demonstrate how many biases people at the mediation table have.

Now we know that people decide differently depending on how you frame the situation to them, how you frame losses they might incur or gains they might have. We do know people are overly optimistic. We do know that they have plenty of cognitive biases. And mediators would have the function of debiasing the errors people make in order to come to a solution. To put it more bluntly, they are able to show participants that there could be a positive sum game, they are not playing a zero sum game but there are possibilities of having a positive sum game. I guess this is also part of what you meant by creativity.

If there is this kind of theory and if there is mediation, let me come to my question, is there any training in the diplomatic service on mediation? Or is this just training on the job? And if there is training, what exactly would be the theory you would refer to in the training?

DIDIER PFIRTER

I am afraid you are asking the wrong person. I am not much of a believer in theoretical training and I have quite a bit of difficulty with the theories of mediation and the way they approach things. I believe more in talent and in learning by doing. I have been through a, fortunately, quite successful process between Israelis and Palestinians representing the whole political spectrum. It went from a founder of the settlement movement in the West Bank all the way to Islamists and they met and they engaged in a very, I would say, prosperous or promising process. We had professional mediators with us to help us in doing this but my impression was that they tend to treat the parties to the conflict like patients in a hospital. And these people of course are as intelligent, as wise, as learned as we are and they resent being treated like that and will not go along with it. So, I think you have to approach it differently. I would use the term *"emotional intelligence"* which has become sort of a fashionable term. People who are parties to a conflict feel so wronged and so misunderstood. If you can show them that you do understand them – but it has to be genuine, it cannot be phoney because they also realise this very quickly – but that you also understand the other side, that they are right does not necessarily mean that the other side is wrong and vice versa because things are more complex than this and one has to find a solution for a situation where they are both right but their two rights are difficult to reconcile. The subject that we had chosen was a Jewish state versus the Palestinian right of return. Both are very legitimate aspirations given the history of the two people but they are very difficult to reconcile.

You referred to creativity in that respect also and I think what is important in the mediator's job is firstly, you have to get the overall balance right, which is difficult enough. So in your first proposal, there has to be, as you said, more positive for both sides than negative. The difficulty in this, of course, is to give things to one side which are more important to that side, than the pain that they inflict on the other side. I think we did succeed in this in Cyprus; it may sound pretentious given the fact that the Annan Plan was rejected by 80% of the Greek Cypriots, but I hold that this was due to political circumstance rather than the content of the plan. The first plan was initially quite well received on the Greek Cypriot side and also virtually everybody on both sides confirmed to the UN in the four revisions that we did, that the plan had become better for their side than the previous one. So it is a bit surprising that after you improve the plan four times (as was admitted also by most Greek Cypriots) they will reject it when in the beginning they thought it was quite acceptable but in the meantime of course, circumstances had changed because the EU had decided to admit the Greek Cypriots by fault of the Turkish Cypriots who had not come on board in time.

When you make changes to a plan once it has been put on the table the sum of the changes has to be more positive for both, so again you have to make the changes in places where it gives a lot to one side and takes little from the other. And the more you do that, of course, the more difficult it becomes. Eventually you run out of further options: it is always a big gamble because it is very difficult to judge how people will ultimately perceive the changes that you make.

CARL BAUDENBACHER
Well, Ambassador, your answer proves that she did not ask the wrong person. There is another question here.

LUKAS RUSCH
My question may be a little bit blasphemous to the world of mediation and I guess it has to be placed somewhere between what you, Ambassador Pfirter, said and Prof. Ehrenzeller in consequence asked. You said that a mediator has to be neutral, which led Prof. Ehrenzeller to question, if that was even possible. What I want to ask, however, is *should* he be neutral? I mean usually when there is a conflict – for instance, between Palestine and Israel or between FARC and the Colombian government –, one state or one party is usually more powerful and can put more pressure on its position.

Now, would it not be pragmatic for a mediator to say, *"I'll make more concessions to the more powerful position instead of to the more sound and reasonable one"*? Because you said that the Colombian government complained that Switzerland was too neutral, which means that it was too balanced. So is that what mediators tend to do, sympathise with the more powerful party to more effectively solve the conflict?

DIDIER PFIRTER
Neutral may actually not be an ideal term because neutral implies also neutral in terms of values. Obviously, we cannot be neutral between a democratically elected government in a state of law and a group of people which for whatever political motives uses completely unacceptable illegal means. And we have to state that clearly, and I think we always did that in the case of Colombia.

When it comes to the conflict as such, however, we have to be impartial. When you suggest an exchange of prisoners, of course, the prisoners in the hands of the government are criminals, they violated the laws, they have been condemned by legal courts, whereas the prisoners in the hands of guerrillas are hostages, they are people who drove their cars on the street and were hijacked. They are not on equal footing. But once the parties have accepted that these people are to be exchanged, as unequal as their status may be, you have to act in an impartial way. You cannot be partial and try to cheat, then you cannot do your job. And I think this is all the more true for a small country like Switzerland which does not project power, or also, if you act – as I did – on behalf of an international organisation like the UN. It may be somewhat different for someone like the United States obviously. The United States in the Mid East conflict is both mediator and party. They are the chief sponsor of the state of Israel: there are stories that sometimes the US mediators jeopardised solutions which the Israelis might actually have accepted. And at the same time, they are basically the only really effective mediator because they are the only one that Israel will accept and the Arabs have learned to live with the situation. But this is, of course, a very different form of mediation than what a country like ours can do.

HANSPETER TSCHÄNI
My name is Hanspeter Tschäni. I work for the Swiss Government, for the SECO to be precise. I have a question that has to do with the time aspect of mediation. I think, the hero of modern times is probably the person who steps in, gets a quick fix done and then shows the results to the press. However, from my point of view, mediation should be more of a long drawn out process. You talked about Colombia, Cyprus, Palestine and Israel and the question I have is, how does one deal with it as a mediator? How does one deal with a process like Israel and Palestine that has been ongoing for 50 years and where the sustainability of a one time mediator is probably rather taxed in a big way? The other question that I have is in terms of the limelight and the secrecy of mediation. If one gets a mandate by an important and prominent person, like for instance Mr. Kofi Annan, then as a mediator, obviously, you are already in the limelight to a certain degree. However, I know of other issues, in which the Swiss government is

involved, that are handled with more secrecy. Can you comment on that in terms of, what it means for the mediator to be in these two circumstances respectively?

DIDIER PFIRTER
Thank you very much. I think you have put the finger on two very pertinent aspects. Indeed, I think successful mediations – especially not in a position like Mr. Holbrook was in Bosnia where you can say *"well that's it, you sign or else you get no more food"* – are drawn out processes that are very frustrating unless you put your expectations very low and you are able to take a certain distance, which is a difficult conundrum because on the one hand you have to get emotionally involved, you have to identify with the parties and their plight and, of course, desire that they should be able to overcome it and on the other hand you have to keep certain distances if you are not to despair. It tends to happen in almost all conflicts in my experience that parties build up positions, big fat red lines that they will never cross. They convince absolutely nobody in the world that they will never cross these lines except their own people. And it then takes a lot of political capital and a lot of courage for a leader to cross these lines. It cost the life of Itzhak Rabin.

We had similar dilemmas in Cyprus. The parties had agreed to sort of an empty formula of a bi-zonal and bi-communal state. The Greek Cypriots associated this with the assurance to all the refugees – they called them refugees even though they are legally speaking internally displaced – would return to their places of origin. This, in the case of Cyprus, is incompatible with a bi-zonal solution which implied that one zone would be predominantly Turkish Cypriot, when it had been before conflict more than three quarters Greek Cypriot. And when we first raised this with Greek Cypriot politicians from the left who were quite willing to solve the conflict but who complained that not all refugees could go back and that this was a violation of human rights. We said, *"Well, you have accepted the bi-zonal solution, how else do you want to have a bi-zonal solution? If you're all going back you will be the majority in both zones. So, did you understand this as meaning two Greek Cypriot zones?"* And they had no answer. They had never really thought it through.

In the case of Israel and Palestine, I think, you can see huge progress in the Israeli public opinion, when you look at where Israelis stood 15 years ago when 80 % of them ruled out a Palestinian state and would not ever even dream of giving back any part of Jerusalem to the Palestinians and now you have – way into the former Likud or even the actual Likud – a realisation that it is in the keen interest of Israel that there be a Palestinian state and there cannot be a Palestinian state without a part of Jerusalem.

So, these things come slowly. I think, as mediators you do have an impact and you do make a contribution to solving the conflict even if you are not standing on a pedestal and assisting the signing of an agreement, because you contribute to the evolution of the thinking of the people and this is the only way. They have to cross the big red lines, these walls that they have built up in their mind and realise in a very painful, difficult process that they have to give up things which they thought could not ever be given up. And this, if it happens from one day to another, is probably not sustainable. People's minds do not work that way. These have to be gradual processes, it has to be digested. It does take time.

The dilemma between limelight and secrecy is a big one, especially for us in Switzerland. Norway is in the favourable position that there is a broad political consensus throughout the political spectrum on the activities in this field that Norway undertakes. And, therefore, there is not much pressure on the politicians to justify what they are doing and to show success. This is different in Switzerland, unfortunately. There is pressure on the Ministry of Foreign Affairs to show that what we are doing is useful, is producing success and this, of course, precisely undermines the success. I think these sorts of processes are like the traditional films: the light ruins them. And therefore it is a big dilemma for our minister to show the success, to justify what she is doing vis-à-vis the parliament, vis-à-vis even her colleagues in government. Things that are said, even among the seven, tend to leak quite often and thus violate the requirement of these processes which have to remain secret. On the other hand, it is also a democratic problem when the other members of government and parliament demand to know what we are doing in the name of the country. It is a legitimate demand but as long as the secrecy cannot be guaranteed it can be fatal for the processes in which we are involved.

BERNHARD EHRENZELLER
Of course there is a need for democratic legitimation of the government's actions, which also includes the foreign policy sphere. It is more or less the same in other countries, also in Norway. But is it possible that the democratic pressure in Switzerland is higher than in other countries?

DIDIER PFIRTER
You will understand, that as a government employee, I am not going to criticise specific things that the Minister has done. It can be that a specific action that comes to be known and is not generally applauded increases the pressure to shed light on what is actually being done. But I think, to begin with, we have had in this country a tradition which is, that the best foreign policy is no foreign policy, because it just disturbs business. I guess this is an appropriate place to say this. Mrs. Calmy-Rey says that many people would like the Foreign Minister of Switzerland to be silent in all four national languages. And her concept of active neutrality has provoked these circles, obviously. I do not think it is as new as people try to make it up to be. Switzerland had a very active neutrality in the 19th century. I mentioned the example of the border between Guayana and Brazil and that between Colombia and Venezuela, there are many others. When there was no UN and there were hardly any multilateral fora, many international conferences were convened by Switzerland; this was a way of active neutrality. I think it is absolutely the right policy in the situation in which we are today, as a small country in Europe which does not belong to the European Union. On details you can always

discuss, but there is the fundamental problem, I think, that the main political forces have not agreed on the principle. I mean if there was agreement that it is desirable that we should have these activities, I think it would be much easier to also discuss in what way it should be done and whether what was done with Iran and other cases was the ultimate wisdom. But when you are in a situation where people do not accept the basis of it and try to undermine that, of course, it is difficult to discuss with them how it should be done because they do not agree that it should be done at all and they will always try to find "hairs in the soup".

CARL BAUDENBACHER
There is probably an additional special feature in Switzerland, namely the attitude that for every single Franc spent, people want to have a short success; they want to see an immediate success in short time. People can hardly wait.

DIDIER PFIRTER
There is a good anecdote for this: I once told one of my superiors in the Ministry who is now retired, that I think we are well placed to play a role in the Caucasus for a number of reasons. His answer was: *"Well, it's been four years that we have been paying this plane to the UN and there still is no peace, I'm losing my patience here"*. Of course, if this is your attitude, you should not even start. These are not conflicts that you solve in a short time.

CARL BAUDENBACHER
Once more, I want to thank the Ambassador very much. That was a very stimulating speech that led to a compelling discussion; a good start for the conference.

Focus:
Diplomacy
v.
Arbitration and Adjudication

Introduction

RUTH MACKENZIE[1]

First of all, let me thank Professor Baudenbacher, Simon Planzer and other colleagues here in St. Gallen for inviting me to take part in this conference and for giving us such a wonderful setting in which to meet.

This Panel addresses the relative roles and the relation between different means of dispute settlement, specifically diplomacy as compared to arbitration and adjudication.

Let me first introduce the panellists so that I can pass straight over to them after a few introductory comments or observations. To my left, Sven Norberg, who I am sure many of you will know as a former director of DG Competition at the European Commission, and who has also worked in the Swedish judiciary, in the Ministry of Commerce, in the Legal Affairs Division of EFTA and has acted as a judge at the EFTA Court. Judge Norberg will speak about EFTA and the relation between the EEA and the European Community.

To my right, Nikos Lavranos, who is Max Weber fellow at the European University Institute in Florence, and previously a senior researcher at the Amsterdam Centre for International Law. He will be talking specifically about the European Court of Justice.

And to his right, Patricia Hansen, who is a professor of law at the University of Texas in Austin, will be speaking about the relationship between adjudication, arbitration and diplomacy in relation to trade issues in the Americas.

I am looking forward to a very interesting set of presentations, hoping that we will still have some time left for questions, discussion and comments at the end. Let me make a few very brief general introductory comments, just to set the scene a little.

The means of dispute settlement in public international law, at least in relation to interstate disputes, are, of course, set out in Article 33 of the UN Charter: negotiation, mediation, adjudication, judicial settlement and arbitration. A distinction is typically made between diplomatic and legal or adjudicatory means. But as Ambassador Pfirter pointed out in his introductory speech, the mechanisms set out in Article 33 have

---

1   BSc, LL.M., UCL, London, Deputy Director and Principal Research Fellow, Centre for International Courts and Tribunals, University College London.

rather fluid boundaries; they are not a hierarchical set of options[2] and nor does resorting to one, necessarily preclude the use of another.

The International Court of Justice itself has on a number of occasions commented upon the relationship between negotiation or other means of diplomatic settlement of disputes and its own adjudicatory process, and clearly the different processes can be rather closely linked in certain circumstances. Diplomatic processes can give rise to a reference to an international court or to an arbitral tribunal and can determine the scope of the questions that are put to that body. Diplomatic processes may lead to the settlement of a dispute notwithstanding that the dispute has been submitted to a judicial body or to an arbitral tribunal and proceedings are pending in that case. And even where a case goes to final judgment on the merits before a court or tribunal, diplomatic processes may play a critical role in the implementation of a judgment or award.

In some cases dispute settlement procedures expressly provide for a period of formal consultation or negotiation or at least make provision for the possibility of exploring a friendly settlement before a case goes to a final decision. A resort to third party dispute settlement can also serve as a tool of diplomacy, used as a bargaining chip or as a means of "publicising" a particular dispute. In other instances, parts of a dispute have been referred to adjudication or to arbitration, while the wider, underlying dispute is subject to a broader diplomatic settlement process.

In other words, there appears to be quite a blurring of the different dispute settlement mechanisms in practice. Yet in other cases one could say that some international courts and tribunals have been established precisely to avoid the need for dispute settlement through diplomacy. One example is the International Center for Settlement of Investment Disputes, designed to provide a depoliticised forum for settlement of disputes between states and foreign investors with a view to doing away with the need for resort to diplomatic protection in such cases.

International courts can also be called upon to play a role as gap fillers in a sense, where diplomats have not fully resolved issues in their negotiation of treaties or other texts, and leave what are sometimes referred to as "constructive ambiguities" (or plain ambiguities) in texts that they adopt, leaving relevant courts or tribunals to sort out differences that may arise in relation to the interpretation or application of those texts.[3]

As we are all aware, recent years have shown an upsurge in the number of international courts and tribunals, and at least some of those courts and tribunals have been busy, if not overloaded, with cases. The question of the relation between diplomacy and dispute settlement or adjudication can arise in different ways before different in-

---

2   J. Collier/V. Lowe, The Settlement of Disputes in International Law, Oxford 1999, 8.
3   See J. Alvarez, International Organizations as Law-Makers, Oxford 2005, 533; L. Boisson de Chazournes/
     S. Heathcote, The Role of the New International Adjudicator, 95 ASIL Proc. (2001) 129, 132–134.

ternational courts and tribunals and some of these will be explored by our panellists. In some tribunals, difficult preliminary questions of jurisdiction might limit the role that adjudication can play – there just might not be any court or tribunal that has jurisdiction to play a role in the resolution of a particular dispute. In other cases, the role of the court might be limited or defined by a particular view of the proper scope of the judicial function that may differ from one court to another, from one regime or region to another. So questions arise about what acts are reviewable, and what is the appropriate scope and standard of review that a court should apply. And finally, there are some issues that might not fit so easily within models of traditional interstate dispute resolution through courts and tribunals. One might think here perhaps of certain global environmental issues, which might demand multilateral, diplomatic solutions rather than bilateral adjudication.

Overall, I am not sure that what we face is always a question of diplomacy **versus** adjudication or arbitration, as the title of this panel suggests, but rather the role, scope and proper relation of each to the other. Some of the questions to be addressed by this panel are to what extent the courts in Europe – the European Court of Justice, the EFTA Court, the European Court of Human Rights – or courts in the Americas dealing with trade issues raise particular considerations in this regard. Where or how do we define the proper role of judicial settlement of disputes, diplomacy and arbitration in those regimes? What are the limits of the dispute settlement bodies established under those regimes? I am sure we can look forward to some very interesting presentations, so let me now turn to our panellists.

Disputes in Intergovernmental Economic Relations of a Traditional Character and in those with Supranational Mechanisms, Respectively

DR. SVEN NORBERG[1]

I will start by simply recalling some of the different institutional solutions that have been laid down in certain European international trade agreements, ranging from intergovernmental relations of a traditional character to relations in a supranational context.

A. Institutional arrangements

I. Traditional intergovernmental relations in the field of trade

The first arrangement in this field that I experienced was of course the 1960 EFTA Convention. The European Free Trade Association (EFTA) was founded by the, at the time so-called, "Outer seven"[2] in response to the "Inner six"[3], which had set out to create the European Economic Community, signing the 1957 Rome Treaty. Through the EFTA Convention the participating countries created a free trade relationship between themselves, mainly for industrial goods. Five of the original founders of the EFTA as well as Finland are now Members of the EU. Today there are four EFTA Member States[4] left.

Within an intergovernmental organisation of a traditional character, which in principle only takes decisions by consensus, the mechanisms for dispute settlement are normally weak. This is also the case with the EFTA. Although in Article 31 of the Convention there is laid down a formal procedure for settlement of disputes on trade issues arising between the EFTA States, this procedure has only been applied six times, the last time being in 1967. Under the formal procedure the Council may as a last

---

1   DR. SVEN NORBERG, Senior Advisor KREAB Strategic Communication Counsellors, Brussels, Former Director in DG Competition of the EC Commission, Former Judge of the EFTA Court.
2   Austria, Denmark, Norway, Portugal, Sweden, Switzerland and United Kingdom. Later also Finland (1986 but associated since 1961), Iceland (1970) and Liechtenstein (1991) have joined EFTA.
3   Belgium, France, Germany, Italy, Luxemburg and the Netherlands.
4   Iceland, Liechtenstein, Norway and Switzerland.

recourse by majority vote make a recommendation. If the party would not follow this recommendation, the consequence would be the traditional trade retaliation measure, suspension of obligations. Even though this formal procedure is very weak, I have to say that as things have developed in practice the settlement in EFTA follows since more than 40 years an entirely informal procedure. This means that it is mostly through "diplomacy" that disputes are addressed.

There are then the Free Trade Agreements (FTAs) that the remaining EFTA Member States concluded in 1972 with the European Economic Communities, when Denmark and the United Kingdom left the EFTA to join the EC. These were the first Free Trade Agreements that the European Community entered into, and the Community was forced to do that by the EFTA States that joined the Community, since otherwise the free trade, once obtained through the EFTA, would have to be abolished in relation to the departing states. Each of the seven remaining EFTA Member States concluded two FTAs. Thus, at the time, 14 Free Trade Areas, seven with the European Economic Community (EEC) and seven with the European Coal and Steel Community (ECSC), were created. The FTAs have no real dispute settlement mechanisms. For each FTA there is a Joint Committee composed of the two parties to the agreement. In every decision they have to agree. In the case of a dispute the two parties cannot settle, the only way out for the other party is to take safeguard measures.

II. The European Economic Area (EEA)[5]

When the EFTA States and the European Community set off to negotiate the EEA, which they did formally in 1990 after one year of preparations, there were two main legal challenges to this.

First of all, creating a new independent legal order, that would deliver the same results as the EC Internal Market for the areas concerned. But since the EEA would be an independent legal order, many experts said that what we were trying to do was comparable to squaring the circle. My reply to such comments was that not being a mathematician I could not know whether that was possible or not, but that I was sure that you could get very close.

The second issue was the legal imbalance that the Community accused the EFTA States of. While the EC had very strong monitoring and judicial institutions as well as direct applicability and effect in national courts of international agreements concluded by the Community, the EFTA States had nothing similar. Thus, we had experienced, for instance, the judgments of the European Court of Justice (ECJ) in the *Polydor*[6] and

---

5   For a more extensive presentation of the EEA, see i.a. Norberg et al.: EEA Law, A Commentary to the EEA Agreement, Kluwer 1993.
6   Case 270/80 – *Polydor Ltd. and Others v. Harlequin Record Shops Ltd. and Others*, ECR 1982 00329.

Kupferberg[7] cases in 1982, through which it had been made clear that EFTA citizens could invoke provisions of the FTAs with the EC and get recognized in EC Courts. This was in stark contrast to the situation in EFTA, where most EFTA States not even recognized direct applicability of any international agreements but only had to rely on diplomacy if there would arise a dispute.

The European Economic Area, which has been in force for almost 15 years, is a "fundamentally improved Free Trade Area" that in practice from its entry into force on 1 January 1994 has extended the EU Internal Market first to five EFTA States[8]. Now there are three countries in the EFTA pillar of the EEA, Liechtenstein, Iceland and Norway. The institutions that in the end were agreed upon are contained in a two-pillar structure with the EU Commission and the European Court of Justice, on the EU side, and two specially created supranational organisations, the EFTA Surveillance Authority and the EFTA Court, on the other side. There is also a Joint Committee with all Contracting Parties represented, with each of the EU and the EFTA States speaking with one voice. Apart from taking Joint Decisions on amendments to Protocols and Annexes to the Agreement, the Joint Committee is also in charge of handling disputes between the two sides. This is of course not a very strong mechanism, as you will see. While each side should settle internal disputes, ultimately by its own court, the Joint Committee can only act by agreement of the two sides. The consequences are that, if there is no possibility to arrive to an agreement in the Joint Committee, there is ultimately only the rather radical solution that the parts of the EEA Agreement, that are directly affected by the dispute, be suspended.[9]

In May 1991, the EFTA States were after one year of negotiations rather frustrated that what they had understood being a promise by the then President of the Commission, Jacques Delors, on one of the most important issues, i.e. Joint Decision Making in Joint Institutions, actually did not mean anything else than the EFTA States having to agree among themselves and then present that position to the EC side without having a possibility to get into a real dialogue with the EC individually. At that moment, there were two issues of great importance for the negotiations outstanding. One was the "Judicial Mechanism", and the other was "Fish". Anyone who has been involved in trade negotiations will know that "Fish" is the issue that you settle last. You never manage to settle "Fish" until everything else is in place. So, the EFTAns managed then to reach an agreement in May 1991 with the EC on a Joint EEA Court composed of five judges from the ECJ and three judges from the EFTA States. That saved the negotiations for the EFTA side, and "Fish" could be put in place. The EFTA side had obtained what was absolutely essential for them, not only politically but also psychologically, a body where all the Contracting Parties were on an equal footing with the body of a Joint Court above them all.

---

7   Case 104/81 – *Hauptzollamt Mainz v. Kupferberg &Cie KG a.A.*, ECR 1982, 3641.
8   Austria, Finland, Iceland, Norway and Sweden.
9   Cf. Articles 111 and 102 of the EEA Agreement.

This first solution, agreed upon by the parties and submitted in autumn of 1991 by the Commission to the ECJ for an opinion under then Article 228 EEC, did, however, not please that Court. Therefore the ECJ turned down that solution, as well as the rest of the draft EEA Agreement in its opinion in December 1991,[10] arguing that such a Joint EEA Court would have presented a serious threat to the autonomy of the Community legal order.

Having, however, put "Fish" in place, everything else was so satisfactory to the EFTAns, that they were able to renegotiate it all with the EC within two months time. They agreed to set up this parallel structure with the EFTA Surveillance Authority and the EFTA Court monitoring the EFTA States' compliance with the EEA Agreement. The main competences of the EFTA Court were determined to be (and still are), similar to the ECJ's: infringement actions, settlement of disputes between EFTA States, preliminary rulings (called advisory opinions) for national courts and actions against the Surveillance Authority and its decisions. Everything has to be related to the application and interpretation of the EEA Agreement. This was the minimum of competences that they had to give to the EFTA Court. The EFTA States had no interest in going further.[11]

The EFTA Court has now been in function for almost 15 years, in which it decided around 100 cases. To anyone that is familiar with the EEA, there is no doubt that it is through the EFTA Court that the EEA Agreement is still credible.

III. The European Union (EU)

Regarding this topic, I will only give a brief summary of some of the main elements. Already at the very beginning, when the first Community, the European Coal and Steel Community, was set up in 1952, the main institutions were the High Authority and the Court of Justice. The main characteristic of the EU, is the particular role given to it and played by the European Commission as Guardian of the Treaty and the ECJ. Oftentimes, when politicians do not manage to settle internal disputes, it is the body that in the end will have to sort out deficiencies, which have their origin in the inability of the political sphere.

B. The settlement of disputes in these different structures

How are disputes addressed in these various places? As a general conclusion one can say, that where there are no real dispute settlement mechanisms, as in the EFTA (FTAs

---

10 Opinion 1/1991, ECR 1991, I-6079.
11 ECJ in Opinion 1/92, ECR 1992, I-2821, now approved the Agreement and the institutional solutions it contained.

with the European Communities; EU-EFTA relationship regarding the EEA), the long-term interdependence of the parties forces them to try all means peacefully to reach a settlement. They are actually tied together in a sort of marriage-like relationship, from which they cannot get out, except if they were to accede to a higher level of integration (i.e. ultimately EU membership). This means that disputes mostly are settled through recourse to diplomacy in one form or the other. It is, however, also extremely rare for an EU Member State to bring a dispute with another Member State before the ECJ. Until about ten years ago, there had only been one such judgment, which was given in 1978, when France brought an action against the UK regarding the size of the meshes of fishing nets in the English Channel. After the more recent enlargements there have, however, been a few new Member States that have brought some disputes before the ECJ, but it is still very rare. Similar is the situation in the EFTA pillar in the EEA. As well as the EC Member States prefer that the Commission does this job, the same situation prevails in EFTA, where the EFTA States prefer the EFTA Surveillance Authority to do this in their place.

The political process is, however, very often such that a considerable number of settlements are so ambiguous that they finally have to be interpreted by the Court.

I will in the following provide a few examples to illustrate what I have said. I will try not to bother you with too many details but only mention a couple of cases from each of these instruments. I will start with EFTA.

I. The EFTA Convention

I would like to mention just two cases. Before the EFTA was founded, the Nordic countries never managed to arrange for free trade between them on their own. It was only through the EFTA that they could do that. For Sweden, in particular, the relationship with Finland was very important. One of the main bilateral difficulties in Sweden's trade relations with Finland, that lasted extremely long, was the establishment of an *IKEA* department store outside Helsinki. The Finns were extremely clever in delaying this. The dispute originated in the 1970s and it was only around ten years ago that the *IKEA* store was established there. The Swedes could never bring that issue up in the EFTA, because they felt embarrassed of not having been able to settle it bilaterally with an old ally as Finland. I can mention in this context that *IKEA* managed to get established in Switzerland, although they could not invoke the establishment provision in the EFTA Convention fully, since they did not manufacture all its products in the EFTA area with EFTA origin as a consequence. *IKEA* instead undertook not to market any products that would be competing with traditional Swiss furniture industry. That meant that, when *IKEA* was established in Switzerland at the end of the 1970s, it enhanced its profile of a company for modern furniture.

Swiss Fodder Products was a rather funny case. It was the regulation in Switzerland of special animal feed products of very odd character, whereby one would introduce import surcharges in order to limit the production of cattle in Switzerland. This became an issue which was discussed at some length in the EFTA Council at the beginning of the 1980s, where Switzerland, in defence of the introduction of such a surcharge, referred to an *"oral reservation"* that they claimed had been made when the EFTA Convention was negotiated in Saltsjöbaden outside Stockholm in 1959. They claimed that this was proven by the fact that the Federal Council at the time had said so before the Swiss Parliament. Everyone in the EFTA Council, knowing the seriousness of Swiss negotiators, had a bit of a difficulty believing that this had taken place. But in the end, the dispute "ran out into the sand" and the matter was forgotten. Nobody bothered to fight over it any longer.

II. The EFTA States' Free Trade Agreements with the European Community

When I joined the Swedish Ministry of Commerce as a legal advisor in 1974, one of the first issues I was asked to look at was the Free Trade Agreement with the EEC. The Commission had just introduced *"paper ceilings"* for the paper exports from Sweden. I studied the FTA and came to the conclusion that this could not be accepted under the wording of the Agreement. When I reported my findings to my colleagues, they only replied: *"Sorry, you don't understand how this functions! We can't really fight with the Commission about this because we have so many other important issues with them that we'll have to accept this one."* From this experience I learnt that, while you may very well have the legal right on your side, if you're too dependent on the other party, you may have to simply accept what the other party is doing.

In 1982, with François Mitterrand as new President, France got a new Minister of Trade with Madame Edith Cresson, and this was the first but not the last time she became famous internationally. In autumn of 1982, in order to stem too high imports of industrial goods in France, she introduced the famous so-called *French import measures*. This meant first, that all Japanese video recorders had to be customs cleared in the middle of France in Poitiers. Secondly, every good imported into France had to be labelled in French and also the instruction manuals had to be in French. This was a very efficient way of blocking imports to France. In the European Community France had to withdraw this very quickly by making exceptions for all imports from other EC States, since the measures otherwise would fall foul of the fundamental provisions on free movement of goods in Articles 30 and 36[12] of the EEC Treaty. In the EFTA a crisis meeting was convened at Ministerial level to urgently discuss this very preoccupying situation. I was at the time the Legal Advisor to the EFTA. It was, however, only with great difficulties that we managed to convince the EFTA States' trade experts that we actually would be

---

12   Now Articles 28 and 30 EC.

in a very good position in Brussels to invoke the FTAs thanks to the two judgments of the ECJ earlier the same year in *Polydor* and *Kupferberg*[13], in which the ECJ had recognised direct effect of the Free Trade Agreements with the EFTA States.

The EFTA States had initially thought that they should base themselves upon the GATT and its case law regarding non-tariff measures. The problem was, however, that in GATT with its more political structure and procedures they would have been treated as any other third country like the US or Japan. This was the first time we succeeded in showing the EFTA States that the FTAs – thanks to their legal standing being recognised by the ECJ – actually were quite valuable. No one on the EFTA side had so far really believed in the FTAs. We thus managed to get things settled by talking to the Commission. One of the experiences I also made in this context was that trade experts in general do not like lawyers to get involved in their matters.

In 1985, the Commission adopted the *Wood Pulp Cartel* decision[14] regarding a number of Swedish, Finnish, Canadian and several other companies that were alleged to have been participating in a cartel, rigging prices for wood pulp. In talks with the Swedish Ambassador to the EEC at the time, I assumed that the companies would challenge the decision before the ECJ. He had been involved quite a lot representing the Swedish companies in talks with the Commission. *"No,"* he said, *"absolutely not! Don't rock the boat! The Commission knows what they are doing and we have so many other important issues going on."* The only companies that did not challenge the Wood Pulp decision were thus four Swedish companies, which had paid the fines imposed in the Commission's decision. When the ECJ a number of years later announced its judgment annulling the Commission decision, the Swedish companies brought an action demanding to be reimbursed the amount they had paid in fines. When the ECJ finally settled this in 1999[15], the Swedish claims were rejected since the companies deliberately had taken a chance in not challenging the Commission decision but paid their fines. This is just an example of where too much of diplomacy can result in.

III. The EEA Agreement

As a part of the EEA Agreement, which was subject to lengthy negotiations, a financial cohesion mechanism was created, intended to – in parallel to what the European Community did – provide support to poorer regions in Greece, Portugal, Spain and the island of Ireland (i.e. both the Republic and Northern Ireland). Under the Agreement this mechanism should last five years. In the EEA Joint Committee the three remaining EFTA States were faced in 1998 with a situation, where the Community claimed that it always had been intended that the mechanism had to be extended. Although

---

13 See notes 6 and 7 above.
14 Joined Cases 89, 104, 114, 116, 117 & 125-129/85 – *Ahlström Oy and Others v. Commission*, (I) ECR 1988, 5193 and (II) ECR 1993, I-1307.
15 Case C-310/07 P – *Commission v. AssiDomän and Others*, ECR 1999, I-5363.

they denied this and there was no evidence to support the claim of the EU side, the EFTA side could not do anything. They tried in vain to seek support from the three former EFTA States who now had acceded to the EU. But with a legal opinion of the Council legal service they finally had to give in and accept the EU claim.

IV. The Swiss Free Trade Agreement with the European Community

There is an ongoing dispute. I have mostly read about it in the Swiss papers and seen television reports thereon. The dispute concerns the application of Article 23 containing the rules of competition in the Free Trade Agreement. This is an Article that more or less contains the essence of the provisions of the Competition Rules in Articles 81, 82 and 87 of the Treaty of Rome. At the signature of the Agreement in 1972, the European Community made a Declaration that they were going to interpret this provision exactly in the same way as the corresponding provisions of the Treaty of Rome are interpreted. This dispute between the EU and Switzerland concerns the famous cantonal tax regimes, where cantons are in competition with each other in having favourable tax conditions to attract establishment of companies. There is a lot of political pressure, in particular from the German and French Governments against the Swiss Confederation. This has also resulted *inter alia* in a Commission Decision concerning the incompatibility of certain Swiss company taxation regimes with the Agreement between the European Economic Community and the Swiss Confederation of 22 July 1972 being adopted on 13 February 2007[16] and subsequently endorsed by the EU Council. Without going further into this matter, it may be observed only, that if Switzerland had been a Member of the EEA, this could have been an internal dispute to be settled within EFTA and ultimately by the EFTA Court.

V. The European Union (EU)

Finally, I would like to mention in a few words the problems that frequently may arise from ambiguous wordings of legal texts, that are the results of political or diplomatic settlements. There are many ECJ judgments regarding the interpretation of wordings having their origin in such "political settlements", which certainly have created a lot of strong reactions in the Member States. I will just mention two recent examples, where unclear and not sufficiently clear legal texts have resulted in disputes that finally have had to be settled by the ECJ.

The first case is the judgment in *Laval*[17] of December 2007 concerning the working and salary conditions for Latvian construction workers engaged to build a school in

---

16 Doc C(2007) 411 final.
17 Case C-341/05 – *Laval un Partneri*, judgment 18 December 2007.

Sweden. This judgment is perceived, at least by some in Sweden, as a major threat to the whole Swedish system for labour relations. *Metoch*[18] is a similar case. That certainly has created upheaval not the least in Denmark. It concerns the right of people married to European Union citizens, but who themselves are not European Union citizens, to settle in the EU.

C. Conclusion

I think the process of the European integration that we have witnessed during the last 55 years, has led to such a complex and rich net of rules and regulations, that it is quite clear that these rules govern not only inter-state relations but also intrastate relations. As well as is the case with Nation States, complex and developed international relations require proper judicial mechanisms for interpretation and dispute settlement. For the overwhelming part, I think it is fair to say, that in the particular European context I mainly have dealt with, this has functioned incredibly and surprisingly well not the least at the national level with the national judiciaries now having more and more of enforcement responsibilities.

Europe is today so dominated by the European Union, which also has created a separate new legal order. One of the particularities of that legal order is, as developed by the ECJ, that international agreements entered into by the European Union become part of Community law and, thus, are subject to the jurisdiction of the ECJ. This means that there also is a need for the ECJ, as it was spelled out in Opinion 1/91, to guarantee the autonomy of the Community legal order. That determines further, as we have seen, how far the European Union can go in accepting other dispute settlement mechanisms. The closer you want to get to the EU, the stronger will also the requirement of reciprocity be. Within these parameters there is still substantial scope for diplomacy, but I think there is another factor that plays an even greater role, *political pressure*.

---

18 Case C-127/08 – *Metoch and Others*, judgment 25 July 2008.

On Misguided Judicial Deference by the ECJ and ECrtHR

NIKOLAOS LAVRANOS[1]

A. Introduction

My contribution will take up Sven Norberg's last point about Community Law being an autonomous legal order and the relationship between Community Law and International Law. I will do that by discussing a number of cases.

The main argument I want to put forward in this contribution is that in my view highly sensitive disputes should rather not be brought before courts and tribunals for adjudication, because, as I will explain below, they tend to show too much – misguided – deference and judicial restraint towards executive bodies. Indeed, the cases at hand will illustrate that this tendency is increasing and spreading – in particular regarding the ECJ and ECrtHR. So, although courts and tribunals are increasingly used – as is also proven by the increasing proliferation of international courts and tribunals – this does not mean that they actually provide for more or better justice and the rule of law.

In order to provide the framework for my analysis, I will first briefly discuss two trends. First, as an introductory trend, I would like to mention the proliferation of international courts and tribunals. Second, I will briefly discuss two examples on the shift from adjudication towards arbitration, which we are currently witnessing. Based on this, I will move on to the main point which is the increasing judicial restraint and deference of courts and tribunals towards executive bodies. This analysis will be wrapped up by some concluding remarks.

I. The proliferation of international courts and tribunals

As regards the proliferation of international courts and tribunals, we know that since the 1990s there has been a clear multiplication of them.[2] We also see that there is a clear increase in the use of adjudication and arbitration as a tool for dispute resolution. Already when we look at the dockets of the International Court of Justice (ICJ), the

---

1 Dr. Nikolaos Lavranos, LL.M; Max Weber Fellow, European University Institute, Florence.
2 Cesare Romano, The Proliferation of International Judicial Bodies: The Pieces of the Puzzle, 31 *NYU Journal of International Law and Politics* (1999), pp. 709–751; Yuval Shany, *Regulating Jurisdictional Relations between National and International Courts* (OUP 2007); Idem., *The Competing Jurisdiction of International Courts and Tribunals* (OUP 2003).

European Court of Justice (ECJ), the European Court of Human Rights (ECrtHR) and the WTO Appellate Body, one can detect a real explosion of their dockets. So, clearly, more cases are coming to these international courts and tribunals.

Moreover, and in line with John Jackson, you clearly see a shift from the classic power-based towards a rule-based dispute resolution.³ Indeed, some even point out that this is a sign of a constitutionalisation of International Law.⁴ Personally, I'd rather speak of an institutionalisation of International Law.

Thus, as a result of these developments, we see that courts are increasingly confronted with highly sensitive cases, such as disputes involving trade law, UN law and environmental law. These are the types of cases I will discuss below.

II. The shift from adjudication towards arbitration

The second trend I wish to highlight is the ongoing shift from adjudication towards arbitration by briefly mentioning two cases, i.e. the *IJzeren Rijn* or *Iron Rhine* case and the *MOX plant* case, on which I have critically commented upon elsewhere.⁵

In the *Iron Rhine* case, Belgium and the Netherlands argued who should pay for the reactivation of this old railway track that runs from the Antwerp harbour through a small piece in the Netherlands to the German Ruhrgebiet. The Belgians want to reactivate this track. However, the problem is that in the meantime, because of the EC Habitat Directive, some small parts in the Netherlands, which the track crosses, have been labelled and dedicated as natural protected area. So, the EC Habitat Directive applies – one would think. As is well known, the Habitat Directive as interpreted by the ECJ allows any economic condition only under extremely strict conditions – if at all.⁶ The Netherlands and Belgium, obviously, knew that, so they really wanted this case not to come before the ECJ. Hence, they set up an ad hoc arbitral tribunal to decide who should pay for the costs of the reactivation of the track. The arbitral tribunal delivered

---

3 See: John H. Jackson, *The World Trading System: Law and Policy of International Economic Relations*, 2nd ed. (MIT Press 1997).
4 See the contributions in the special issue of the *Leiden Journal of International Law* 2006, issue 3.
5 Nikolaos Lavranos, The MOX Plant and IJzeren Rijn Disputes: Which Court is the Supreme Arbiter? 19 *Leiden Journal of International Law* (2006), 223–246; Idem., Jurisdictional Competition between ECJ and other international courts and tribunals, *European Law Reporter* 2007, pp. 156–171.
6 See for recent cases concerning Art. 6 Habitat Directive: ECJ Case C-418/04 (*Commission v. Ireland*) [2007] ECR I-10947; ECJ Case C-388/05 (*Commission v. Italy*), [2007] ECR-7555, available at <http://eur-lex.europa.eu>.

its award without taking EC law, in particular the EC Habitat Directive, into account.[7] The arbitral tribunal delivered its award as if we were back in the 1870s, when the treaties between Belgium and the Netherlands concerning the use of the Iron Rhine track were signed. In my view, this was a clear violation of Article 292 EC, which states that all Community law related cases between EC Member States must come exclusively before the ECJ.

The other example refers to the MOX *plant* dispute between the UK and Ireland.[8] For many years, Ireland has been concerned about the radioactive emissions of the MOX plant situated in Sellafield, UK. Ireland argued that by operating the MOX plant the UK has been violating the UN Law of the Sea Convention (UNCLOS) and the Convention for the Protection of the Marine Environment of the North East Atlantic (OSPAR), which provides a right to access to information concerning possible pollution. As in the *Iron Rhine* case, we have again EC law provisions, which are clearly applicable in this case and which therefore would have triggered the exclusive jurisdiction of the ECJ under Article 292 EC. But both parties decided to bring the dispute before two separate arbitral tribunals, one established under UNCLOS and the other established under OSPAR.

The OSPAR arbitral tribunal completely ignored the EC law provisions, including Article 292 EC, and delivered its award purely on the basis of the OSPAR Convention.[9] The UNCLOS arbitral tribunal was more open to Article 292 EC by staying the proceedings and asking the parties to check out whether the jurisdiction of the ECJ is involved in this dispute. Indeed, the case eventually came through the European Commission before the ECJ.[10] Of course, in its judgment the ECJ claimed exclusive jurisdiction by referring to the autonomous character of the Community legal order. If a dispute would be brought before another court or tribunal, this – according to the ECJ – would endanger the autonomous legal order as well as the uniformity and consistency of EC law.[11] Since the ECJ indeed exercised its exclusive jurisdiction, the UNCLOS arbitral tribunal recently terminated the case.[12] Thus, after a couple of years, and the case having been brought before a number of courts and tribunals, we still

---

7 The details of the dispute can be found at the website of the Permanent Court of Arbitration, available at http://www.pca-cpa.org/ENGLISH/RPC/#Belgium/Netherlands; See further: I. van Bladel, *The Iron Rhine Arbitration Case: On the Right Legal Track? An analysis of the award and of its relation to the Law of the European Community*, 18 Hague Yearbook of International Law (2005), pp. 3–22; C. Warbrick, The *"Iron Rhine" ("Ijzeren Rijn") Arbitration: its contribution to international law*, THE IRON RHINE ARBITRATON AWARD 2005, (T.M.C. Asser Press 2007), pp. 153–193.
8 Nikolaos Lavranos, Protecting its exclusive jurisdiction: The MOX plant-judgment of the ECJ, *The Law & Practice of International Courts and Tribunals* 2006, pp. 479–493.
9 OSPAR Arbitral Award, available at:< http://www.pca-cpa.org/showpage.asp?pag_id=1158>.
10 ECJ Case C-459/03 (*Commission v Ireland*) [2006] ECR I-4635; see for a detailed analysis: Cesare Romano, Case-note on *Commission of the European Communities v. Ireland*, 101 *American Journal of International Law* (2007), pp. 171–179.
11 ECJ Case C-459/03 (supra note 9), paras. 123 ff.
12 UNCLOS Arbitral Tribunal, MOX *plant case*, Order No. 6, Termination of proceedings, 6 June 2008, available at: <http://www.pca-cpa.org/upload/files/ MOX%20Plant%20Press%20Release%20Order%20 No.%206.pdf>.

don't know whether the UK actually violated its UNCLOS obligations. I think that's very interesting.

So, we can observe a tendency for a preference of the EC Member States to circumvent the exclusive jurisdiction of the ECJ by bringing disputes before other (arbitral) tribunals rather than before the ECJ. This, in my view, can sometimes endanger the uniform and consistent application and interpretation of Community Law. We can see this in particular in the *Iron Rhine* case. However, I am hopeful that it will still come before the ECJ. Dutch inhabitants who are living close to the railway track probably will start proceedings against its reactivation which would probably lead to a preliminary question by a Dutch court to the ECJ, which in turn would have to apply the EC Habitat Directive.

B. The case-studies on the increasing misguided judicial deference towards executive bodies

I. GATT/WTO law

Let's start with the old story of the GATT 1947. We all know what the ECJ was saying back in the time.[13] According to the ECJ the GATT 1947 was predominantly still power-based and therefore any direct effect of GATT provisions was excluded.[14] But even after the WTO was established in 1994, both the CFI and the ECJ continue to refuse to review the conformity of Community law measures with WTO law.[15] The ECJ essentially uses three arguments for refusing to review GATT/WTO provisions. Next to the negotiation-based argument, the ECJ introduced the separation of powers-argument, arguing that if the ECJ would step in, it would limit the room of manoeuvre of the EC executive bodies vis-à-vis the other WTO members. In addition, the ECJ came up with the reciprocity-argument, arguing that since the US doesn't accept direct effect neither should the EC.[16]

Thus, in the context of WTO law we clearly can detect a reluctance of the ECJ and CFI to get involved in this – mainly – because of possible negative economic repercussions as the ECJ itself quite explicitly stated in the *Portugal* case.[17]

---

13 See eg: H.G. Schermers, Community Law and International Law, 12 *Common Market Law Review* (1975), pp. 77–90.
14 See eg: ECJ Joined cases 21-24/72 (*International Fruit Company*) [1972] ECR 1219. The ECJ has been repeating its position ever since, see eg: Case C-280/93 (*Germany v. Commission*) [1994] ECR I-4973.
15 See eg: ECJ Joined cases C-120/06 P and C-121/06 P (*FIAMM*) judgment of 9 September 2008.
16 See for an illustrative summary of the ECJ's approach: ECJ **Case C-149/96** (*Portugal v. Council*) [1999] ECR I-8395, *paras. 40–47*; See for a general discussion with opposing views: Nikolaos Lavranos, The *Chiquita* and *Van Parys* Judgments: An Exception to the Rule of Law, 32 *Legal Issues of Economic Integration* 2005, pp. 449–460; Antonis Antoniadis, The Chiquita and Van Parys Judgments: Rules, Exceptions and the Law, 32 *Legal Issues of Economic Integration* 2005, pp. 460–476.
17 Ibid.

More recently, reference must be made to the *IKEA* case[18], which was adjudicated in September 2007. The case concerned the validity of the use of the zeroing-method in anti-dumping. The WTO Appellate Body had ruled in the *Bed linen* case[19] that zeroing was not in conformity with WTO rules.[20] However, the EC, like many WTO members, had been applying the zeroing-method. As a result, IKEA paid too many customs duties, which IKEA asked back from the UK Treasury, i.e. the EC. IKEA relied *inter alia* on the WTO *Bed linen* ruling. The ECJ, however, only looked at the EC Regulation, which contained the zeroing-method without looking at all at the WTO *Bed linen* case. In the end, the ECJ found that indeed the zeroing-method is inconsistent with EC law (!) not mentioning the inconsistency with WTO law. Accordingly, in this case the ECJ is using a very interesting new strategy, which I call the de-coupling of international and EC law obligations.

Notwithstanding this new de-coupling strategy, there is in principle no judicial review of EC law measures vis-à-vis WTO law available, unless the *Fediol/Nakajima*-exceptions are met.[21]

II. UN law

Now, let's move on to another very interesting area, namely the use of UN sanctions and their status and effect in the Community legal order.

To me the CFI's *Yusuf/Kadi*-judgments[22] in which the CFI showed complete deference towards the UN Security Council, with the exception of *ius cogens*, came as a shock. In particular, since the CFI failed to show any regard to fundamental rights, the rule of law or the ECHR. In my opinion, that was really a misguided judgment.[23]

---

18 ECJ Case C-351/04 (*IKEA Wholesale Ltd v Commissioners of Customs & Excise*) judgment of 27 September 2007, available at: <http://curia.europa.eu/jurisp/cgi-bin/form.pl?lang=en>; see further: Nikolaos Lavranos, Case-note on the IKEA case, 56 *SEW* (2008), pp. 256–261.
19 WTO Panel Report, *EC – Anti-dumping duties on imports of Cotton-type bed linen from India* (WT/DS141/R) of 30 October 2000; Appellate Body Report, *EC – Anti-dumping duties on imports of Cotton-type bed linen from India* (WT/DS141/AB/R) of 1 March 2001, all available at: http://www.wto.org/english/tratop_e/dispu_e/cases_e/ds141_e.htm.
20 See on the WTO jurisprudence regarding zeroing: Sungjoon Cho, Constitutional Adjudication in the World Trade Organization, *NYU Jean Monnet Working Paper 04/08*, available at: <http://www.jeanmonnetprogram.org/papers/08/080401.html>.
21 ECJ Case 70/87 (*Fediol*) [1989] ECR 1781; Case C-69/89 (*Nakajima*) [1991] ECR I-2069.
22 CFI Case T-315/01 (*Kadi*) [2005] ECR II-3649 and CFI Case T-306/01 (*Yusuf*) [2005] ECR II-3533.
23 See extensively: Nikolaos Lavranos, UN sanctions and judicial review, 76 *Nordic Journal of International Law* 2007, pp. 1–18.

Fortunately, and luckily, the ECJ's *Kadi*-judgment[24] came out before this conference was timed, so now we know where we stand. We know that the EC is based on the rule of law. We know that fundamental rights do apply fully to UN sanctions as implemented by the EC. And we know that the ECJ will provide for full judicial review against measures implementing UN sanctions. So, I am very pleased with this judgment and I think the ECJ should be praised for that.

But let's move on to the *Bosphorus* case, which is a slightly different story – unfortunately. As is well-known, the *Bosphorus* case came first before the ECJ. In its judgment, the ECJ ruled that Bosphorus had to accept substantial limitations of its right to property for the sake of full implementation of UN sanctions.[25] This judgement is of the old school so to speak, that is, showing clear deference towards the EC executive bodies and the UN Security Council.

Subsequently, the *Bosphorus* case came before the ECrtHR.[26] The interesting aspect about this case is that the ECrtHR was called upon to review – indirectly, of course – the ECJ's *Bosphorus*-ruling. The case also raised the issue of which court is the final court in terms of fundamental rights protection in Europe. Clearly, this is a huge political and diplomatic mine field, while at the same time there is mutual respect and diplomatic *contenance*[27] between those two courts. In other words, top judges do not criticise each other openly. Hence, the ECrtHR had to think hard on how to get a way out of this situation. The ECrtHR started by emphasising the importance of cooperation between international organisations.[28] Indeed, states increasingly cooperate in international organisations such as the EC, UN, NATO etc. The ECrtHR has to respect that to a certain extent, especially when there are common problems that have to be dealt with such as terrorism, peace, security etc.

---

24 ECJ Joined Cases C-402/05 P and C-415/05 P (*Yassin Abdullah Kadi, Al Barakaat International Foundation v Council of the European Union, Commission of the European Communities, United Kingdom of Great Britain and Northern Ireland*), judgment of 3 September 2008, available at: <http://curia.europa.eu/jurisp/cgi-bin/form.pl?lang=en&newform=newform&Submit=Submit&alljur=alljur&jurcdj=jurcdj&jurtpi=jurtpi&jurtfp=jurtfp&alldocrec=alldocrec&docj=docj&docor=docor&docop=docop&docav=docav&docsom=docsom&docinf=docinf&alldocnorec=alldocnorec&docnoj=docnoj&docnoor=docnoor&typeord=ALL&docnodecision=docnodecision&allcommjo=allcommjo&affint=affint&affclose=affclose&numaff=&ddatefs=&mdatefs=&ydatefs=&ddatefe=&mdatefe=&ydatefe=&nomusuel=&domaine=&mots=kadi&resmax=100>. See for a detailed analysis: Nikolaos Lavranos, Case-note on Kadi, 36 *Legal Issues of Economic Integration* 2009, issue 2 forthcoming.
25 ECJ Case C-84/95 (*Bosphorus*) [1996] ECR I-3953.
26 ECrtHR *Bosphorus Hava v Ireland* (App no 45036/98), judgment of 30 June 2005, available at: <http://cmiskp.echr.coe.int/tkp197/view.asp?item=1&portal=hbkm&action=html&highlight=bosphorus&sessionid=15918426&skin=hudoc-en>.
27 Contenance is defined as:
   1) Faire bonne contenance, montrer de la sérénité dans une circonstance difficile.
   2) Perdre contenance, perdre son sang-froid, se troubler: Quelqu'un le contredit et on le vit perdre contenance.
   3) Se donner une contenance, adopter une attitude pour dissimuler son embarras, sa gêne: Elle boutonna sa veste pour se donner. Source: <http://fr.thefreedictionary.com/contenance>.
28 ECrtHR *Bosphorus* (supra note 25) para. 150.

The next step in the ECrtHR's analysis was to establish a rebuttable assumption that the EC protects fundamental rights almost as equivalent to the ECHR.[29] However, in this context, it should be recalled that the ECJ concluded in its *Kadi*-judgment that the rights of Yusuf and Kadi were "patently not respected" by the CFI's *Yusuf/Kadi*-rulings.[30] In my view, there is a gap between this rebuttable assumption of being ECHR-proof and what the CFI had stated in this case.

But the ECrtHR still maintained this rebuttable presumption, while at the same time there is this exception of "manifestly deficient" that was introduced by the ECrtHR's *Bosphorus*-judgment.[31] Accordingly, only when fundamental rights are not protected sufficiently enough by the ECJ and CFI, would the ECrtHR step in. Admittedly, this "Solange"-method is a very elegant way since it shows deference towards the ECJ and at the same time leaves the question unanswered as to which is the final court.[32] Unfortunately, the answer to this question is the one we all are waiting for!

The next example I would like to discuss is the *Behrami* case[33], which is a very interesting case indeed. It deals with the responsibility of states, EC Member States and contracting parties to the ECHR, regarding acts or omissions of peacekeeping forces in Kosovo, i.e. UNMIK and KFOR. In essence, the ECrtHR was asked to review the conformity of acts and omissions of UNMIK and KFOR and, more precisely, to what extent the states remain responsible even though the forces were established and operated under UN auspices.

The ECrtHR started off its analysis by emphasising the importance of UN Security Council resolutions.[34] In a second step, the ECrtHR argued that reviewing the acts or omissions of UNMIK and KFOR would in effect mean reviewing the UN Security Council and "would be tantamount to imposing conditions on the implementation

---

29 Ibid., paras. 155–156.
30 ECJ Case C-402/05 P (*Kadi*) (supra note 23), para. 334.
31 ECrtHR *Bosphorus* (supra note 25) para. 156:
"156. If such equivalent protection is considered to be provided by the organisation, the presumption will be that a State has not departed from the requirements of the Convention when it does no more than implement legal obligations flowing from its membership of the organisation. However, any such presumption can be rebutted if, in the circumstances of a particular case, it is considered that the protection of Convention rights was *manifestly deficient*. In such cases, the interest of international cooperation would be outweighed by the Convention's role as a "constitutional instrument of European public order" in the field of human rights (see *Loizidou v. Turkey* (preliminary objections), judgment of 23 March 1995, Series A no. 310, pp. 27–28, § 75)." [emphasis added].
32 See extensively: Nikolaos Lavranos, Towards a Solange-Method between International Courts and Tribunals?, in: T. Broude/Y. Shany, *The Shifting Allocation of Authority in International Law: Considering Sovereignty, Supremacy and Subsidiarity* (Hart Publishing 2008), pp. 217–235.
33 ECrtHR *Behrami* (Application no. 71412/01) and *Saramati* (Application no. 78166/01), Admissibility decision of 2 May 2007, available at: <http://cmiskp.echr.coe.int/tkp197/view.asp?item=1&portal=hbkm&action=html&highlight=behrami&sessionid=15918426&skin=hudoc-en>.
34 Ibid., paras. 146 ff.

of UN Security Council resolutions, which were not provided for in the text of the resolution."[35]

This sounds similar to the CFI's *Yusuf/Kadi*-judgment.[36] As a result, the ECrtHR did not admit the case. The ECrtHR tried to differentiate the *Behrami* case from the *Bosphorus* case[37], but in my opinion there really is no difference between those cases regarding the point of final responsibility because it always lies with the states and not with the UN Security Council. Thus, in my view, the ECrtHR should have fully reviewed the acts and omissions of UNMIK and KFOR, thereby offering some fundamental rights protection. Particularly considering the fact that no judicial review is provided for by UNMIK, KFOR, NATO or the UN Security Council, which means that this situation meets the "manifestly deficient"-test as established by the ECrtHR in its *Bosphorus*-judgment. Thus, the situation remains unchanged inasmuch as that the ECrtHR offers

---

35 Ibid., para. 149.
36 CFI Case T-315/01 (*Kadi*) [2005] ECR II-3649:
"284 Nor does it fall to the Court [CFI] to verify that there has been no error of assessment of the facts and evidence relied on by the [UN] Security Council in support of the measures it has taken or, subject to the limited extent defined in paragraph 282 above, to check indirectly the appropriateness and proportionality of those measures. *It would be impossible to carry out such a check without trespassing on the Security Council's prerogatives under Chapter VII of the Charter of the United Nations* in relation to determining, first, whether there exists a threat to international peace and security and, second, the appropriate measures for confronting or settling such a threat. Moreover, the question whether an individual or organisation poses a threat to international peace and security, like the question of what measures must be adopted vis-à-vis the persons concerned in order to frustrate that threat, entails a political assessment and value judgments which in principle fall within the exclusive competence of the authority to which the international community has entrusted primary responsibility for the maintenance of international peace and security." [emphasis added].
37 ECrtHR *Behrami* (supra note 32):
"150. The applicants argued that the substantive and procedural protection of fundamental rights provided by KFOR was in any event not 'equivalent' to that under the Convention within the meaning of the Court's [ECrtHR] *Bosphorus* judgment, with the consequence that the presumption of Convention compliance on the part of the respondent States was rebutted.
151. The Court, however, considers that the circumstances of the present cases are essentially different from those with which the Court was concerned in the *Bosphorus* case. In its judgment in that case, the Court noted that the impugned act (seizure of the applicant's leased aircraft) had been carried out by the respondent State authorities, on its territory and following a decision by one of its Ministers (§ 137 of that judgment). The Court did not therefore consider that any question arose as to its competence, notably *ratione personae*, vis-à-vis the respondent State despite the fact that the source of the impugned seizure was an EC Council Regulation which, in turn, applied a UNSC Resolution. In the present cases, the impugned acts and omissions of KFOR and UNMIK cannot be attributed to the respondent States and, moreover, did not take place on the territory of those States or by virtue of a decision of their authorities. The present cases are therefore clearly distinguishable from the *Bosphorus* case in terms both of the responsibility of the respondent States under Article 1 and of the Court's competence *ratione personae*.
There exists, in any event, a fundamental distinction between the nature of the international organisation and of the international cooperation with which the Court was there concerned and those in the present cases. As the Court has found above, UNMIK was a subsidiary organ of the UN created under Chapter VII and KFOR was exercising powers lawfully delegated under Chapter VII of the Charter by the UNSC. As such, their actions were directly attributable to the UN, an organisation of universal jurisdiction fulfilling its imperative collective security objective.
152. In these circumstances, the Court concludes that the applicants' complaints must be declared incompatible *ratione personae* with the provisions of the Convention."

no protection against UN Security Council resolutions or acts or omissions adopted for the purpose of implementing UN Security Council resolutions. In my opinion, this is unacceptable.

III. International and European environmental law

With the final example we come back to the environmental law area. I refer to the recent *Intertanko* case[38], which also involved UNCLOS and Marpol (International Convention for the Prevention of Pollution from Ships of 1973) treaties. In this case the international association of independent tanker owners (Intertanko) asked the UK High Court to request a preliminary ruling from the ECJ regarding the validity of an EC Directive, which introduced a stricter standard of liability for tanker owners compared to what is contained in UNCLOS and in Marpol.

The main question was whether the EC is competent to introduce a different – stricter – liability standard, in particular, in view of the fact that the EC is not a contracting party to Marpol, although the EC is next to the EC Member States party to UNCLOS.

The ECJ found a very elegant way to avoid the whole discussion. It argued that since the EC is not party to Marpol and since there was not a full transfer of the Member States' competence in this field to the EC, Marpol is not binding on the EC.[39] Therefore, the ECJ considered itself unable to review the compatibility of the EC Directive vis-à-vis Marpol.

With regard to UNCLOS, the ECJ stated that:

> "*UNCLOS does not establish rules intended to apply directly and immediately to individuals and confer upon them rights or freedoms capable of being relied upon against states.*"[40]

As a result, Intertanko could not rely on UNCLOS or Marpol provisions. Thus, the ECJ concluded that the validity of this EC Directive cannot be reviewed neither in the light of UNCLOS nor in the light of Marpol. So, there was no judicial review available. Let me emphasise that I am, of course, very happy that the stricter liability standard remained applicable at the end. However, this should in my view not exclude the possibility of judicial review.

---

38 ECJ Case C-308/06 (*Intertanko*) judgment of 3 June 2008.
39 Ibid., paras. 44 ff.; see also the previous judgment of the ECJ regarding the non-binding effect of Marpol on the EC, Case C-379/92 (*Peralta*) [1994] ECR I-3453.
40 ECJ Case C-308/06 (*Intertanko*), para. 64.

Indeed, the approach of the ECJ is very strange and unconvincing compared to the opinion of Advocate General Kokott in this case.[41] In her excellent opinion, she explained quite clearly that since the EC is bound by UNCLOS and since Marpol is referring to UNCLOS and since the EC Directive pursues similar aims as UNCLOS and Marpol, there is no reason at all why the EC Directive should not be reviewed in the light of those two treaties.[42] In my view, this approach is much more convincing.

C. Conclusions

In my view, the cases discussed above show substantial deference and judicial restraint of the European courts towards all of these executive bodies (Council, Commission, Member States, UN Security Council etc.). As a result, even though these disputes are brought before courts and tribunals, thereby suggesting the availability of judicial review and resolution of the disputes on the basis of justice and the rule of law, it is clear that this is very often not the case because courts and tribunals avoid giving clear answers.

Actually, one can see the creation of "self-contained" regimes by the courts, which they are using as a tool for excluding the normally applicable judicial review standards. One can see this trend with regard to the GATT/WTO, with regard to UN Security Council resolutions and, surprisingly, in my view, also with regard to International Environmental Law.

If this is a correct observation, the only conclusion should be that courts should not lend themselves as being used for "window dressing", that is, for giving legitimacy to pseudo dispute resolution, while in fact they avoid dealing with the substantive issues by showing this significant restraint and deference. Instead, it would be better if in those cases, courts and tribunals either fully exercise their jurisdiction to the very end, including the substantive part, or should just leave the job to diplomacy.

---

41 Opinion AG Kokott in case C-308/06 (*Intertanko*) of 20 November 2007.
42 Ibid.: "70. Consequently, through the *reference* in the above provisions of the Convention on the Law of the Sea concluded by the Community Marpol 73/78 is the test standard applicable to Directive 2005/35 outside the territorial sea. In this respect it should be borne in mind that under the Convention on the Law of the Sea only rules which comply with Marpol 73/78, that is to say, rules which implement the standard of protection laid down therein, are permitted. By contrast, rules which go beyond Marpol 73/78 are not permitted in these sea areas. [emphasis added]."
[...]
107. However, provisions of secondary Community law must, so far as possible, be *interpreted in a manner that is consistent with the international agreements concluded by the Community*. Under Article 300(7) EC, those agreements are binding on the institutions. Secondary law may not infringe them. They have primacy over secondary law. [emphasis added].
108. Accordingly, *interpretation in conformity with international law must be given priority over other methods of interpretation*. This requirement is limited only by rules and principles which take precedence over the Community's obligations under international law. Such rules and principles include, for example, general legal principles and in particular the principle of legal certainty. Therefore, an interpretation contra legem is not possible." [emphasis added].

Thus, in the end, more cases before courts does not necessarily mean more justice!

We have to think about this aspect, because it has become fashionable to always emphasise the proliferation of international courts and tribunals and the constitutionalisation of international law, but there is another side to it, too.

Perspectives on Diplomacy, Arbitration and Adjudication from the United States and Latin America

PATRICIA HANSEN[1]

I also would like to thank Carl Baudenbacher for inviting me, and I am delighted to be here in this beautiful place on this very beautiful day. As Ruth Mackenzie mentioned, my main contribution to this panel will be to provide a perspective from the United States and Latin America, both of which had very different experiences from those of Europe in relation to international diplomacy and adjudication.

I would like to begin by discussing the classic debate that Dr. Lavranos referred to: the debate between diplomacy and adjudication, also known as the conflict between power-based and rule-based approaches to international law. Critics of the diplomatic or power-based approach generally argue that it is too closed and secretive, gives too much power to larger and richer countries, and compromises core values such as fairness, consistency, and predictability. Critics of the adjudicative or rule-based approach, on the other hand, focus on political realities. They point out, as Dr. Lavranos did, the dangers of having international courts take on "wrong" cases – meaning, cases that defy politically acceptable solutions. In their view, adjudication of a "wrong" case poses two separate dangers: the risk of undermining the political legitimacy of international adjudicatory institutions; and the risk of "poisoning the atmosphere" for future diplomatic negotiations.

Ironically, prior to the establishment of the WTO, the European Union favoured a "soft" diplomatic approach to resolving international trade disputes, while the United States favoured a "hard" legal enforcement mechanism. The United States backed up its view with a policy known as "aggressive unilateralism", in which the United States set *itself* up as adjudicator and enforcer of international trade rules. One result of this policy is the current WTO dispute settlement mechanism, which relies on a newer and much stronger dispute settlement process. Decisions issued in this process are automatically adopted unless there is a "reverse consensus" – i.e., if every member of the WTO agrees that the decision should *not* be adopted. Moreover, the prevailing party in the dispute is automatically entitled to impose trade sanctions against the losing party if it fails to comply with a WTO decision within a "reasonable" time.

---

1   JD, MPA, AB, J. Waddy Bullion Professor of Law at the University of Texas School of Law, Austin, Director of the dual degree programme in Law and Latin American Studies.

A similar framework for dispute settlement was established one year earlier in the North American Free Trade Agreement (NAFTA). Although neither the WTO nor NAFTA establish any "courts", both systems are more "adjudicatory" than "diplomatic." NAFTA is perhaps a bit less adjudicatory than the WTO, since it lacks a permanent Appellate Body such as the one created in the WTO. But in NAFTA, as in the WTO, there is a presumption that members should ordinarily comply with panel decisions, and a provision authorizing the prevailing party in a dispute to impose trade sanctions against parties that fail to comply with these decisions in a reasonable time. Under NAFTA, this time is set out as 30 days for all cases.

In the last few years, the United States has entered a number of additional bilateral and regional trade agreements that have spread the NAFTA model to many other countries. The United States now participates in NAFTA-like dispute settlement processes with Chile and Peru, as well as with the Dominican Republic and the five Central American countries that signed an agreement known as "DR-CAFTA". It has also agreed to similar dispute settlement processes in separate agreements with Australia, Bahrain, Jordan, Oman, Morocco and Singapore.

South American countries have also been busy developing their own regional trade agreements and dispute settlement institutions. The Andean Community, which includes Peru, Colombia, Ecuador, Bolivia and now Venezuela, was established in the 1960s and strengthened in the 1990s based on the EU model. In addition, Brazil, Argentina, Paraguay and Uruguay have created an important new common market known as "MERCOSUR", which recently created its own permanent appellate court.

During the past decade, each of these different agreements have had to confront a number of very important and widely-publicized disputes. The results of these disputes provide us with an initial basis to assess the success of the new "adjudicative" approach to dispute settlement.

In general, the WTO dispute settlement process has proven to be quite productive and effective. However, there have been a few highly-publicized cases of noncompliance. As I am sure you know, the EU has refused to comply with a WTO decision requiring it to change its regulation of meat hormones. The EU has also been slow to change its biotechnology policies in response to the WTO's decision in this area. Just this past year, the United States announced that it would not change its rules on internet gambling to comply with a decision issued in a case brought by the small island nation of Antigua. Instead, it will withdraw the GATS commitments that these regulations were found to violate. The United States has also dragged its feet before complying with a number of other WTO decisions.

Advocates of adjudication will probably be even more depressed by the NAFTA dispute settlement experience. In the fourteen years since NAFTA was established, only three panel decisions have been issued under its general dispute settlement provisions. None of these decisions was issued in the last seven years. The last panel decision issued under NAFTA's general dispute settlement provisions found that NAFTA required the United States to permit Mexican trucks to cross the border into the United States. Seven years later – despite the enormous economic costs generated by requiring goods to be transferred from Mexican trucks to U.S. trucks in order to cross the border – the United States still has not come into compliance with that ruling. The Bush Administration has proposed an experimental program that would permit entry by a limited number of Mexican trucks, but even this proposal is facing strong Congressional opposition. Recrimination against NAFTA is so strong that, during the recent presidential campaign, both Democratic presidential candidates called for renegotiation of the agreement – including, and perhaps especially, its dispute settlement provisions.

NAFTA also sets out special procedures for resolving anti-dumping and countervailing duty disputes. These procedures have been much more widely used than NAFTA's general disputes settlement provisions, in part because the procedures for resolving anti-dumping and countervailing disputes can be invoked directly by private parties, while the procedures for resolving other types of disputes may only be invoked by national governments. However, they have proved to be of limited use in highly political disputes. For example, the U.S. and Canada have been engaged for many years in a seemingly endless dispute over softwood lumber. Despite a series of panel decisions in both the WTO and NAFTA, there has been no permanent solution to this dispute. Instead, the two countries have found themselves repeatedly returning to the negotiating table to cobble together new temporary solutions.

Outside NAFTA, the results of the adjudicative approach to trade disputes are even less promising. The Andean Community, modelled on the European Union, has achieved little in real terms and is widely dismissed as a failure. After a number of early setbacks, MERCOSUR may be on a different path, but it is too soon to tell.

Viewing this panorama, it is easy to conclude that the adjudicatory approach to trade disputes has been a failure. However, defenders of adjudication have been quick to rebut this perception. In the famous words of Professor Henkin, most countries have in fact complied with most decisions most of the time. Moreover, the scarcity of panel decisions under agreements such as NAFTA may in part reflect the parties' ability to arrive at successful diplomatic resolutions to their disputes.

The repeated instances of non-compliance are clearly not cause for giving up on adjudication altogether. However, they remain problematic. Professor Alan Sykes from the University of Chicago argues that non-compliance with WTO decisions is in fact efficient and legitimate, so long as non-complying parties are required to pay compensation to the countries that are harmed by their violation of trade rules. He reasons that, if a party is actually willing to compensate others for the damages caused by its non-compliance, the benefits of the violations must exceed the costs. "Breach" of the rules is therefore efficient and legitimate. However, this argument is an inadequate response to the problem of non-compliance for two reasons. First, it appears to invite rich and powerful countries to buy their way out of their treaty commitments. Moreover, as Antigua has convincingly argued in the internet gambling case, the sanctions authorised under trade agreements do not always fully compensate for the losses that are caused by noncompliance.

I would like to put forward an alternative view. In my view, the perceived conflict between adjudication and diplomacy in international trade law is greatly overrated. We should regard the two approaches as complimentary, rather than competing models. By interpreting rules, adjudicatory bodies provide an open and neutral forum for reasoned discourse about issues such as the regulation of food or of internet gambling. As Dr. Lavranos pointed out, these kinds of issues can have significant and emotionally resonant political implications. Unlike Dr. Lavranos, however, I believe that the adjudicatory process need not and should not have the final word on these matters. I would argue that adjudication *should not* produce clear answers. Instead, it should produce guidelines and signals that will facilitate the negotiation of more informed and legitimate *political* solutions to the underlying problems. Viewed in this light, adjudication and diplomacy are equally important parts of the larger process of legal development.

If we view adjudication as just one part of a larger political dialogue, we begin to see noncompliance as a catalyst for what I would call "creative and principled" diplomacy. Let me give a few examples of where this appears to have already happened.

First, let me return to the WTO internet gambling case. That decision signalled a number of important areas where the rules quite frankly need to be reworked. The panel found that the United States did not *intend* to include internet gambling in its schedule of commitments, though it apparently accidentally did so. This ruling sent out an important message that countries should take great care in making their commitments and make sure they are very clear. On the other hand, it is not exactly surprising that a party would prefer to renegotiate and compensate others for a commitment that was not intentionally made.

The Gambling decision also signalled two other areas where "creative and principled" diplomacy are needed. First, the Appellate Body found that any regulation that generally prohibits a particular mode of services trade – for example, trade over the internet – is prohibited if a party has made a GATS commitment to refrain from "market access" restrictions. As Professor Joost Pauwelyn has pointed out, this ruling calls a very wide variety of regulatory restrictions into question. WTO members clearly need to revisit the provision that produced this unanticipated consequence, and negotiate a solution that takes into account the differing social concerns raised by different modes of supply for services trade.

The Gambling decision also represents the first adjudicatory attempt to address the WTO's mysterious "public morals" exception. The panel wisely recognized that WTO members should have significant leeway in defining the scope of that exception. In my view, the best way to define the limits of this exception is through the negotiation of treaties on human rights and other related areas, rather than through adjudication alone.

Arbitration has also been a catalyst for diplomatic and political solutions in the NAFTA. Although there have been only three panel decisions on intergovernmental trade disputes, dozens of decisions have been issued under NAFTA's provisions for investor-state arbitration. In many cases, arbitrators have been required to determine whether environmental and other regulatory matters violate a vague NAFTA provision requiring countries to give investors "fair and equitable" treatment. Interpretation of this provision has developed through a series of interrelated steps. First, arbitrators issued a series of decisions setting out their views on what kinds of treatment should be considered "fair and equitable". The NAFTA parties responded by agreeing to an "interpretation" designed to cabin the arbitrators' discretion, by requiring them to apply standards set out in customary international law. Of course, the interpretation does not spell out what kind of treatment customary international law requires, or answers the question of whether customary law has changed as a result of recent investment treaties. These issues require further input from well-researched and well-reasoned arbitration decisions. Political actors can and should review the results of these decisions, and adopt further interpretations to the extent they appear necessary. This is exactly the kind of interplay and exchange that I think is healthy for the development of international law.

Panel decisions have also acted as catalysts for political action in the Andean Community. As I mentioned earlier, the Andean Community is widely dismissed as a failure. However, a very interesting study by Professor Lawrence Helfer concludes that the Andean Tribunal of Justice is actually the third most active international court in the world, after the European Court of Human Rights and the European Court of Justice. Interestingly, the Andean court's rulings have focused almost entirely on Intellectual Property. In three of its rulings, the court found that Community rules prohibited individual members from complying with certain International Property provisions set out in agreements they had negotiated separately with the United States. In one of these cases, however, Colombia was able to persuade the members of the Andean Community to adopt an interpretation of Community rules that produced a different result. The new interpretation permitted Colombia to change its Intellectual Property laws in a way that accommodated its agreement with the United States.

Of course, political processes are not always able to resolve the problems caused by problematic adjudicatory decisions. As I mentioned earlier, the U.S. and Mexico have not yet been able to resolve their dispute over trucking. And despite seven years of negotiation, members of the WTO have been unable to complete the Doha round of negotiations. I remain hopeful, however, that new leadership will lead to more political and diplomatic cooperation in areas that have up to now been relegated solely to adjudication and arbitration.

I am particularly hopeful about the call for re-thinking of the NAFTA. When NAFTA was first signed, Mexico had just become a member of the GATT, and had very weak democratic and judicial institutions. The political and economic situation in Mexico is now quite different. Moreover, the NAFTA doesn't address some of the most critical issues in the hemisphere, such as immigration and energy. NAFTA's provisions on trucking were negotiated without any prior public discussion of the environmental or safety consequences involved. The same can be said regarding the US-Canada controversy over softwood lumber, which involves important issues relating to the sustainable level of logging on the continent, but has instead focused on technical requirements of countervailing duty laws that nobody really understands. It is time now to discuss the real issues.

Finally, let me give one brief example from MERCOSUR, where political authorities are confronting somewhat different lessons concerning the need to incorporate political realities into legal arguments *during* adjudication. Some years back, both Brazil and Argentina decided to ban imports of retreaded tyres. Uruguay, a country that exports retreaded tyres, initiated proceedings to challenge Brazil's ban under MERCOSUR rules. Brazil argued, unsuccessfully, that its ban was justified by MERCOSUR rules permitting member states to restrict imports of "used" tyres. After the panel rejected this argument, Brazil modified its ban so that it applied only to imports from *non*-MERCOSUR countries. Uruguay then initiated a second MERCOSUR proceeding, this time challenging Argentina's ban on imports of retreaded tyres. Surprisingly, the second MERCOSUR panel upheld Argentina's ban, based on the environmental and public health concerns associated with retreaded tyres. Amazingly, Brazil had made no mention of these concerns when defending its own import ban! As a result, Brazil was not allowed to ban retreaded tire imports from Uruguay, while Argentina was. Meanwhile, the European Union initiated WTO proceedings challenging Brazil's remaining ban on non-MERCOSUR tyre imports. This time, Brazil managed to persuade the WTO Appellate Body that its ban also addressed legitimate and important environmental and health concerns. However, the Appellate Body determined that these concerns were insufficient to justify a ban that applied only to some countries, and not others. Not surprisingly, the inconsistent results for Brazil and Argentina have produced a huge political outcry in Brazil.

The *Tyres* case illustrates that creative and principled diplomacy is not enough. In addition, legal institutions *within* each country must have a solid understanding of the social and political dimensions of trade disputes. Trade tribunals cannot provide satisfactory solutions to trade disputes unless trade lawyers themselves become aware of these dimensions and bring them to the tribunals' attention.

As I see my time is up, let me quickly sum up my main point: diplomacy and adjudication should not be viewed as competing approaches, but as complementary parts of a larger process of legal development, where diplomacy is based on law, and law is based on an adequate understanding of political and diplomatic concerns.

Discussion

RUTH MACKENZIE
Thank you very much. I am sure you will join with me in thanking all the panellists for their fascinating interventions on the interplay of diplomacy and adjudication and arbitration in each of these different contexts. We have some time now for discussion.

ALAN RAU
I have a question for Dr. Lavranos' paper, particularly, what he calls the second trend. I think there is a strong and interesting parallel with private law, which I am most familiar with. There, the overriding, overwhelming imperative is that parties are free to opt out, to withdraw from the litigation process if they prefer to settle their disputes privately. And that is without regard to what would otherwise be the exclusive jurisdiction of the court, because nobody is forced to litigate. And that is without regard to what the law is. Now arbitration I think fundamentally is an exercise of the settlement prerogative at the same time.

What becomes problematical is the presence of externalities, that is to say third party effects because the parties themselves or their agents, their arbitrators, have no reason to take into account third party effects. Still, it is rather startling that the party's freedom to arbitrate or to opt out of litigation would be in any way impeded or prevented by this public interest. There are public law enforcement bodies that exist for cases where the public interest is implicated.

So, the model I am just giving, which is parallel private and public jurisdictions, depending on who is invoking it, seems quite at odds with what you are suggesting. Am I correct in assuming that? I thought you were suggesting that it was somehow undesirable – for instance in the *Iron Rhine* case – to allow parties to opt out of what would be the exclusive jurisdiction of a court in order to choose the settlement prerogative. But that choice is what is inherent in the entire private system.

NIKOLAOS LAVRANOS
No, I think maybe I was not clear. My starting point or my general point is that, unfortunately or fortunately, you have Article 292 EC which gives exclusive jurisdiction to the European Court of Justice when it comes to disputes between two EC Member States involving potentially EC law. So if the Member States do not like this anymore, they can simply change or add another paragraph to this Article. The point I am making is that if every time EC Member States, for whatever reason, consider that it is better to bring the case before an arbitral tribunal, it undermines the consistency of

EC law. Clearly, there are advantages for choosing arbitration, for instance, because it is much quicker; arbitration maybe takes a few months whereas an ECJ case takes two years and you can select your arbitrators etc. So there are a number of advantages for the EC Member States, but since they are part of this EC law system they are limited by their choice and they have to live with it or have to change the rules. What they are doing now is in a way not consistent with their obligations. So, I think it is not the contrast between public or private, choosing a private or public forum, the problem is that you have obligations written in the treaty and these have to be first amended and then you can start forum shopping or combining, even, if you like, public and private methods of dispute resolution. Just to add, in the *Iron Rhine* case they framed the dispute as if it was about who should pay the cost. You could leave that to an arbitral tribunal, no problem; but the actual problem was the circumvention of the EC Habitat Directive. If the Habitat Directive would have been applied, it would clearly block any reactivation of the railway line. So, I think we do not really disagree it is just a different point I was mentioning.

ANNE VAN AAKEN

Certainly, fragmentation as a problem in International Law has been much discussed in the last years; best example of this is the ILC Report on fragmentation authored by Martti Koskenniemi. Since states do not always take into account other, potentially conflicting public international law when negotiating treaties, interpretation by international courts tribunals becomes crucial for defragmentation. That has been much discussed within the "trade and... issues". But it is also a problem in other areas. The Vienna Convention on the Law of Treaties may provide for a solution, in Art. 31 (3)(c), which has been called the master key in the building of international law. In my view, clarity and transparency in interpretational matters is a desideratum for international law. I would be interested in your point of view.

CARL BAUDENBACHER

Just concerning this last point, fragmentation. My own experience as a European judge makes me reluctant to take that very seriously. This statement that this so-called proliferation of international courts leads to a fragmentation of an overall system is based on the assumption that there used to be a comprehensive system which is now fragmentised and that is simply not true. If you look at the development in Europe, with the European Court of Justice and the European Court of Human Rights and even my court, the EFTA Court, these are new developments. These are courts that are based on parameters that were not there in traditional public international law. Access to justice for individuals and economic operators, direct effect, interpretation not according to the interpretation rules of the Vienna Convention but according to the normal rules that every national Supreme or Constitutional Court applies. I can see the argument from a theoretical perspective, but in practice I would rather focus on the dialogue situation which we should foster among these courts and to a certain extent also on the fact that with this spreading out of courts there is some competition involved. Competition of ideas and competition of reasons. That will bring us forward.

MARIA AGIUS

Thank you very much for very interesting speeches. I am from Uppsala University in Sweden and my question pertains to the judicial restraint and deference that was raised by Dr. Lavranos. And I was wondering if you or other panel members could give your views on what considerations a court or a tribunal must give to the objective of the treaty regime under which it is established and whether there should be consideration when the full resolve of an issue implies the application of law from a different treaty regime with perhaps different objectives and intentions of the parties upon conclusion of that treaty. What consideration that should be given in the choice of applicable law and the judicial interaction and dialogue that was also raised by Professor Baudenbacher? Thank you.

RUTH MACKENZIE

That is the end of the questions but I need to give the panellists a few minutes to answer. So let me go perhaps in the reverse order of speakers and call on Patricia Hansen first.

PATRICIA HANSEN

I just have a few comments. I agree with Carl on the fragmentation issue. At least in NAFTA, tribunals are citing and reading decisions issued by other tribunals under other agreements. If they were not doing this I would really worry about fragmentation. But tribunals do in fact appear to be working together to help develop a coherent understanding of similarities and differences in the way all these treaties address related problems. Also, Article 31 of the Vienna Convention clearly allows tribunals to use principles taken from other areas of international law when interpreting a specific treaty provision.

However, the emergence of so many different investment treaties with so many different provisions has produced a significant problem with respect to the Most Favoured Nation obligation. Each treaty provides that investors from the signatory countries are entitled to Most Favoured Nation treatment. Does this mean that the provisions of each treaty are automatically superceded by more generous provisions in other investment treaties? If not, then there is certainly a need to make these investment treaties more coherent.

NIKOLAOS LAVRANOS

My starting point to a number of questions is that we have to consider the European constitutional traditions when we look at the European Court of Justice and the Strasbourg Court. This is a common denominator and this should enable at least those regional courts to take into account the objectives, which is to protect fundamental rights and to provide full judicial review. If this is an objective for both the European Court of Justice and the Strasbourg Court, there should be no problem of taking each other into account. They do so in most cases but there are cases, I know I was very selective in pointing out the one percent cases which are problematic, but these are exactly the cases where it is interesting to see if there is a real dialogue. And when you look at the *"Solange"*-method which has been used in the *Bosphorus* case by the Strasbourg Court, there is no dialogue anymore. The dialogue is closed because they say, we are not going to exercise our judicial review unless in manifestly deficient cases.

There is another example I did not yet mention. I am referring to the interaction between the International Court of Justice (ICJ) and the International Criminal Tribunal for the former Yugoslavia (ICTY) regarding their respective views on the application of the rules on state responsibility.

In one of the most discussed ICTY cases, *Tadić*[1], the Tribunal had to look into the rules on state responsibility. The ICTY Chamber identified two degrees of control, the ICJ's *Nicaragua* "effective control" test and the previously established "overall control" test. The ICTY Chamber decided in favour of the former alternative, which conflicted with the view of the ICJ on the issue of use of force in customary international law. In its judgment[2] it even went as far as to expressly argue that the law as stated by the ICJ on the use of force was not "persuasive" and was "unconvincing" and went on to declare that the law was to the contrary of what the ICJ had said it was.[3]

In the *Genocide* Judgment[4] the ICJ reacted quite strongly to the ICTY's "reasoning" in the *Tadić* case. It argued that the findings on questions of state responsibility were outside the scope of the ICTY's jurisdiction and even though it will accept the factual and legal findings made by the ICTY on criminal liability of an accused, it will not accept its positions on issues of general public international law, especially when this is outside its jurisdiction and unnecessary.

Now, can this interaction be described as a dialogue? Professor Simma, who two days ago gave a speech in Florence, defended it as a sort of dialogue. But when you read the judgement, this is not a dialogue, at least in my opinion, this is a form of correction or even reprehension. So, obviously there is no clear definition of what dialogue is. But I think, and this is a very important point that was raised, that there is no unified international law and so there cannot be fragmentation, but more important is the aspect of an uncoordinated system. In the EC we have this hierarchical coordinated system between the ECJ and national courts. That solves a lot of problems. And because we

---

1 *Tadic*, IT-94-1-A.
2 ICTY Appeals Chamber, *Tadic* judgment, 15 July 1999.
3 *Tadic*, IT-94-1-A, paras. 115 and 116.
4 Application of the Convention on the Prevention and Punishment of the Crime of Genocide, ICJ judgment of 26 February 2007.

do not have that at the international level, I think we have to search for other tools and means and that is exactly where the Vienna Convention comes in and also other instruments like teleological interpretation, dynamic interpretation, looking at what is the best solution for the interests involved; these are instruments and tools every court can and should use.

So even though I may have sounded too pessimistic, it is possible that in the end we can overcome this with the tools we already have at our disposal. But that would require for judges to be a bit more open and just do their job.

SVEN NORBERG
You mentioned the definition of judicial dialogue. I am convinced that we will get to listen to a very interesting keynote speech tomorrow morning by Carl Baudenbacher on that issue.

I would simply like to pick up on what Carl mentioned before – competition between courts. In my opinion, competition between courts is healthy. Especially considering the tremendous developments the judicial systems in Europe went through during the European integration process, it would be unreasonable to expect everything to be perfect from the very beginning. It will take time. However, the progress made over the last ten to twenty years is impressive. Of course, the European courts and the national courts may be struggling with their dialogue but I am confident that after a while they will get it right.

The cases Nikos brought up, in which he criticised the deference in the relationship between the European Court of Justice (ECJ) and the European Court of Human Rights (ECrtHR) were very interesting. They raise the question of what will happen the day the European Union accedes to the European Convention on Human Rights (ECHR). Because by doing that, a system would be created in which the risk of two European Courts mutually undermining each other's authority would be very real. I will give you an example of what I mean.

The national courts of most European countries have to apply the ECHR. However, they do not have the possibility to get a preliminary ruling from the ECrtHR to guide them in the interpretation of the provisions of the Human Rights Convention. This possibility exists, on the other hand, with regard to all provisions of EC law thanks to the competence of the ECJ under Article 234 EC. If the EU would adhere to the ECHR, the provisions thereof would, under the established case law of the ECJ[5], automatically become Community Law. This would in turn mean that a national court in an EU State could make a reference under Article 234 EC to the ECJ with regard to provisions of the ECHR. At the same time, someone who is dissatisfied with a legal act

---

5   Cf. Cases *Haegeman v. Belgium* (1974) ECR 449 and 104/81 *Hauptzollamt Mainz v. Kupferberg* (1982) ECR 3641.

or behaviour by the EU could under the relevant procedures launch a challenge against the EU before the Strasbourg Court. Thus, nearly unsolvable conflicts between the two European Courts in Strasbourg and Luxembourg could risk to be created.

Having that in mind, I have a somewhat larger sympathy for the courts not wanting to get too close to the conflict but rather stepping back a bit. I can agree it is not always satisfactory but let us not "make the best the enemy of the good".

RUTH MACKENZIE

Thank you very much. I feel sure that we will continue to discuss these issues over the next couple of days, so please just join me in thanking the panellists for this rich introduction to the interplay between diplomacy and adjudication.

Focus:
Effect, Non-Compliance and Enforcement of Judgments of International / Supranational Courts

Introduction

ULRICH HALTERN[1]

Ladies and Gentlemen, the next panel promises to be truly intriguing. This is due to both to its subject and to the panellists which I have the pleasure of introducing to you. On my left is Dr. Reto Malacrida. He is Counsellor with the Legal Affairs Division of the WTO and a specialist on retaliation. One of his recent articles on fair WTO retaliation has just appeared in the 2008 volume of the Journal of World Trade.

On my right is Dr. Diana Panke who worked a lot with Professor Tanja Börzel and who is now lecturer at the School of Politics and International Relations at the University College Dublin in Ireland. She has published extensively on Europeanization and European governance. One of her recent articles is about the European Court of Justice as an Agent of Europeanization.

On the very right hand is Professor Paul Mahoney, who hardly needs introducing. He is now President of the Civil Service Tribunal of the European Union. As you all know, Paul Mahoney was Registrar at the European Court of Human Rights, and I understand that the Strasbourg Court will be the focus of his contribution today.

Today's topic is "Effect, non-compliance, and enforcement of judgements of international and supranational courts". Let me share with you just a few brief thoughts before we dive into the subject matter.

It is well known that political science has taken a decisive normative turn. The impression you get from literature in political science and political theory is that of the law being the safe haven of all theory. It seems as if the vectors of history's trajectory all point to the law, which, in the light of mounting evidence to an increasingly violent world, becomes something of a last straw. The law is also the focal point of our belief in a narrative of political progress. That narrative has three elements: First, a transition from personal to democratic forms of power, in which the people become the sole legitimate power. Second, a movement from a world of torture to one of procedure, from the spectacle of the scaffold to the science of penology. The rule of the people is, in this way, simultaneously the rule of law. Third, the displacement of war by law. Every aspect of this threefold narrative of progress appeals to the law. Indeed, the rule of law is the dominant theme of the entire narrative. Accordingly, compliance with the law turns out to be the centre piece not only of the focus of lawyers, but also of everybody

---

1 Professor and Chair at Leibniz University of Hannover, Director of the Hannover Institute for National and Transnational Integration Studies.

who believes in, and desires, political progress. No wonder, then, that we passionately discuss, reform, and work on compliance issues: Nothing less than our political identity is at stake.

More down to earth, I would like to share with you a quote I came across in a speech by Pascal Lami to the United States Chamber of Commerce. Lami, as you all know, is a former European Commissioner and the Director-General of the WTO, with ample experience in the weal and woe of compliance. He composed a "Hymn to Compliance", which goes as follows:

> *Hymn to Compliance*
> *Consult before you legislate,*
> *negotiate before you litigate,*
> *compensate before you retaliate, and*
> *comply at any rate.*

Lami sang his hymn tongue in cheek, I am sure. Still, it might structure our discussion. Comply at any rate – is there an obligation to comply? Ask professors of international law, and they will surely answer in the affirmative: Of course you have to comply, it is "the law". Ask international diplomats, and they will talk of efficient breach: There is no obligation to comply if you are willing to pay.

Consult before you legislate, negotiate before you litigate: What is the meaning of consultations and negotiations? Is this a discursive element or a power element in international relations? How do they relate to international law? Can international law perhaps co-opt power relations or transform them into discursive relations? And how does litigation before national and international courts figure in this equation?

Finally, compensate before retaliate: What instruments do we have to drive sovereign nation-states towards compliance? Surely, the mechanisms in the European Union are vastly different from those in the WTO or the ECHR. In addition, these mechanisms are embedded in very different contexts. The EU context is that of a quasi-constitutional environment, with direct effect, supremacy, human rights protection, a powerful court, and national courts and civil society highly involved in law enforcement. Things may be different in WTO and ECHR law.

Now, let us first hear from Diana who told me she is going to speak about issues of a more general nature. We will then hear from Paul and, finally, from Reto.

The European Court of Justice as an Instance of High Legalisation: What Have We Learned on the Prospects to Foster Compliance with EU Law?

DIANA PANKE[1]

It is remarkable how international cooperation has mushroomed in the last decades. On the international level, there is hardly any policy field in which cooperation across borders does not take place. Yet, even though states agree on particular hard and soft laws within a broad range of international organisations and regimes, they nevertheless have lots of incentives to violate it afterwards. For example, governments can change, interests of states can vary over time, or states discover that free riding saves implementation costs, while they nevertheless profit from cooperation, if other cooperation partners comply with the created law beyond the nation-state. Hence, each and every international organisation grapples with instances of non-compliance. Since norm violations impair the power of law beyond the nation-state, international organisations and regimes incorporate a broad empirical variety of compliance facilitating mechanisms. The most important means to increase compliance with law beyond the nation-state is to introduce legalised compliance monitoring and dispute settlement mechanisms. The former shall detect instances of non-compliance and the latter shall turn detected norm violations into compliance.

Against this background, this chapter addresses the following question: Can high legalisation of international organisations foster compliance and reduce non-compliance? Since the European Union (EU) has a highly legalised compliance management system, this chapter will exclusively focus on non-compliance in the EU, more specifically on the means and records of the European Court of Justice (ECJ) in settling hard cases of non-compliance with EU law.

In principle, states can violate EU and international law in three ways. Firstly, they can abstain from transposing it into national law altogether or not notify the European Commission or the responsible international secretariats of measures undertaken (delayed transpositions). Secondly, law beyond the nation-state is violated, if governments and parliaments incompletely or incorrectly transpose it into national law (incorrect

---

1   Dr. Diana Panke, Lecturer in European Politics, School of Politics and International Relations, University College Dublin.

transposition). Thirdly, due to administrative malpractices at central, regional, or local levels, Member States can fail to practically implement European or international law correctly (incorrect implementation).[2]

If the European Commission as the guardian of the treaties suspects a Member State to violate EU law in one of the three manners outlined above, the Commission can open an infringement proceeding against the respective state (Article 226 ECT).[3] In doing that, the Commission sends letters of formal notice to the respective government and governments react with written statements. If this unofficial step cannot solve the compliance problems, the Commission initiates first formal steps of the infringement procedure by issuing reasoned opinions (Art. 226 ECT). This is followed by bilateral negotiations, in which the Commission and the state exchange clarifications and political considerations. If compliance problems persist, the Commission refers the cases to the ECJ. The ECJ is highly independent and can resort to *judicial discourses* and *judgments* as the two judicial compliance instruments. Once cases reach the ECJ, it starts a judicial discourse (Art. 226 ECT). State and European advocates exchange judicial arguments in an oral and a written procedure. After both stages of the discourse ended, since the two parties had exchanged all legal arguments, the European Advocate General prepares a written opinion for the ECJ, summarising the arguments and developing own views on the cases. In the next step, the ECJ issues binding judgments on how to interpret the disputed norm (Art. 226 ECT). Should governments still refuse to comply and abstain from domestic legal changes after both judicial compliance instruments had been applied, the enforcement phase follows the adjudication stage and expands the toolbox through *sanction threats* as the third available compliance instrument. The European Economic Community Treaty (ECT) of 1957 entailed no provisions for centralised but only for decentralised sanctions.[4] If the Member States did not comply with rulings, the ECJ referred to a violation of Art. 171 ECT. Through these references, instances of persistent non-compliance became transparent and opened windows of

---

2   In its empirical analysis, this chapter focuses on delayed and incorrect transpositions and not on failures of practical implementation, because the number of actors responsible for compliance is lower for the former (ministries) than the latter (ministries and bureaucracy).

3   This chapter focuses on direct actions (infringement procedure based on Art. 226–228 ECT) and not on the preliminary rulings (based on Art. 234 ECT) as a decentralised compliance mechanism (e.g. (Stone Sweet and Brunell 1998; Carrubba and Murrah 2005)). The reason for this empirical limitation is that many of the compliance monitoring and restoring instruments (as outlined by Art. 226–228 ECT) can also be found in other international organisations, while the decentralised preliminary ruling system has hardly been copied by other IOs so that the findings cannot be easily generalised beyond the EU context.

4   The treaty basis for the infringement procedure, the European Community Treaty (ECT), was changed in 1993 and in 1997. The European Economic Community Treaty of 1957 provided the legal framework for the infringement procedure (Arts. 169, 170 and 171) and Art. 171 had no second paragraph allowing for financial sanctions until 1993. If Member States did not comply with ECJ rulings, the ECJ could only refer to a violation of Art.171, which stated that Member States are obliged to comply with ECJ rulings. Since the Treaty of Amsterdam, the infringement procedure is regulated by Arts. 226–228 ECT (which correspond to the old Arts. 169, 170 and 171). For reasons of simplicity, this study refers to the newer numbers even for cases before 1997, when it would for example be formally correct to refer to Art. 169 instead of Art. 226 ECT, or to Art. 171 instead of Art. 228 ECT.

opportunity for informal sanctions by other states.⁵ The Maastricht Treaty introduced a centralised sanctioning mechanism in 1993. If states fail to comply with judgments, the Commission will send second letters of formal notice⁶ followed by second reasoned opinions based on Art. 228 ECT. Thereby, a second infringement procedure is initiated that resembles the first procedure with one exception. As the Commission refers the case to the ECJ, it additionally proposes daily penalties and lump sums. In its second judgment, the ECJ then imposes monetary sanctions.

Informed by neoliberal theory, legalisation approaches in regard to the free rider problem as the central obstacle for international institutionalised cooperation⁷. While some states comply with law beyond the nation-state, others abstain from investing resources and fail to implement it timely and legally correct. In order to prevent norm violations, legalisation approaches point to hard law and its high degree of obligation and precision and to institutional transparency-creating mechanisms, such as centralised or decentralised monitoring systems.⁸ If norm violations have been detected, legalisation approaches propose a variety of institutional mechanisms to restore compliance. Institutions are highly legalised if third parties and not only states have the right to file complaints, if dispute and infringement procedures are obligatory and not voluntary, if courts can issue binding rulings and if judges are independent. Based on those criteria, the European Union is an instance of high legalisation.

Does this mean that the EU has a particularly good compliance record due to its highly legalised compliance monitoring system? If we are looking into empirical instances of non-compliance in the European Union, we see that among the almost 17 000 proceedings which the Commission opened through a letter of formal notice between 1978 and 1999 for the EU-12 Member States (on all three types of violation),⁹ only 4142 infringements, in which the EU-12 Member States violated EU secondary law because they did not transpose it at all or transposed it incorrectly, reached the first official stage (reasoned opinions, based on Art. 226 ECT).¹⁰ Moreover, if we control the number of Member States and the acquis communautaire as violative opportuni-

---

5   Examples of informal sanctions are losses of reputation or credibility, which could negatively affect a state's bargaining power in policy-making processes.
6   However, as for the first letter of formal notice, the European Commission keeps no publicly available track of the letters. Thus, it is not possible to acquire comprehensive data on second letters of formal notice.
7   Abbott, Kenneth W., Robert O. Keohane, Andrew Moravcsik, Anne Marie Slaughter, and Duncan Snidal. 2000. "The Concept of Legalization." *International Organization* 54 (3):401-19.
8   Goldstein, Judith, Miles Kahler, Robert O. Keohane, and Anne-Marie Slaughter. 2000. "Introduction: Legalization and World Politics." *International Organization* 54 (3):386-7; Mitchell, Ronald. 1996. "Compliance Theory: An Overview." In Improving Compliance with *International Environmental Law*, ed. J. C. u. J. W. u. P. Roderick. London: Earthscan: 17-20.
9   Börzel, Tanja A., Meike Dudziak, Tobias Hofmann, Diana Panke, and Carina Sprungk. 2007. "Recalcitrance, Inefficiency, and Support for European Integration: Why Member States do (not) Comply with European Law." *Harvard University. Center for European Studies Working Paper Series* No. 153: 6.
10 The data is based on the Annual Reports of the European Commission and stems from a research project on the occurrence of non-compliance with EU law, headed by Prof. Tanja Börzel and funded by the German Research Council. For more information see (Börzel et al. 2007).

ties, the level of detected norm violations is more or less constant over time and the EU does not face a growing implementation deficit.[11] Is that good news? Is the high legalisation of the EU's compliance monitoring system a success?

Since the first annual report of the Commission and 1999, the European Commission, as the guardian of the treaties, detected over 4000 instances in which Member States did not implement European secondary law timely or legally correct. Since the personnel, financial and administrative resources of the European Commission are not endless, it might be the case that the Commission did not detect all instances of norm violations. Against this background, researchers can only speculate whether the infringement cases reported in the annual reports represent the total number of cases or whether they are the tip of an iceberg.[12] Hence, the only two conclusions we can safely make for the high legalisation of the compliance monitoring system is that it worked in so far as the EU is not facing an increasing problem of norm violations over time and that the detected instances of norm violations do not show very high levels of non-compliance, if we control for the violative opportunities and assume that each state can violate each EU law once a year.[13]

Hard cases of non-compliance are infringements that cannot be settled in non-judicial bilateral interactions with the European Commission but reach the ECJ. Those hard cases get then confronted with the EU compliance restoring system, which is also highly legalised. In the European Union, infringement proceedings are not voluntary, judges are independent and the ECJ can rely on a big toolbox of compliance instruments combining judicial discourses, binding judgements, sanction threats and since 1993 even financial penalties. An empirical analysis[14] shows that less than a third of the cases on delayed or incorrect legal transpositions of EU secondary law of the EU-12 States, in which the Commission had sent a reasoned opinion, were referred to the ECJ in order to be subject to a *judicial discourse*. Of those 1110 referrals, the ECJ issued *judgments* in 439 cases. In more than 90% of the occasions, the ECJ sided with most of the complaints of the European Commission and not with the Member States. Only 66 cases in which the ECJ issued a judgment (based on Art. 226 ECT) became subject to a second infringement proceeding and to *threats of sanctions* (reasoned opinions based on Art. 228 ECT). In only eight instances, cases on delayed or incorrect transposition of EU secondary law were actually referred to the ECJ for a second time but with one exception resolved before the ECJ issued second judgments and financial penalties.[15] This shows that the judicial EU compliance restoring system is overall highly success-

---

11 Börzel, Tanja A. 2001. "Non-Compliance in the European Union: Pathology or Statistical Artefact?" *Journal of European Public Policy* 8 (5):803-24.
12 Cf. (Börzel 2001).
13 Cf. (Börzel et al. 2007).
14 The data is based on the Annual Reports of the European Commission and stems from a research project on the occurrence of non-compliance with EU law, headed by Prof. Tanja Börzel and funded by the German Research Council. For more information see (Börzel et al. 2007).
15 The ECJ convicted Greece for an incorrect transposition to a penalty of 20 000 € a day (Case C-387/97 – *Commission of the European Communities v Hellenic Republic*, ECR 2000, I-05047).

ful. With each and every applied compliance instrument the number of open cases declines and enforcement measures in the form of actual financial sanctions come rarely into play. In the end all cases are settled, even though some norm violations might drag on for a total of 16 years after being detected.

While the EU compliance restoring system is highly successful in general, the European Commission's infringement data (cf. the annual reports) also shows that not every compliance instrument is effective all the time. Why is it that for example a judicial discourse sometimes fosters very quick transpositions and very quick shifts from non-compliance into compliance, sometimes even before the European Court of Justice issues its judgement? And why is it that at other times even a sanction threat is necessary for Member States to push Member States out of non-compliance? Why do judicial instruments vary in their effectiveness even against one and the same state, even against one and the same government? Under which conditions are those instruments successful? When do judicial discourses talk Member States into compliance? When do judgements end in non-compliance and when are sanction threats effective?

In order to answer these questions, it is necessary to take a closer look on judicial discourses, judgments, and sanction threats in turn. A judicial discourse requires between one and a half and two and a half years on average in the EU. It consists of a written and an oral stage in which judicial arguments are exchanged by the advocates of the parties. Judicial discourses take place for all cases referred to the ECJ, but do not always lead to quick transformations into compliance. Only sometimes do Member States already start to adapt domestic acts and shift into compliance during judicial discourses. Why is it that judicial discourses can be successful in talking Member States into compliance, but that they can also fail to do so? In order to quickly foster compliance, governments have to become ideationally entrapped by the judicial arguments exchanged in the judicial discourse.[16] This requires that the advocates of the parties do not talk at cross purposes but instead commonly apply a technique of judicial interpretation that also fits to the complexity of the interpretational problem.[17] If, for example, an interpretational dispute is not complex, because the relevant paragraph is relatively precise (e.g. no unspecified concepts, no complex list of exceptional rules, no cross references to other parts of the legal norm etc.) and if at one point both advocates applied the wording method of judicial interpretation, then it is very likely that the legal experts came to the same conclusion of how to best interpret the norm in question. In such cases, a national advocate can basically communicate to her ministry that there is really no way that non-compliance can be defended with good arguments anymore. This, in turn, argumentatively entraps ministries and makes them shift into compliance. However, not in all cases the advocates of the parties actually agree on the applied technique of interpretation and not in all cases the technique of inter-

---

16 Panke (forthcoming) "Why Discourses are Only Sometimes Successful" in Review of International Studies.
17 Panke (forthcoming) "Why Discourses are Only Sometimes Successful" in Review of International Studies.

pretation fits to the complexity of the problem at stake (e.g. wording method cannot solve highly complex issues, in which more than one paragraph is relevant but point to different conclusions). Whenever the advocates of the parties argue at cross purposes, the governments may still have hope to be able to defend their initial norm interpretation with good arguments and do not initiate legal changes that resemble compliance before the ECJ judgment.[18]

Judgments are also not always successful in fostering compliance, as, for example, the number of applied sanction threats shows (reasoned opinions based on Art. 228 ECT). Judgments summarise the major cleavages of the cases, authoritatively define content

---

18 The UK case on the collective redundancy directive (75/129) is an example for a successful judicial discourse that argumentatively entrapped a government and fostered compliance. The European directive prescribes informational rights and consultations between employers and employees' representatives in order to protect employees in the event of collective dismissals. Yet, the latest UK transposition (the 1985 EPA) only incompletely transposed the directive, since protective rights only applied to some redundancies. Also, information of and consultation with trade unions were ultimately voluntary for employers. Hence, the Commission opened an infringement proceeding. Westminster strongly opposed collective worker rights, because they did not fit to the liberal economic approach and were regarded as costly burden for employers (Ashford, Douglas E. 1981. *Policy and Politics in Britain*. Philadelphia, PA: Temple University Press: 101-114; House of Commons. 1989. "House of Commons Hansard Debates for 6 July 1989." Hansard Debates: 475; House of Commons 1992. "House of Commons Hansard Debates for 17 November 1992." Hansard Debates: 476.) Non-compliance interests were strong, so that the Commission referred the case to the ECJ in 1992 and a judicial discourse began. Most importantly, the parties disagreed whether employers have to recognise trade unions (1994. "Court Judgment of June 8th 1994. European Commission Against the United Kingdom Regarding the Incomplete Legal Transposition of Directive 75/129, C-383/92." Official Journal of the European Communities 1994: I-02479.). It affected the very heart of the directive's aim: employees were considerably less protected, if employers could simply reject to collaborate with trade unions and if worker representatives only had a voice in consultation processes, which employers could easily ignore. In the course of the judicial discourse the advocates of the parties both used the teleological method of judicial reasoning ((European Court of Justice 1994): 14, 20, 24-25). They inquired into the aim of the norm and placed the disputed paragraphs in the context of the directive's purpose. Does an interpretation positively contribute to the aim of the directive or does it thwart it? For both parties the aim of the directive was not to harmonise systems of worker's representation, but to harmonise the protective legislation in cases of collective redundancies ((European Court of Justice 1994): 14). It followed that the directive could not achieve partial harmonization of worker protection in collective redundancies, if workers were not represented at all ((European Court of Justice 1994): 24-25). Prior to the judicial discourse, the Major-government defended voluntary recognition of trade unions by employers (e.g. (House of Commons 1992): 172). After the British advocate disseminated the norm interpretation as developed in the judicial discourse, the Major-government became argumentatively entrapped and shifted into compliance. Subsequently, the government changed the legal landscape and no longer denied that the directive puts an obligation on employers to consult and inform worker representatives and stopped claiming that recognition is voluntary. "We reached a point of considerable uncertainty where it looked as though an employer had to consult in cases of collective redundancy only if there were a recognised trade union. If there were no recognised trade unions, the employer was apparently under no obligation to consult anyone, *which cannot be right.*" (Minister for Competition and Consumer Affairs (Mr. John M. Taylor) in House of Commons. 1996. " House of Commons Hansard Debates for 6 February 1996." Hansard Debates: 205, emphasis added. In line with that, the UK already started with legal adaptations during the ongoing judicial discourse and quickly finalised the legal changes shortly after the ECJ judgment (Collective Redundancies and Transfer of Undertakings Regulations). Afterwards, workers were protected from negative consequences of collective redundancies, even in enterprises without trade union representatives. Employers were no longer free to ignore worker representatives and thereby ignore collective worker rights, but had to either recognise a trade union or other representatives, elected by the employees (House of Commons 1996).

and scope of contested norms, and reduce the complexity of disputed issues. While the written and oral stages of the judicial discourse excluded the public, judgments are openly accessible and increase the publicity of cases. Thereby they disseminate new ideas into the domestic sphere and clarify how the state concerned violated EU law. This differentially empowers domestic compliance constituencies vis-à-vis domestic compliance opponents.[19] Norm proponents gain additional attention, new ideas on the issue-matter, and the normative backing of the Court, while non-compliance proponents are disempowered through authoritative norm definitions of the ECJ because they can no longer use the legal uncertainty for their purposes, can no longer claim to be in line with EU law, and cannot hardly argue to ignore the ECJ.[20] Differentially empowered societal actors, most notably interest groups, can use judgments to push their states into compliance.[21] Compliance constituencies can threaten their respective governments with losses of reputation and votes (shaming campaigns) and, thereby change governmental cost-benefit calculations and facilitate domestic changes in line

---

19 Dai, Xinyuan. 2005. "Why Comply? The Domestic Constituency Mechanism." *International Organization* 59 (02):363-98; Finnemore, Martha, and Sikkink, Kathryn. 1998. "International Norm Dynamics and Political Change." International Organization 52 (4):887-917; Börzel 2006; Conant, Lisa J. 2002. *Justice Contained. Law and Politics in the European Union*. Ithaca, NY: Cornell University Press.
20 Cichowski, Rachel. 2006. "Courts, Rights, and Democratic Participation." *Comparative Political Studies* 39 (1):50-75; Alter, Karen, and Jeannette Vargas. 2000. "Explaining Variation in the Use of European Litigation Strategies: EC Law and UK Gender Equality Policy." *Comparative Political Studies* 24 (4):535-61.
21 Cf. (Panke 2007).

with the ECJ judgment. This is successful if the judgment resonates well with already domestically institutionalised norms.[22]

The third instrument at the disposal of European authorities is a sanction threat. The European Commission can introduce first measures towards a second binding judgement and penalties (issued by the ECJ) with a second letter of formal notice followed by a second recent opinion (both Art. 228 ECT). Under which conditions are sanction

---

22 An example for a differential empowerment effect of an ECJ judgment is the German case on the residence of foreign workers and their families (c.f. (Panke 2007)). Directive number 1990/364 aims to provide legal certainty to affected persons in creating transparent and clear standards for the permission and the deprivation of residence entitlements of foreign workers and their families within the EU. The EU directive created adaptational demands, but the German government hesitated to transpose it. They framed foreign workers as short-term guests and regarded Germany not as an immigration country (e.g. Minister Schäuble (Bundestag. 1990a. "Plenarprotokoll vom 26.04.1990.): 16281. Therefore and in order to save social security expenses, the government opted for restrictions regarding the entry and residence of foreign workers (Bundestag. 1990b. "Plenarprotokoll vom 31.05.1990.): 16893-5. They claimed that there was no need to transpose the foreign workers directive, since the general clause (§ 2 II) of the law on foreigners mentioned the supremacy of EU over domestic laws. In addition, in 1992 the federal interior ministry composed an internal circular letter informing the bureaucracy on the existence of the directive. The European Commission detected non-compliance and referred the case to the ECJ in 1995. The issue at stake was, whether the general clause § 2 II of the law on foreigners was a sufficient legal transposition. During the ongoing judicial discourse, the German government did not initiate legal changes and did also not rhetorically accept the norm interpretation of the Commission. In 1997, the ECJ ruled that Germany failed to legally transpose the foreign workers directive (European Court of Justice 1997). After the ECJ ruling, the Interior Ministry issued a regulation ("Freizügigkeitsverordnung") that legally transposed the ruling in a minimal patching-up manner. This was a response to shaming campaigns of differentially empowered domestic actors. The 1997 ECJ judgment created publicity and reinforced the arguments of societal norm proponents. German catholic and protestant church associations strongly opposed sentiments against foreigners (Süddeutsche Zeitung. 1996. "Kirchen und DGB fordern Reform des Ausländerrechts."). They argued for policies broadening legal rights of foreigners and criticised that existing laws suffer from two elements: they leave too wide administrative margins and are insufficient as regards long-term stays of foreigners (Evangelische Kirche Deutschland. 1997. *"Offen für Europa – offen für andere"*. Gemeinsames Wort der Kirchen zur Woche der ausländischen Mitbürger, 1997: Evangelische Kirche Deutschland; Barth, Hermann 1997. "Die Christen und Europa. Der Vizepräsident des EKD-Kirchenamtes, Hermann Barth, zu Herausforderungen und Aufgaben für Christen im heutigen Europa." *In Evangelische Kirche Deutschland (EKD)*: Evangelische Kirche Deutschland (EKD); Bundestag. 1998b. "Plenarprotokoll vom 29.05.1998.). Churches were important societal actors, not the least because the membership in the catholic or the protestant church was relatively broad in Germany. Also the conservative party (CDU) identified itself strongly with Christianity (the commitment to Christian Democracy is even part of the party's name) and could not neglect the position of the Catholic Church altogether (Pombeni, Paolo. 2000. "The Ideology of Christian Democracy." Journal of Political Ideologies 5 (3):289-300.). The high goodness of fit between the judgment on residence permissions of foreign workers and their families and Christian values on charity, on integration, and equal value of human lives, on the other hand allowed churches and also trade unions to successfully shame the Christian-democratic/ liberal government in highlighting how inappropriate non-compliance is (Bundestag 1998b; Evangelische Kirche Deutschland 1997; Süddeutsche Zeitung 1997; Die Welt. 1997. "Katholische Kirche fordert Hilfe für Ausländer ohne Aufenthaltsrecht." Die Welt, 22.11.1997. (This created a threat of reputational losses and electoral sanctions and, in turn, increased non-compliance costs from below, especially since the government's policy vis-à-vis children of foreigners came under wide public attack in spring 1997 (cf. Panke 2007). The government could neither publicly justify the strong restriction of residence entitlements with arguments of appropriateness, nor with any judicial argument after the ECJ judgment of 1997 clearly defined the German practice as constituting a violation of EU secondary law (e.g. Die Welt 1997). In this context, the Ministry of the Interior shifted into compliance and issued a regulation, which circumvented losses in reputational and electoral support.

threats effective? When is it necessary to actually have penalties? Enforcement theory suggests that sanction threats are effective if a government can expect to be punished during its incumbency and if the norm violation constitutes a serious infringement because then the amount of anticipated sanctions is relatively high. Under these conditions, even a government that does not like to comply with a particular European legal act adapts cost benefit calculations to the external threat and shifts into compliance once it becomes less costly than maintaining non-compliance. However, if the government can either not expect to be penalised while still being in office, for example, because elections are coming very soon and they are not sure of whether they make it again into the government, or if the infringement was simply not serious based on the criteria laid out by the European Commission, then the amount of sanction is not really high and the sanctions threat does not become deterrent. In such instances, we would expect that the sanctions threat fails, non-compliance prevails and the ECJ will issue a second judgement and financial penalties.[23]

---

23 The German case on the transposition of the Environmental Impact Assessment directive (EIA, 1985/337) exemplifies the effectiveness of the compliance instrument "sanction-threat". The EU directive prescribes a mandatory procedure for the evaluation of projects' impacts on the environment. It seeks to prevent environmental damages: only when a project will not significantly impact the environment concerning all media, it may be approved. Germany transposed the EIA directive with a two years delay with the environmental impact assessment law (UVPG) in 1990. Yet, the adaptation to EU law remained incomplete and rested on a very restricted interpretation of the EC directive. Already in 1990, the Commission sent a letter of formal notice, followed a reasoned opinion of 1994 in which it accused Germany for the incorrect legal transposition. The German government never responded and the case was referred to the ECJ in 1995. During the ongoing judicial discourse, the government did not introduce first steps towards domestic changes and did not change their compliance-adverse policy interests. Hence in 1998, the ECJ issued its ruling and clarified that Germany was not in compliance with the EIA directive (European Court of Justice. 1998. "Court Judgment of October 22nd 1998. European Commission Against the Federal Republic of Germany Regarding the Incomplete Legal Transposition of Directive 85/337." *Official Journal of the European Communities* C-301-95:I-06135: 45, 46). Almost directly after the ECJ ruling a new government of Social Democrats and Greens came into office. Their policy interests were already in line with compliance (compare (Bundestag. 1996. "Plenarprotokoll vom 27.06.1996") with (Bundestag. 1998a. "Plenarprotokoll vom 05.03.1998") and they opted for a comprehensive legal reform (environmental code, (Trittin, Jürgen. 1999. "Perspektiven der deutschen Umweltpolitik." In Speech in the German Bundestag, 29.09.1999. Berlin: *Speech in the German Bundestag, 29.09.1999*, 18th Session of the Committee on Environment, Nature and Nuclear Safety; Trittin, Jürgen. 2000. "Die ökologische Erneuerung der Bundesrepublik. Speech at the Heinrich Böll Foundation." Berlin: Heinrich-Böll Stiftung.), although such a comprehensive reform of the complex issue required additional time – during which the newly elected government continued non-compliance. Yet, the environmental code was never realised, because federal competencies were lacking (Bundestag. 2001. "Plenarprotokoll vom 05.04.2001"). As a consequence, non-compliance prevailed several months after the comprehensive reform failed and sanction threats came into play. Since the infringement was serious, the amount of the proposed daily penalties was high: 237 600 € a day (Bundestag 2001: 16076). Once the Commission issued a second reasoned opinion (based on Art. 228 ECT), the government feared to become penalised during their incumbency. As a result, the sanction threat was deterrent and induced compliance. The Schröder-government wanted to avoid financial penalties and speeded up the process of legal change – although this led to the trade off of giving up the plan to push for Constitutional change in order to obtain the federal competence to pursue an environmental code as a comprehensive legal reform. The result was a less demanding compound law ("Artikelgesetz") that allowed to circumvent sanctions, but fell short of the legal reform that the Social-Democratic/Green government would have been preferred (Bundesrat. 2000. "Plenarprotokoll vom 21.12.2000": 625, Bundestag 2001: 16076).

Hence, the in-depth analysis of the operation of judicial discourses, judgements and sanction threats as well as the aggregate compliance data of the European Commission indicate that institutional design matters for the transformation of non-compliance into compliance. In highly legalised compliance management systems, all instances of norm violations can in the end be transformed into compliance. Yet, the presence of highly legalised institutional features, such as judicial discourses, independent judges, binding judgments, and sanction threats, is only the necessary condition for restoring compliance, while policy-related variables (e.g. the fit of interpretational techniques and scopes of interpretational problems, the fit between judgments and domestic norms, or the seriousness of the infringement) crucially influence whether an applied instrument is effective in inducing domestic changes or fails to end the norm violation.

In conclusion, this chapter argues that high legalisation of the EU compliance monitoring system cannot totally prevent norm violations. Yet, it is scientifically not possible to assess whether and in how far the high legalisation of the EU's compliance management system fosters high levels of compliance, because we do not have any means to estimate whether the Commissions infringement data on Art. 226 ECT cases (as reported in the annual reports) captures all or nearly all instances of norm violations or whether detected cases of non-compliance are really just the tip of an iceberg.[24] Some insights are nevertheless possible. Firstly, an analysis plotting of the Commission's non-compliance data over time showed that the EU is not facing an increasing implementation deficit.[25] Secondly, in the EU many but not all detected infringements by EU Member States can be settled quickly in bilateral non-judicial settings. Hard cases of non-compliance, in which the interests of affected governments to pursue less demanding norm interpretations, than preferred by EU actors, and save compliance costs at the expense of others are very strong and rigid, reach the ECJ. Thirdly, the Court is well equipped to deal with these instances of persistent non-compliance. The ECJ can apply judicial discourses, judgements, and sanction threats. These instruments transform norm violations of states into compliance but do so only under specific policy-related conditions. Judicial discourses can only argumentatively entrap lead ministries if the advocates of the parties share a judicial method of interpretation that also fits the scope of the interpretational problem at hand. Otherwise, judicial discourses do not produce a single superior norm interpretation and states maintain non-compliance. Judgments foster compliance of states if they resonate well with domestic norms, so that differentially empowered pro-compliance actors can shame the reluctant government into compliance. Finally, sanction threats end norm violations, if they are deterrent, which requires that they are looming and that the penalties are sufficiently high (e.g. that the infringement was seriousness). This chapter also argued that the legalisation of the EU has been overall very successful. On total, in the EU there are more than 4000 instances of non-compliance due to delayed or incorrect legal transpositions of EU secondary law between 1978 and 1999 by the EU-12 Member States (based on Art.

---

24 (Börzel 2001).
25 (Börzel 2001).

226 ECT). Yet, among the cases of delayed or incorrect legal transpositions, the ECJ issued financial penalties in only one instance. Thus, overall the ECJ is well equipped with judicial discourses, judgments and sanction threats to induce compliance and we can conclude that the high legalisation of the EU has been a story of success in ending norm violations even against the strong will of the involved state-actors.

The European Court of Human Rights as a Case-Study

PAUL MAHONEY[1]

A. Introduction

It is a truism that international courts cannot be assimilated to national courts in all respects, primarily because they operate in a fragmented and undeveloped context, namely the international legal order, which is far from being as stable and as structured as most national legal orders. While the multiplication of international courts over the last sixty years or so can be seen as positively contributing to what has been described as the progressive "judicialisation" or "legalisation of world politics",[2] the inherent imbrication with international politics brings with it a degree of dependence on Governments not found in a national setting – in a democratic one at least. The resultant institutional fragility of international courts and tribunals, unsupported by the integrated structures which ensure the operation of the rule of law in a democratic legal order, is particularly apparent, both in legal and practical terms, in relation to the implementation and enforcement of their judgments.

As international human rights courts were set up from the end of the Second World War onwards, they were considered as fitting into the traditional mould of international justice. However, like international criminal courts and international courts for economic integration, they have special features which have prompted the development of variations on the classic international-law model, notably in relation to implementation and enforcement of decisions rendered.[3] They thus provide an interesting case study.[4] The European Court of Human Rights ("the Strasbourg Court"), with its 50 years of accumulated rulings, is particularly well placed to shed light, hopefully instructive, on the topic of the enforcement and effect of international judgments.

---

1   President of the European Civil Service Tribunal (Luxembourg), former Registrar of the European Court of Human Rights (Strasbourg). Any views expressed are personal.
2   Daniel Terris, Cesare P.R. Romano and Leigh Swigart, *The International Judge*, p. 6 (Brandeis University Press, 2007).
3   For an analysis of the incidence of international human rights law on the evolution of general international law, see Gérard Cohen-Jonathan, "Du caractère objectif des obligations internationales relatives aux droits de l'homme – Quelques observations", in Andreas Auer, Alexandre Flückiger and Michael Hottelier, eds., *Les droits de l'homme et la constitution: Études en honneur du professeur Giorgio Malinverni*, pp. 109–133 (Schulthess, 2007).
4   See Ireneu Cabral Barreto, "L'excécution des décisions des cours internationales des droits de l'homme", in Vytautas Andriulis and Saulius Katuoka, eds., *Law in The Changing Europe: Liber Amicorum Pranas Kuris*, pp. 35–57 (Mykolo Romerio Universitetas, 2008).

The present paper discusses

- first, the process, at international level, of executing the judgments of the Strasbourg Court in individual cases, including the handling of instances of unsatisfactory compliance with the judgment and with a sideways glance at the Inter-American Court of Human Rights;

- then, the applicability and binding effect or not of individual judgments within the internal legal order of the respondent Contracting State;

- and, finally, the general effect of Strasbourg judgments, that is to say the case law, as between the Contracting States to the European Convention on Human Rights ("the ECHR") and within the national legal orders of the Contracting States.

Without there necessarily being any watertight division between those three aspects of the subject.

The main conclusions reached after looking at the ECHR experience are that

- *the ideal of a purely judicial mechanism for the execution of judgments, as found within national legal orders, is not (yet) realistic on the international level;*

- *political pressure exerted on a hesitant or recalcitrant State by the collectivity of other Contracting States to the treaty, despite its limits and its drawbacks, is not to be decried as an effective means of securing proper enforcement of international judgments, especially when, as in the ECHR system, it becomes institutionalised;*

- *(perhaps most interestingly) the phenomenon that can be perceived of an increasingly closer legal relationship between the international judgment and the internal legal orders of the Contracting States represents the development most likely to be susceptible of improving the effectiveness of the international enforcement process;*

- *given time to consolidate and the right conditions, international courts and tribunals can develop their own specific systems which build on the tools available to them under international law, so as to reinforce what at first sight appears to be a rather weak enforcement structure;*

- *in short, a generally effective process of execution of its judgments, appropriate to the mission assigned to it under the relevant treaty, is not a wholly unattainable ideal for an international court or tribunal.*

B. The legal framework

Bearing in mind that the possible effect of an international judgment and the implementation obligation of the States concerned largely depend on what the court is empowered to hold or order in its ruling, it is important first to identify the particularity of the legal framework. The relevant clauses of the ECHR provide that:

– if the Court finds a violation of the ECHR or its protocols and the internal law of the respondent State allows only partial reparation to be made, the Court "shall if necessary, award just satisfaction to the injured party" (Article 41);

– the judgments, subject to certain conditions, are or become "final" (Articles 42 and 44);

– the Contracting States "undertake to abide by the final judgment of the Court in any case to which they are parties" (Article 46 § 1), this provision being clearly inspired by classic international law, that is the similarly worded Article 94 of the Charter of the United Nations;[5]

– final judgments of the Court are transmitted to the Committee of Ministers of the Council of Europe, "which shall supervise [their] execution" (Article 46 § 2).

In line with classic international law, the Strasbourg Court in its early caselaw read the following implications into those texts:

– a judgment finding a violation of an ECHR right or freedom imposes on the respondent State a legal obligation to put an end to the violation and make reparation for its consequences in such a way as to restore as far as possible the situation existing before the violation, that is to achieve *restitutio in integrum*;

– the judgments are essentially declaratory in character, not prescriptive;

– consequently, while the Court can declare a national administrative act (or omission), judicial decision or legislative text to be incompatible with the international standards laid down in the ECHR, it is not empowered to invalidate, overrule or abrogate the offending act, decision or text;

– likewise, with one exception, it has no power to order consequential measures in the event of its finding that some conduct by the national authorities violates the ECHR;

---

5   Article 94 § 1 of the UN Charter provides: "Each Member of the United Nations undertakes to comply with the decision of the International Court of Justice in any case to which it is a party."

- the one exception being the power to award "just satisfaction" (financial compensation for prejudice suffered, reimbursement of costs incurred) if *restitutio in integrum* is not possible (for example, where there has been deprivation of liberty);

- the primary responsibility for executing the judgment and for deciding on what measures of implementation should be taken is conferred on the respondent State, which is left free to choose the means for executing the judgment within its own domestic legal order (the principle of subsidiarity);

- the Committee of Ministers in the performance of its collective task of "supervision", not the Court in the context of a fresh application brought by a successful applicant, is the body empowered to review whether the respondent State, in the exercise of its freedom of choice, has complied with its treaty obligation to "abide by" a judgment delivered against it.[6]

Under this traditional scheme, the prerogatives for the execution process are located in the political sphere, namely with the respondent State and the Committee of Ministers, and the judgment has no direct or binding effect under the treaty within the national legal order. Two questions may be asked. Firstly, how effective in practice is this political (rather than judicial) scheme? And secondly, has there been any evolution, in law or in practice, notably towards diluting its political and discretionary colouring?

C. Results in practice

I. General assessment

The Committee of Ministers' role of supervision of execution of the Strasbourg Court's judgments can be summarised as involving a reporting procedure under which the respondent State informs the Committee of the measures taken and, when satisfied, the Committee declares – by means of a Final Resolution – that it has discharged itself of its supervisory duty under the ECHR. The general assessment is that the vast majority of the judgments delivered by the Court are executed by the respondent State in good

---

[6] For accounts of the development of the caselaw, see Joël Andriantsimbazovina, "La réouverture d'une instance juridictionnelle administrative après condamnation de la France par la Cour européenne des Droits de l'Homme", *Revue française de droit administratif*, 21st year, no. 1 (January–February 2005), pp. 163–172, at pp. 165–167; Luzius Wildhaber, "The Execution of Judgments of the European Court of Human Rights", in *Common Values in International Law: Essays in Honour of Christian Tomuschat*, pp. 671–679 (N.P. Engel Verlag, 2006); Lucius Caflisch, "La mise en oeuvre des arrêts de la Cour: ouvelles tendances", in *La nouvelle procedure devant la Cour européenne des Droits de l'Homme après le Protocole no. 14: actes du colloque tenu à Ferrara les 29 et 30 avril 2005*, sous la direction de Francesco Salerno ("*Colloque de Ferrara*"), pp. 157–174, at pp. 157–159 (Bruylant, 2007).

faith in a satisfactory manner.[7] The ECHR system has nonetheless had to cope with some cases of non-execution or of defective or unsatisfactory execution.

To begin with, there have been instances of long delays in the adoption of remedial measures, one early example occurring in relation to the 1979 case of *Marckx v. Belgium*[8] where, in the absence of corrective jurisprudential rulings by Belgian courts[9] and because of the vicissitudes of the national legislative process, it took the respondent State nearly 8 years to modify its offending laws on the legal status of unmarried mothers and children born out of wedlock. There have also been instances of States doing the strict minimum: by ensuring formal compliance in the individual case, rather than removing the root-cause of the problem underlying the violations found. The outstanding illustration of this phenomenon is the omission by Italy over decades to reform its civil justice system with a view to avoiding unreasonable duration of court proceedings, the sole concrete measure of execution which was taken being the payment of just satisfaction to each successive successful applicant. On the other hand, outright refusal to comply with a judgment is extremely rare, even in politically sensitive, controversial cases where national interests are at stake and which provoke negative reactions in public opinion in the country concerned. Despite the 50 years of operation of the Strasbourg Court and the 10,000 judgments so far delivered, such instances – adverted to below – can be counted on half the fingers of one hand. More typical is the judgment in the *"Death-on-the-Rock"* case (which concerned the killing of three IRA terrorists by British security forces in Gibraltar), which, despite all the bellicose statements of outrage in political circles and in the popular media in the United Kingdom, was fully and promptly executed by the respondent Government.[10]

---

7   See *Report of the Evaluation Group to the Committee of Ministers of the Council of Europe on the means of guaranteeing the continued effectiveness of the [Strasbourg] Court* ("*Evaluation Group Report*") (2001), §§ 33, 43(b): "In the great majority of cases" "the supervisory system works well" and "the Committee [of Ministers] is able to fulfil its function under Article 46 [ECHR] without difficulty". The group was composed of the Irish Ambassador to the Council of Europe, the Deputy Secretary General of the Council of Europe and the President of the Court.
8   13 June 1979, Series A vol. 33. See also *Sporrong and Lönnroth v. Sweden*, 23 September 1982, Series A vol. 52, where almost 6 years elapsed before amending legislation (on expropriation permits and prohibitions on construction) was enacted.
9   In the subsequent case of *Vermeire v. Belgium*, 29 November 1991, Series A vol. 214-C, 1125-27, the Court stated that, as a matter of Belgian law, "it [could] not be seen what could have prevented the Brussels Court of Appeal and the Court of Cassation [in 1985 and 1987] from complying with the findings of the [1979] *Marckx* judgment, as the Court of First Instance had done" by interpreting the non-discrimination clause in the Belgian Constitution according to the reasoning of the *Marckx* judgment. The Brussels Court of Appeal followed by the Court of Cassation had refused to give direct effect to the passage in the *Marckx* judgment relating to inheritance rights, under Belgian law, of children born out of wedlock (*ibid.*, §§ 10 –12). This is an early example of the Strasbourg Court indicating a precise means, albeit *ex post facto*, for satisfactory execution of its judgment and encouraging national courts to give direct effect to its judgments whenever possible (as to which, see the discussion below).
10 *McCann and Others v. United Kingdom*, 27 September 1995, Series A vol. 324.

II. Sanctions for non-compliance

The sole formal sanctions at the disposal of the Committee of Ministers for non-execution of a judgment are suspension and expulsion of the State from membership of the Council of Europe. These sanctions are not provided for in the ECHR, but derive from the powers conferred by the Statute of the Council of Europe – a separate and earlier international treaty – on the Committee of Ministers in its capacity as the governing organ of the Council of Europe.[11] Recourse to these drastic options has been openly contemplated on one occasion only, in 1970 in relation to Greece at the time of the Colonels' regime. What was in issue on that occasion was not, however, the non-execution of a judgment but the alleged large-scale violation of the ECHR rights and freedoms before the famous inter-State application under the ECHR had even been lodged against Greece;[12] and, in any event, Greece withdrew from the Council of Europe of its own volition before the Committee of Ministers took the matter any further. Suspension and expulsion from membership of the Council of Europe are therefore more theoretical than realistic tools as far as the day-to-day responsibility of supervising the proper execution of judgments is concerned.

The main means employed by the Committee of Ministers in ensuring the proper execution of judgments by recalcitrant or hesitant respondent States is largely informal exercise of political pressure. In cases deemed to be serious this pressure may be given formal and public expression by the adoption of Interim Resolutions expressing concern, making suggestions and, if need be, drawing attention to the lack of execution and calling on the State concerned to take appropriate measures.[13] The first time this occurred was in 1996 in a high-profile case in which the Greek Government were unwilling to pay, immediately and in one instalment, the (admittedly high) financial compensation awarded by the Court to the applicants by way of just satisfaction. Following publication of an Interim Resolution, the Greek Government rapidly complied with the Court's judgment and paid the compensation in full.[14]

Other responses to such Interim Resolutions have not been so rapid. The Turkish Government, despite several Interim Resolutions, waited five years after the delivery of the Court's judgment on just satisfaction in the *Loizidou* case (in 1998) before finally paying (in 2003) the financial compensation awarded to a Greek Cypriot applicant in respect of the unjustified interference, for which Turkey was held responsible, with her

---

11   Articles 3 and 8, Statute of the Council of Europe.
12   See Committee of Ministers Resolution DH(70)1 on the case of *Denmark, Norway, Sweden and Netherlands v. Greece*; and the discussion in *Cabral-Barreto*, footnote 3 above, pp. 44–45.
13   A practice now embodied in the Rules of the Committee of Ministers for the supervision of the execution of judgments and of the terms of friendly settlements ("CM Rules") (adopted in May 2006), Rules 16 and 17. In 2007, for example, 15 such Interim Resolutions were adopted.
14   *Stran Greek Refineries and Stratis Andreadis v. Greece*, 9 December 1994, Series A vol. 301-B; Interim Resolution DH (96)251 and Final Resolution DH(97)184.

enjoyment of her right of property in the northern part of Cyprus.[15] Turkey's continuing attitude of non-execution up till 2003 had been prompted by one of the guiding principles of its foreign policy: Turkey could not accept the judgment's finding that it exercised effective control and, hence, "jurisdiction" over the northern part of Cyprus. As the political situation, under the impulse of the United Nations and the European Union in particular, evolved towards a possible reunification of the island, so Turkey became more amenable to the political pressure of its fellow members of the Council of Europe to fulfil its treaty obligation to execute the *Loizidou* judgment. More recently, the Russian Government, held responsible in 2004 for an arbitrary deprivation of liberty by a secessionist regime in Transnystria, a breakaway region of Moldova, promptly paid the financial compensation awarded, but took no action to secure the applicants' immediate release from prison as directed by the Court (as to this, see section IV-B below), despite several Interim Resolutions.[16]

The institutionalisation of the collective exertion of political pressure has greatly enhanced the effectiveness of the ECHR enforcement process. Non-compliance with judgments – now running into thousands – has all but been eliminated in practice. On the other side of the coin, the limits on what can be achieved by collective political pressure within the Committee of Ministers are to be found in the few extreme cases where the respondent State chooses not to implement the judgment for what it considers to be overriding political reasons going to its national interest. For the moment, in order to confront such a situation, there is available to the Committee of Ministers no intermediate tool between the two extremes represented by the nuclear option of suspension or exclusion from membership of the Council of Europe and the purely "persuasive" means of public political pressure exercised through Interim Resolutions.

III. Delays on the part of the Committee of Ministers

As the caseload of the Court and its capacity to take greater numbers of cases to judgment increase, so does the execution workload of the Committee of Ministers. This has brought in its wake a problem of growing delays in the treatment of cases by the Committee of Ministers itself. A problem exacerbated by the phenomenon of repetitive cases, that is series of applications (tens, hundreds, sometimes thousands) against the same country and in which the violation found has its origin in the same source (the same legislative scheme, the same administrative practice), the most notorious

---

15 *Loizidou v. Turkey (Just Satisfaction)*, Reports 1998-IV; Committee of Ministers Resolutions DH (2003)174 and 190. See also the inter-State case of *Cyprus v. Turkey*, ECHR 2001-IV, which covered some of the same ground as in *Loizidou*.
16 See, e.g., Committee of Ministers Resolutions DH(2005)42, DH(2005)84, DH(2006)11 and DH(2006)26 in relation to the judgment delivered in *Ilaşcu and Others v. Moldova and Russia*, ECHR 2004-VII. The applicants were finally released in July 2007 after having served their sentences.

example here being the thousands and thousands of applications at one time pending against Italy in which the issue – largely uncontested – was the unreasonable length of civil proceedings.

IV. Unclear judgments

One factor sometimes cited until recently as contributing to the unsatisfactory execution of judgments was their drafting – in the sense that the Court's reasoning was often too casuistic or lacking in clarity, without providing either the respondent Government or the Committee of Ministers with sufficient pointers as to what was required to ensure proper execution.[17]

D. Development of the traditional model

I. General measures

From the early years of the Strasbourg system, the idea was progressively abandoned that a State held to be in breach of the ECHR was only obliged, by virtue of its treaty duty to "abide by a judgment", to make good the consequences of the breach in the concrete case and in respect of the individual applicant, and that, if *restitutio in integrum* was not possible, "just satisfaction" (in the form of financial compensation) for the individual applicant was the maximum that could ever be required by way of remedial action. Instead, when supervising the execution of the judgment, the Committee of Ministers soon came to accept that, in cases where legislation or administrative practice was judged by the Court to have been defective, it should also review whether appropriate general measures removing the defect had been taken.[18] In the words of Professor Rudolph Bernhardt, among other things former President of the Strasbourg Court, "the supervisory machinery in Strasbourg has tried to induce the State concerned not only to make good the violation ... in the concrete case, but also to change

---

17 See, e.g., Resolution 1226(2000) of the Parliamentary Assembly of the Council of Europe on Execution of Judgments of the European Court of Human Rights, which lists seven causes of defective execution: the scope of the remedial reforms required, practical reasons linked to national legislative procedures, budgetary reasons, political considerations, pressure of public opinion, the drafting of the judgments and conflict with obligations arising on other grounds.

18 In the follow-up to the judgment in *Luedicke, Belkacem and Koç v. Germany* (28 November 1978, Series A vol. 29), although the German Government merely referred to the payment to the applicants of compensation by way of "just satisfaction" in the information supplied to the Committee of Ministers, the Resolution (DH(83)4) of the Committee of Ministers closing the file nevertheless adverted to the intervening amending legislation (on interpretation costs in criminal proceedings), which the German Government had scrupulously passed over in silence. See the discussion on this in Hans-Jürgen Bartsch, "The Supervisory Function of the Committee of Ministers under Article 54 [now renumbered Article 46 ECHR] – A Postscript to Luedicke, Belkacem and Koç", in Franz Matscher and Herbert Petzold, eds., *Protecting Human Rights: The European Dimension – Studies in Honour of Gérard Wiarda*, pp. 47–55 (Carl Heymanns Verlag, 1988).

its laws and practices in future cases".[19] The existence of such a treaty obligation on a respondent State to take general remedial measures, not for the benefit of the individual applicant with a view to granting him or her reparation for past prejudice, but for the future in order to prevent other people being victims of similar violations, is now well established in the caselaw.[20] It can be said that general measures going beyond the facts of the particular case have become one of the most important facets of the process of supervision of ECHR judgments. In this way, continuing progress in the overall level of protection of human rights in the ECHR countries is assured, this being one of the essential objects of the treaty.[21]

II. Ordering of specific individual measures

In addition, while there has been no radical rejection or dismantling of the traditional international law approach to execution of judgments, the last few years have seen some innovatory developments initiated by both the Court and the Governments, aimed at curtailing some of the weaknesses outlined above.[22]

In right-of-property cases from the early 1990s onwards, the Court has on appropriate occasions directed the respondent State to return wrongfully expropriated property (as being the most adequate manner of placing the applicants in the situation in which they would have been but for the violation – *restitutio in integrum*) or, failing that, to pay monetary compensation (the classic "just satisfaction").[23] In two cases in 2004, *Assanidze v. Georgia* and *Ilaşcu and Others v. Moldova and Russia*, the Grand Chamber of the Court took a step further and directed, in the operative provisions of the judgment, that the applicants should be immediately released from custody, without any alternative of paying financial compensation.[24] At first sight, this appears to be the ordering of a consequential measure going beyond the Court's declaratory competence, in disregard of the usual rule of subsidiarity that it is for the respondent Government alone to choose the appropriate means for executing a judgment. However, the particular circumstances – namely a deprivation of liberty that not merely was contrary to

---

19 Rudolph Bernhardt, "Judgments of International Human Rights Courts and Their Effects in the Internal Legal Order of States", in *Studi di diritto internazionale in onore di Gaetano Arangio-Ruiz*, pp. 429–440, at p. 435 (Ed. Scientifica, 2004).
20 See, e.g., *Papamichalopoulos and Others v. Greece (Just Satisfaction)*, 31 October 1995, Series A vol. 330-B, § 34; *Scozzari and Giunta v. Italy*, ECHR 2000-VIII, § 249.
21 See ECHR, preamble, which speaks of the "maintenance *and further realisation* of human rights and fundamental freedoms" (emphasis supplied) as being one of the methods by which the Council of Europe's aim of achieving greater unity between its Members is to be pursued.
22 See the discussion in *Caflisch*, footnote 5 above, pp. 159 et seq.
23 E.g., *Papamichalopoulos*, footnote 19 above, §§ 38–39 and operative provisions 2–3; *Brumarescu v. Romania (Just Satisfaction)*, ECHR 2001-I, §§ 19–23 and operative provisions 1–2.
24 *Assanidze v. Georgia*, ECHR 2004-II, §§ 202–203 and operative provision 14(a); *Ilaşcu*, footnote 15 above, § 490 and operative provision 22. See the discussion in Laurent Sermet, "L'exécution des arrêts de la Cour européenne des Droits de l'Homme", in Laurent Sermet, ed., *Adaptation des institutions et des législations nationales à la Convention européenne des Droits de l'Homme*, Annuaire de droit européen, vol. 3 (2005), pp. 297–358, at pp. 299–301.

procedural safeguards laid down by the ECHR but was the product of a flagrant denial of justice, wholly arbitrary and offensive to the rule of law – meant that the violation found could only be satisfactorily remedied in one possible and urgent manner: release from custody.[25]

It is worth noting that the Inter-American Court of Human Rights has issued more prescriptive directions, on the basis of the more generous wording of the American Convention on Human Rights which empowers it, in the event of finding a violation, not only to award compensation but also to "rule, if appropriate, that the consequences of the measure or situation that constituted the breach ... be remedied".[26] The Inter-American Court has thus ordered, in the operative provisions of judgments, the taking of consequential measures within the national legal order, such as the investigation of certain facts and the punishment of their instigators, the amendment of laws held to be in violation of the Convention, and the reinstatement in her post of a public servant with full retirement benefits.[27] It has even declared that national legal proceedings "are invalid" before directing a retrial.[28] In the view of Professor Bernhardt, "this ... far-reaching pronouncement" – which, as in the ECHR cases of *Assanidze* and *Ilaşcu*, "can probably only be justified by the extraordinary arbitrariness of the decision of the national authorities in that case" – "can hardly be reconciled with the dualistic approach to the relationship of international law and municipal law as developed by Triepel and Anzilotti at the beginning of the twentieth century". So there is something new in the air, Professor Bernhardt surmises.[29]

Cases such as these, where the necessary remedial action is required as a matter of urgency and so evident as, in effect, to deprive the State of any margin of choice, will be very rare indeed and unlikely ever to involve specific general, as opposed to individual, measures being ordered. In 2005, in the high-profile case of *Öcalan v. Turkey*, the Grand Chamber of the Court pulled back from the position where previously some chamber judgments had explicitly stated that in the particular case a retrial or re-opening of criminal proceedings constituted the most appropriate manner of redressing

---

25 This is also the analysis of *Caflisch*, footnote 5 above, pp. 161–165: "Dans le cas d'espèce, la nature de la violation appelait une seule mesure et celle-ci était urgente." In *Assanidze*, footnote 23 above, the Court expressly explained that, "by virtue of its very nature, the violation [of the right to liberty under Article 5 ECHR] found in the ... case [did] not leave any real choice as to the measures required to remedy it", before directing that the respondent State "must secure the applicant's release at the earliest possible date". Cf. also Hans-Jürgen Papier, "Execution and Effects of the Judgments of the European Court of Human Rights from the Perspective of German National Courts", 27 *Human Rights Law Journal* 1–4, footnote 8 (2006), who makes the further point that the explicit direction issued in the *Assanidze* case "is ... an exception [to the habitual rule] to the extent that the national Georgian court had already passed a final judgment ordering the release, but this judgment had not been complied with on the national level".
26 American Convention on Human Rights, Article 63 § 1.
27 E.g. *Loayza-Tamayo v. Peru* and *Castillo Páez v. Peru*, 27 November 1998, Series C No. 42, § 192, and No. 43, § 118; *Barrios Altos Case* (*Chumbipuma Aguirre et al. v. Peru*) (Merits), 14 March 2001, Series C No. 75 – also reported in *International Law Materials*, Vol. XLI (2002), p. 93, at pp. 106–108.
28 *Castillo Petruzzi v. Peru*, 30 May 1999, Series C No. 52, §§ 221, 226.
29 *Bernhardt*, footnote 18 above, pp. 439–440. See also the discussion along similar lines in *Andriantsimbazovina*, footnote 5 above, pp. 168–169.

the violation found (of the applicant's right to trial by an independent and impartial court), by reformulating redress by retrial or by reopening of criminal proceedings as a principle to be applied by the national authorities wherever possible when executing judgments finding such a violation, rather than as a binding direction given by the Strasbourg Court in the circumstances of the specific case.[30]

The dangers of the Strasbourg Court trying to substitute itself for the competent national decision-makers by specifying precise individual measures of redress are illustrated by another 2004 case, *Görgülü v. Germany*,[31] and the subsequent follow-up to that case before the German Constitutional Court,[32] which together have provoked much controversy in legal writings, in Germany in particular.[33] A violation of the right to respect for family life (Article 8 ECHR) was found by the Strasbourg Court as a result of lower court's decision denying the applicant – of Turkish origin, as his name suggests – custody of and access to his child born out of wedlock. The respondent State's freedom to choose the appropriate remedial measures was stated to be subject to the obligation "to make it possible for the applicant to have access to the child".[34] Some analysts feel that, in issuing this prescription, the Strasbourg Court strayed beyond its given role.[35] Was this one particular outcome, among others possible under domestic law, the only conceivable one compatible with the requirements of the ECHR? Even if it had been at the time of the contested national decision, the relevant facts regarding custody and access might have changed in the meantime. The German Constitutional Court, when reviewing the lower court's reaction to the Strasbourg judgment, was clearly uneasy with the prescriptive formulation of that judgment and its relation to the role of national courts. As the President of the Constitutional Court, Hans-Jürgen Papier, explained in an article commenting on his own Court's decision in the *Görgülü* case, where conflicting interests of individuals are at stake (not all of whom will have been represented in the proceedings in Strasbourg), so that the execution of the Strasbourg judgment is characterised by "multipolar legal relations" in connection with the fundamental rights issue, the correctness as such of the national court's decision on the facts should not be reviewed but only the national court's analysis of the significance of the human right in question for the outcome of the case before it.[36]

---

30 Öcalan v. Turkey, ECHR 2005-IV, § 210. For previous chamber judgments, see, e.g., *Gençel v. Turkey*, application no. 53431/99, 23 October 2003, § 27, unreported; and *Somogyi v. Italy*, ECHR 2004-IV, § 86. See also the discussion in *Caflisch*, footnote 5 above, pp. 160–161.
31 *Görgülü v. Germany*, ECHR 2004-II.
32 *Görgülü*, 14 October 2004, Entscheidungen des Bundesverfassungsgerichts – BVerfGe (Decisions of the Federal Constitutional Court), 111, 307 (319). An English translation of the decision may be found in 25 *Human Rights Law Journal* 99 (2004).
33 See Jens Meyer-Ladewig, "The German Federal Constitutional Court and the Binding Force of Judgments of the European Court of Human Rights under Article 46 ECHR", in Hanno Hartig, ed., *Trente ans de droit européen des droits de l'homme – Études à la mémoire de Wolfgang Strasser ("Mélanges Strasser")*, pp. 215–228 and the references given there to material published in German (Bruylant-Nemesis, 2007).
34 *Görgülü*, footnote 30 above, § 64 *in fine*.
35 See, e.g., the discussion in *Papier*, footnote 24 above, and *Meyer-Ladewig*, footnote 32 above.
36 *Papier*, footnote 24 above.

From the perspective of a national judge, such a point of view is more than understandable. In the sphere of relations governed by civil law, the variables, and the constant need to balance and evaluate conflicting interests, are such that it is difficult to conceive of the specific solution on the particular facts being so evident at the international level that the Strasbourg Court can prescribe it to the competent domestic authorities, notably the national courts.

III. Guidance on general measures

There has also been movement towards the Strasbourg Court's issuing, if not specific, detailed instructions on execution as in *Assanidze*, *Ilaşçu* and *Görgülü*, at least guidance as to the scope and import of general measures that should be taken in order to properly execute a judgment. The best illustration of this is the so-called pilot-judgment procedure initiated by the Court in the Polish case of *Broniowski* in 2004.[37] Under the pilot-judgment procedure one test case among numerous similar pending or potential applications prompted by the same systemic situation in the respondent country is taken for adjudication, so as (if necessary) to facilitate the most speedy and effective resolution of a dysfunction in national human rights protection affecting a lot of people and also to serve as a basis for preserving the Court (and the Committee of Ministers) from the burden of processing in the normal, work-intensive manner every single one of those other pending or potential applications. The *Broniowski* judgment had been preceded by a Resolution of the Committee of Ministers inviting the Court "to identify, in its judgments finding a violation of the Convention, what it considers to be an underlying systemic problem and the source of that problem, in particular when it is likely to give rise to numerous applications, so as to assist the States in finding the appropriate solution and the Committee of Ministers in supervising the execution of judgments".[38]

In *Broniowski*, which concerned the enjoyment of a property right under a legislative scheme in Poland, the Court stated (in line with similar general dicta in previous cases)

---

37 *Broniowski v. Poland (Merits)*, ECHR 2004-V and *Broniowski v. Poland (Friendly Settlement)*, ECHR 2005-IX. See also the admissibility decision reported in ECHR 2002-X. For a commentary on this and subsequent "pilot" cases, see Renata Degener and Paul Mahoney, "The Prospects for a Test Case Procedure in the European Court of Human Rights", in *Mélanges Strasser*, footnote 32 above, pp. 173–207; *Caflisch*, footnote 5 above, pp.165–174; Vladimiro Zagrabelsky, "Violations structurelles et jurisprudence de la Cour européenne des Droits de l'Homme", in *Colloque de Ferrara*, footnote 5 above, at pp. 149–156, and in Lucius Caflisch, Johan Callewaert, Roderick Liddell, Paul Mahoney and Mark Villiger, eds., *Human Rights – Strasbourg Views: Liber Amicorum Luzius Wildhaber*, pp. 521–535, under the title "Questions autour de Broniowski" (N.P. Engel Verlag, 2007); *Sermet*, footnote 23 above, pp. 303–313; Elisabeth Lambert-Abdelgawad, "La Cour européenne au secours du Comité des ministres pour une meilleures exécution des arrêts "pilote" (en marge de l'arrêt Broniowski)", *Revue trimestrielle des droits de l'homme*, no. 61 (1 January 2005), pp. 221–224; David Szymczak, "L'arrêt pilote: un remède efficace contre l'engorgement d'un rôle de la Cour européenne des Droits de l'Homme ... à condition de bien lire la notice!", *La semaine juridique: édition administrations et collectivités territoriales*, no. 21 (22 May 2006), pp. 661–664.

38 Resolution of 12 May 2004, adopted by the Committee of Ministers of the Council of Europe, on judgments revealing an underlying systemic problem (DH Res (2004)3).

that not only individual measures in favour of the successful applicant, Mr. Broniowski, but also general measures at national level in favour of other potential victims were called for in execution of the judgment. In addition, the Court specified that, as part of its obligation to execute the judgment, Poland was required, through appropriate legal measures and administrative practice, to secure the implementation of the property-right in question in respect of the other, remaining claimants under legislative scheme or to provide them with equivalent redress in lieu.[39] The aim of the pilot-judgment procedure is to incite the respondent Government, not only to eliminate for the future the causes of the violation and to afford adequate reparation to the individual applicant in the pilot case, but also to make rapidly available within the domestic legal order a remedy, with retroactive effect, capable of redressing the prejudice sustained by other victims of the same structural or systemic defect.[40] This was done by the Polish Government in the *Broniowski* case, with the consequence that the Court did not have to take to judgment all the other applications prompted by the same defective operation of the legislative scheme but could redirect those applicants back to the Polish legal system where a remedy for obtaining individualised relief now existed.[41]

The Court's initiative has been met with some reservations, by Governments and commentators who feel that the Court, by purporting also to specify the appropriate solution, has gone beyond the invitation issued by the Committee of Ministers in its 2004 Resolution simply to "identify" more clearly any systemic problems underlying a violation found; and that the new practice runs the risk of nullifying the principle of subsidiarity (whereby States are free to choose the means of executing judgments) and lacks a clear basis in law.[42] Such fears are, the present writer believes, misconceived. The formula used by the Court in *Broniowski* (the Government being called on to secure the implementation of the property right in question for the other remaining claimants "*or [to] provide them with equivalent redress in lieu*") acknowledges that, in accordance with the principle of subsidiarity, Poland enjoyed considerable freedom of

---

39 *Broniowski (Merits)*, footnote 36 above, §§ 193–194 and operative provisions 3-4.
40 See the "Position Paper" of 12 September 2003 submitted by the Strasbourg Court to the committee of governmental experts responsible for drafting what became Protocol No. 14 to the ECHR: "[A pilot] judgment would trigger an accelerated execution process before the Committee of Ministers which would entail not just the obligation to eliminate for the future the causes of the violation, but also the obligation to introduce a remedy with retroactive effect within the domestic system to redress the prejudice sustained by other victims of the same structural or systemic violation. Whilst awaiting the accelerated execution of the pilot judgment, the Court would suspend the treatment of pending applications raising the same grievance against the respondent State, in anticipation of that grievance being covered by the retroactive domestic remedy. It was stressed in the Court's discussions that, in the event of the respondent State's failing to take appropriate measures within a reasonable time, it should be possible for the Court to re-open the adjourned applications."
41 See *Wolkenberg and Others v. Poland*, to be reported in ECHR 2007, where the Court took note of the compensation system introduced by a statute enacted subsequent to the *Broniowski* judgments and struck the application out of the list on the basis that "the matter ha[d] been resolved" (Article 37 § 1 ECHR).
42 See, e.g., the pleading of the Italian Government in *Sejdovic v. Italy*, ECHR 2006-II, discussed in *Degener and Mahoney*, footnote 36 above, at pp. 191–192; and the reservations adverted to by *Lambert-Abdelgawad*, footnote 36 above, by *Caflisch*, footnote 4 above, by *Zagrabelsky*, footnote 36 above, and by *Szymczak*, footnote 36 above.

choice as to the general remedial measures to be taken, although the Court did thereby attenuate the rigour of the previous traditional judicial policy of refraining from giving any indications *at all* to the respondent State as to how to execute the judgment.[43] Some guidance was given, but there was no encroachment on the State's prerogative to decide on complex matters of legislative and administrative policy at national level.

The pilot-judgment procedure is not a wonder-solution adapted to all scenarios of structural systemic defects at national level, it has its limitations[44] and it very much depends for its success on the willing and active collaboration of the respondent State; but it does represent an innovative, pragmatic and flexible approach to execution of a judgment in an individual case whereby, if all the conditions are present, redress can be assured at national level for a whole category of victims, as opposed to redress for one victim at a time at international level, and the risk of overloading the international court's docket with numerous repetitive cases is reduced, if not even avoided.

IV. Association of the applicant in the execution process and greater publicity

Although excluded in the early years of the ECHR's existence from the ongoing process of "supervision" of execution of judgments (the deliberations of the Committee of Ministers being in principle confidential),[45] this exclusion has subsequently (from 2000 onwards) been progressively attenuated. Thus, under the Committee's current rules, its agenda in human rights meetings is public and information provided by the State to the Committee and the documents relating thereto are, unless otherwise decided, accessible to the public.[46] Information on the progress of execution of judgments is also usually rendered public a few days after each meeting. Such public access "has the advantage of ensuring that applicants and their lawyers are kept duly informed about

---

43   In *Botazzi v. Italy*, ECHR 1999-V, for example, while holding that there had been an accumulation of identical breaches which were sufficiently numerous to disclose, not a series of isolated incidents, but rather the existence in Italy of an administrative practice as a result of which the civil justice system was incapable of providing litigants with a trial within a reasonable time, the Court did not attempt to give any guidance to the Italian Government as to what general measures should be taken or even state the obvious point that general measures were called for.

44   See, e.g., the unsuccessful attempt by a Chamber of the Court in *Xenides-Arestis v. Turkey (Merits)*, application no. 46347/99, 22 December 2005, unreported, to apply the pilot-judgment procedure to the property situation in northern Cyprus. Although, with over 1,500 similar applications pending, the Court was faced with the prospect of being turned into a property-claims commission for northern Cyprus, some hesitation may be expressed as to the enforceability in practice of the Chamber's ruling calling on Turkey to introduce, within three months, an effective remedy for property-owners residing in the southern part of the island and to afford actual redress within three months after that. In the event no global solution was secured: the parties failed to reach a friendly settlement (unlike in *Broniowski*) and the Chamber was obliged to assess the detailed compensation in the circumstances of the particular case – *Xenides-Arestis v. Turkey (Just Satisfaction)*, application no. 46347/99, 7 December 2006, unreported.

45   Article 21, Statute of the Council of Europe.

46   CM Rules 2 § 1, 8 § 2.

the state of proceedings before the Committee".[47] In addition, applicants are now entitled to submit their observations "with regard to payment of the just satisfaction or the taking of individual measures"; and the Committee may consider "any communication from non-governmental organisations, as well as national institutions for the promotion of human rights, with regard to the execution of judgments".[48] An annual report is to be adopted on the Committee's activities regarding execution of judgments under the ECHR; this report is to be made public and transmitted to the Court, as well as to the Secretary General, the Parliamentary Assembly and the Commissioner for Human Rights of the Council of Europe.[49]

The doors of the Committee of Ministers are thus no longer closed to applicants or to the public in general. This development marks a steps towards adversarial proceedings and at least quasi-judicialisation of the ECHR execution process.

E. Execution of ECHR judgments in the internal legal order of the respondent state

It has been said that "the international supervision [of execution of ECHR judgments] is one side of the coin, the national implementation the other".[50] The general rule in international law, however, is that international decisions are not immediately applicable and binding in the internal legal order of States unless this is provided for (explicitly or implicitly) in the treaty – as is so, for example, in European Community law.[51] This classic doctrine is replicated in the ECHR system: while the Strasbourg Court's decisions are internationally binding on the respondent State(s) concerned in the particular case, they do not, by virtue of the treaty, automatically carry over any obligation of implementation binding on the national authorities within the domestic legal order.[52] Just as the ECHR is directly applicable inside the Contracting States only in so far as this is provided for in the law of each State, so the enforceability of the Court's judgment is similarly circumscribed.[53]

---

47 *Evaluation Group Report*, footnote 6 above, § 33.
48 CM Rule 9 §§ 1–2
49 CM Rule 5. The first such annual report was adopted in 2007 ("CM Annual Report 2007"). According to its foreword, "the report demonstrates, in particular, the breadth of questions examined by the Committee in this area of its work, the number of different actors involved in the execution process, and the important number of reforms which are eventually adopted to ensure that legal systems and practices develop in conformity with the standards of the [ECHR]".
50 *Bernhardt*, footnote 18 above, p. 435.
51 Articles 244 and 256, Treaty Establishing the European Community (consolidated version) ("EC Treaty"). See the interesting discussion on the authority of preliminary rulings of the European Court of Justice in Sean van Raepenbusch, *Droit institutionnel de l'Union européenne*, 4th edition, pp. 577–580 (Editions Larcier, 2005).
52 See the discussion in *Andriantsimbazovina*, footnote 5 above, at pp. 165–167.
53 To take a unique example, in Malta the European Convention Act 1987 (section 6(1)) provides a special mechanism for enforcement of Strasbourg judgments at national level: "Any judgment of the [Strasbourg Court] ... may be enforced by the Constitutional Court in Malta, in the same manner as judgments delivered by that court and enforceable by it ..."

In this connection, more and more countries are now providing, under legislation or through judicial practice, for the reopening of criminal and sometimes also civil and administrative proceedings in the event of a Strasbourg judgment holding that the original trial, conviction or proceedings at national level were contrary to the ECHR (usually its fair trial guarantee).[54]

In an interesting development in Germany in the controversial *Görgülü* case referred to above, the Constitutional Court set aside a decision of the lower (regional) court on the ground that it had not properly taken into account the Strasbourg Court's earlier judgment in the same matter – namely, Mr. Görgülü's continuing efforts to gain custody of and access to his child.[55] In so doing, the Constitutional Court, to use the words of its own decision, "[was] indirectly [acting] in the service of enforcing international law".[56] This is hopefully reminiscent of the often heard dictum in European Union circles to the effect that the national judge is the principal judge applying Community law.[57]

This is not the place to carry out a comparative survey of similar developments within the national legal order of each of the 47 ECHR Contracting States.[58] What can be perceived is a growing trend towards injecting into national law in as direct a manner as possible the concrete implications of a Strasbourg judgment in the particular case, thereby bringing the international judgment and its national implementation closer together as a matter of law, rather than being a consequence of the exercise of political discretion enjoyed by the Government.[59]

F. General effect of judgments

The strict legal position, as enunciated in the very first judgment delivered by the Strasbourg Court in 1960 (in the case of *Lawless v. Ireland*) is that only the Contracting

---

54   See Recommendation R (2000)2 of the Committee of Ministers of the Council of Europe to Member States on the re-examination or re-opening of certain cases at domestic level following judgments of the European Court of Human Rights.
55   See footnote 31 above.
56   Quoted in *Papier*, footnote 24 above, p. 3. See also the discussion in *Meyer-Ladewig*, footnote 32 above, pp. 222, 227–228.
57   See, most recently, the Resolution of the European Parliament on the role of the national judge in the European judicial system (2007/2027(INI)), adopted at its session of July 2008, § 1, and the accompanying report of the Committee on Legal Affairs, rapporteur: Diana Wallis (doc. A6-0224/2008).
58   See the survey concerning the situation in 2005, given in *Sermet*, footnote 23 above, pp. 319–325, under the head "La contribution des États à l'exécution des arrêts par la réouverture des procédures internes" ["The contribution of the States to the execution of judgments by means of reopening of domestic proceedings"].
59   For convincing pleas for movement towards such co-operation between the national and the European legal orders, see, as regards France, Pierre-Yves Gautier, "De l'obligation pour le juge civil de réexaminer le procès après une condamnation par la Cour européenne des Droits de l'Homme", *Recueil Dalloz*, 181st year, no. 40 (10 November 2005), pp. 2773–2776; and *Andriantsimbazovina*, footnote 5 above (as regards proceedings before administrative courts).

States which are "parties to the proceedings" are bound by the Court's decision.⁶⁰ In broader terms, however, "the Court's judgments ... serve not only to decide those cases brought before the Court but, more generally, to elucidate, safeguard and develop the rules instituted by the [ECHR], thereby contributing to the observance by the States of the engagements undertaken by them as Contracting Parties".⁶¹ The mission of the Strasbourg Court is not only to decide such individual cases as are put before it, but also to build up a "common law" of human rights for the ECHR community of countries. The ECHR has been incorporated, in one way or another, into the domestic law of all the Contracting States. This being so, its case law serves as an authoritative source of interpretative guidance for national authorities, in particular the courts. Although the judgments are sometimes described as having a "precedential effect", this does not mean that they are binding in the formal sense. More often than not the resolution of human rights issues involves balancing conflicting interests in society. The national judge will very rarely, if ever, find in the ECHR jurisprudence the concrete answer to the particular case being adjudicated on. Rather, to the extent that it elucidates the relevant criteria for setting and using the analytical "weighing scales" necessary for effecting the balancing exercise in different kinds of situations, the ECHR jurisprudence provides the domestic courts (as well as the legislature and the executive) with authoritative guidance.

The broad conclusion on the effect of ECHR jurisprudence for national judges is that it is to be treated not as a series of specific precedents for a limited number of applications of the ECHR safeguards in particular, given contexts, but as a source of guidance as to the philosophy, values or considerations to be weighed in the balance by national courts when applying their own domestic law. Principles, not precedents. While the Governments of the Contracting States to the ECHR have undertaken the international commitment that their domestic authorities, including the courts, will observe the standards laid down in the treaty, the relevant ECHR law (that is to say, the text of the article(s) in the treaty, not read in a vacuum but *as elucidated* by the accompanying interpretative jurisprudence) does not furnish anything like a detailed blueprint calling for rigorous and uniform application throughout the ECHR community of participating countries. As regards both the regulatory framework and, above all, the outcome in individual cases, the scope for different solutions deemed appropriate for each ECHR country remains, provided that the relevant ECHR values and considerations are in substance integrated into the national analysis. That is the subsidiarity that is inherent in the ECHR system of protection. The ECHR and therefore the judgments delivered by the Strasbourg Court differ in this respect from the "legal systems" created under other international instruments which are aimed at laying down unifying, if not even uniform, rules in specific, often technical, domains.

---

60 *Lawless v. Ireland*, 14 November 1960, Series A vol. 1, p. 11.
61 *Ireland v. United Kingdom*, 18 January 1978, Series A vol. 25, § 154.

In some countries, in line with a recommendation by the Committee of Ministers of the Council of Europe to Member States,[62] parliamentary committees examine draft legislation for compatibility with the ECHR and its jurisprudence, such that the effects of the judgments are felt in a routine manner in the ongoing work of the legislature as well as that of the judicature (and the executive). The Council's Parliamentary Assembly has recently invited all national parliaments to add a further level of scrutiny by introducing specific mechanisms for effective parliamentary oversight of the implementation of ECHR judgments on the basis of regular reports by responsible ministries.[63]

G. Proposed treaty amendments and alternative solutions

An amending protocol to the ECHR which has yet to come into force (Protocol No. 14) provides for two innovations which would enable the Committee of Ministers to refer a matter to the Court for a further ruling in connection with execution of a final judgment. The Committee of Ministers would be able, firstly, to seek an interpretation of a final judgment if "the supervision of the execution of [the] judgment is hindered by a problem of interpretation" and, secondly, to institute what are called "infringement proceedings" against a respondent State which is considered to be "refus[ing] to abide by a final judgment".[64] In the event of finding that the respondent State had violated its treaty obligation of proper execution, the Court would have no power to impose any sanction, such as a financial penalty (as is possible, for example, under European Community law[65]), but would be required to refer the case back to the Committee of Ministers "for consideration of the measures to be taken".[66] According to the Explanatory Report to this amending Protocol, infringement proceedings, which would be brought "only in exceptional circumstances", are intended to furnish the Committee of Minis-

---

62 Recommendation (Rec (2004)5) of the Committee of Ministers to Member States on the verification of the compatibility of draft laws, existing laws and administrative practices with the standards laid down in the EHCR.
63 CM Annual Report 2007, p. 10. In this connection the British Parliament (lower and upper chambers) has appointed a Joint Committee on Human Rights, which operates a regular screening both of draft legislation going through parliament (for compatibility with the country's obligations under the ECHR and other international human rights instruments) and of the Government's responses to key ECHR judgments against the United Kingdom, as well as *ad hoc* scrutiny of the practical effect of existing legislation and administrative practice in human rights terms – see Lord Onslow, "Legislative Scrutiny in the United Kingdom: Who We Are and What We Do", in *Towards Stronger Implementation of the ECHR at National Level*, Proceedings of the Colloquy organised under the Swedish chairmanship of the Committee of Ministers of the Council of Europe, Stockholm, 9–10 June 2008, pp. 78–85 (Council of Europe, 2008).
64 Article 46 §§ 3 and 4 ECHR, as amended by Protocol No. 14 (Article 16).
65 Under Article 228 EC Treaty, the Commission of the European Communities may bring a case back before the European Court of Justice if it considers that a Member State "has fail[ed] to take the necessary measures to comply with the Court's judgment" in the case. The Member State concerned may be ordered by the Court to pay a lump sum or penalty payment. This procedure is without prejudice Article 227 EC Treaty, which generally empowers a Member State to institute proceedings before the European Court of Justice if it considers that another Member State "has failed to fulfil an obligation under [the] Treaty".
66 Article 46 § 5 ECHR, as amended by Protocol No. 14 (Article 16).

ters with a supplementary means of pressure, explicitly characterised as "political", to exert on recalcitrant respondent States, more muscular than the simple adoption of "persuasive" Interim Resolutions but falling some way short of the extreme sanction of suspension or expulsion from membership of the Council of Europe.[67] Hesitations have however been expressed in some quarters as to the feasibility of such infringement proceedings.[68]

As far as reinforcing the Court's involvement in the actual process of execution of judgments is concerned, one conceivable alternative solution to infringement proceedings brought solely at the initiative of the Committee of Ministers would be to invest the Court with direct jurisdiction to entertain applications from aggrieved individual applicants alleging non-compliance by a State with its treaty obligation (under Article 46 ECHR) to abide by the judgment in their case (something which would appear to be excluded by the current wording of the ECHR[69]). The argument in favour of such an amendment to the treaty is that individual applicants personally would benefit from a veritable action for infringement, enabling them to obtain redress for the prejudice caused to their legitimate interest in seeing the judgment in their case properly executed. The present author however tends to the view that such attribution of jurisdiction would not be desirable as a matter of judicial policy, since it would in effect place the Court in competition with the Committee of Ministers and be liable to provoke a disproportionate number of unmeritorious applications.

Finally, it might at first sight appear to be an attractive and natural progression to reinforce the universal character of human rights standards for the States by formally endowing the Court's judgments with a binding legal effect *erga omnes* and not only *inter partes*, as per the strict orthodoxy enunciated in the *Lawless* judgment. However, such a formal binding effect *erga omnes* for each and every judgment is difficult to reconcile with the essentially declaratory character of the Strasbourg judgments, measuring a given factual situation against the ECHR standards. As pointed out above, the infinite variety of differing circumstances, combined with the ECHR's underlying principle of subsidiarity and the margin of appreciation enjoyed by each country's national authorities, renders it almost materially impossible to envisage making the specifics

---

67 Explanatory Report, §§ 42–43, 95–100.
68 E.g. Steven Greer, "Protocol No. 14 and the Future of the European Court of Human Rights", *Public Law*, Spring 2005, pp. 83–106, at p. 93.
69 Article 46 ECHR does not embody any of the "rights" in respect of which individuals are empowered, by virtue of Article 34 ECHR, to bring an application before the Court. See *Haase and Others v. Germany*, application no. 34499/04, 12 February 2008, unreported, p. 20, where, when rejecting a complaint under Article 46 in conjunction with Article 8 ECHR that the German authorities had failed to "abide by" earlier judgments of the Court concerning the applicants' enjoyment of their right to respect for their family life, the Court simply ruled: "It is not for the Court to verify whether a Contracting Party has complied with the obligations imposed on it by one of the Court's judgments." The wider wording of Article 33 ECHR (on inter-State applications) would however appear to empower a Contracting State to ground an application against another Contracting State on an alleged failure to comply with a judgment: "Any High Contracting Party may refer to the Court any alleged breach of the provisions of the [ECHR] and the protocols thereto by another High Contracting Party."

of a Strasbourg judgment legally binding throughout the community of Contracting States. As far as *erga omnes* effect of judgments is concerned, looking to the Strasbourg jurisprudence for authoritative guidance and orientation (on interpretation of the text of the ECHR, on the concrete requirements of the vaguely worded ECHR standards in given kinds of situations or contexts, on how to set the weighing scales for evaluating competing interests in relation to the enjoyment of a given right or freedom, and so on) is frequently just about the most that can be expected of the national authorities, notably the courts, when confronted with taking a decision with human rights connotations in a given case.[70]

H. Conclusion

The proper execution of judgments is essential for the effectiveness of the international system of protection of human rights under the ECHR, especially as regards the taking of general remedial measures at national level.[71] Yet the inherent dependence of international courts on participating Governments and the former's resultant institutional fragility, referred to in the introductory remarks made at the outset of this paper, are likewise found in the process of enforcement of ECHR judgments. The new initiative of the pilot judgment procedure, for example, in order to be successful in dealing effectively with the problem of repetitive cases, relies on the willing and active cooperation of the respondent State, with whom the ultimate choice of remedial ac-

---

70 See *Cohen-Jonathan*, footnote 2 above, p. 123: "C'est tels qu'ils sont interprétés et façonnés par le jurisprudence de la Cour européenne que les droits garantis de la Convention sont opposables *erga omnes*. C'est bien cela qu'avait en vue Pierre-Henri Teitgen quand il expliquait que le nouveau "système" était dominé par une Cour à laquelle les États avaient concédé un pouvoir d'interprétation authentique. Il était entendu que tout État devrait non seulement exécuter les arrêts de la Cour le concernant (autorité de la chose jugée), mais qu'il devrait appliquer la convention telle qu'elle était interprétée par le juge de Strasbourg dans les arrêts rendus à l'égard de n'importe quel État partie (authorité de la chose interprétée) *dans la mesure où sont perceptibles des enseignements généraux au-delà du cas d'espèce*." (Emphasis supplied.) [Free translation by the author: "It is as interpreted and developed by the jurisprudence of the European Court that the rights guaranteed by the ECHR have an *erga omnes* effect. This was precisely what Pierre-Henri Teitgen had in mind when he explained that the new "system" was dominated by a Court to which the States had conceded a power of authoritative interpretation. By this was meant that every State had not only to execute the judgments of the Court concerning it (the rule of *res iudicata* as between the parties) but also to apply the ECHR as interpreted by the Strasbourg judges in judgments rendered in regard to any other Contracting State (interpretative authority) *to the extent that general guiding principles going beyond the particular case are discernible*." (Emphasis supplied.)]
71 See Explanatory Report to Protocol No. 14, § 16: "Execution of the Court's judgments is an integral part of the [ECHR] system. ... The Court's authority and the system's credibility both depend to a large extent on the effectiveness of this process." See likewise CM Annual Report 2007, p. 7: "Good execution is essential from many different perspectives. Its primary purpose is to improve and promote the protection of human rights by remedying (as far as possible) violations which have already occurred, and by taking measures necessary to prevent similar violations or putting an end to continuing violations. Good execution fosters good governance, respect for the rule of law and for the human rights of citizens and of all other persons within the State's jurisdiction. It also fosters the trust which must exist between the authorities in the various Member States if there is to be democratic stability and efficient cooperation in Europe. The quality of execution is crucial. Redress provided to victims must be effective and general reforms taken should truly be able to prevent further violations. Supervision of execution is thereby an essential element of the credibility of the system and the efficiency of the actions of the Court."

tion or inaction resides. In extreme cases of political sensitivity, the treaty obligation to comply with the judgment cedes before what are regarded by the respondent State as overriding national interests, and the other States are reluctant ever to apply the only formal sanction at their disposal, namely suspension/expulsion from membership of the Council of Europe, because of its dramatic consequences. As a matter of pure principle, the existence of this small space of "non-law" is less than ideal, but it is doubtless inevitable "at least while sovereign States remain the building blocks of the international community".[72] However, it cannot be said that the inherent traits of international law as reflected in the legal framework and practical operation of the enforcement machinery established under the ECHR have significantly undermined the process of execution of the judgments delivered by the Strasbourg Court.[73]

Instances of outright refusal to comply with a judgment are extremely rare in the ECHR system, even in controversial cases; and the States, both individually as respondent Parties and collectively when acting as the supervising Committee of Ministers, display good faith in relation to the execution of judgments. Collective political pressure within the cloistered confines of Committee of Ministers' meetings is more often than not likely to be more effective than other, perhaps more judicial means in difficult human rights cases, which are difficult precisely because of political considerations (foreign relations, public opinion in the country, and so on). Problems do exist, as the first annual report of the Committee of Ministers concedes, "not least the question of redress to individual applicants in certain situations and the length of time sometimes required for legislative and other reforms, as well as the related problem of clone and repetitive cases that come before the Court".[74] Efforts are being made within the existing legal framework to cure perceived weaknesses – for example, better drafting of judgments so as to specify the nature and source of any violation found, the introduction of a pilot-judgment procedure in order to help cope better with the phenomenon of repetitive cases, the setting up by the Committee of Ministers of a special execution assistance programme, greater publicity being afforded to the execution process by the Committee of Ministers, and the preparation of a vademecum on execution practice. Further procedural reforms aimed at improving the process of execution of judgments (request for interpretation, infringement proceedings) are foreseen in Protocol No. 14.

The present writer's overall conclusion is situated on the side of the optimists rather than that of the pessimists: despite some avoidable weaknesses (notably delays), the

---

72 *Terris, Romano and Swigart*, footnote 1 above, p. 37 (when talking of the process of selection of international judges rather than the execution of international judgments).
73 For a more critical approach, see Natalie Fricero, "L'effectivité des arrêts de la Cour européenne des Droits de l'Homme: un enjeu pour l'Europe", in N. Nikas et al., eds., *Studia in honorem Pelayia Yessiou-Faitsi*, pp. 107–117 (Sakkoulas, 2007), and also in *Petites affiches, la loi, le quotidian juridique*, no. 44 (2 March 2006), pp. 37–40. Fricero's analysis is organised under the two headings "*Des attributs procéduraux insuffisants pour une execution effective*" ["Inadequate procedural tools for an effective execution"] and "*Des mécanismes de contrôle insuffisants pour une execution garantie*" ["Inadequate control mechanisms for ensuring proper execution"].
74 CM Annual Report 2007, p. 7.

bill of health regarding execution of ECHR judgments is on the whole good, will hopefully even improve once the projected treaty reforms enter into force, and does not disclose any fatal flaws in the enforcement tools with which international law provides the European system of human rights protection. What the present writer at the start of his career once heard described by a noted international lawyer as "little short of a miracle" – that is, States ceding their sovereignty in human rights issues to an independent international control machinery and being willing to implement unpopular, unwanted judgments – has become an accepted, routine fact of life in international law. Since judicial rulings became part of the ECHR framework in 1959 (with the setting up of the Strasbourg Court), there has been consolidation of practice into rules, institutionalisation of the way in which collective political pressure is exerted on hesitant or recalcitrant States, evolution of attitudes at both international and national levels towards facilitating compliance with judgments, and the pragmatic progressive development of a process for execution of judgments which is appropriate for international protection of human rights, a process which is not as judicial as purists would want but which on the whole works.

To pick out one noteworthy development, the execution process under the ECHR displays an evolving relationship between international law and national law, bringing the two closer together. Following the express invitation made to it by the Governments in the 2004 Resolution of the Committee of Ministers with a view to improving and expediting the execution process, the Strasbourg Court has visibly displayed a greater tendency to spell out the implications of its judgments in terms of the measures required to be taken at domestic level in order to comply with the judgment. Correspondingly, a greater willingness can be discerned on the part of the national authorities, in particular the judicial authorities, to translate the implications of individual judgments directly into national law. As the first annual report of the Committee of Ministers in 2007 pointed out, if nowadays "in many cases reforms progress rapidly and efficiently and supervision of execution does not pose major problems", this is largely attributable to "the increasingly important role played by domestic courts and authorities, as the direct effect of the [Strasbourg Court] is more and more extensively recognised in domestic law" – given that "acknowledgement of direct effect often spares States more complex and lengthy legislative work".[75]

It is not that there has occurred a revolution in the relationship between national law and international law, but rather a welcome drift towards integrating the two, so as to form, for the purposes of the execution of ECHR judgments, a seamless fabric, without the dividing wall of the discretionary will of the executing Government between the two. The integration is far from complete; there has been no marriage yet between the two partners in the ECHR system, but at least there is an engagement. Although there are evident differences between human rights treaties and other international legal instruments, the phenomenon (of the national legal system coming to the aid of the

---

75 CM Annual Report 2007, p. 11.

international system) may perhaps be one of relevance for the process of execution of judgments by international courts other than human rights courts. As Professor Bernhardt put it, "all these and other developments indicate that a new approach might be necessary in respect of the traditional doctrines concerning the relationship between public international law and municipal law".⁷⁶

---

76 *Bernhardt*, footnote 18 above, p. 440. Similarly, *Andriantsimbazovina*, footnote 5 above, pp. 168, 169: "L'interpénétration réciproque des deux ordres publics implique une autre approche des rapports entre les juridictions nationales et européennes. Ces rapports sont régis ni par la hiérarchie ni par la subordination, mais par la complémentarité et l'effectivité. La protection des droits de l'homme y est une fonction assumée en commun (…)." "La protection des droits de l'homme organisée et assurée en coopération par les deux systèmes et en leur sein implique le dépassement de la logique séparatiste des ordres et systèmes juridiques européens et nationaux." [Free translation by the author: "The reciprocal interpenetration of the two legal orders entails another approach in the relations between the domestic courts and the European Court. These relations are governed neither by hierarchy nor by subordination, but by complementarity and effectiveness, their raison d'être being that the protection of human rights is a shared task…" "The protection of human rights, organised and ensured in cooperation by the two systems and in parallel within both systems, requires going beyond the logic of separate legal orders on the national and European levels."]

Legal Consequences of Non-Compliance with Dispute Settlement Decisions: The Case of the WTO as a "Benefits-Centred" Organization

RETO MALACRIDA[1]

A. Introduction

This contribution begins with an overview of the dispute settlement rules of the World Trade Organization ("WTO"), with particular reference to the rules applicable in cases where a WTO Member has failed to comply with an adverse dispute settlement decision. An attempt is then undertaken at ascertaining the intent behind these rules. Finally, some observations are offered concerning possible reform and improvement of WTO rules on non-compliance with dispute settlement decisions.

B. Overview of relevant WTO dispute settlement rules

I. Access to the WTO dispute settlement mechanism

The WTO dispute settlement mechanism is set forth in the WTO *Understanding on Rules and Procedures Governing the Settlement of Disputes* ("Dispute Settlement Understanding" or "DSU"). It is available to members – i.e., states or customs territories (like the European Communities[2]) – for the settlement of disputes arising under one or more WTO agreements.[3] WTO agreements confer rights, and impose obligations, only on Members. Thus, WTO disputes are, by definition, Member-to-Member disputes.[4] WTO bodies (councils or committees) or the WTO Secretariat cannot file complaints against Members. Similarly, non-governmental entities (companies, NGOs, etc.) or

---

1 Counsellor, WTO Legal Affairs Division. The views and ideas expressed in this article are those of the author acting in a personal capacity and do not represent a position, official or unofficial, of the WTO Secretariat. The author wishes to acknowledge useful comments from, and discussion with, Bruce Wilson as well as Thomas Cottier and other participants in the International Dispute Settlement Conference 2008, organised by the University of St. Gallen and held in St. Gallen, Switzerland, on 2/3 October 2008. Data contained in this article are up to date as of 13 November 2008.
2 At the WTO, the European Community is officially referred to as the "European Communities".
3 See Article 1.1 of the DSU.
4 It is possible for several Members jointly to complain against another Member.

individuals cannot bring complaints on their own behalf against Members. However, complaining Members may, and do, bring complaints to protect the commercial interests of private parties.[5]

II. Binding effect of WTO dispute settlement decisions

Except where the disputing parties resolve a dispute through bilateral consultations, WTO dispute settlement decisions are made by the WTO Dispute Settlement Body ("DSB").[6] The DSB is a political body in which all Members are represented.[7] It makes dispute settlement decisions based upon reports prepared by WTO adjudicating bodies – *ad hoc* dispute settlement "panels" and, in case of an appeal against a report of a panel, the standing Appellate Body. The DSB is under an obligation to "adopt" such reports, which contain recommended legal conclusions and findings, unless all Members, including the parties to the dispute upon which a decision is to be made, agree not to adopt such reports.[8] In practice, adoption has been a formality.[9]

It is a settled point of WTO jurisprudence that the DSB's dispute settlement decisions are legally binding as between the parties to the relevant dispute.[10] In contrast, it is not entirely clear whether the DSU imposes a strict legal obligation to comply with adverse dispute settlement decisions and take implementing action, or whether compliance is merely strongly preferred to other types of specified responses to adverse decisions (essentially, the provision of voluntary compensation or retaliation by the complaining Member).[11] In practice, both complaining Members and responding Members have treated adverse dispute settlement decisions as requiring implementation.[12]

---

5   For instance, an aircraft manufacturer might convince its government to file a complaint at the WTO against another Member, e.g., because it believes that this other Member is subsidizing its own aircraft manufaturer in a manner inconsistent with its WTO obligations.
6   See Article 2.1 of the DSU.
7   See Article IV of the *Marrakesh Agreement Establishing the WTO*.
8   See Articles 16.4 and 17.14 of the DSU.
9   There has been no instance to date in which the DSB decided not to adopt a panel or Appellate Body report.
10 See Appellate Body Report, *Japan – Taxes on Alcoholic Beverages*, WT/DS8/AB/R, WT/DS10/AB/R, WT/DS11/AB/R, adopted 1 November 1996, DSR 1996:I, 97, 108.
11 For relevant DSU provisions, see, in particular, Articles 3.7, 19.1, 21.1, 21.5, 21.6, 22.1, 22.2, 22.8 and 26.1(d) of the DSU. See also John H. Jackson, "The WTO Dispute Settlement Understanding – Misunderstandings on the Nature of Legal Obligation", *American Journal of International Law* 91:1 (1997), 60 *et seq.*
12 Of course, in certain cases no implementing action may be required, e.g., where the measure found to be WTO-inconsistent has been repealed in the course of the dispute settlement proceedings.

Responding Members are expected to comply with adverse dispute settlement decisions prospectively. In other words, there is, in principle, no obligation to make reparation for injury caused prior to the due date for compliance with an adverse dispute settlement decision.[13]

III. Implementation period and multilateral surveillance

Within 30 days after adoption of a WTO panel or Appellate Body report, the responding Member is to make known to the DSB its "intentions" in respect of implementation of an adverse dispute settlement decision, including in respect of the time frame for compliance.[14] In this regard, the DSU stipulates that the responding Member is to comply "immediately", unless this would be impracticable, in which case the Member concerned "shall have" a "reasonable period of time" to bring itself into conformity with its WTO obligations.[15] Usually, Members state that they require a reasonable period of time. The reasonable period of time to be granted in such cases is determined, in practice, either by mutual agreement of the parties or through binding WTO arbitration.[16] The DSU provides as a guideline for WTO arbitrators that 15 months should not be exceeded.[17] This being a mere guideline, arbitrators have sometimes granted significantly less time.[18] In this respect, more time is generally granted in cases where implementation requires legislative action than in cases where implementation could be achieved through administrative action. Also, in a number of cases the complaining Member has agreed to a request of the responding Member to extend the reasonable period of time for implementing an adverse dispute settlement decision.

The DSB is to keep the implementation of adverse dispute settlement decisions under multilateral surveillance. To that end, the responding Member is to provide the DSB with periodic written reports on its progress in respect of implementation. The first such status report is due no later than six months after the reasonable period of time has been determined. Additional status reports are to be submitted in advance of each subsequent and regular DSB meeting until the dispute is resolved.[19]

---

13   In one case, however, a WTO panel determined that a prohibited subsidy granted by Australia on a "one-off" basis needed to be repaid in full. The panel based this determination on the requirement, contained in the WTO *Agreement on Subsidies and Countervailing Measures*, that prohibited subsidies must be "withdrawn". See Panel Report, *Australia – Subsidies Provided to Producers and Exporters of Automotive Leather – Recourse to Article 21.5 of the DSU by the United States*, WT/DS126/RW and Corr.1, adopted 11 February 2000, DSR 2000:III, 1189, para. 6.48. This report was quite controversial among Members, but it was nonetheless adopted without appeal.
14   See Article 21.3 of the DSU.
15   See *ibid*.
16   See *ibid*.
17   See Article 21.3(c) of the DSU.
18   There has been no case to date in which the reasonable period of time was determined significantly to exceed 15 months.
19   See Article 21.6 of the DSU.

IV. Disagreement over compliance with an adverse dispute settlement decision

If, at the end of the reasonable period of time, there is disagreement as to whether the responding Member has complied with an adverse dispute settlement decision, the complaining Member has the right to request the DSB to refer the matter to a so-called "compliance panel" for examination.[20] Compliance panel proceedings are accelerated dispute settlement proceedings.[21] The reports of compliance panels are, however, subject to appeal to the Appellate Body.[22] The reports of compliance panels and, where relevant, of the Appellate Body must be adopted by the DSB in the same way as ordinary panel and Appellate Body reports. Successive compliance panel proceedings are a possibility.[23] This might be necessary in cases where a complaining Member considers that an amended measure of the responding Member still falls short of that Member's WTO obligations.

V. Legal consequences of a failure to comply with an adverse dispute settlement decision

If the DSB decides that a responding Member has failed to comply with a prior DSB dispute settlement decision, the complaining Member may allow more time for the responding Member to comply and, if necessary, challenge any further measures taken to comply. Alternatively, the complaining Member can protect its interests by taking, or accepting, specified "temporary measures".[24] Such measures are temporary in the sense that they must be discontinued if, and when, the responding Member has complied with the adverse dispute settlement decision.[25]

One of the available temporary measures is compensation. Usually, this takes the form of trade compensation, that is to say, of measures taken by the responding Member to provide additional market access opportunities, such as a temporary lowering of import duties on specific goods.[26] Compensation must be provided in a WTO-consistent manner.[27] In the case of trade compensation, this means that compensation cannot be pro-

---

20   See Article 21.5 of the DSU.
21   Pursuant to Article 21.5 of the DSU, they are to be completed within 90 days.
22   The DSU does not explicitly say so, but the Appellate Body has accepted numerous appeals against reports of compliance panels. The Appellate Body typically takes 90 days to complete appellate review proceedings.
23   There have been four disputes so far in which the complaining Member has had recourse to compliance panels twice.
24   See Article 22.1 of the DSU.
25   See, e.g., Article 22.8 of the DSU.
26   Monetary compensation is not explicitly excluded. In fact, in one dispute – *United States - Section 110(5) of the US Copyright Act* – monetary compensation was provided by the United States to the European Communities. See WTO document WT/DS160/23. Some Members have raised concerns over this, however.
27   See Article 22.1 of the DSU.

vided exclusively to the complaining Member. In other words, it is not permissible to lower import duties only in respect of imported goods originating in the territory of the complaining Member. It is, however, possible to provide compensation which, in effect, benefits exclusively, or at least primarily, the complaining Member. A further limiting condition is that compensation is "voluntary", which means that the complaining Member cannot require the responding Member to provide compensation.[28] Nonetheless, the responding Member is under an obligation to enter into negotiations with a view to agreeing on mutually acceptable compensation (*pactum de negotiando*).[29]

If, and only if, the disputing parties are unable to agree on satisfactory compensation, the complaining Member may request authorization from the DSB to suspend the application, to the responding Member, of concessions or other WTO obligations (hereafter "suspension of WTO obligations").[30] This "last-resort"[31] temporary measure is often referred to as "retaliation".[32] As indicated, retaliatory measures must take the form of a suspension (i.e., non-performance) of WTO obligations. Also, such measures may only be applied to the responding Member. In other words, they are discriminatory measures.[33] Another important substantive requirement is that the DSB may authorize a requested level of suspension of WTO obligations only if that level is "equivalent" to the level of nullification or impairment of economic benefits resulting from the failure of the responding Member to comply with the relevant DSB dispute settlement decision.[34] Typically, the level of suspension is expressed in value terms and relates to a one-year period, e.g., USD 200 million per annum. This means that the complaining Member is authorized to suspend specified obligations in such a way that they restrict imports from the responding Member up to a maximum value of USD 200 million per year.[35]

Regarding the design of retaliatory measures, the complaining Member faces no significant legal constraints if it proposes to retaliate in the same "sector".[36] In the case of

---

28 See *ibid*.
29 See Article 22.2 of the DSU.
30 See *ibid*. The provisions of the DSU are less than clear regarding whether authorization to suspend WTO obligations may be granted before the DSB has determined, in accordance with Article 21.5 of the DSU, that the responding Member has failed to implement an adverse dispute settlement decision of the DSB. This is known to WTO experts as the "sequencing issue". In practice, disputing parties nowadays conclude bilateral understandings in order to prevent this from becoming a problem. Typically, disputing parties agree to a *modus procedendi* under which the complaining Member cannot be granted authorization to suspend WTO obligations until after Article 21.5 proceedings have run their course.
31 See Article 3.7 of the DSU.
32 The term "retaliation" does not appear in the DSU.
33 See Articles 3.7 and 22.2 of the DSU.
34 See Article 22.4 of the DSU.
35 A complaining Member might, e.g., try to identify several goods for which the total value of imports from the responding Member during a past representative period amounts to no more than USD 200 million per year and impose a 100 percent *ad valorem* duty on the importation of such goods if they originate in the responding Member. The expectation would be that a 100 percent duty would effectively prevent imports of the goods concerned.
36 See Article 22.3(a) of the DSU.

goods, all goods are considered as one single sector.[37] Thus, if the WTO-inconsistent measure maintained by the responding Member adversely affects, say, soybean exports of the complaining Member, the complaining Member is free to determine whether its retaliatory measure should target, e.g., passenger car exports of the responding Member, or computer chip exports, or steel exports, or exports of all those products.

Where same-sector retaliation is not considered "practicable" or "effective", the complaining Member is entitled to retaliate in another sector under the WTO agreement that has been breached.[38] For instance, if the WTO-inconsistent measure maintained by the responding Member affects, say, the provision of construction services through commercial presence by service providers of the complaining Member, the complaining Member could target another services sector for retaliation, such as cross-border communication services provided by service providers of the responding Member. The complaining Member could not, however, target passenger car exports of the responding Member.

Finally, where different-sector retaliation is not considered "practicable" or "effective", and the circumstances are "serious enough"[39], the complaining Member may retaliate under a WTO agreement other than the one that has been breached.[40] Accordingly, if the WTO-inconsistent measure maintained by the responding Member affects soybean exports of the complaining Member, the complaining Member would be entitled to target cross-border communication services provided by service providers of the responding Member. Alternatively, the complaining Member would, in principle, be entitled to suspend WTO-mandated protection of intellectual property rights in respect of right holders of the responding Member.[41]

Procedurally, the DSB is obligated to authorize a retaliatory measure proposed by the complaining Member, except in either of two situations. The first, unlikely, situation is where the DSB, which includes the complaining Member, decides by consensus not to grant a request by the complaining Member for authorization to retaliate.[42] The other situation is where the responding Member objects to the proposed level of suspen-

---

37 See Article 22.3(f) of the DSU.
38 See Article 22.3(b) of the DSU.
39 This might possibly be the case where, e.g., a poor complaining Member is heavily dependent on imports of essential goods originating in the territory of the responding Member. By restricting imports of such goods from that Member, the complaining Member might inflict considerably more economic harm upon itself than upon the responding Member.
40 See Article 22.3(c) of the DSU. This has been authorized by arbitrators in two instances so far. See (1) Decision by the Arbitrators, *European Communities – Regime for the Importation, Sale and Distribution of Bananas – Recourse to Arbitration by the European Communities under Article 22.6 of the DSU*, WT/DS27/ARB/ECU, 24 March 2000, DSR 2000:V, 2237; and (2) Decision by the Arbitrator, *United States – Measures Affecting the Cross-Border Supply of Gambling and Betting Services – Arbitration under Article 22.6 of the DSU*, WT/DS285/ARB, 21 December 2007.
41 The two identified alternatives to same-sector retaliation – retaliation in a different sector or under a different agreement – are commonly referred to as "cross-retaliation".
42 See Article 22.6 of the DSU.

sion, or claims that the request is otherwise inconsistent with applicable DSU rules, including the above-noted rules on resort to cross-retaliation.[43] In the latter situation, which is the norm, the matter is referred to arbitration.[44] The mandate of the WTO arbitrators is to determine whether the proposed level of suspension is equivalent to the level of nullification or impairment, and/or whether the request is consistent with other applicable requirements. The decision of the arbitrators is not subject to appeal, nor does it need to be submitted to the DSB for adoption.[45]

During the course of the arbitration, the complaining Member may not impose the proposed retaliatory measure.[46] After completion of the arbitration, the complaining Member needs to re-submit its original request to the DSB for authorization, if it has been upheld by the arbitrators, or submit a modified request that is consistent with the arbitrators' decision. If the request submitted to the DSB is consistent with the arbitrators' decision, the DSB must grant the request, unless it decides by consensus to reject the request.[47] The grant of a request entitles a complaining Member to impose a retaliatory measure as from the date of authorization. The complaining Member does not need, however, to impose such a measure immediately or at all. Nor, if a measure is imposed at some point, is it necessary to maintain it until the responding Member complies with the adverse dispute settlement decision. Nonetheless, as explained, retaliatory measures being temporary measures, they are to be discontinued once the responding Member has taken all necessary steps to implement a dispute settlement decision.

C. WTO Members' compliance record

It is fair to say that, overall, Members' record of compliance with adverse dispute settlement decisions has been neither perfect nor poor. Whether one considers Members' record to be closer to one end of this spectrum or the other is a matter of opinion and perspective. Some would argue that any instance of prolonged non-compliance with a multilateral dispute settlement decision reveals a shortcoming in the WTO's dispute settlement system. Others might consider that in view of the absence, in general international law as well as WTO law, of effective means of coercion and the fact that Members at the WTO do not have the option of submitting to the jurisdiction of the DSB only on an *ad hoc* basis, it is remarkable that Members do, in fact, comply with an adverse dispute settlement decision.

---

43 See *ibid.*
44 Pursuant to Article 22.6 of the DSU, the arbitration is to be completed within 60 days.
45 See Article 22.7 of the DSU.
46 See Article 22.6 of the DSU.
47 See Article 22.7 of the DSU. There has as yet been no instance in which the DSB did not grant a request for authorization to retaliate.

Another difficulty lies in the identification of a suitable objective standard against which to measure Members' compliance. Is it realistic, as a factual matter, to expect prompt compliance with adverse decisions in every case? If not, at what point does a delay in complying become persistent non-compliance which might give rise to justifiable systemic concerns? Even assuming that a standard could be agreed upon, there would still be the separate problem of the "missing" cases which do not appear in any dispute settlement statistics. This category includes cases of anticipated non-compliance, i.e., cases in which it is expected that another Member would be either unwilling or unable to comply with an adverse dispute settlement decision, with the consequence that (i) no complaint is filed or (ii) no action is taken in response to non-compliance with an adverse dispute settlement decision, either at the end of the reasonable period of time or at a subsequent stage.

These conceptual difficulties notwithstanding, it is interesting to note how Members' overall record of compliance with dispute settlement decisions has been assessed by the Director of the WTO Legal Affairs Division:

> "*The record indicates that, generally speaking, WTO Members found in violation of their WTO obligations in dispute settlement proceedings have done a reasonably good job in taking steps to correct these violations within a reasonable period of time. While there have been cases where compliance has been delayed or where full compliance has yet to be achieved, this should not detract from the fact that the overall compliance record of WTO Members has been quite positive [...].*"[48]

Thus, according to this observer, Members' overall record is closer to the "perfect record" end of the spectrum than to the "poor record" end.[49] As noted by the observer, his "quite positive" assessment of Members' overall compliance record relates to "ultimate" compliance, which includes cases where compliance has been achieved only after some delay.[50] In this regard, from a legal perspective, there is a delay in compliance whenever the responding Member has failed to comply with an adverse dispute settlement decision by the end of the reasonable period of time.

WTO dispute settlement practice shows that no less than 23 compliance panel reports have been adopted so far, and in a majority of these cases it was found that the

---

48 Bruce Wilson, "Compliance by WTO Members with Adverse WTO Dispute Settlement Rulings: The Record to Date", *Journal of International Economic Law* 10:2 (2007), 398 (emphasis added). According to Wilson, it is not surprising that "compliance has usually been more rapid where WTO violations could be corrected through administrative action under the control of the Executive as opposed to legislative action" (*Ibid.*, 399).

49 See also Raimund Raith, "How does the World Trade Organization's dispute settlement system work?" in *Global trade governance: the WTO at a crossroads*, European Policy Centre Working Paper No. 26 (2006), 46 (stating that "[t]he track record of implementation by members – including the EC and US 'elephants' and the developing countries – is excellent, even in the most politically sensitive and economically important cases").

50 Wilson also notes that only about 30 percent of Members have ever been the object of adverse dispute settlement decisions. See Wilson, *Compliance by WTO Members*, 398.

responding Member had not fully complied. This number should be compared to the number of cases where the reasonable period of time for implementation has expired. The present author has estimated, though somewhat roughly, that the number of cases in that category by now exceeds 60.[51] This suggests that delays in compliance are not entirely uncommon.[52] In three disputes so far, the DSB has determined that even a responding Member's second attempt at complying with an adverse dispute settlement decision was inadequate.

As explained earlier, temporary measures are available to complaining Members if a responding Member fails to comply with a dispute settlement decision by the end of the reasonable period of time. The preferred temporary measure – compensation – has hardly ever been used.[53] Arguably, this is due, above all, to the fact that the disputing parties need to agree to the amount and manner of compensation. Also, by accepting compensation the complaining Member might compromise its ability to induce the responding Member to comply with a dispute settlement decision.[54]

On the other hand, the temporary measure of last resort – suspension of WTO obligations, or retaliation – has been repeatedly used. As of the time of writing, Members have requested authorization to retaliate in 18 different disputes. In four of those disputes retaliatory measures have been actually imposed.[55] The Members who have imposed such measures are Canada, the European Communities, Japan, Mexico and the United States. Those Members' retaliatory measures were directed against either the European Communities or the United States. Comparing the four disputes in which complaining Members have resorted to retaliation to the above-mentioned 60-plus disputes in which the reasonable period of time has expired, it can be said that retaliation has not been a negligible occurrence, although it has definitely been the exception rather than the rule.

Regarding the effectiveness of retaliatory measures, experience with the measures that have been imposed until now suggests that retaliation does not necessarily induce compliance promptly, or at all. Retaliatory measures have been in place in one of the four

---

51 See Malacrida, *Towards Sounder and Fairer WTO Retaliation*, 7.
52 Some of these delays may be the result of failed *bona fide* attempts at implementing adverse dispute settlement decisions. In other words, there may be some cases in which it cannot be considered that the Member concerned could have foreseen that a compliance panel would find that full compliance had not yet been achieved.
53 As pointed out above, compensation was provided, although for only three years, in *United States - Section 110(5) of the US Copyright Act*.
54 For a discussion of possible reasons why one or both parties may be unable or unwilling to agree on compensation, see Malacrida, *Towards Sounder and Fairer WTO Retaliation*, 24 et seq.
55 The four disputes are: (1) *European Communities – Regime for the Importation, Sale and Distribution of Bananas* (retaliation by the United States against the European Communities), (2) *European Communities – Measures Concerning Meat and Meat Products (Hormones)* (retaliation by the United States and Canada against the European Communities), (3) *United States – Tax Treatment for "Foreign Sales Corporations"* (retaliation by the European Communities against the United States) and (4) *United States – Continued Dumping and Subsidy Offset Act of 2000 (Byrd Amendment)* (retaliation by Canada, the European Communities, Japan and Mexico against the United States).

relevant disputes since 1999, and in another since 2005.[56] In a further dispute, however, the retaliatory measure appears to have contributed to inducing compliance by the responding Member. At any rate, the retaliatory measure was withdrawn within less than one year of its imposition.[57] In the remaining dispute, a settlement was reached about two years after a retaliatory measure had been imposed.[58] As an additional matter, it should be noted that in some cases the mere fact of obtaining authorization to retaliate – i.e., the threat of retaliation – appears to have made a difference.

D. Understanding WTO rules on non-compliance with dispute settlement decisions

I. Comparison with European Community law

In attempting to understand, and make sense of, the above-described WTO rules concerning non-compliance with DSB dispute settlement decisions, it is instructive for comparative purposes to look at the corresponding rules of the European Community. Article 228(2) of the *Treaty Establishing the European Community* ("TEC") provides in relevant part:

> *If the Member State concerned fails to take the necessary measures to comply with the Court's judgment within the time limit laid down by the Commission, the latter may bring the case before the Court of Justice. In so doing it shall specify the amount of the lump sum or penalty payment to be paid by the Member State concerned which it considers appropriate in the circumstances.*

> *If the Court of Justice finds that the Member State concerned has not complied with its judgment it may impose a lump sum or penalty payment on it.*

Article 244 of the TEC further provides that judgments of the Court of Justice are enforceable under the conditions laid down in Article 256 of the TEC. Article 256 stipulates that enforcement of pecuniary obligations is governed by the rules of civil procedure in force in the EC Member State in which it is to be carried out.[59]

In *Commission v France*, the Court of Justice explained the provisions of Article 228(2) in the following terms:[60]

---

56 The disputes are *European Communities – Measures Concerning Meat and Meat Products (Hormones)* and *United States – Continued Dumping and Subsidy Offset Act of 2000 (Byrd Amendment)*, respectively.
57 The dispute in question is *United States – Tax Treatment for "Foreign Sales Corporations"*.
58 The dispute in question is *European Communities – Regime for the Importation, Sale and Distribution of Bananas*.
59 It should be noted, however, that the money collected by the EC Member State goes to the European Community.
60 Case C-304/02 *Commission v. France* [2005], ECR I.6263, paras. 80–81 and 91 (emphasis added).

> The procedure laid down in Article 228(2) EC has the objective of inducing a defaulting Member State to comply with a judgment establishing a breach of obligations and thereby of ensuring that Community law is in fact applied. The measures provided for by that provision, namely a lump sum and a penalty payment, are both intended to achieve this objective.
>
> ... While the imposition of a penalty payment seems particularly suited to inducing a Member State to put an end as soon as possible to a breach of obligations which, in the absence of such a measure, would tend to persist, the imposition of a lump sum is based more on assessment of the effects on public and private interests of the failure of the Member State concerned to comply with its obligations, in particular where the breach has persisted for a long period since the judgment which initially established it.
>
> ...
>
> The order imposing a penalty payment and/or a lump sum is not intended to compensate for damage caused by the Member State concerned, but to place it under economic pressure which induces it to put an end to the breach established. The financial penalties imposed must therefore be decided upon according to the degree of persuasion needed in order for the Member State in question to alter its conduct.

The Advocate General's opinion in the same case also illuminates the rationale underpinning the financial sanction (penalty payment and/or lump sum) envisaged in Article 228(2):[61]

> The rationale for imposing such a financial sanction lies firstly in the fact that the Member State concerned has disregarded a judgment of the Court. This is particularly serious in a Community based on the the rule of law and equality of all Member States in respect of their rights and obligations under the Treaty. Non-compliance with a judgment finding that a Member State has infringed its Treaty obligations strikes at the heart of the legal order of the Community and seriously threatens the credibility of the Community legal order.

The provisions of Article 228(2) of the TEC as well as the statements by the Court of Justice and the Advocate General serve to demonstrate that the European Community can be regarded as a "law-centred" organization. Indeed, what is at the centre of the procedure set out in Article 228(2) is a concern to protect the integrity of the objective EC legal order. As observed by the Advocate General, a failure to end a breach of EC law would, in his view, "strike[ ] at the heart" of the Community's legal order and "seriously threaten[ ]" the "credibility" of that order as a legal order.

---

61 Opinion of Advocate General Geelhoed, delivered on 18 November 2004, Case C-304/02 *Commission v. France*, para. 7 (emphasis added).

This law-centred perspective leads to what might be called a *"satisfaction – or else!"* attitude towards non-compliance with judgments by the Court of Justice. Accordingly, an EC Member State which fails to put an end to a breach of EC law is "sanctioned", that is to say, it is "penalized". The financial sanction that may be imposed is not, however, intended as "punishment" in the penal law sense of the term.[62] As confirmed by the Court of Justice, the only purpose of the financial sanction it has the authority to impose is to "induce compliance" with its judgment, and the level of any financial sanction would be a function of the "persuasion needed" to get the relevant EC Member State to comply.

II. Main purpose of WTO rules on non-compliance with dispute settlement decisions

In the WTO, neither a complaining Member nor the DSB is authorized to impose a financial sanction, be it a penalty payment or a lump sum. It is therefore pertinent to ask the question whether the WTO can, nevertheless, be regarded as a law-centred organization, i.e., as an organization for which the protection of the integrity of the objective "WTO legal order" is the primary concern, or whether it would be more appropriate to conceive of it as a different type of organization.

In examining this issue, it should be recalled at the outset that in accordance with the DSU the level of suspension of WTO obligations must be "equivalent" to the level of nullification or impairment of economic benefits caused by a breach of a WTO obligation. By necessary implication, therefore, where the level of nullification or impairment is low, the level of suspension cannot exceed that low level. Conversely, where the level of nullification or impairment is high, concessions or other obligations may be suspended up to that high level. What this means is that it may be substantially more difficult for complaining Members to secure compliance in cases in which the level of nullified or impaired benefits is low than in cases where that level is high. This is because in "low impairment" cases the "cost" of non-compliance for a responding Member would be correspondingly low. The cost of non-compliance could thus be relatively low even in cases involving a serious breach, e.g., because the WTO provision that has been breached is a fundamental one or the breach is egregious.

Accordingly, as currently envisaged in the DSU, suspension of WTO obligations may not constitute an effective "sanction" for a breach of law, except in circumstances where the level of nullified or impaired benefits is high. In the light of this, it seems doubtful that suspension of WTO obligations is first and foremost about "sanctioning"

---

62 See Denys Simon, "The Sanction of Member States' Serious Violations of Community Law" in *Liber Amicorum in Honour of Lord Slynn of Hadley*, Vol. I (Judicial Review in European Union Law), eds. David O'Keeffe and Antonio Bavasso (The Hague/London/Boston: Kluwer Law International, 2000), 279 (Article 228(2) does not provide for "a sanction mechanism *stricto sensu*, aimed at "punishing" Member States in a way which, by analogy, pertains more to penal law").

breaches of law as such. If a breach of a WTO obligation were considered reprehensible because it hurts the integrity of the WTO legal order, there is an argument to be made that this breach should then be subject to an effective sanction, independently of whether such breach is minor or major. This could have been achieved, for instance, by allowing the level of suspension of WTO obligations to vary according to the "persuasion needed" to get a responding Member to comply (e.g., its ability to accept a "price" for non-compliance, or the seriousness of a breach and the resulting urgency for prompt compliance).

But if suspension of WTO obligations is not primarily about "sanctioning" breaches of law as such, what is its main purpose? In attempting to answer this question, it is instructive to look at the similar effects of a breach of a WTO obligation and suspension of WTO obligations. Just like a breach of a WTO obligation ordinarily results in economic benefits being denied to a complaining Member, so also a suspension of a WTO obligation ordinarily results in economic benefits being denied to a responding Member. The DSU requires that the level of benefits which may be denied by suspending WTO obligations be "equivalent" to the level of benefits nullified or impaired as a result of the breach of a WTO obligation. What suspension of WTO obligations does, therefore, is to re-establish a balance of benefits, i.e., an equilibrium, as between the responding Member and the complaining Member. This effect of equivalent suspension of WTO obligations is sometimes referred to as "re-balancing".

Thus, judging by what suspension of WTO obligations actually does (and assuming that it does what it is designed to do), it would appear that its main purpose is to establish a new balance of benefits.[63] The view that re-balancing is the main purpose of suspension of WTO obligations fits well with the fact that mutually agreed compensation constitutes the alternative temporary measure available to a complaining Member in the event of non-compliance with a dispute settlement decision. Indeed, mutually agreed compensation is also about re-balancing. The DSU stipulates, in effect, that if the responding Member fails to offer satisfactory compensation which would re-balance the level of benefits by providing compensatory new benefits, the complaining Member may bring about such re-balancing of benefits by itself, by suspending WTO obligations. Seen in this light, suspension of WTO obligations is a form of "self-compensation" in response to an unjustified denial of benefits. Accordingly, both types of temporary measures allowed under the DSU, i.e., mutually agreed compensation and "self-compensation" in the form of suspension of obligations, can be viewed as serving a common purpose, which is to reestablish a balance of benefits.[64]

---

63 See also David Palmeter and Stanimir A. Alexandrov, "'Inducing compliance' in WTO dispute settlement," in *The Political Economy of International Trade Law – Essays in Honor of Robert E. Hudec*, eds. Daniel L. M. Kennedy and James D. Southwick (Cambridge: Cambridge University Press, 2002), 665.
64 It is important to realize that in the case of *agreed compensation*, the new level of benefits accruing to the complaining Member and the responding Member would ordinarily be equivalent to the originally agreed level. In contrast, in the case of *"self-compensation"*, the new level of benefits would be lower than the originally agreed level. This, of course, is why the DSU expresses a preference for voluntary compensation and suspension of WTO obligations is only to come into play as a last resort.

As pointed out, it is arguable that re-balancing is the main purpose of suspension of WTO obligations. Another important purpose is to induce the responding Member to comply with a dispute settlement decision of the DSB. This assertion draws support from the fact that suspension of WTO obligations is a temporary measure, to be discontinued if and when the responding Member complies with the decision of the DSB. The DSU therefore contemplates that suspension of WTO obligations might induce a responding Member to comply. Furthermore, it has been explained above that, subject to specified limitations, the complaining Member enjoys discretion as to which WTO obligations to suspend.[65] In practice, Members use this flexibility to withhold benefits from the responding Member in a way that maximizes the political costs for that Member.[66] The goal is to try to change the political dynamics in the responding Member in such a way that it will reconsider its position and comply with the relevant dispute settlement decision of the DSB.

While complaining Members can thus seek to induce compliance by selecting the *WTO obligations* to be suspended, they cannot do so by varying the *level of benefits* to be suspended. The level of suspension must pursuant to DSU rules be "equivalent" to the level of nullification or impairment. As noted previously, particularly in cases where the level of nullification or impairment is low, the "equivalence" condition may hamper the ability of a complaining Member to induce prompt compliance, no matter how carefully or cleverly it selects the WTO obligations to be suspended. Conversely, and it is important to underline this, the "equivalence" condition does not limit the ability of a complaining Member to re-establish a balance of benefits. For these reasons, it would seem that the purpose of inducing compliance is subordinate to the purpose of re-establishing a new balance of benefits.[67]

---

65 To recall, there are no significant constraints if a complaining Member retaliates in the same sector. If same-sector retaliation would "not [be] practicable or effective", the complaining Member has the option of cross-retaliation, i.e., retaliation in different sectors or under different agreements. See Article 22.3(b) and (c) of the DSU. The term "not effective" in Article 22.3(b) and (c) supports the view that the WTO obligations to be suspended would be selected with a view to ensuring, as much as possible, that the suspension is effective in inducing compliance.

66 For example, a complaining Member might seek to target export-oriented industries which, e.g., (i) are important for the economy of the responding Member, (ii) export products with a high symbolic value for the responding Member and thus guarantee high visibility if targeted (e.g., Roquefort cheese for France), or (iii) have an electoral significance, for instance because they maintain production facilities in the constituency of political decision-makers of the responding Member. For further discussion of how Members design retaliatory measures, see Malacrida, *Towards Sounder and Fairer WTO Retaliation*, 14 *et seq.* and 30 *et seq.*

67 See also Warren F. Schwartz and Alan O. Sykes, "The Economic Structure of Renegotiation and Dispute Resolution in the World Trade Organization", *Journal of Legal Studies* XXXI (January 2002), 191 (arguing that "[i]f WTO members really wanted to make compliance with dispute resolution findings mandatory, they would have imposed some greater penalty for noncompliance to induce it").

The foregoing considerations lead to the conclusion that DSU rules concerning non-compliance with DSB dispute settlement decisions serve two important purposes: (i) to safeguard, and maintain, a balance of economic benefits between complaining Members and non-compliant responding Members, and (ii) to protect the integrity of the WTO legal order, including by inducing compliance with dispute settlement decisions of the DSB. Significantly, however, WTO dispute settlement rules appear to give priority to the former purpose. This view is reinforced by two further elements.

III. Additional supporting elements

The first additional element relates to the possibility that Members may file so-called "non-violation" complaints.[68] This type of WTO complaint may be initiated by a Member to challenge a measure taken by another Member which does not conflict with the provisions of a particular WTO agreement, but which is nonetheless considered to nullify or impair benefits that should accrue to the complaining Member under that WTO agreement. In other words, the DSU contemplates a possible cause of action even in situations where no WTO provision has been breached.[69] If the DSB decides that a challenged measure has nullified or impaired benefits, the responding Member is not required to withdraw the measure, since it is not WTO-inconsistent. But the responding Member is nonetheless required to make a "satisfactory adjustment". This may take the form of mutually agreed compensation as final (i.e., not merely as temporary) settlement of the dispute.[70]

The possibility of filing non-violation complaints confirms that the notion of "balance of benefits" occupies a central place in the WTO, so much so that Members may need to provide compensatory benefits in situations where their measures upset the agreed

---

68 See Article 26(1) of the DSU. Article 26(1) does not use the term "non-violation" complaint.
69 To illustrate, if Member X has agreed to bind its customs duty on product p at 20 percent *ad valorem*, but subsequently decides to pay a subsidy to producers of product p, the benefit to foreign exporters of product p would be nullified or impaired, depending on the amount of the subsidy. In effect, this would be a situation where Member X initially gives with one hand, but subsequently takes away with the other hand.
70 See Article 26(1)(b) and (d) of the DSU.

balance of benefits, irrespective of whether such measures breach any WTO obligations. This also suggests that what matters to Members above all is the balance of *benefits* between complaining Members and responding Members, and not the balance of *rights and obligations* between complaining Members and responding Members.[71]

The other element reinforcing the view that re-balancing is the primary purpose of the relevant DSU rules is Article 4.10 of the WTO *Agreement on Subsidies and Countervailing Measures* ("SCM Agreement"). Article 4.10 deals with cases where the DSB has found that a Member has granted a prohibited subsidy. In such cases, the prohibited subsidy must be "withdrawn without delay".[72] In the event of non-compliance with such a DSB decision, the DSB, upon request of the complaining Member, must authorize the complaining Member to take "appropriate countermeasures" against the responding Member, unless the DSB decides by consensus to reject the request. A footnote to Article 4.10 clarifies the expression "appropriate", stating that "[t]his expression is not meant to allow countermeasures that are disproportionate in light of the fact that the subsidies dealt ... are prohibited".

Article 4.10 is a very interesting provision, because it refers to "appropriate" countermeasures, not "equivalent" countermeasures, and because it indicates that it would only allow countermeasures that are not "disproportionate". Thus, Article 4.10 appears to contemplate temporary measures that are directed, not so much at re-establishing a balance of benefits, but at inducing the responding Member to comply with a DSB decision. In other words, Article 4.10 appears to contemplate that in some cases the level of benefits suspended need not be "equivalent", but could actually exceed, the level of nullified or impaired benefits. The only limitation is that Article 4.10 countermeasures must not be disproportionate.[73]

---

71 It is useful to note in this context the International Law Commission's 2001 Draft Articles on Responsibility of States for Internationally Wrongful Acts. See UN General Assembly, Resolution on responsibility of States for internationally wrongful acts, A/RES/56/83, adopted on 12 December 2001. According to Article 49, the object of countermeasures is to "induce" the State which is responsible for an internationally wrongful act "to comply" with, inter alia, its obligation to cease that act. Countermeasures are limited to the "non-performance" of international obligations of the State taking the measures towards the responsible State. Article 51 states that countermeasures must be "commensurate with the injury suffered, taking into account the gravity of the internationally wrongful act and the rights in question". These draft rules governing countermeasures are plainly similar to current WTO rules governing the suspension of WTO obligations. Nevertheless, it has been observed in respect of general international law that "the suspension of performance is aimed at restoring the normative balance altered by the breach". See Enzo Cannizzaro, "The Role of Proportionality in the Law of International Countermeasures", European Journal of International Law, 12:5 (2001), 894 (emphasis added). In contrast, in the case of the WTO, the existence of non-violation complaints suggests that the balance that matters is not so much, or at least not merely, the normative balance (i.e., the balance of rights and obligations), but the balance of economic benefits.

72 See Article 4.7 of the SCM Agreement.

73 See Decision by the Arbitrators, *Brazil – Export Financing Programme for Aircraft – Recourse to Arbitration by Brazil under Article 22.6 of the DSU and Article 4.11 of the SCM Agreement*, WT/DS46/ARB, 28 August 2000, DSR 2002:I, 19, para. 3.57 (stating that "there is no legal obligation that countermeasures in the form of suspension of concessions or other obligations be equivalent to the level of nullification or impairment").

Article 4.10, if understood as suggested above, gives meaning to the distinction made in the *SCM Agreement* between prohibited subsidies and so-called "actionable" subsidies. Prohibited subsidies are subsidies which Members may neither grant nor maintain. They comprise export subsidies and import substitution subsidies.[74] These types of subsidies are prohibited because they are considered to be highly trade-distorting. It makes sense, therefore, to require that if a subsidy is found by the DSB to constitute a prohibited subsidy, that subsidy should be withdrawn without delay. So far as concerns actionable subsidies, Members may grant or maintain them, provided they do not cause adverse effects to the interests of other Members.[75] If an actionable subsidy is found by the DSB to cause adverse effects, the responding Member must either withdraw it or take steps to remove its adverse effects.[76]

Now, if it is correct that suspension of WTO obligations as contemplated in Article 22 of the DSU is primarily designed, not to protect the integrity of the WTO legal order by securing compliance, but to ensure a re-balancing of benefits, it makes sense that a special rule would need to be added – Article 4.10 of the *SCM Agreement* – to allow Members to take temporary measures that are primarily intended to secure compliance. Indeed, since inducing compliance arguably is not the main purpose of Article 22 of the DSU, it is conceivable that without the threat of "appropriate" countermeasures as envisaged in Article 4.10, a responding Member would decide not to withdraw a prohibited subsidy and to accept "equivalent" suspension of WTO obligations by the complaining Member, as set out in Article 22. If this were to happen, it might render largely academic the distinction in the *SCM Agreement* between prohibited subsidies, which are not to be granted or maintained, and actionable subsidies, which can be granted or maintained. Presumably, it is precisely to prevent this from happening that the *SCM Agreement* imposes a higher cost – "appropriate" countermeasures – on noncompliance with a DSB decision in prohibited subsidy cases, as an "inducement" to Members to comply with their obligation not to grant or maintain prohibited subsidies.

Thus, the fact that Article 4.10 exceptionally allows "appropriate" countermeasures, to induce compliance with DSB decisions in prohibited subsidy cases, would appear to confirm that "equivalent" suspension of WTO obligations is primarily designed to secure the maintenance of a balance of benefits between the complaining Member and the responding Member, and not to secure compliance with a DSB decision. Since Article 4.10 provides for an exception to the general rule set out in Article 22, it can be regarded as the proverbial exception that confirms the rule – that WTO dispute settlement rules are designed, first and foremost, to safeguard a balance of benefits between complaining Members and non-compliant responding Members.[77]

---

74 See Article 3.1 of the *SCM Agreement*.
75 See Article 5 of the *SCM Agreement*.
76 See Article 7.8 of the *SCM Agreement*.
77 See also Joost Pauwelyn, "Enforcement and Countermeasures in the WTO: Rules are Rules – Toward a More Collective Approach", *American Journal of International Law* 94:2 (2000), 340.

IV. The WTO as a "benefits-centred" organization

In view of the above considerations, it does not seem entirely appropriate to characterize the WTO as a law-centred organization. On the other hand, based upon the foregoing, it does seem appropriate to characterize the WTO as a "benefits-centred" organization. Needless to say, characterizing the WTO as "benefits-centred" does not at all imply that the law does not play an essential part in the WTO, much less that it is not taken seriously by Members. Indeed, to suggest otherwise would be far from the truth. There is nothing strange about conceiving of the WTO as a benefits-centred organization. In fact, doing so is consistent with the fundamental mission of the WTO. At its core, the WTO is what might be called a "benefit exchange". That is to say, the WTO is a place and organization where economic benefits – essentially, market access opportunities – are exchanged by its Members. Members "buy", and "pay" for, benefits by providing benefits themselves, usually in the context of multilateral trade negotiations, i.e., so-called trade "rounds".[78] If and when Members strike bargains in the context of multilateral trade negotiations, there is, naturally, a political concern with balance. It is costly in political terms for elected politicians to open up their domestic market to suppliers of other Members. Members are therefore keen to make sure that the benefits they provide to others do not exceed the benefits others provide to them. Otherwise, the benefits to be received from other Members would, politically speaking, be "overpaid". Or to put it differently, the benefits received would not justify the political costs incurred. Arguably, this sort of political logic explains the importance of the notion of "balance of benefits" for the WTO in general and the DSU in particular.[79] The same logic arguably also explains why the law is viewed and used in the WTO in pragmatic fashion. It is considered not so much as an end in itself, but as an instrument. Its main function is to provide a legal framework for the exchange of benefits and to establish disciplines that serve to protect the benefits exchanged from being nullified or impaired.[80]

Conceiving of the WTO as a benefits-centred organization also contributes significantly to understanding, and making sense of, the requirement in Article 22.4 of the DSU

---

78 As the preamble to the *Marrakesh Agreement Establishing the WTO* makes clear, the WTO seeks to realize its trade-liberalizing mission through "reciprocal" and "mutually advantageous" arrangements.
79 See also Warren F. Schwartz and Alan O. Sykes, *The Economic Structure of Renegotiation and Dispute Resolution*, 180 (characterizing WTO agreements as being, in effect, "contracts among the political actors who negotiated and signed them" and referring to an underlying "logic of joint political welfare maximization").
80 Not all disciplines depend on the existence of market access commitments or directly serve to protect such commitments from being undermined or circumvented. Some also serve a systemic function. But even then, there often is a link to the main function of the law in the WTO, i.e., that of facilitating the exchange of benefits. For instance, Article III:2 of the GATT 1994 provides that Members may not impose internal taxes on imported products so as to afford protection to domestic production. This obligation applies regardless of whether a tariff concession has been made in respect of a particular product. The objective underlying Article III:2 is that only tariffs (customs duties) should have a protective element, because the level of tariff protection is subject to negotiation in the context of multilateral trade rounds, whereas this is not the case for the level of internal taxation.

that the benefits suspended must be "equivalent", i.e., equal in value, to the benefits nullified or impaired. From a "benefits-centred" perspective, it is by no means inevitable that when a responding Member persists in denying a benefit without justification, that Member needs to be "sanctioned", or "penalized" for doing so.[81] Indeed, from a benefits-centred perspective, it seems entirely logical and adequate for a complaining Member to respond by withholding the same level of benefits from the responding Member – i.e., an "equivalent" level of benefits – so as to avoid "paying" for benefits that are not being provided. Thus, it would appear that a benefits-centred perspective does not inherently lead to a *"satisfaction – or else!"* attitude towards non-compliance with DSB dispute settlement decisions. Instead, it is more likely that it would lead, as in the case of the DSU, to a *"satisfaction – or take back your money's worth"* attitude. As explained, the way a complaining Member takes back its "money's worth" under the DSU is by suspending WTO obligations *vis-à-vis* the responding Member. As also explained, however, under the DSU a complaining Member is still bound by the original bargain it struck, in the sense that it is required to cease suspending WTO obligations once the responding Member comes into compliance. Or to put it another way, a complaining Member cannot walk away from the original bargain, but must accept "satisfaction" if and when it is offered.[82]

In sum, it emerges from the above observations that the European Community's law-centred approach and the WTO's benefits-centred approach lead to significantly different responses to non-compliance with, respectively, EC Court judgments and WTO dispute settlement decisions. Under the European Community's law-centred approach, priority is given to inducing compliance – to robust "persuasion" through financial sanctions. Under the WTO's benefits-centred approach, greater emphasis is placed upon re-establishing a balance of economic benefits through compensation (agreed compensation or "self-compensation").

E. Looking ahead

Besides helping to understand WTO rules concerning non-compliance with dispute settlement decisions, and to contrast the WTO with law-centred organizations like the European Community, the conclusion that the WTO may be best characterized as a benefits-centred organization also provides a useful starting and reference point for the ongoing academic debate about possible reform and improvement of the relevant WTO dispute settlement rules. In concluding this contribution, an attempt is therefore

---

81 See also Decision by the Arbitrator, *European Communities – Regime for the Importation, Sale and Distribution of Bananas – Recourse to Arbitration by the European Communities under Article 22.6 of the DSU*, WT/DS27/ARB, 9 April 1999, DSR 1999:II, 725, para. 6.3 (stating that "there is nothing in Article 22.1 of the DSU, let alone in paragraphs 4 and 7 of Article 22, that could be read as a justification for countermeasures of a punitive nature").

82 Presumably, the rationale for this approach is that the complaining Member agreed to the original bargain, and that that bargain would result in a higher level of benefits for both the complaining Member and the responding Member.

made at looking ahead and considering how the direction and shape of any future reform might differ depending on whether one takes a benefits-centred or a law-centred perspective. This is not a purely academic exercise, inasmuch as WTO Members are, in fact, engaged in ongoing negotiations aimed at improving the WTO dispute settlement rules (hereafter the "DSU negotiations").[83]

I. DSU reform from a "law-centred" perspective

If one approaches the issue of reform from a law-centred perspective, the key concern would probably be to give greater weight and prominence to the objective of compliance inducement. It might be proposed, for instance, that the standard of "appropriate countermeasures", currently applicable only in prohibited subsidies cases, could be extended to all cases, thus replacing the general standard of "equivalent" suspension of WTO obligations as set forth in Article 22.4 of the DSU. Alternatively, conditions could be defined under which a departure from the strict "equivalence" standard would be permissible. Thus, it could be established that in cases where the level of suspension is low because the level of nullification or impairment is low – e.g., where the equivalent level of suspension would fall below a defined percentage of the non-compliant responding Member's annual GDP or exports – the DSB could authorize a level of suspension which corresponds to $(100 + x)$ percent of the level of nullification or impairment, with the parameter "x" being specified in the DSU. Another suggestion that has been put forward is to allow complaining Members to increase the level of suspension of WTO obligations over time.[84] Presumably, this suggestion contemplates that the initial level would be the "equivalent" level and that if that level of suspension proves to be ineffective in inducing compliance within a specified period of time, the level could be increased on a periodic basis in accordance with a predetermined formula.

Interestingly, in the context of the DSU negotiations, Members have shown limited interest in revisiting the strict standard of "equivalent" suspension of WTO obligations.[85] This suggests that it would be difficult to achieve consensus among Members on strengthening the compliance-inducing features of the DSU along such lines.[86] The precise reasons are unclear and probably complex. Nonetheless, WTO dispute

---

83 These negotiations were begun in late 2001.
84 See William J. Davey, "Evaluating WTO Dispute Settlement: What Results Have Been Achieved Through Consultations and Implementation of Panel Reports?", in *The WTO in the Twenty-First Century: Dispute Settlement, Negotiations and Regionalism in Asia*, eds. Y. Taniguchi, A. Yanovich & J. Bohanes (Cambridge: Cambridge University Press 2007), 132.
85 There are proposals by developing country Members which contemplate introducing the possibility of authorizing collective retaliation in cases involving developing country Members, or least-developed country Members, as complaining parties. Some of these proposals appear to envisage a departure from the provisions of Article 22.4 of the DSU, to allow the level of benefits collectively suspended to exceed the level of nullified or impaired benefits. See WTO documents TN/DS/W/17, TN/DS/W/37, TN/DS/W/40 and TN/DS/W/92.
86 Note that the DSU negotiations can be brought to a successful conclusion only with the consent of all Members.

settlement practice shows that Members who frequently have recourse to the system as complaining parties often also find themselves having to defend cases as responding parties. To use a sports analogy, these Members regularly play offence and defence. In the light of this, for these Members it could be a double-edged sword to enhance the compliance-inducing features of the DSU, in that doing so could help them when they are on the offensive, but could hurt them when they are on the defensive.[87] It should be remembered in this connection that "being on the defensive" could in some cases be the result of conduct adopted for political benefit.[88]

II. DSU reform from a "benefits-centred" perspective

If, for this and/or other reasons, the WTO effectively needed to continue to evolve along a different path, what possible improvements would be consistent with a benefits-centred approach to reform? Arguably, the principal objective would be to make sure that a balance of benefits can, in all cases and promptly, be re-established in the event of a failure to comply with a DSB dispute settlement decision. That is to say, a key objective would be to ensure that effective compensation can be obtained by all Members and without undue delay.

In this respect, some developing country WTO Members have expressed concern that suspending WTO obligations would not be a viable option for them. The argument is that suspension of WTO obligations might be counterproductive, in that it could hurt developing country Members more than the targeted responding Members that might be wealthy developed country Members.[89] Developing country Members could, therefore, encounter difficulties in trying to reestablish a balance of benefits.[90]

It is not surprising, then, that in the context of the DSU negotiations, developing country WTO Members have put forward a series of proposals that are designed to address this perceived problem.[91] One of these is designed to permit developing country Members to cross-retaliate in all cases.[92] This could enhance the ability of such Members to select the WTO obligations to be suspended in a way that minimizes adverse effects on

---

87 See also John Magnus, "Compliance with WTO dispute settlement decisions: is there a crisis?", in *Key Issues in WTO Dispute Settlement: The first ten years*, eds. R. Yerxa and B. Wilson (Cambridge: Cambridge University Press 2005), 250.
88 See Schwartz and Sykes, *The Economic Structure of Renegotiation and Dispute Resolution*, 184 (stating that "even where the [trade-liberalizing] bargain ... is initially beneficial, changing circumstances may make it politically unappealing").
89 For instance, it may be difficult for a developing country Member to suspend tariff concessions on goods imported from the responding Member. This could be the case, e.g., where imports are relatively insignificant in value terms, or where a large portion of imported goods are considered essential (agricultural products, textiles, pharmaceutical products, etc.) or are important inputs for the domestic industry.
90 As indicated above, disputing Members have rarely been able to agree upon voluntary compensation.
91 For further discussion of some of these proposals, see Malacrida, *Towards Sounder and Fairer WTO Retaliation*, 20 et seq.
92 See WTO documents TN/DS/W/19 and TN/DS/W/47.

their own economies. Another proposal would create the possibility of authorizing collective retaliation at the request of a developing country complaining Member.[93] Members other than the developing country complaining Member would then be allowed to suspend WTO obligations *vis-à-vis* the responding Member. A further proposal would make it possible to "sell" the right to suspend WTO obligations to another Member, e.g., the highest bidder.[94] That other Member could then suspend WTO obligations *vis-à-vis* the responding Member, while the developing country Member would receive monetary or trade compensation from the Member "buying" the right to suspend WTO obligations. Finally, it has been proposed that there should be a possibility of receiving mandatory monetary compensation from the responding Member in cases where the complaining Member is a developing country Member.[95]

Taking a benefits-centred perspective, another concern about the existing WTO rules on non-compliance might be that a complaining Member cannot suspend WTO obligations and thus reestablish a balance of benefits until the DSB authorizes the suspension, which may in some cases be up to two years after the DSB has decided that a breach has occurred. In the light of this, it could be considered whether the DSU should provide that in those cases where a responding Member is found to have failed to comply with a dispute settlement decision by the end of the reasonable period of time, the complaining Member should be "compensated" for the fact that there is a period of time during which it is legally barred from reestablishing a balance of benefits. Specifically, this period of time would include the period from the date of adoption by the DSB of an adverse dispute settlement decision until the end of the reasonable period of time. It would also include the period of time during which there is further litigation (before a compliance panel, the Appellate Body and an arbitrator). However, the latter period of time would probably best be calculated using the minimum time-lines provided for in the DSU so as to prevent delays caused by WTO adjudicative bodies, or the complaining Member, from being attributed to the responding Member.

The "compensation" referred to could take the form of a one-off additional amount of suspension of benefits. If the "uncompensated" period of time amounts to, say, one and a half years, the complaining Member could be granted an additional amount of suspension that corresponds to the ordinary (forward-looking) level of annual suspension multiplied by a factor of 1.5. To illustrate, if the ordinary level of suspension is, say, USD 200 million per annum, the additional amount would be USD 300 million. It could be left to the complaining Member's discretion to determine how it uses the additional amount of USD 300 million. This would allow the complaining Member

---

93 See WTO documents TN/DS/W/17, TN/DS/W/37, TN/DS/W/40 and TN/DS/W/92. As indicated previously, these proposals appear to envisage a departure from the strict "equivalence" standard. However, this does not appear to be an essential feature. The main purpose of these proposals appears to be to make it less costly for developing country Members to retaliate. This could be achieved even if the "equivalence" standard were maintained.
94 See WTO documents TN/DS/W/23 and TN/DS/W/40.
95 See WTO documents TN/DS/W/9 and TN/DS/W/17.

to adopt a front-loaded approach and suspend WTO obligations in the first year at a level of USD 500 million. In any subsequent years, the level of suspension of WTO obligations would need to go back to USD 200 million. This could be a potentially interesting approach, inasmuch as it might enable the complaining Member to induce the responding Member to comply promptly, including in cases where the ordinary level of suspension is low. Alternatively, if the complaining Member anticipates that the responding Member will not comply promptly, it could choose, for instance, to add USD 100 million to the ordinary level of suspension of USD 200 million during the first three years of suspension.

To conclude, it is apparent from the foregoing that there are ways in which WTO rules on non-compliance could be improved, irrespective of whether one approaches the issue from a law-centred or a benefits-centred perspective. It is also clear, however, that the two perspectives are likely to lead to priority being given to reforms that are quite different. Those Members who would prefer to see the WTO remain a benefits-centred organization are unlikely to be willing to support reform proposals that emanate from a law-centred perspective. Conversely, it would appear that, in principle, Members who would like to see the WTO move in the direction of a law-centred organization are unlikely to have major philosophical problems with reform proposals that flow from a benefits-centred perspective. For those Members, benefits-centred reform proposals would, however, not go far enough. Against this background, proposals of the latter type might possibly stand a better chance of attracting the necessary consensus of all Members.

Discussion

ULRICH HALTERN
Let me start the discussion by getting some numbers straight. Robert Hudec calculated that 88% of all cases under the GATT dispute settlement worked; only 12% did not. Those 12% were sufficient to destroy the credibility of GATT, enough for a major change in the dispute settlement mechanism. Now let us look at the numbers on the WTO. There were 98 decisions since 1996. In 85 cases a violation was found. Out of those 85 cases, in six cases the compliance period is still running, and in two compliance is unclear, which leaves us with 77 cases. Out of those 77 cases, almost 70% ended with more or less full compliance. 25% ended with partial compliance, debatable compliance or sleazy settlements. Approximately 6% ended with open, overt unabashed non-compliance. Now, 6% overt non-compliance is not so bad after all. However, 25% of all cases with less than full compliance seems problematic, considering that under GATT, 12% of cases with less than full compliance was enough to change the system. So what makes you think that the compliance pull under WTO is satisfactory?

Taking us a step further, should we focus on high visibility cases – those cases that make headlines – rather than 80% of all cases where compliance is satisfactory?

RETO MALACRIDA
Thank you, Professor Haltern, for your questions. I would say that it depends on whether you see the glass as half full or half empty. I think the general sense in Geneva is that the WTO dispute settlement system works well and that, in the great majority of cases, Members' record of compliance with dispute settlement decisions has been very good. But it is correct that there are a handful of cases where there has been no compliance or delayed compliance.

As regards the GATT statistics, one has to be careful when comparing the WTO to the GATT. One of the big differences is that in the WTO Members can actually have their day in court. A WTO Member can bring a case, and if it has merit, a WTO dispute settlement panel will hand down a favourable ruling. The fact of being able to obtain a formal ruling counts for a lot. With GATT this was not possible in all cases because of so-called "blocking" of dispute settlement panels. Under GATT, a responding party could actually prevent a GATT panel from adjudicating the matter in the first place. As a consequence, it is possible that some of the WTO cases where there have been compliance problems are cases which might have been "blocked" under the GATT.

Similarly, with respect to retaliation, under GATT, when a responding party lost a case, it could prevent retaliatory action from being taken against it in the event it did not comply with the ruling. It is probably no coincidence that in about 50 years of GATT dispute settlement history there was only one instance where retaliatory action was authorised, and it is not even clear whether it was implemented. Compare this to the WTO, where in less than 15 years we have already had four disputes in which retaliatory meaures were imposed. I think this reflects the different institutional set-up, because in the WTO there no longer is a possibility of "blocking" retaliatory action. So here, too, it is quite possible that in one or more of the WTO disputes in which retaliatory action was taken, such action might have been "blocked" if it had been possible to do so. I hope this illustrates that it is not always easy to compare GATT and WTO figures on compliance with dispute settlement rulings.

ERICH SCHANZE
My name is Erich Schanze and I would like to know if Reto Malacrida when talking of enforcement did so solely in the WTO context. Furthermore, I would like to ask a question regarding the compliance in the WTO. Usually, when people talk about compliance, they mean compliance with laws. However, in context of the WTO, compliance is to be understood as compliance with panel rulings, which obviously has to be distinguished. My question is, do legal costs matter in terms of compliance?

NIKOLAOS LAVRANOS
I really appreciate Reto's presentation and it certainly reflects what we tell our students, how the WTO should be and should function. I missed one aspect though and that is the *amicus curiae* brief. In particular I would like to ask, if you agree that the WTO should take into account the rights of those who are affected by measures which have no say at all in the whole process. In other words, is there not a need to open up the WTO towards a less state-centred approach?

PATRICIA HANSEN
I also have some questions for Reto. One has to do with your characterisation of the WTO as a benefit-centred organisation which implies that the WTO is indifferent between whether you actually comply with the rules or whether you just pay off for them. And that is first of all a pretty controversial way of characterising the organisation and seems inconsistent with the provisions of the dispute settlement understanding that retaliation is just a temporary measure intended to ensure compliance.

Second and sort of related to Nikos' point in terms of the benefits balancing, how much of a balance is there for very small countries, for example, to the countries that have not retaliated even though they were authorised to do so. Mexico and Brazil are fairly large developed countries but Antigua and Ecuador were both authorised to suspend intellectual property protection. Neither one of them did, partly because of concerns of third parties and partly because of concerns about themselves.

RETO MALACRIDA
Thank you all for your questions. I will try to answer them one by one.

First, do costs matter? The WTO does not charge any fees for the initiation and conduct of WTO dispute settlement proceedings. The WTO also does not award lawyers' fees, however. In this respect, that is to say, lawyers' fees, most WTO Members use their own government lawyers. When Member States do not have the necessary expertise "in-house", they usually retain outside council in the private sector and this can be expensive. That is why some WTO Members have established what is called the "Advisory Centre on WTO Law", which is a separate international organisation. Its purpose is to provide high-quality legal advice to developing countries at favourable fees, that is to say, fees that are lower than those of private sector law firms. Many developing countries have already made use of this option. Nevertheless, some developing countries continue to express concern that it remains very expensive for them to bring cases.

As far as Nikos Lavranos' question about *amicus curiae* briefs is concerned, in most cases it is already possible to file such briefs. Thus, it is possible to have non-governmental participants in WTO dispute settlement proceedings. As to whether the WTO should give greater access to non-State actors, I would merely note that this is a complex issue, and that there is a wide range of views among Members regarding whether or not this would be appropriate.

Finally, let me turn briefly to Patricia Hansen's comments. Hopefully, the written version of my contribution will clarify various points which I have had to make in abbreviated form in my presentation today. At this juncture, let me just say that it is not at all my contention that the WTO, or its Members, are indifferent between whether a Member complies with an adverse dispute settlement ruling or not. I am interested in why we have the dispute settlement rules which we currently have, particularly those that are applicable in cases where a Member fails to comply with an adverse dispute settlement ruling. In conversations with lawyer colleagues, I often hear it said that there are not enough teeth in the system and that new mechanisms are needed to make sure that Members comply with WTO rulings in dispute settlement cases. I understand how one can come to that conclusion and I am not saying that it is wrong. But maybe we should ask ourselves first whether the system is actually designed to ensure compliance in all cases. In my view, there is an argument to be made that inducing compliance with WTO rulings is an important purpose, but not necessarily the central purpose, of the current WTO rules. And so I am asking the question: why is that? Is it because public international law does not yet provide the enforcement tools that would be needed to ensure compliance, or is it because maybe not all Members think that ensuring compliance in all cases is, or should be, the objective of the WTO dispute settlement system? It seems to me worthwhile to reflect on these questions. As I explain in the written contribution, they notably have implications for the nature and direction of any reform of the system. The examples given of Ecuador and Antigua and Barbuda go to precisely this issue of reform of the dispute settlement system.

CARL BAUDENBACHER

I would like to take up another compliance mechanism; in Community law as well as in EEA law, at least partly, there is the famous triad of direct effect, supremacy or primacy and state liability. I think it was an American professor who once wrote that state liability is in fact the most effective tool to secure compliance of Member States in the interest of individuals and economic operators. Ulrich Haltern has written a lot about it in his seminal book „Europarecht – Dogmatik im Kontext".[1] If I see it correctly, state liability is not handled in the same way in all the Member States. First of all, the references tend to come always from the same countries, essentially the six founding Member States plus the UK and a couple of others, Austria is among them. But if you go a little bit further east or further south, it looks different. So my questions are directed at Diana Panke: Are there any studies in this respect? Who makes references? Who complies with the judgement of the ECJ or in our case of the EFTA Court? If I remember correctly, Mr. Francovich[2] has never seen a single Lira although he has heavily contributed to the development of the standard of individual protection all over Europe. The EFTA Court has, against a lot of opposition, also accepted state liability as being part of EEA law exactly ten years ago.[3] And this has been accepted by all the courts actually with the exception of the Supreme Court of Liechtenstein. The Norwegians, for instance, have fully complied with this. When they have lost a case in the national court, the government has set out a notice on the website of the Ministry of Justice and has invited other individuals who have suffered damage to present their claims, back to a certain number of years. I have not seen such an attitude in countries a little bit further south. So my question is whether this most important tool to secure compliance with EC and with EEA law is handled in the same way in all the countries? Are there studies on their way or is at least the political science branch aware of the problem?

DIANA PANKE

There are plenty of studies on the question of who is making references under the preliminary reference clause. And the first line you will find therein is „*the bigger the Member State, the bigger the population, the more references are made.*" In a certain way, this compliance mechanism works differently whether you have a small Member State or a big Member State, because the latter is more likely to face a preliminary reference and this alternative leans towards compliance.

Besides, there are differences between sectors. In some of them you have higher levels of organisation of societal actors. Therefore, these have more financial means to actually put cases to national courts who then get referenced under the preliminary ruling procedures.

---

1   Ulrich Haltern, Europarecht – Dogmatik im Kontext, 2. Aufl., N 788 ff.
2   Joined cases C-6/90 and 9/90 - *Francovich & Bonifaci*, ECR 1991, I-5357.
3   Case E-9/97 - *Erla María Sveinbjörnsdóttir v. Iceland*.

HJALTE RASMUSSEN

Diana Panke's presentation was admirable from the point of view that it was quantifying compliance patterns but not qualifying them. However, Denmark was cited as a positive example of a Member State with a positive compliance record. I happen to come from that country and I have considerable years of experience fighting the government in cases when it did not comply with its obligations. In my opinion, Denmark is everything but a positive example for compliance. One of the reasons, why it does not appear that way from an outside perspective, can be attributed to the Danish language. It is hard to understand and therefore easy to hide a lot of litigation that is contrary to Community Law or Union Law simply by writing it in Danish, which we Danes have a habit of doing.

I have collected clear evidence over a long period of time, which proves that when the political branches of my government want to violate Community Law in matters of political importance, the courts of my country will actively cooperate with the government to get away with the violation, simply by not making references under the preliminary ruling procedure. To put it in Shakespeare's words: "Something is rotten in the state of Denmark".[4] I would be surprised, however, if we were the only black sheep in this aspect.

ERICH SCHANZE

I have another question for Diana Panke. There is a lot of discretion in law enforcement. In some areas, law is more partially enforced than in others. Did you take that into account in your methodology?

THOMAS COTTIER

A look at the record on implementing decisions shows that there is a self interest of nations to essentially comply. But if we broaden the vision a little bit, go further than just looking at implementation of decisions and ask about the role of courts in general in implementation, I wonder whether the picture is as rosy? And I would like to have your comments about the overcharging of the European Courts on Human Rights, since the docket they have is just tremendous. Can the law still deliver in that respect? And regarding the EU, especially after listening to our Danish colleague, Professor Hjalte Rasmussen, the question comes up if all of the non-compliance cases brought before the court, are actually chased up by the Commission. How many instances are left out? With the WTO we know that many violations are not brought up and there is hardly any case brought up against these developed countries because nobody cares. They do not comply with a lot of things here. So if we take the picture slightly broader than that, do the courts actually deliver in the process of complying with the law in a larger size?

---

4 *William Shakespeare*, Hamlet Act 1, scene 4, 87–91.

HANSPETER TSCHÄNI
I also have a question for Diana Panke. You qualified the EC compliance mechanism as a successful one. And indeed, what you said was, that eventually all the cases get resolved. According to your presentation, however, there is still a rather impressive number of non-compliance that you would not expect from a successful system. Is there a higher deterrent effect than what seems to be indicated by such a high number?

PAUL MAHONEY
My paper addressed non-compliance with the judgments of the Strasbourg Court, not non-compliance with the primary obligations under the ECHR. These are two distinct things.

On the issue of international review of compliance with the primary ECHR obligations, the question to be asked is: what is the Strasbourg Court there for, what is its purpose? With a population of 800 million people in the ECHR community, the Court cannot possibly be expected to deal with every alleged violation of one of the rights or freedoms that are protected by the ECHR. It must have some other role. And the main aspect of that role – you can call it a constitutional-court role, whatever you like – is to create a sort of common law of human rights which the national courts should then apply. But the Court in Strasbourg cannot be expected to be the main tool for ensuring day-to-day compliance by the national authorities with the obligations that are stated in the ECHR. The number cases being lodged in Strasbourg is rising inexorably. The whole system on the international level will seize up unless something is done to relieve the caseload of the Court. The machinery of human rights protection under the ECHR needs to be reformed – I would agree with that. One crying need is to tip more cases back into the national legal system where they more properly belong.

Consequently, when looking at what the Strasbourg Court does, one should not expect it to do too much. It is not there to give a full judicial ruling in every application lodged, or to "split hairs" by going into every little factual and legal issue raised in every single case. The doctrine of the margin of appreciation and the principle of subsidiarity reflect that philosophy. The mission of the Court is to determine whether States have really gone beyond the line of what is acceptable in modern European democratic society. The Court, in its judgments, must allow the States, which have their elected parliaments, their governments and their courts, to do their own business; its mission is not to substitute itself for the national authorities, but to set the main rules for the proper protection of human rights.

Russia poses a different problem. The problem with Russia is that it was, I think, pushed into acceding to the ECHR long before it was ready. There are thousands of cases pending against Russia, with a potential for far more to come. For example, 40% of civil judgments are not executed in Russia. Every one of those litigants could theoretically bring a case to Strasbourg. To take another example, it was held in a given case that the applicant's prison conditions were unacceptable, inhuman and degrading. The defence of the Russian Government was: *"What is this man complaining about? This is what every Russian prisoner has to put up with."* The conclusion to be drawn from that judgment is therefore, that every prisoner in pretty well every Russian prison can bring a case before the Court and the case will be well founded. So the situation of Russia in regard to observance of the ECHR rights is particular. It was probably a political mistake forcing Russia to sign up to the ECHR before it had had the time to put its internal legal order into a state where it could withstand being measured against the standards of human rights protection laid down in the ECHR.

That said, the main point made, that there are too many applications coming to the Strasbourg Court for it to function effectively, is correct. It is the responsibility of the Contracting States – the governments – to do something about the perilous situation of the Strasbourg Court, which has over 100,000 cases pending before it at the moment. But that is another issue that is not on the agenda today.

DIANA PANKE
I will try to be brief. In the questions, the issue that came up the most, was the data used in the study, and more specifically, if it was biased regarding the law enforcement?

First of all, the data represents a sample collected by the European Commission who has been monitoring the enforcement authorities of the Member States. It would not have been possible to record all the data, since the Commission does not have the capacity to systematically analyze the entirety of every Member State's enforcement practice.

As far as the possible bias of the data is concerned, the same question was directed at the European Commission and the answer was clear, namely that it is not the case. None of the Member States feels under- or over-represented. However, you have to bear in mind that over the years the European Commission's priorities changed multiple times, in the sense that depending on the political priorities some areas were looked at more closely, which obviously lead to more detailed data. From that perspective one cannot deny that the data is biased. The extend, however, is unclear, since at this point there is no scientifically reliable method of measuring it.

Nevertheless, since the data used by the research group is the same the Commission works with, it can be said that it is the most comprehensive data available.

Regarding the comment about Denmark and its behaviour, one has to accept that Member States can sometimes succeed in convincing the European Commission that the domestic implementation or transposition is completely in line with Community Law. And obviously, those cases are not dragged on. In other instances Member States can easily be convinced that it is necessary to adjust domestic orders and then comply with it. In that regard, there might also be a bias, but as long as there is no bias against a particular set of Member States, we are fine.

ULRICH HALTERN
I am very happy with the way the discussion went. It turns out we are in an ongoing discussion and we have, I believe, a lot to look forward to tonight and tomorrow. Thank you very much to the panellists, to all interveners, and to all listeners.

Keynote

The Relation of International/ Supranational and National Law: The Case of Competition Law

JACQUELINE RIFFAULT-SILK[1]

A. Introduction: The framework set up by the Treaty in competition matters, the New Deal resulting from 1/2003 Regulation

To begin, I would like to stress the simplicity and strength of the framework that was set up in the Treaty in competition matters, and its specificity compared to other economic domains subject to EU regulations.

It encompasses, firstly, an integrated legal order and a communal substantive law applicable as soon as communal interests are or may be affected, characterized by primacy and uniformity; secondly, a communal Constitutional Court – the ECJ – in charge of the interpretation of the Treaty; thirdly, a centralised regulatory authority – the European Commission – to implement and enforce EU competition rules.

As a result, some principles essential to the functioning of the Treaty in competition matters were affirmed, such as the direct effect of European law, since not only the Member States but also their nationals are the subjects of the legal order created by the Treaty. Procedural autonomy is derived from the principle of subsidiarity, under which each Member State designates the courts having jurisdiction in these matters and prescribes the procedural rules governing the actions brought before them, notwithstanding the application of national competition law, parallel to the EU law when the interests of the Community are or may be affected, solely when only national economic interests are at stake.

The reform brought by Regulation 1/2003, in force since May 1st 2004, and its follow-up, the Green and White Papers issued by the Commission, may be seen as a New Deal between all the institutional actors involved: European institutions, national courts and authorities.

Indeed, the new principles enacted by the Regulation deeply transformed the balance between those actors: suppression of the European Commission's monopoly in granting authorisations beforehand for agreements restricting competition, and decentralisation

---

1   Judge at the French Cour de Cassation, Paris.

of the application of EU rules. Since the reform, national courts, as well as national competition authorities, may directly apply the provisions of Articles 81 and 82 EC, in their entirety.

Even the role of the economic actors evolved. Regulation 1/2003 stresses[2] how important the private enforcement of these rules has nowadays become to protecting subjective rights and complementing the role of NCAs. The Commission insisted it could therefore focus its activity on the most important infringements of European competition law, such as hard-core cartels. As a consequence, economic actors, undertakings and individuals, including natural persons and consumers, were invited to participate in the enforcement of European competition law, in bringing private actions before national courts. For this, they possess a powerful weapon, again provided for by the ECJ, and which is the direct effect of EU rules.

Thus, the general balance of antitrust legislation in Europe has evolved, and the question arises whether these changes may affect, beyond the strict competition domain, national legal systems.

At first sight, procedural rules – national ones given the principle of subsidiarity – and substantive law – European competition law –, seem to follow opposite regimes. The principle applicable to procedure is autonomy and relativity. In the domain of substantive law, it is uniqueness and primacy.

However, it can be seen, on the one hand, that this contrast is smoothed by significant nuances and exceptions and on the other hand, that the new balance leads far beyond the new organisation, the decentralisation decided by the European institutions. It leads indeed to nothing less than a transformation in depth of structures, rules and principles applicable to the judicial systems of the Member States within the Union.

To that extent, procedural autonomy (B.) and substantive law (C.) provide interesting examples of the relation of national, international and supranational law in the competition law field. Lastly, cooperation must be discussed, in its two aspects, the first relating to the relations between competition authorities and courts in the course of the judicial proceedings, and the second to the sensitive question of the binding effect of regulatory authorities' decisions on national courts, when taken on the grounds of EU competition law (D.).

---

2   Preamble, recital 7.

B. Procedural autonomy, versus efficiency and equivalence principles and ECHR requirements

Let us first have a brief look at the Treaty's provisions which provide a basis for our topic: primacy and direct effect of EU rules, subsidiarity, cooperation and reciprocity. There are no specific provisions in the Treaty relating to the principles of primacy and direct effect of EU rules, which were consecrated by ECJ decisions[3].

But Article 5 EC[4] lays down the principle of subsidiarity, according to which the Community exercises its powers within the limits conferred by the Treaty. However, the same Article adds that the principle of subsidiarity does not prevent the Community from intervening beyond these limits, particularly when the objectives of the Treaty cannot be adequately achieved by the Member States: such a wording leaves some margin of action to the European institutions, which was used in procedural matters as examined below.

According to Article 10[5] and its interpretation by the ECJ, not only the Member State institutions and courts have to cooperate with European bodies to ensure fulfilment of obligations arising out of the Treaty, but European bodies too must cooperate with national institutions: these duties of cooperation are reciprocal.

These principles led to various applications in procedural matters.

I. Procedural autonomy: the case of interim measures

In procedural matters, Member States and the Commission are symmetrically bound by the principle of subsidiarity, here autonomy, as noted by the ECJ[6].

Interim measures provide an interesting example of this in French case-law. Stricter

---

3   ECJ, Costa v. Enel, 15.07.64.; Van Gend en Loos, 5.02.63, aff. 26/62. In France, the Cour de Cassation stated that the principle of primacy derived from Article 55 of the Constitution (Cass. Cafés Jacques Vabre, 24.05.75).
4   Article 5 EC: The Community shall act within the limits of the powers conferred upon it by this Treaty and of the objectives assigned to it herein. In areas which do not fall within its exclusive competence, the Community shall take action, in accordance with the principle of subsidiarity, only if and in so far as the objectives of the proposed action cannot be sufficiently achieved by the Member States and can therefore, by reason of the scale or effects of the proposed action, be better achieved by the Community. Any action by the Community shall not go beyond what is necessary to achieve the objectives of the Treaty.
5   Article 10 EC: Member States shall take all appropriate measures, whether general or particular, to ensure fulfilment of the obligations arising out of this Treaty or resulting from action taken by the institutions of the Community. They shall facilitate the achievement of the Community's tasks. They shall abstain from any measures which could jeopardize the attainment of the objectives of this Treaty.
6   ECJ, 22.10.02, C-94/00, Roquette Frères.

rules have been defined by the ECJ[7], lately enacted in Regulation 1/2003[8], mainly the requirement of a *prima facie* case, whereas French rules contain lighter procedural requirements relating notably to the *presumption* that the alleged practices are in breach of competition rules[9].

The question arose whether European or national requirements should be applicable to grant or refuse interim measures, when Article 81 or 82 EC was to be applied to the alleged infringement itself.

The Court of Appeal of Paris, before which an appeal had been lodged against a decision of the Competition Council granting interim measures, decided that since the alleged practices infringed European competition law, the ECJ requirements of a *prima facie* case had to be applied accordingly. The decision was quashed by the Cour de Cassation, which held that, given their procedural nature as well as the principle of subsidiarity, EU rules could not be applied[10]. The French Supreme Court eventually approved the Court of Appeal, in another case, for having used a criterion of "reasonable presumption"[11].

II. Symmetry

One can recall the ruling of the ECJ in the *Roquette* case, under which national courts cannot control the lawfulness of the Commission's decision asking for coercive measures[12]. The question was about the extent of national judicial control before ordering entry upon premises and seizures in private domiciles, at the demand of the Commission. For French courts, the question was all the more difficult since the French Constitution contains strict provisions to ensure that the rights of the defense, human rights, are protected. Accordingly, the French Commercial Code provides that evidence must be produced before the court, in order to prove that the case is strong enough to justify these coercive measures. The problem was then whether or not the national judge could impose such a production of evidence on the European body, and could refuse to grant the order, for lack of information or evidence. This was denied by the ECJ, which ruled that the Commission's decision to have recourse to coercive measures cannot be questioned by national courts, but only by the ECJ. It added that national courts are not deprived of every power when answering the Commission's demand: they may control the authenticity of its decision, and the proportionality of the measure asked for, given the seriousness of the case. These rules have been since laid down in Regulation 1/2003[13].

---

7   ECJ, Ordinance 17.01.1980, Camera Care, n° 792/79; TPICE, 24.01.92, La Cinq.
8   Article 8, Reg. 1/2003.
9   Article L. 464-1 French Commercial Code.
10 Com. 14.12.04, Bull. 225, PharmaLab; Com. 8.11.05, Bull. 220, Neuf Telecom.
11 Com. 28.01.05, Orange Caraïbes.
12 ECJ, 22.10.02, C-94/00, Roquette Frères.
13 Article 20 § 8, Reg. 1/2003.

III. Mutual duties of loyal cooperation: the principles of equivalence and effectiveness

As was stated in decisions of the Community courts[14], Article 10 EC imposes on European institutions and Member State judicial authorities, mutual duties of loyal cooperation with views to attaining the objectives of the Treaty, and it is for national courts to ensure the legal protection which individuals derive from the direct effect of Community law. Given the subsidiarity principle, it is for Member States to designate courts and tribunals having jurisdiction to hear actions for damages based on an infringement of Community competition law and to lay down the detailed procedural rules governing these actions.

The Commission notice on cooperation insists again on the latter, also adding that the independence of both national courts and the Commission must be safeguarded[15].

Two principles of paramount importance, consecrated by the Community court decisions, derive from the principle of loyal cooperation laid in Article 10 EC: the principle of equivalence and the principle of effectiveness[16].

According to the former, procedural rules applicable to actions for safeguarding rights that individuals derive from Community law must not be less favourable than those governing similar domestic actions. Under the latter, these rules must not render the exercise of rights conferred by Community law practically impossible or excessively difficult.

IV. Equivalence and effectiveness: examples

Examples of these duties to cooperate are numerous.

National rules of procedure can be set aside by courts on their own motion, provided they do not run counter the principle that, in civil litigation, the parties have power to define the ambit of the dispute, which cannot be modified by the court.

---

14 ECJ, 14/83, Von Colson and Kamann, § 26; 230/81, Luxembourg v. Parliament, § 38; 22.10.02, Roquette Frères, cited above.
15 Article 19, Reg. 1/2003: It should be recalled that whatever form the cooperation with national courts takes, the Commission will respect the independence of national courts (...) The Commission has also to make sure it respects its duty of professional secrecy and that it safeguards its own functioning and independence (...).
16 ECJ, 14.12.95, C-312/93, Peterbroeck; 14.12.95, joined cases C-430/93 and C-431/93, Van Schijndel; 1.06.99, C-126/97, Eco Swiss China; 20.09.01, C-453/99, Crehan; 13.07.06, joined cases C-295-04 to C-298-/04, Manfredi.

This explains why the cases *Peterbroeck*[17] and *Van Schijndel*[18] led to different outcomes. The first one raised the question whether a limitation period, which forbade the parties to submit a new plea based on Community law, was objectionable. The ECJ decided that, although it was not objectionable *per se*, such a limitation period had to be set aside if it prevented the court from raising this point on its own motion.

But in the second one, what was at stake was the ambit of the dispute between the parties and the power the parties, not the court, have in its definition. The ECJ ruled, as a national court would have done, that the limits of the dispute, defined by the parties, must remain untouched. Courts cannot raise an issue concerning the breach of provisions of Community law on their own motion, if the examination of that issue would oblige them to abandon the passive role assigned to them by going beyond the ambit of the dispute defined by the parties themselves and relying on facts and circumstances other than those on which the party with an interest in application of those provisions bases his claim. This refers to the passive role of the judge in civil litigation.

Another application of the principle of effectiveness can be found in the relaxation of national rules applicable to standing. In Member States like Italy or Spain – whereas under domestic rules, only enterprises were considered as economic actors and therefore were able to bring actions based on national competition law before civil judges – national Supreme Courts overturned their case-law when applying EU competition law and decided that the consumers were also part of the market[19].

In Spain, after having held that civil courts were not competent to apply EC competition rules ("Campsa doctrine")[20], the Spanish Supreme Court also reversed its doctrine and decided to apply EC rules directly, leaving the door open to future requests[21]. But it was not until the reform of the Spanish Competition Act, which came into force on 1 September 2007, that private enforcement was also allowed under national competition rules. Thus, national courts played an active role in putting into effect the principles of effectiveness and direct effect of EU rules, consecrated by the ECJ.

Again in the standing chapter, the adoption of measures of collective redress, as recommended by the Commission's Green and White papers, must be noted. In Denmark a collective redress was instituted by law, based on both opt in and opt out models[22]. The opt out one, the most dangerous one under some European critiques, has been put under the control of the ombudsman and can be brought to the court only through him. The opt in procedure is more open, and its requirements are lighter.

---

17 See above.
18 See above.
19 Italian Supreme Court, 4.02.05, Ricciarelli v. Spa Unipol Assicurrazioni.
20 Tribunal Supremo, 30.12.93, dec 1262/1993, Rodriguez & al. v. Campsa.
21 Tribunal Supremo, 2.06.00, dec 540/2000, Rafael v. Disa.
22 Danish Parliament, 22.02.07, 2006-07- L 41.

But the most impressive innovation was the *de facto* class action imagined by a Belgium company, CDC, and recently approved by the Düsseldorf Court of Appeal[23]. According to the CDC system, the victims of a cartel are invited to sell their claims to the CDC, a private company, for a merely symbolic amount of one hundred euros. But CDC in exchange has taken an obligation to pass on to them 85% of the damages it could obtain from the court. In the said case, the Cement cartel members objected immediately as to the lawfulness of CDC's action, claiming that it lacked standing. But the courts supported the system, the Court of Appeal even denied the cartelists any rights to appeal. It is clear indeed that, on an economic point of view and on a legal one, the courts' decisions must be approved: the right to sue, the possession of a claim is an asset that can be sold.

The principles of equivalence and effectiveness had another brilliant application in the definition of damages. In the *Courage* decision, the ECJ has ruled that it derives from the direct effect of the Treaty that individuals must be able to seek compensation for harm caused by infringements of EU competition law.

What harm? What kind of damages? In this respect, concepts in Europe are various, and the majority of them differ deeply from the American ones. Whereas in the US the notion of exemplary, restitutionary and/or punitive damages is accepted, in the majority of EU Member States, on the contrary, only the principle of full compensation is unanimously admitted.

In this regard, it is remarkable that the European Court of Justice decided to use both principles in the definition of damages[24]: the ECJ ruled that, according to the principle of effectiveness, the victim of anti-competitive practices must be able to seek compensation not only for loss but also loss of profit, plus interest. But it added that the principle of equivalence allows awards of particular damages, such as exemplary or punitive damages, if these exist in domestic actions.

Such an invitation was quickly understood: in the UK, victims of the Vitamins cartel argued that they should be able, as a matter of law under the principle of equivalence laid down by the ECJ, to seek exemplary damages, restitutionary damages or an account of profits since such damages could be granted under national law. The High Court rejected these arguments in a strongly motivated decision[25]. It held, firstly, that the allocation of exemplary damages, which serve the same aim as fines, namely to punish and deter anticompetitive behaviour, would contradict not only the principle of *non bis in idem*, but also, in follow-on cases, the rule laid down in Article 16 of Regulation 1/2003, under which national courts cannot rule in a manner which runs counter a decision already adopted by the Commission. Secondly, the Court said that

---

23 Court of Appeal of Düsseldorf, 14.05.08, Cement cartel case.
24 ECJ, 13.07.06, Manfredi v. Lloyd Adriatico, see above.
25 High Court, Chancery Division, 19.10.07, Devenish Nutrition Ltd & al. v. Sanofi Aventis & al., Vitamins cartel.

in current English law, a restitutionary award is not available as a remedy in private antitrust litigation cases, unless a higher court decides conversely. Thirdly, the Court stated that the claimants were precluded as a matter of law from seeking an account of profits from the defendants, on the grounds that compensatory damages were an adequate remedy in the case, also given the practical difficulties in allocating any amount of profits between all relevant claimants.

One cannot leave the damages chapter without citing the final step taken by the Giudice di Pace di Bitondo in the *Manfredi* case, after the referral made to the ECJ which prompted, after the *Crehan* case, a second ruling on antitrust damages[26]. Despite the absence in Italian law of any punitive, restitutionary or exemplary damages, the judge held that the damages awards must be such as to deter the defendant and third parties from adopting practices similar to those sanctioned by the NCA in this particular case. Accordingly, the claimant was awarded a sum which doubled his loss and was meant to set off any economic benefit gained by the infringer. Although Italian law allows for small claims adjudication of damages upon "*secondo equità*", i.e. on an equitable basis[27], one can wonder whether the discretion given to the judge includes the liberty to motivate its decision on grounds that Italian law does not recognize.

V. Autonomy also subject to supranational rules: the ECHR requirements

The principle of autonomy is also subject to supranational rules. Thus, the Convention for Human Rights and the decisions taken by the Strasbourg Court provide a set of rules, national courts must observe.

An interesting application of these rules was recently noted in the field of the duty of fairness in the collection of evidence, relating to the use of recordings made without warning[28]. It is remarkable that the French Cour de Cassation, on the grounds of Article 6 of the Convention, echoed the decision taken by the European Commission in a similar case, rejecting such evidence as unfairly obtained and non-admissible. But in the French case-law, the criminal Chamber of the Cour de Cassation has always allowed such evidence as admissible, only with the reservation that the judge must appreciate to what extent this evidence has to be taken into consideration[29]. Thus, the Commercial Chamber of the Cour de Cassation decided, in a procedural matter, to diverge from the Criminal Chamber doctrine and to follow the opinion of a European Institution.

---

26   See above.
27   Article 113 (2) of Italian Code of Civil Procedure.
28   French Cour de Cassation, Commercial Chamber. 3.06.08, Sony France et Philips France.
29   French Cour de Cassation, Criminal Chamber, 13.10.04, Bull. 243.

C. Substantive law: primacy and uniform application of EU rules

Contrary to procedural rules, EU competition law is characterised by primacy and uniqueness.

According to the primacy principle[30], laid down in Article 3 paragraph 2 of Regulation 1/2003, application of national competition law may not lead to prohibit agreements that are justified under Article 81 paragraph 3 EC. This rule which abandons the previous system under which it was possible for Member States to apply stricter rules to a practice allowed under EU rules, consecrates the absolute primacy of EU competition law when the interests of the Community are at stake.

The principle of uniform application, laid down in Article 16 of the Regulation, forbids national courts to take decisions running counter to decisions adopted by the Commission and insists that they must avoid giving decisions which would conflict with a decision contemplated by the Commission. It can be noted that these provisions are silent about the effect of national competition authorities' decisions on civil courts, belonging or not to the same Member State.

One significant illustration of these principles can be found in the *Crehan* case. The referral made to the EU court asked whether a party to a contract liable to restrict or distort competition, could rely on the breach of Article 81 EC before a national court to obtain relief from the other contracting party. Since English law does not allow a party to an illegal agreement to claim damages from another party, the ECJ had to decide whether EU provisions could paralyze the general contract law applicable in a Member State.

The ECJ recalled that the Treaty had created its own legal order which is integrated into the legal systems of the Member States and which their courts are bound to apply. It ruled that the sole ground that a claimant is party to the contract is insufficient *per se* to set aside European antitrust rules, although it may be different if that party bears significant responsibility for the distortion of competition. One can think that the ECJ decision simply echoes the Roman maxime *Nemo auditur propriam turpitudinem allegans*, recognised in most of the legal systems of the Member States as noted by the Court.

In other cases, national decisions show the influence of the EU competition regulations and case law on national courts.

Thus, the notion of complex cartel schemes created by the ECJ in 1999[31], under which complex agreements may be qualified as a single infringement provided they pursuit a

---

30 Article 3, Regulation 1/2003.
31 ECJ, 8.07.99, C-49/92, Anic Anichem; 7.01.04, C-204/00, Aalborg Portland.

common objective, with consequences notably for time limits, and for the liability of the participants, each of them being held responsible for the entire matter, provided their intention to contribute, knowledge and acceptance of risks have been proven, was recently adopted by the French Supreme Court[32].

Such an influence does not exclude nuances, as shown in the case of implicit agreements on oligopolistic markets. Whereas the ECJ had ruled, in the *John Deere* case[33], that the exchange of sensitive information on an oligopolistic market amounts to concerted action between competitors with a view to reducing competition on the market, the French Cour de Cassation took a more restrictive approach in a case involving the three operators of the French mobile telephony market, sanctioned by the Competition Council whose decision had been approved by the Court of appeal. The Supreme Court ruled that the exchange of retrospective non-public information on activity, on a regular basis, was not sufficient *per se* to assess an adequate reduction of the operators' commercial autonomy and consequently characterized it as anticompetitive practices under Article 81 EC and national equivalent provisions[34].

It is also reciprocal. Thus, the De Minimis doctrine was used by the French Competition Council as "useful guidelines" when applying national competition rules[35], before similar provisions were enacted in French law[36]. Symmetrically, in the field of negotiated procedures, one may note the influence exerted on EU regulation reforms by national legislations where settlement procedures had been initially created.[37]

D. Cooperation, harmonisation: the relationship between regulatory and judicial bodies

I. Cooperation, to what extent: information, opinion, co-investigation?

Article 15 of Regulation 1/2003 organizes the cooperation between national courts and the Commission, and provides that the Commission may act as *amicus curiae* for national courts, in various ways:

– national courts may ask the Commission for information and/or opinion concerning the application of EU competition rules,

---

32 Com. 15.01.08, Bull. 208, Colas Ile de France & al.
33 ECJ, 28.05.98, John Deere Ltd v. Commission.
34 Com. 29.06.07, Bouygues, Telecom, Orange, SFR, quashing Court of appeal of Paris, 12.12.06.
 On this topic of implicit agreements on oligopolistic markets, see also Court of appeal of Paris, 29.06.06, Palaces.
35 Competition Council, dec n° 03-D-53, 26.11.03, Biotherm.
36 Articles L. 464-6-1 and L. 464-6-2 of the commercial Code, modified by Ordinance 25.03.04.
37 In France, article L. 464-2-III of the commercial Code, added by the New Economic Regulations Act (NER Reform), dated 15.05.01.

- national courts forward to the Commission, "without delay after the full written judgement is notified to the parties", a copy of any written judgment deciding on application of article 81 or article 82 EC,

- NCAs may submit written observations to the national courts of their Member State, on their own motion, as the Commission can do, equally on its own motion, "when the coherent application of Articles 81 or 82 EC so requires",

- NCAs and the Commission may submit oral observations with the permission of the court.

Adding to these principles, the European Commission notice on cooperation emphasizes that its assistance cannot bind the courts, and the courts must as well respect its independence and duty of professional secrecy[38]. Also the notice insists that the Commission's assistance to the national courts is part of its duty to defend the public interest, and therefore it has *"no intention to serve the private interests of the parties involved in the case pending before the national court"*[39].

A request made by the Supreme Court of Sweden in 2006, asking the Commission's opinion on the definition of the relevant market in a case concerning alleged excessive prices for port services[40] led the Commission to explain more clearly what cooperation stood for[41].

In its response, the EU body stated that it limited itself to only providing the factual information or the economic or legal clarification asked for, without considering the merits of the case. Since the definition of a relevant market is dependent on case-specific elements such as the characteristics and specificity of the services offered, the Commission could only clarify the criteria and evidence that could have been used in a case similar to the one pending before the Swedish court. The Commission also noted that, contrary to referrals made to the ECJ asking for interpretation of the Treaty[42], Commission opinions are not binding on national courts.

One may note that, as far as referrals before the ECJ are concerned, other constraints restrict their scope, such as the inability of NCAs, given their administrative nature, to refer a case to the EU courts[43] and the fact that these referrals are aimed only at interpreting the treaty.

---

38 EC Notice on cooperation, paragraphs 17–19.
39 EC Notice on cooperation, para. 19.
40 Sweden Supreme Court (Högsta Domstolen), request to the Commission in the Bornholms Trafikken A./S case.
41 Commission opinion, 1.03.07, Port of Ysad.
42 Article 234 EC.
43 ECJ, 31.05.05, Syfait.

French rules on cooperation differ from the EU ones. Contrary to the latter, Article L. 462-3 of the Commercial Code allows the regulatory authority to express its opinion, although not binding, on the facts of the case and on their qualification. Furthermore, the authority may make some investigation in order to respond properly to the questions asked by the court: this "pro-active" cooperation proved to be very useful, especially in stand-alone actions which would have been dismissed by national courts for lack of evidence either on the definition of the relevant market, or the alleged position of domination of the defendant, or the characterisation of the practices, led to damages awarded to victims of anticompetitive practices, sustained by the elements provided by the Competition Council[44].

One can wonder why the doctrine taken by the Commission on the application of the said article remained so restrictive, while the role of economic actors, and of private enforcement, was held essential for the implementation of the EU competition rules.

II. Uniform application of Community competition law, the binding effect of the Commission and EU Court decisions

Article 16 of Regulation 1/2003 is meant to ensure a uniform application of Community competition law. Thus, it provides that national courts, when ruling on decisions or practices under Article 81 or 82 EC which are already the subject of a decision of the Commission, cannot take a decision running counter the decision adopted by the Commission. It adds that national courts must also avoid giving decisions which would conflict with a decision contemplated by the Commission, and to that effect, stay their proceedings if necessary. Finally, Article 16 recalls that this obligation is without prejudice to the referral procedure before the ECJ, set up in article 234 EC.

At first sight, it seems obvious that there can be no identity between administrative punitive decisions as those taken by the Commission on public interest grounds, and civil actions brought by undertakings or individuals before national courts in order to obtain personal compensation, analogous to the requirements applicable to the *res judicata* rule in national legislations (i.e. identity of parties, demand and cause)[45]. And the approval of those regulatory decisions, by courts, should not modify their analysis, given the administrative nature of this control even when exerted by judicial institutions.

Instead, it is a concept of "decided/determined matter" that seems to emerge from both, the EU and some national legislations, and recent case-law.

---

44   Court of Appeal of Paris, Ugap v Camif, 13.01.98, 22.10.01; Paris, court of first instance, 26.01.05, Luk Lamellen.
45   See article 1351 of the French Civil Code.

With regard to the EU institution decisions, national courts had soon to precise the extent of the obligations laid down in Article 16.

III. The extent of the binding effect of the Commission's decisions

The first question dealt with by the House of Lords in the *Crehan* case, was whether the British courts were bound, under the response of the ECJ to their referral, by the decisions initially taken by the EU Commission in the case.

It was argued before the British courts that neither the defendant – nor the claimant – had been specifically addressed by the decisions of the Commission, although they were actors on the market it investigated.

The Law Lords observed that there was no previous decision of the Commission dealing specifically with the beer tie arrangements between the claimant and the defendant, and overturned the decision of the Court of Appeal which had ruled that the High Court was under an obligation to follow the conclusions reached by the Commission in its decisions preceding the referral made before the ECJ.

They ruled that national courts are not required to follow a decision of the Commission when considering an issue arising between different parties in respect with a different subject matter, and added that the Commission decisions were then to be treated as evidence that the court could consider, although not binding[46].

A second question arose about the duty for national courts to stay the proceedings, in follow-on actions, until the EU – or NCA's – decision was final. In Germany, the defendants to a follow-on action launched by the alleged victims of a cartel sanctioned by the Bundeskartellamt, objected that the appeal to the NCA's decision was still pending and asked the civil court to stay the proceedings. The Regional Court rejected their request[47], on the grounds that the purpose of paragraph 33 of the German Competition Act (ARC) is to facilitate private damages actions and that the defendants were not entitled to make their request on this legal basis. One can note, firstly, that under general procedure rules in Member States, national courts are usually entitled to organize the course of the trial and notably to suspend the proceedings if a proper administration of justice so requires. Secondly, if the infringement case had been decided by the EU Commission instead of the NCA, the court would have been under an obligation to stay the proceedings under Article 16 of the Regulation 1/2003, or at least to consider the necessity of interim measures in order to safeguard the interests of the parties pending final judgement, as the ECJ ruled in the *Masterfood* case[48].

---

46 House of Lords, 19.07.06, [2006], UKHL 38, Inntrepreneur Pub Company CPC v. Crehan; Court of Appeal, 21.05.04, Crehan v. Inntrepreneur Pub Company, case n° A3/2003/1725.
47 Regional court of Düsseldorf, 3.05.06, Cement cartel case, VI-W (Kart) 6/06.
48 ECJ, 14.12.00, C-344/98, paragraphs 57–58.

IV. The causation link requirement

As noted by the ECJ, the civil liability of undertakings for breach of EC antitrust law requires a causal relationship between the harm alleged by the claimant, and an agreement or a practice which was found to infringe upon EC competition rules[49]. These conditions meet the general conditions for civil liability in every national tort law.

Thus, it is not sufficient for civil courts to refer to the decision assessing an infringement to the EC or national competition law in order to uphold the claim brought before them: the court must assess that the alleged harm resulted certainly and directly from the said infringement. These principles also raised some sensitive difficulties.

In Italy, in a follow-on action relating to the exchange on a regular basis of sensitive commercial information among several Italian insurance companies, the defendants argued that the national authority had only ascertained that the concerted practices had the object of restricting competition, but had not investigated its effects. Rejecting the argument, the Court of Appeal had held that once ascertained that the premium had increased, the causal link between the infringement and this increase could be "automatically" inferred from the NCA's decision. The Italian Supreme Court took a more nuanced approach, and ruled that, although the causal link may be inferred on the basis of probability and presumptions, the judge must take into account any evidence provided by the defendant at proving that other factors have caused or contributed to causing the loss[50].

In other words, the presumption under which the infringement caused the harm suffered by the claimant is a rebuttable one, and the judge is under a duty to consider the converse elements provided by the defendant.

In the assessment of the prejudice, NCA's decisions may also bring some useful elements for the victims of anticompetitive practices. Thus, the German Federal Supreme Court[51] decided that the existence of the cartel is sufficient ground for the presumption that the cartelists have derived profits from this infringement. Such a presumption is all the more notable in that, in German civil law, profits gained by the infringer may contribute to the assessment of the prejudice.

---

49   ECJ, joined cases C-295/04 to C-298/04, 13.07.06, Manfredi.
50   Corte di Cassazione, 15.12.06, Fondiaria Societa Assicuratrice Industriale v. Nigriello.
51   BGH, Ready-mixed concrete cartel, 28.06.05, KRB 2/05, Berliner Transportbeton.

E. Conclusion

Two remarks to conclude.

The first relates to the characteristics of harmonisation in Europe of competition rules: bottom-up, or top-down? Undoubtedly both, at many levels. EU and national authorities, EU and national courts, undertakings and consumers, everybody takes part in this process of harmonisation, of construction of a communal competition law.

I would like to stress, on this point, how the framework set up in competition matters proved to be consistent and dynamic.

Furthermore, the dynamics in these matters proved to go far beyond a satisfactory implementation of European competition rules. As shown, hopefully, in this presentation, they already led to harmonising procedural rules and substantive law in Member States, and necessarily to bringing national concepts and practices closer.

In these regards, competition law proves to be the core of the construction of the Union.

Discussion

CARL BAUDENBACHER
Thank you very much, Judge Riffault-Silk, for a most interesting and inspiring speech. In fact, your final statement made it very clear what this is all about. I remember the time when this new regulation was set up and Judge Norberg was part of it. A lot of people had doubts about whether this was the right thing to do and now it turns out that it has become the most important tool, formally, in the field of competition law, even though, as you mentioned, many other areas are being affected by it. And not only that, it could also serve as some sort of a role model for other policy fields to be deepened and to be subject to uniform rules in European integration law on a broad scale.

Furthermore, it was particularly interesting to see that in the field of private enforcement, where until a few years ago everybody thought there would not be any progress made in Europe, a lot is moving. I am particularly pleased that we have also been able to put the focus on the role of the courts. Because at competition law conferences all over the world the focus is always on the regulators. The agencies tend to believe that it is them, who call the shots, but ultimately it is the judges who have the control over the agencies.

Let me add one last point. With all this development going on now in the European Union and also in the European Economic Area in the field of competition law, Switzerland is obviously in difficulty because according to the Swiss Competition Act, Switzerland is supposed to follow the way the European Union paves. All the key notions and key concepts of EC competition law have been taken over in this country in 1995 but Switzerland and its Competition Agency and courts are not part of this network. And by network I mean a formal EC competition network in case of the agencies and an informal network in the case of the courts. I am impressed how well the latter works and I suppose this functioning is essentially based on judicial dialogue, on the willingness to look to each other and to cross-fertilize each other. That is why last summer, the Swiss government has commissioned a big study on the status of competition law in this country and on further possibilities of development. And part of it was in fact about private enforcement. A lot of people may have seen with great interest what is going on in this court case in Düsseldorf where a Belgian company, in a follow-on case after a cartel has been discovered, buys claims and brings them to court.

Similar developments are going on in the field of passing on defence and I suspect, the Swiss legislator will have to keep its eyes open. As Ambassador Pfirter already mentioned today, remaining off side will become more and more costly for Switzerland.

SVEN NORBERG

Thank you. First of all, I would like to thank you very much Jacqueline for a fantastic presentation. There were so many things you managed to carry and so many new developments. I would have two comments and one question. The first comment was regarding the fact that the Swedish Supreme Court (Högsta Domstolen) decided to ask the European Commission regarding the application of Article 81 EC. And that is a very interesting phenomenon, considering that the Swedish Supreme Court has a history of being extremely reluctant to make references to the ECJ. This changed about two years ago. But the reason why the Supreme Court in that case referred to the Commission and not to the ECJ was that this was on a particular topic where the Commission is much better placed, I dare to say, than the ECJ. It concerned a market definition on the ferry traffic line between the port of Ystad in southern Sweden and the Danish island of Bornholm. It would have been difficult to get a relevant answer from the ECJ whereas the Commission could draw on its extensive experiences in the field of market definition.[1]

My second comment refers to what Carl said regarding the spreading of this to other fields. The Commission has recently published a draft Notice regarding a similar assistance to National Courts in the field of State aid.[2] One can only hope that this sort of assistance to the National Judiciaries will continue to spread to many other areas where National Judges are faced with interpreting complex pieces of EC legislation.

But now I come to the question to Jacqueline. I remember, two, three years ago, that there was a lot of discussion in France regarding the introduction of a system for collective actions, but I did not see anything reflected on that on your slides. Could you enlighten us on that?

JACQUELINE RIFFAULT-SILK

This is a painfully difficult subject. Measures of collective redress in France are still extremely restricted, and almost non-existent in competition matters. The reason for this may be found, for a significant part, in the reluctance of the business community to support such reforms. As a matter of fact, collective redress systems are designed to alleviate the burden of proof that victims have to bear, and also to facilitate the course of the proceedings by concentrating the dispute between a few representatives of the victims, and the defendants. It seems that the business community is not confident that there would be enough control, judicial control, on these kinds of actions.

One cannot but recognize that the schemes we have in France, either actions in representation, taken by consumers associations, for instance, provided they received an agreement for this at national level, or joined actions, do not work well.

---

1 Case T-2808/05 Damska Staten through Brornholmstrafikken v. Ystad Hamn Logistik AB, judgment 19.2.2008.
2 Now final as Commission Notice on the enforcement of State aid law by national courts, OJ 9.4.2009 C85/1.

This was recently illustrated by a decision of the Commercial Court of Paris, taken in a follow-on action brought before the court by the victims of the mobile telephony cartel. Each victim of the cartel had brought its action before the court and, in addition to these amounting some thousands claims, a national consumers association had also brought an action on its own behalf, for the defense of collective interests.

The Commercial Court declared inadmissible all the claims[3] and dismissed the case, on the grounds that the consumers association had made illegal solicitation to collect mandates from harmed victims of the cartel, then organized an action in representation "in disguise", in violation of the French Consumers Code. One can wonder where was the fraud, since what was proposed on the website of the association was nothing but a method of calculation of the personal prejudice resulting from the cartel, and the actions brought before the court were nothing but personal.

CARL BAUDENBACHER
Let us take another question before we have to finish.

ERICH SCHANZE
The Düsseldorf case, Carl mentioned, shows a startling development. I doubt however, that it has much to do with the European development itself. In my opinion, it has its origin in the enforcement system of the United States. The problem is that the cement cartel was already fined in proportion to the damage done to the market. And the private claim doubles more or less that effort. At this point it is pending on appeal and it is very unclear whether the Federal Supreme Court will really take up that view. Especially since in this particular case a cost risk aspect has to be considered in the sense that this Belgian company will get immediately insolvent if it loses the action. The company's reasoning is simple: *"If we are active, we can collect and if we do not win, we simply quit."*

JACQUELINE RIFFAULT-SILK
You make a very good point about the costs aspect, which is an important chapter of the White Paper proposals. Rules about judicial costs are of paramount importance when considering starting an action, and they differ quite a lot from one Member State to another. What is proposed seems inspired by some practices already existing in the United Kingdom, under which the court may impose to the parties to calculate and pay in advance, or secure the litigation costs, with a possibility for the public body in charge to take those foreseen costs in advance. In fact, it is exactly what a private company like CDC is aimed at, with the difference that CDC would lose any chance of reimbursement of its expenses in case the action fails. These various mechanisms are necessary, because they safeguard all of the system, to some extent.

---

3   Paris, Commercial Court, 6.12.2007, Amblard, UFC-Que Choisir & al. v. Bouygues Telecom, RG 2006057440.

Finally, about cooperation, may I tell you that national judges in Europe founded, a few years ago, an association aiming at sharing experience and knowledge, in competition and judicial matters. The association holds conferences and meetings on a regular basis every year, in one or the other Member State. The results of this were interesting. There is more and more understanding of the different cultures and rules in Europe, which turn out to be closer than imagined at first sight.

CARL BAUDENBACHER
Thank you very much.

Keynote

Some Considerations on the Dialogue between High Courts

CARL BAUDENBACHER [1]

A. Theory of international judicial dialogue

I. General

In the last 10 years Canadian and American authors have postulated a systematic dialogue between high court judges all over the world. It is argued that in times of globalization, a global dialogue among supreme courts and international courts is inevitable. Those who are in favor of such comparison argue that a functionalist approach is needed "in which the relevant unit of analysis is not a geographic entity, such as a country or a region, but is rather the problem and its legal solution[2]". It is stated that there should not be any limitations as to the geographic origin of an argument. One is reminded of *Habermas'* concept of *herrschaftsfreier Diskurs*[3].

Two women made especially important contributions. (1) Ten years ago, Canadian Supreme Court Justice *Claire L'Heureux-Dubé*[4] pointed to the fact that unlike in the past, when colonial powers such as Britain and France and later the United States were the most influential sources of foreign authority on most matters, today, "[j]udges no longer simply receive the cases of other jurisdictions and then apply them or modify them for their own jurisdiction. Rather, cross-pollination and dialogue between jurisdictions is increasingly occurring. As judgments in different countries increasingly build on each other, mutual respect and dialogue are fostered among appellate courts. Judges around the world look to each other for persuasive authority, rather than some judges being 'givers' of law while others are 'receivers'. Reception is turning to dialogue." Justice *Claire L'Heureux-Dubé* stated that certain Supreme Courts were open-minded in that respect, whereas others were reluctant to engage in this. (2) Former Dean of the Woodrow Wilson School for Public Affairs at Princeton University and former

---

1 President of the EFTA Court and Director of the Institute of European and International Business Law at the University of St. Gallen.
2 See Ruti Teitel, Comparative Constitutional Law in a Global Age, 117 Harv. L. Rev. 2570, 2574 (2004) (referring to the famous German comparatist Rudolf von Ihering's statement that "[T]he reception of foreign legal institutions is not a matter of nationality, but of usefulness and need. No one bother to fetch a thing from afar when he has one as good or better at home, but only a fool would refuse quinine just because it didn't grow in his back garden"); see also Konrad Zweigert & Hein Kötz, Introduction to Comparative Law 17 (Tony Weir trans., 3d ed. 1998).
3 See generally Jürgen Habermas, 2 Theory of Communicative Action (1981).
4 Claire L'Heureux-Dubé, The Importance of Dialogue: Globalization and the International Impact of the Rehnquist Court, 34 Tulsa L.J. 15, 15-16 (1998).

Harvard-Professor *Anne-Marie Slaughter* has postulated a worldwide dialogue of Courts. As early as 2000 she spoke of a vision of a global community of law, "established by national courts working together around the world" and added: "It is also a vision of a shift from deference to dialogue, from passive acceptance to active interaction, from negative comity to positive comity".[5]

II. Reasons

The main reasons for the increasing dialogue between courts are the following: (1) Legal problems arising in different jurisdictions tend to be increasingly **similar**. Human rights are by their very nature international. The same goes for environmental law. Other fields where legal problems are comparable concern antidiscrimination legislation. There is a high amount of convergence in fields such as antitrust and IP law, corporate governance, accounting law, money laundering law, counterterrorism measures and their limits. Moreover, it has been rightly stated that "[t]he global economy creates global litigation"[6]. (2) In a globalized world, legal problems arising in various jurisdictions may even be **identical** (Examples: Patentability of one and the same invention [e.g. the Harvard oncomouse], registration of one and the same trademark [e.g. the shape of the *Coca Cola* bottle or the color of the *Milka* cow], cross-border marketing [Examples: reproduction of *Lego* cubes, lawfulness of the *Benetton* shock advertising], worldwide operating price cartels [Example: Vitamin cartel]). (3) New technologies facilitate the dialogue: e-mail, internet. (4) There is an increased mobility of judges. Personal contacts are more frequent than in the past.

III. Exporting and importing courts

(1) In the past, the courts of Great Britain and of France were able to export their case law[7]. After 1945, the most influential **idea giver** was the **U.S. Supreme Court**. Anthony Lester stated in 1988:

> "[t]he Bill of Rights is more than an historical inspiration for the creation of charters and institutions dedicated to the protection of liberty. Currently, there is a vigorous overseas trade in the Bill of Rights, in international and constitutional litigation involving norms derived from American constitutional law. When life or liberty is at stake, the landmark judgments of the Supreme Court of the United States, giving fresh meaning to the principles of the Bill of Rights, are studied with as much attention in New Delhi or Strasbourg as they are in Washington, D.C., or the State of Washington, or Springfield, Illinois."[8]

---

5   Anne-Marie Slaughter, Judicial Globalization, 40 Va. J. Int'l L., 1103, 1114 (2000).
6   Anne-Marie Slaughter, A Global Community of Courts, 44 Harv. Int'l L.J., 191, 204 (2003).
7   L'Heureux-Dubé, loc. cit., 17 ff.
8   Anthony Lester, The Overseas Trade in the American Bill of Rights, 88 Colum. L. Rev. 537, 541 (1988).

A famous example is the worldwide triumph of the *Miranda*-Rule which was formulated in a 1966 Supreme Court case called *Miranda v. Arizona*[9]. When a person is in custody, some version of the Miranda rights, such as the following, is read to the individual before questioning: "You have the right to remain silent. If you give up the right to remain silent, anything you say can and will be used against you in a court of law. You have the right to an attorney. If you desire an attorney and cannot afford one, an attorney will be obtained for you before police questioning." [10]

The **European Court of Human Rights** too is a significant exporter. Its judgments have, for instance, been referred to by the U.S. Supreme Court, the Canadian Supreme Court, the High Court of Australia and the Inter-American Court of Human Rights[11].

The ECJ has been referred to in a number of judgments of the European Court of Human Rights[12].

(2) It has been said that **Canadian Courts** are particularly open-minded when it comes to the question of whether they should **look abroad** when interpreting Canadian law [13].

The **U.S. Supreme Court** has referred to non-U.S. views in a relatively small number of cases. The most prominent example is the judgment in *Lawrence v. Texas*, in which the U.S. Supreme Court found a Texas sodomy statute to be unconstitutional.[14] In that case, the Supreme Court referred to the judgment of the **European Court of Human Rights** in *Dudgeon v. United Kingdom*[15]. The Court of Justice of the European Communities (ECJ) has not been referred to by the U.S. Supreme Court. In *Intel Corp. v. Advanced Micro Devices, Inc.* (2003) the ECJ and the CFI are mentioned, but only in the framework of a general description of the enforcement of European competition

---

9   384 U.S. 436 (1966).
10 384 U.S. 436 (1966).
11 E.g. U.S. Supreme Court: Lawrence v. Texas, 539 U.S. 558 (2003); Canadian Supreme Court: Kindler v. Canada, [1991] 2 S.C.R. 779, 1991 SCC 70 and United States v. Burns, [2001] 1 S.C.R. 283, 2001 SCC 7; High Court of Australia: Applicant NABD of 2002 v. Minister for Immigration and Multicultural and Indigenous Affairs, [2005] 79 ALJR 1142, 216 ALR 1, Inter-American Court of Human Rights: Montero-Aranguren et al (Detention Center of Catia) v. Venezuela, Inter-Am. Ct. HR, 5 July 2006. Further examples of Supreme Courts referring to the European Court of Human Rights encompass the South-African Constitutional Court, e.g. National Coalition for Gay and Lesbian Equality and Another v. Minister of Justice and Others, [1998] ZACC 15; 1999 (1) SA 6; or the Zimbabwian Supreme Court, e.g. Catholic Commission for Justice and Peace in Zimbabwe v. Attorney-General, Zimbabwe, and Others, [1993] 4 SA 239 (ZS), 2 SACR 432.
12 See, e.g., Sergey Zolotukhin v. Russia, Application No. 14939/03, judgment of 10.02.2009; Sheffield and Horsham v. the United Kingdom, 1998-V Eur. H.R. Rep.; Stec and Others v. the United Kingdom, 2005-X Eur. H.R. Rep.
13 See L'Heureux-Dubé, loc. cit., 19 ff.
14 539 U.S. 558, 576 (2003).
15 See id. at 573, citing Dudgeon v. United Kingdom, [1982] 4 Eur. H.R. Rep. 149.

law. In the oral hearing in *Quality King Distributors, Inc. v. L'Anza Research Int'l, Inc.*[16], the case law of the ECJ on regional exhaustion of copyright has been referred to in a rather unspecified way[17].

The European Court of Human Rights has made some references to case law of the **Inter-American Court of Human Rights**[18]. Moreover, it has cited U.S. Supreme Court judgments on a number of occasions.[19] In *G.B. v. Bulgaria* (2004), the Strasbourg Court also dwelled on considerations of the Supreme Court of India and of the Supreme Court of Canada[20]. In the *Allan v. The United Kingdom* ruling from 2002 reference was made to the 1998 judgment of the High Court of Australia in *R. v. Swaffield and Pavic*[21].

The ECJ itself does not make reference to foreign Supreme Courts, but its Advocates-General do[22].

For Supreme Courts of **European countries** it is not at all revolutionary to look across borders. In small countries like Switzerland, Austria or Norway, this is even deemed to be a necessity, not least because there is a limited number of cases. The framework conditions are particularly favorable in countries whose legal orders are based on common values and have a common basis in Roman Law. In the case of Germany, Austria and Switzerland there is no language barrier. Switzerland is not a Member State of the EU nor of the EEA. The country has joined the UN late. It is usually not seen as particularly open-minded. Nevertheless, the **Swiss Supreme Court** has long used the comparative method much more frequently than any other Supreme Court in Europe. The **Austrian Supreme Court** has obtained inspiration from the German and the Swiss

---

16   98 F.3d 1109.
17   1997 WL 765595 (U.S.), the judgment does not contain any reference (523 U.S. 135).
18   E.g. Mamatkulov and Askarov v. Turkey, [2005] 41 Eur. Ct. H.R. 25; Anguelova v. Bulgaria, 2002-IV Eur. H.R. Rep. 355, 399 (Bonello, J., dissenting); Çiçek v. Turkey, [2001] 934 Eur. Ct. H.R. 56 (Maruste, J., concurring).
19   See the references to U.S. Supreme Court Knight v. Florida from 1999 in G.B. v. Bulgaria, Application No. 42346/98, 2004 and to U.S. Supreme Court Rochin v. California from 1952 in Jalloh v. Germany (Application No. 54810/00, 2006). In Dickson v. The United Kingdom (Application No. 44362/04, 2006) the Joint Dissenting Opinion of Judges Casadevall and Garlicki mentions the U.S. Supreme Court's 1942 judgment in Skinner v. Oklahoma. In Sergey Zolotukhin v. Russia, Application No. 14939/03, judgment of 10.02.2009, the Grand Chamber mentions Blockburger v. United States (1932), Grady v. Corbin (1990) and United States v. Dixon (1993) as relevant and comparative international law in order to assess the principle of ne bis in idem.
20   Vatheeswaran v. State of Tamil Nadu [1983] 2 S.C.R. 348, Sher Singh and Others v. the State of Punjab [1983] 2 S.C.R. 582 and Smt. Treveniben v. State of Gujarat [1989] 1 S.C.J. 383; Kindler v. Canada, [1991] 2 S.C.R. 779.
21   Allan v. The United Kingdom, 2002-IX Eur. Ct. H.R.; R. v. Swaffield and Pavic, [1998] HCA 1.
22   See Peter Herzog, United States Supreme Court Cases in the Court of Justice of the European Communities, 21 Hastings Int'l & Comp. L. Rev. 903 (1998); Carl Baudenbacher, Judicial Globalisation: New Development or Old Wine in New Bottles?, 38 Tex. Int'l L.J., 505, 516 ff. (2003); Les Faircloth Peoples, The Use of Foreign Law by the Advocates General of the Court of Justice of the European Communities, Symposium: 21st Century International, Foreign and Comparative Law Research Issues, 35 Syracuse J. Int'l L. & Com. 219 (2008).

Supreme Court. The **German Supreme Court**, for its part, would occasionally make reference to the Supreme Courts of the two other German speaking countries [23].

A famous example of judicial globalization is the *Fairchild* judgment of the **House of Lords**[24]. Mr Fairchild had worked for a number of different employers, all of whom had negligently exposed him to asbestos. As a consequence, he contracted *mesothelioma*. A single asbestos fibre, inhaled at any time, can trigger mesothelioma. The risk of contracting an asbestos related disease increases depending on the degree of exposure to it. However, because of long latency periods (it takes 25 to 50 years before symptoms of disease become evident) it is impossible to know when the crucial moment was. It was therefore impossible for Mr Fairchild to identify the employer whose fiber was causal. The House of Lords held that the employers were joint and severally liable. Their Lordships reviewed jurisprudence from as far afield as Australia, Austria, Canada, Germany, Greece, Italy, France, the Netherlands, Norway, South Africa, Spain, Switzerland and the United States; reference was also made to opinions of classical Roman jurists.

IV. Critique

In **Europe** as in Canada, judicial dialogue is usually seen as a positive development. The situation is different in the **U.S.** There are basically two types of criticism put forward: On the one hand, it is argued that judges enter an international dialogue in order to gain more power, that using non-U.S. opinions in constitutional interpretation undermines U.S. sovereignty, that it sets aside the domestic **majoritarian impulse**, that it is incompatible with the supremacy of the U.S. Constitution over international law, that getting inspiration from foreign judges is without democratic legitimation[25]. The debate has, at least from a European perspective, some slightly bizarre traits. Supreme Court Justice *Antonin Scalia* defined any reference to foreign law meaningless, but dangerous dicta[26]. Republican members of the House of Representatives called for the impeachment of judges who "substitute foreign law for American law or the American Constitution"[27]. Now, Chief Justice *John Roberts* was asked during his confirmation hearing in the Senate Judiciary Committee whether, if put on the bench, he would make reference to foreign judgments[28].

---

23 See Baudenbacher, Judicial Globalization, 507 ff.; Joachim Bornkamm, The German Supreme Court: An Actor in the Global Conversation of High Courts, 39 Tex. Int'l L.J. 415, 417 f. (2004).
24 Fairchild (suing on her own behalf) etc. v. Glenhaven Funeral Services Ltd and others etc., [2002] UKHL 22: see with regard to that judgment Sir Basil Markesinis, Judicial Mentality: Mental Disposition or Outlook as a Factor Impeding Recourse to Foreign Law, 80 Tul. L. Rev. 1325, 1373 (2006).
25 See Roger P. Alford, Misusing International Sources to Interpret the Constitution, 98 Am. J. Int'l L. 57 (2004).
26 Dissenting opinion in 539 U.S. 558 Lawrence v. Texas (2003).
27 See Tom Curry, A flap over foreign matter at the Supreme Court, http://www.msnbc.msn.com/id/4506232 (last visited on 1 June 2009).
28 See, e.g., Emily Bazelon, Moments of Truth, What John Roberts really thinks, http://www.slate.com/id/2126311/ (last visited on 1 June 2009).

On the other hand, critics complain that judges are ill-suited to carry out comprehensive research so that there is a danger of them acting as "bricoleurs" and that international and foreign materials may be used selectively[29].

B. Systematizations

I. General

Judicial dialogue can take many forms. The traditional exchange among courts in European countries is largely **unstructured**. Whether it happens or not depends also on coincidences such as whether the competent judge has studied abroad and speaks the language in question.

There have been, however, attempts to systematically assess the individual forms and types of judicial cooperation. In the following three theories will be presented before this writer introduces its own approach.

II. Claire L'Heureux-Dubé[30]

Former Canadian Supreme Court Justice *Claire L'Heureux-Dubé* distinguishes between reception of other courts' decisions in a broad sense and dialogue. **Reception** in her view occurs in cases in which the importing court is bound to follow the case law of the exporting court as well as in cases in which foreign case law is imported due to its prominence. **Dialogue** differs from one-way transmission in that judges who are on eye-level take into account a broad spectrum of sources.

III. Joachim Bornkamm

Joachim Bornkamm, President of Chamber at the German Supreme Court distinguishes **five degrees of cooperation**: (1) Cooperation of judges as a means of generating a supply of solutions, (2) referencing judgments of foreign courts as persuasive authority, (3) cooperation of judges in order to secure a homogeneous application of international law, (4) harmonization under the control of the WTO Dispute Settlement mechanism, (5) harmonization under the control of the ECJ.

(1) An example of the **first level** would be that judges from several jurisdictions meet each other and discuss issues of common interest. This type of cooperation "is nursed

---

29 See in particular Alford, loc. cit., 57 f.; Ronald J. Krotoszynski, "I'd Like to Teach the World to Sing (in Perfect Harmony)": International Judicial Dialogue and the Muses – Reflections on the Perils and the Promise of International Judicial Dialogue, 104 Mich.L.Rev., 1321, 1329 (2006).
30 Supra, fn. 3.

more by academic curiosity than by legal necessity. At this step we are looking at legal systems that hardly have any common ground. What they have in common are the tasks to be solved. But they do it with different means".[31]

(2) On the **second level**, there is still no necessity for dialogue, but dialogue makes the judge's life easier and is therefore of more than an academic interest. Legal systems have a common background or fields of the law may be similar in spite of differences between the legal systems at large. Examples are references of the Swiss and the Austrian Supreme Court to the German Supreme Court and of the German Supreme Court to the Swiss, the Austrian and even the U.S. Supreme Court. The latter happened in cases concerning trademark law[32], the right of privacy[33], antitrust[34], and the use of weapons by government agents[35].

(3) Examples of **third level** cooperation would be the dialogue among judges applying provisions of multilateral IP law conventions such as the Paris Convention for the Protection of Industrial Property, the Berne Convention for the Protection of Literary and Artistic Works, and the European Patent Convention. Here, judicial dialogue becomes a **necessity**, since homogeneous application of international law in the individual Member States must be assured. The law is uniform, but there is no institution that would effectively supervise the Member States.

The judges applying provisions of the said Conventions in many countries are specialists of IP law. That holds particularly true for the European Patent Convention. Under this Treaty, an inventor may apply for a European patent which will eventually be granted by the European Patent Office in Munich. In reality, the European patent is, however, not a single patent, but a bundle of national patents. National patent laws have been harmonized, so that the **law is identical in substance**, but it is for the national courts to interpret them without there being a higher institution. Dialogue is therefore essential. Obviously, the framework conditions for such cooperation are ideal. Bornkamm observed that cooperation is so smooth that there may even be an overkill effect[36]. An example would be provided by the *Epilady* cases. A women's hair-shaving device with the name "Epilady" had been patented. The patent owner brought infringement actions against the defendant whose product bore the name "Lady Remington" in London and in Düsseldorf. In London, the Patent Court dismissed the application for an interlocutory injunction whereas the Düsseldorf *Landgericht* granted such preliminary protection. On appeal, counsel for the plaintiff submitted the Düsseldorf judgment to the Court of Appeal in London, and counsel for the defendant did

---

31 Joachim Bornkamm, loc. cit., 416.
32 BGHZ 140, 193 (199); see also the references to the ECJ in Joined Cases C-53/01, C-54/01 & C-55/01, Linde AG, Winward Industries Inc., and Rado Uhren AG, [2003] E.T.M.R. 963, 963.
33 BGHZ 131, 332 (337).
34 BGH Case KZR 35/97, 102 GRUR 95 (2000).
35 Judgment of Nov. 3, 1992, Entscheidungen des Bundesgerichtshofes in Strafsachen [BGHSt] 39, 1 (20–21).
36 Bornkamm, 421.

the same with the Patent Court judgment before the *Oberlandesgericht* in Düsseldorf. Both courts of appeal followed the first instance judgment delivered by the foreign court, the Court of Appeal in London, referring to the ruling of the Düsseldorf Landgericht, decided in favor of the plaintiff and granted patent protection. The German Appeal Court followed the example of the Patent Court in London and dismissed the application[37].

(4) The **fourth level** of cooperation has been developed under the TRIPs Agreement. TRIPs has integrated the Paris and the Berne Convention and added certain points. The pivotal novelty is that in the context of the TRIPs Agreement provisions of the Paris and the Berne Convention can be enforced in a more effective way by using the **WTO Dispute Settlement Mechanism**. This makes dialogue among the national courts a necessity, at least up to a certain degree.

(5) The **fifth level** of cooperation in Bornkamm's system is the dialogue between the ECJ and the national courts of the EC Member States in the framework of the Article 234 EC preliminary ruling procedure. This clearly is the most advanced type of cooperation. There is a common court which has sole competence to interpret the law and whose task it is to to secure a uniform application of the law by the national courts. Direct effect follows from Community law. Courts of last resort are, as a matter of principle, obliged to seize the ECJ, and the latter's rulings are legally binding on the referring court and factually binding on all other national courts in the Community. It is to be noted that the ECJ exerts influence on the jurisprudence of the courts of the Member States also under the infringement procedure under Articles 226/227 EC.

IV. Allan Rosas

Allan Rosas, President of Chamber at the Court of Justice of the European Communities, distinguishes five types of relationship of international courts, thereby having a strong focus on his own court, the ECJ[38].

(1) The first type consists of international courts with **overlapping or competing jurisdiction**. This means that the same dispute could go to either of the two. An example are the competences of the International Court of Justice in The Hague and of the Tribunal for the Law of the Sea in Hamburg.

---

37 See Epilady Before the Courts – A Case Study on Infringement Procedure, 24 Int'l Rev. Indus. Prop. & Copyright L. 803, 803 (1993); Decision of the Court of Appeal, August 12, 1988, Improver Corp. v. Remington Consumer Prod. Ltd., 21 Int'l Rev. Indus. Prop. & Copyright L. 561 (1990); Decision of the Düsseldorf Court of Appeals (Oberlandesgericht), October 27, 1988 – Case No. 2 U 181/88, Improver Corp. & Sicommerce AG v. Remington Prod. Inc., 21 Int'l Rev. Indus. Prop. & Copyright L. 572, 575 (1990).

38 Allan Rosas, Methods of Interpretation – Judicial Dialogue, in: Baudenbacher/Busek, The Role of International Courts, Heidelberg 2008, 185 ff.

(2) As another extreme, Rosas mentions a rather strict **vertical, hierarchical system**. Examples are many, first of all in national systems where there is a court hierarchy, but also in the European Community (at least in certain fields) with a Court of Justice, a Court of First Instance and a Civil Service Tribunal.

(3) The third type is the relationship between **the ECJ and the national courts** in the Member States under the Article 234 EC preliminary ruling procedure. This is close to the second type, but there is not a relation of hierarchy *stricto sensu*. Still, the ECJ's preliminary rulings are binding on the national judge.

(4) The **fourth category** occurs in a situation where the EU or a State or another actor is committed to a certain set of international rules. An example is the relationship between the ECJ and the **WTO Appellate Body**. This relationship is a formal one because the EU is a Contracting Party to the WTO system. Rosas also mentions the relationship between the ECJ and the **European Court of Human Rights**, although the EU or the EC is not a Contracting Party to the European Human Rights Convention. The commitment of the EC is twofold: On the one hand, the Treaty itself contains respective provisions. On the other hand, the case law of the ECJ is closely linked to the one of the Strasbourg Court.

(5) The **fifth category** is referred to as horizontal judicial dialogue. It describes a cooperation between courts more or less at the same level that are looking at what their neighbours are doing. In that respect, Rosas mentions "a certain tendency that the national judges are also looking at what their neighbours are doing and that they are also citing judgments from these neighbouring or maybe even more far away countries"[39]. This would apply to Supreme Courts making reference to other Supreme Courts (e.g. Swiss Supreme Court – German Supreme Court and vice versa; Indian Supreme Court – U.S. Supreme Court; U.S. Supreme Court – European Court of Human Rights; Advocates General of the ECJ – U.S. Supreme Court). As far as the European Economic Area system is concerned, the relationship between the ECJ and the **EFTA Court** would in Rosas' view be the best example. Since EEA law which the EFTA Court applies and interprets is largely identical in substance with EC law, the EFTA Court is supposed to follow ECJ case law under special homogeneity rules. The court is in fact citing judgments of the EC courts quite frequently. The crucial point is, however, that the ECJ, for its part, refers to the EFTA Court when dealing with a legal question that as such it has not decided before[40].

---

39   Methods of Interpretation, loc. cit., 190.
40   See Carl Baudenbacher, The EFTA Court, the ECJ, and the Latter's Advocates General – a Tale of Judicial Dialogue, in: Arnull/Eeckhout/Tridimas, Eds., Continuity and Change in EU Law: Essays in Honour of Sir Francis Jacobs, Oxford 2007, 90 ff.

C. This writer's own approach

This writer would suggest to distinguish three levels of judicial cooperation depending on whether and to what extent the importing court is bound to take over foreign jurisprudence.

I. Prescribed cooperation

(1) Historically, prescribed cooperation existed, e.g., in the jurisdictions whose courts were bound to follow the jurisprudence of the Privy Council[41].

(2) Today, the cooperation between the **ECJ and the national courts of the EC Member States** in the framework of the Article 234 EC preliminary ruling procedure may be characterized as prescribed. This cooperation is vertical in nature, since it is the ECJ which is calling the shots. The referring national courts are bound to follow the ECJ's ruling. The latter will, moreover, have factual *erga omnes* effect[42]. But the procedure is initiated by the referring national court. And at the end of the day, national courts can hardly be forced to make such references. That means that the ECJ will have to consider whether its jurisprudence may diminish the national courts' willingness to send questions for preliminary rulings. As a matter of principle, the ECJ does not quote judgments of the national courts.

(3) The same applies *mutatis mutandis* with regard to the relationship between the EFTA Court and the national courts of the EEA/EFTA States[43].

(4) Prescribed cooperation also exists (at least in effect) between the **European Court of Human Rights and the national Supreme Courts of the Member States** to the European Human Rights Convention.

(5) The ECJ is not only the court which, by way of different procedures, sets the tone in the European Union, but also the center of gravity when it comes to the application and interpretation of the so-called extension agreements that have been concluded between the EU (and in some cases its Member States) on the one hand and the EFTA States on the other. The **extension of Community law to the EFTA States** is a specifically European phenomenon. Under the Agreement on the European Economic Area (EEA) EC single market law has largely been extended to Iceland, Liechtenstein and Norway[44]. Under the Lugano Convention on jurisdiction and the enforcement of judg-

---

41 L'Heureux-Dubé, loc. cit., 17 f.
42 Carl Baudenbacher, The Implementation of Decisions of the ECJ and of the EFTA Court in Member States' Domestic Legal Orders. 40 Tex. Int'l L.J., 383 ff. (2005).
43 Baudenbacher, The Implementation, loc. cit.
44 http://www.efta.int/content/legal-texts/eea.

ments in civil and commercial matters[45] the same happened with the Brussels Convention and the Brussels Regulation to Iceland, Norway and Switzerland. The bilateral agreements with Switzerland extend certain parts of Community law to that country[46]. This results each time in there being separate legal orders with separate courts, but law that is identical in substance. Thereby the question arises how a homogeneous development of the case law can be secured.

(i) The **Lugano Convention** contains a mutual homogeneity mechanism, according to which the courts of the EFTA States Iceland, Norway and Switzerland ought to take into account the jurisprudence of the ECJ, whereas the ECJ should consider the case law of the courts of the said EFTA States. Special emphasis is put on the old ECJ case law, i.e. judgments rendered before the signature of the agreement in 1988. In reality, there is only one way street homogeneity[47].

(ii) The homogeneity regime of the **EEA Agreement** of 1992 is, on its face, unilateral. The EFTA Court, according to Articles 6 EEA and 3 II Surveillance and Court Agreement, is supposed to follow old and to take into account new ECJ case law. It has always complied with these provisions. The ECJ, for its part, is making reference to EFTA Court case law which deals with a fresh legal question[48]. The latter form of cooperation constitutes **dialogue**. One will notice in this context that when dealing with ECJ case law, the EFTA Court has sometimes pursued an approach which has been characterized as "creative homogeneity"[49].

(iii) The more recent **bilateral agreements** concluded between the EU and Switzerland, too, contain homogeneity clauses. According to them, the Swiss Supreme Court is bound to follow the case law of the ECJ delivered before the date of signature and to take into account the case law rendered since[50]. The Supreme Court's jurisprudence concerning the EU-Switzerland Free Movement of Persons Agreement is full of references to ECJ case law[51].

---

45 http://curia.europa.eu/common/recdoc/convention/en/c-textes/lug-idx.htm.
46 http://www.europa.admin.ch/themen/00500/index.html?lang=en.
47 See Christian Kohler, Dialog der Gerichte im europäischen Justizraum: zur Rolle des EuGH bei der Auslegung des neuen Übereinkommens von Lugano, in: Monti/Prinz Nikolaus von und zu Liechtenstein/Vesterdorf/Westbrook/Wildhaber, Eds., Festschrift for Carl Baudenbacher, Baden-Baden 2007, 141.
48 See supra, fn. 39.
49 Christiaan Timmermans, Creative Homogeneity, Liber Amicorum for Sven Norberg, Bruxelles 2006, 471 ff.
50 Article 16(2) of the Free Movement of Persons Agreement Switzerland – EU.
51 E.g, A.X. et B.X. contre Service de la population du canton de Vaud, BGE 134 II 10; X. gegen Staatsanwaltschaft des Kantons Aargau, BGE 134 IV 57; X. gegen Regierungsrat sowie Verwaltungsgericht des Kantons Zürich, BGE 130 II 176.

II. Necessary cooperation

Examples of necessary cooperation are the constellations mentioned by *Joachim Bornkamm* under the Paris and Berne Conventions, the European Patent Convention, and the TRIPs Agreement, where there is **uniform law**, but no common court. Articles 28 of the Paris Convention and 33 of the Berne Convention which state that disputes may ultimately be brought before the International Court of Justice are without any practical relevance. In the same vein, *Allan Rosas* has pointed to the longstanding practice of the ECJ to make reference to the case law of the European Court of Human Rights when dealing with fundamental rights. A similar situation exists with respect to the relationship between the ECJ and the WTO Dispute Settlement Mechanism. As far as citation practice is concerned, the ECJ in one judgment in which it had to interpret the TRIPs Agreement made reference to an individual decision of the WTO Appellate Body[52]. Reference to the case law of the Strasbourg court has become routine[53].

A further example is provided by the 1951 **Convention Relating to the Status of Refugees**. When dealing with asylum seekers, national courts have entered an intensive cooperation. It was observed that "[t]his judicial dialogue can be traced to the early 1990s, when a 1993 judgment of the Canadian Supreme Court ... cited a 1985 decision of the United States Board of Immigration tribunal, ... to be cited itself later by the High Court of Australia in 1997, the New Zealand Refugee Status Authority in 1998, and the House of Lords in 1999 ... In the latter judgment, the Law Lords commend the New Zealand Refugee Status Authority for its 'impressive judgment,' which draws on 'the case law and practice in Germany, The Netherlands, Sweden, Denmark, Canada, Australia and the U.S.A.' ... In 2000 the U.S. Court of Appeals for the Ninth Circuit retreated from its prior interpretation, ... which these other courts had refused to follow, and endorsed the evolving common position, acknowledging that this position is also taken by the neighboring Canadian court."[54]

III. Cooperation by choice (= dialogue)

The only constellation of cooperation which deserves to be called dialogue is the **voluntary referencing of courts** located in different jurisdictions which are on equal footing. This is essentially what *Allan Rosas* describes as the fifth step in his system; in *Joachim Bornkamm's* system it is the second step, and the same holds true of *Claire L'Heureux-Dubé's* classification.

---

52 Case 145/02 Anheuser-Busch, 2004 ECR, I-10989, paras 49, 67.
53 See, e.g., Allan Rosas, Fundamental Rights in the Luxembourg and Strasbourg Courts, in: Baudenbacher et al., The EFTA Court Ten Years On, Oxford and Portland Oregon 2005, 163 ff.
54 Eyal Benvenisti, Reclaiming Democracy: The Strategic Uses of Foreign and International Law by National Courts, 102 Am. J. Int'l L. 241, 264 f.

As far as the EEA Agreement is concerned, it is to be noticed that national courts of EEA/EFTA States do not only make reference to the EFTA Court, but also to the ECJ und and that national courts of EC Member States have in a number of important cases cited EFTA Court jurisprudence[55].

IV. Combination of several constellations

Experience finally shows that in reality, cooperation may occur among several courts and that it may involve different constellations. Part of it may be prescribed by homogeneity rules whereas other elements may constitute voluntary dialogue.

D. Functions of judicial dialogue

I. Indicating the origin of the considerations underlying the judgment

It would seem that indicating the origin of the considerations a judgment is based on is simply a matter of intellectual honesty. The borrowing court would thereby **pay respect** to the lending court. In some jurisdictions like France and Italy, the traditional judicial style may, however, make it difficult to openly refer to foreign judgments.

II. Enhancing the rationality and the quality of judgments

Consulting foreign judgments gives additional input. Other judges have already thought the problem through. Taking into account foreign rulings will therefore enhance the rationality and quality of the judgment.

III. Securing influence on other courts

It has been said that high courts who take part in the modern global judicial dialogue have a better chance to export their own case law to other jurisdictions than courts which prefer to stand aside[56]. Courts of other countries may be reluctant to adopt jurisprudence from a court that does hardly actively participate in the global dialogue of judges.

---

55 See Baudenbacher, The EFTA Court, the ECJ, and the Latter's Advocates General, loc. cit., 109 ff.
56 L'Heureux-Dubé, loc. cit., 37 ff.

IV. Giving support to the referred court

Depending on the circumstances, this may constitute a very important function. The European Court of Human Rights has made reference to the case law of the Inter-American Court of Human Rights on a number of occasions[57]. It thereby beefs up the latter which is working in **politically difficult circumstances**. The EFTA Court too has profited from this kind of backing when the ECJ in its 1999 *Rechberger* judgment made reference to it's 1998 *Sveinbjörnsdóttir* ruling[58]. In *Sveinbjörnsdóttir*, the EFTA Court had acknowledged, against the opposition of the Governments of Iceland, Norway and Sweden as well as of the European Commission, that State liability is part of EEA law[59]. In the *Karlsson* case, which was decided in 2002, the Norwegian Government called on the EFTA Court to overrule *Sveinbjörnsdóttir*. The latter confirmed that ruling and explicitly mentioned the fact that the ECJ had cited *Sveinbjörnsdóttir* in *Rechberger*[60]. One will finally have to assume that support by another court may in certain conditions also be appreciated by a big and powerful court. This could, for instance, be so in **politically sensitive cases**. It may also happen that if a big court is split, the previous judgment of a small court on the same legal question will tip the balance.

V. Avoiding judicial conflicts

Experience finally shows that judicial dialogue is capable to secure the development of coherent case law across national boundaries. In times of globalization this is of particular significance. As Lord Bingham stated in House of Lords *Fairchild*:

> "In a shrinking world (in which the employees of asbestos companies may work for those companies in any one or more of several countries), there must be some uniformity of outcome, whatever the diversity of approach in reaching that outcome."[61]

E. Chances and risks of judicial dialogue

Judicial globalization means, as a matter of principle, that high courts must be prepared to take into account **judgments from every jurisdiction around the globe**, not just the jurisprudence of the most powerful Supreme Courts such as the ones of the United States, Britain, France, Germany, or the European Union. Judges' networks and judges' meetings may play an important role in that regard. One of the special features of judicial globalization is in fact that judges see each other in person.

---

57   See supra, footnote 17.
58   C-140/97, 1999 ECR, I-3499, at paragraph 39.
59   Case E-9/97, 1998 Rep. EFTA Ct., 115.
60   Case E-4/01, 2002 Rep. EFTA Ct., 240, 248 (at paragraph 25).
61   Cited in http://www.parliament.the-stationery-office.co.uk/pa/ld200102/ldjudgmt/jd020620/fchild-3.htm, last visited on 1 June 2009.

Concerns regarding the countermajoritarian problem and the democratic legitimacy of international judicial dialogue are exaggerated. They appear to be an American specialty. Lee Faircloth Peoples has rightly stated that the Advocates-General of the ECJ who routinely reference foreign case law have never been attacked in academic literature or in the press[62]. It is clear though that a court will not take over foreign solutions blindfoldedly, but will assess them in their specific context and if it concludes that they are persuasive it will make reference to them.

But there are **pitfalls**: First of all, it is debatable whether courts are able to fully understand the foreign judgment in context. Critics emphasize the dangers of selectivity and of bricolage. The language issue must also be mentioned in that respect. Moreover, the question arises what the **purpose** of judges' conversation is. Is it only an additional tool that would allow a court to confirm a result that it has found based on the interpretation of domestic law? Or does it have a similar significance as, for instance, the wording, the history, the purpose, and the overall scheme of a given provision? In many cases, the global conversation will simply provide a confirmation. That does not mean that it is useless. It may still serve as an additional support for the deciding court's approach to the matter[63].

There are, however, cases, where it was the look abroad that convinced a high court to opt for a certain solution. Examples of this are particularly to be found in cases where a high court fills gaps or overrules its earlier case law. In its 1971 *Agfa* judgment, the Austrian Supreme Court switched from national to international exhaustion in trademark law, explicitly following the examples of the German and the Swiss Supreme Court[64]. Experience also shows that courts may refer to a foreign judgment in a dialectic way by concluding that for certain reasons it should not be adopted into the case law of the court. Another dialectic technique is sometimes used in courts which adhere to an open vote and dissenting opinion system: Whereas the majority decides the case based on considerations stemming from national law, dissenting judges refer to judgments of foreign courts[65].

A practical question is whether a court should carry out a comparative analysis on its own motion or only if the parties plead accordingly. In most cases, the parties' **lawyers** will put the comparative material on the court's table. In the case of the ECJ, the **Advocates-General** will play an important part in that respect. But even in these cases, the Court will have to verify whether the foreign material can and should be used. The ECJ is in a particularly favorable situation in this regard since it has its own research department which may be asked to write a *note de recherche* in a given case. In addition,

---

62 Loc. cit., 221.
63 A case in point is the ruling in which the Swiss Supreme Court held that patents are not subject to international exhaustion. The judgment mentions a whole range of foreign jurisdictions (ATF 126 III 129 Kodak).
64 1974 Österreichische Blätter für Gewerblichen Rechtsschutz und Urheberrecht, 84.
65 See Baudenbacher, Judicial Globalization: New Development or Old Wine in New Bottles, 523 f.

the ECJ has the advantage of having a judge from each Member State. German courts may ask one of the Max Planck Institutes for expertise and, in Switzerland, the Swiss Institute of Comparative Law will provide assistance. Courts which do not have the resources for comparative research will hardly be able to participate in the global conversation. Generally speaking, there seems to be room for improvement in many courts. Databases containing foreign judgments should be established. But there may also be new challenges for attorneys as well as for universities and university institutes.

F. Conclusions

High courts are important players in a globalized and regionalized world. International judicial dialogue is a **necessity**. It works best in the fields of law which are characterized by convergence, such as IP law and competition law. Other areas are human rights law, and so-called borderline problems like assisted suicide, abortion, hate speech, gay and lesbian rights. The nature of democracy and the functioning of federal systems are further examples.

Allan Rosas has stated:

> *"I would end by saying that for me the question as to whether judges should be open to the outside world and be aware of discussions taking place in other relevant jurisdictions, is not any longer a question of opinion. It is a question of whether you are competent or incompetent. If you close your eyes, you belong to the latter category."* [66]

This writer concurs with that statement.

---

66 Methods of Interpretation – Judicial Dialogue, loc. cit., 191.

Discussion

CARL BAUDENBACHER
The floor is yours.

ERICH SCHANZE
Well this was a wonderful presentation which I enjoyed quite a bit. Obviously, there is a lot of *bricolage* going on even at distinguished courts and that is exactly what you were talking about. One of the most recent and famous examples, is the *Liechtenstein* case before the German Federal Supreme Court on the recognition of Liechtenstein companies. The Federal Supreme Court made the right decision by finally recognising Liechtenstein entities as juridical persons. But it did not understand the mechanism, it just followed the respective judgement of the ECJ, which is absolutely ridiculous, since the Federal Supreme Court had to decide a problem of private and national law. In the end, we got a correct decision, however, the reasoning was slightly off the mark.

Now a more fascinating example is the case of Scotland in the UK. That is going back to the beginnings of my teaching career, 40 years ago, when I started teaching in Edinburgh. The fact is, that there are two separate jurisdictions and only one court which does not really have a coordination function but is simply a final court, the House of Lords. And there are Scottish and English judges sitting together if a Scottish case comes on appeal. The most famous case in which an English judge misunderstood the Scottish law is *Donoghue v. Stevenson*[1]. By introducing the liability for negligence Lord Atkins, the English judge, had misinterpreted the Scottish rule of culpa. There was an old culpa liability in Scotland and he just wanted to re-reason it in his own terms. And so by mere accident he formed this new rule of negligence.

CARL BAUDENBACHER
Thank you very much. I may add that courts are obviously more likely to cooperate, if they have a huge research department, such as the ECJ. If the ECJ gets a major case, the Advocate General or the Judge Rapporteure will order a so-called *note de recherche*, which is very a efficient way of avoiding the *bricolage* problem. My court, The EFTA Court, unfortunately, does not have that. So we draw on opinions of Advocates General. We once had a case[2], in which, at least in my opinion, we should have made reference to the US Supreme Court. The case was about the question of whether collective

---

1   Donoghue v. Stevenson (1932) AC 562.
2   Case E-8/00 – Landsorganisasjonen i Norge (Norwegian Federation of Trade Unions) with Norsk Kommuneforbund (Norwegian Union of Municipal Employees).

agreements may fall foul of the competition law provisions of the EEA Agreements, which are identical in substance with those of the EC Treaty. The European Court of Justice was rather formal in its judgements in *Albany*[3] and related cases, by saying that as long as there was a collective agreement, whose purpose was to improve the working conditions of workers, the Court would not look into it.

Former Advocate General, Francis Geoffrey Jacobs, who wrote the opinion on the *Albany* case, was more open-minded towards competition and although the ECJ did not follow him, the EFTA Court did and even quoted him on this. So that is an example of creative homogeneity. But at the same time we realised that Advocate General Jacobs was basing his opinion on US Supreme Court case law, so it would have been the most natural thing for the EFTA Court to make that reference as well. But in a court with a majority of Nordic judges, to make a reference to the US Supreme Court in a labour law case would have been a deadly sin.

ULRICH HALTERN

I am a great admirer of judicial dialogue, and its existence and impact are utterly undeniable. I remember my time at the German Federal Constitutional Court as a legal clerk to Justice Dieter Grimm, where I was involved in drafting the *Caroline von Hannover*[4] decision which later fell into the hands of the European Court of Human Rights[5]. So you might think I am the burnt child that dreads the fire. But no – I am a great admirer of your idea that conceptualizing judicial dialogue is a matter of intellectual honesty, and there is much-needed legal realism behind what you are trying to achieve.

Still, let me try and pour some water into the wine by contextualising judicial dialogue and by making explicit what, it seems to me, is merely implicit in the notion of courts talking to each other. There is, I believe, a tacit deep-structure behind it that informs judicial dialogue and that fuels our hopes in a global rule of law.

Contemporary scholars of law tend to argue that what matters is not the origin of a rule, but the rationality of a rule. Rationality is based on reason; reason, like morality, knows no borders. Viewed from such a principled perspective, there is no reason to give priority to the state. Law thereby overcomes the limits of its own originating sources. In their place, scholars put human rights, global markets and the global protection of the environment. There is a strong normative pull towards functionality and management which leaves little space for state sovereignty: The world looks like a network of entangled expert regimes, generating social cooperation and organization on the local, regional, national, inter- and supranational level. This is the deep structure of global constitutionalism: the autonomy of the reasonable displaces the autonomy of the political. Globalized problems call for globalized solutions, and the way to get there

---

3   Case C-67/96 – Albany, ECR 1999, I-5751.
4   BVerfG, 1 BvR 653/96 vom 15.12.1999, BVerfGE 101, 361.
5   Appl.-No. 59320/00, June 24, 2004.

is through globalized reasonableness, working its way through law that pushes towards the universal. There is no reason, then, why judges should not be able to learn from their brethren in other countries. If the problems are the same, perhaps the solution might be the same as well. Obviously, this is a narrative of progress. If borders cease to matter, the dawning empire of reason, and of law, will level differences that seem atavistic. The political, tainted by nation-state myths, loses its demonic power. Rather than going to war over perceived national interests we will enter into reasonable deliberations over shared problems; rather than being bound to cloudy, mythical and organic national identities we will understand ourselves as fluid and rational. It is this narrative of progress that turns global constitutionalism – and its progeny, judicial dialogue – into an almost metaphysical promise.

We know enough to be suspicious of narratives of progress. We only need to gaze at the world as it is today to understand that we have not left behind political identities shaped by nation-states, that borders have meaning, that the empire of reason and law is far off, and that law has not at all overcome the limits of its own originating sources. Constitutions, for instance, appear to us as the words that have spoken the nation-state, and ourselves as citizens of that state, into existence. They embody ideal historical meaning which links the present to the past, to some point of imagined origin, and they construct an imaginative fabric that allows a state to inscribe its own identity into the identity of its citizens. They form a counter-narrative: a metaphysical and political deep structure that is largely ignored by theory but still has an important place in political practice. Law, in this sense, is more than the rationality of its contents. It also matters who spoke the words of the law – was it "our" popular sovereign? Or was it the result of some horse-trading between diplomats? Law, in the nation-state, is the storage space for political action we imagine to be the origin of "our" political community. It bears authentic witness to "our" history, to the lessons "we" have learned, and to the sacrifices "our" ancestors have made. Law is part of the memory of a political community, with all the mythical, mystical, and miraculous ingredients we thought we had left behind. In law, there is more at stake than solving problems and finding answers to the question of "what we should do". It is just as much about political identity and finding answers to the question of "who we are". Law sometimes appears as an expression of universal reason. But it is just as much the expression of a bounded, rooted, and totally contingent self-narrative of a political community. Memory is very different from history. Law is informed by both.

We see this everywhere. International law exerts little normative pull even with liberal western nation-states despite the fact that it is informed by the same values as they are. There is still a space for violence beyond law. Even liberal democracies torture. The United States Supreme Court is reluctant to rely on, cite, or even acknowledge decisions by other courts, even if those courts are as important and powerful as the European Court of Justice, the European Court of Human Rights, or the constitutional courts of other nation-states. The law that those courts expound is "different"; it is not informed by the peculiar American revolutionary tradition; it is not the storage space for revolutionary action; it was not handed down by the founding fathers, and young men in Gettysburg did not die for it. It is not part of the bounded American self-narrative that the Supreme Court is assigned to tell and maintain. In law, there is always an imagined, deep commonality at stake.

Judicial dialogue, then, may be part of the European experience. But it would be overly optimistic to expect a Europeanization of the world. Here, precisely, is the pitfall. When we talk about judicial dialogue and the globalisation of the law, there is always this counter-drive of political communities trying to understand and imagine themselves as political communities with all the myths, and all the "crazy" stuff that is still at work in the undercurrents of politics and of law. I believe we should not be too optimistic and not howl in triumph about the globalisation of law. Rather, we ought to realise that what we are actually doing is little more than to scratch the surface of political imagination.

CARL BAUDENBACHER

Thank you very much for this votum. I would agree with that. My own experience is limited to the European Economic Area. There we have common values, we even have a law that is identical in substance, which makes it an easy exercise. But if you go beyond such an organisation, there are a lot of pitfalls.

Still, there are areas of the law where this must be done and can be done in a very meaningful way, antitrust for instance. We saw yesterday how much antitrust is now moving towards convergence in Europe. But it goes beyond Europe. Antitrust and intellectual property law are probably the areas of economic law where you have global convergence. A patent is defined in exactly the same way all over the world, as well as a trademark. And a price cartel is the same as well, meaning that these are areas, that lend themselves to judicial dialogue. In the field of human rights however it is a whole other story. There are different traditions and different beliefs come into play. A perfect example would be capital punishment, which obviously is one of the concerns of American authors when it comes to this.

HANSPETER TSCHÄNI

Thank you for your presentation. I enjoyed it very much. I have a remark and a question. The remark pertains to something that you mentioned, that is a peculiar thing in the bilateral agreement between Switzerland and the European Union. I am speaking about the fact that Switzerland is only taking over the ECJ judgements delivered up until the point the bilateral agreement was signed. Now, I understand, that this may look a bit peculiar from the outside, but it is quite consistent with our approach when it comes to dealing with *acquis communautaire* in general, since it is the same thing when it comes to both, directives and ordinances. However, when it comes to the further development of *acquis communautaire*, there is another mechanism, that comes into play, and it is a tricky one, which is currently very disputed because of its political nature.

Then maybe a bit of an innocent question from a non-judge: Why is it so difficult for judges and courts to cooperate or to have a dialogue? All the countries that you mentioned in here are part of the OECD and one of the things that they do at the OECD – in a very successful manner I might add – is peer reviews for instance. Now, peer reviews at the beginning were looked at with a bit of suspicion because they could be interpreted as interference. But in the meantime the advantages have become pretty widely accepted. And competition authorities submit to peer reviews in the context of the OECD on a regular basis. So the innocent question is: Why has that idea not spread to the courts and to judges?

CARL BAUDENBACHER
Thank you very much for your remarks and for your questions. That is a tricky question but a very interesting one and I will have to think about it. Right now I would just say that a court is still very different from a competition authority. Whether competition authorities are truly independent is debatable. You always have the Ministers of Economic Affairs trying to interfere, and even strong competition authorities, like the Dutch one, seem to be in trouble because of that. It pretty much depends on whether your Minister of Economic Affairs is willing to let you do what you should or if he prefers to politically interfere. In Switzerland you hear a lot of stories about the Minister not wishing this and not wishing that. For the future I would not exclude anything, but peer reviews in the case of a court may also be politically dangerous. I give you an example. It is probably atypical but it just crossed my mind:

Let us assume that the following happens in a Member State either of the European Union or of EEA/EFTA. A judge's term comes to the end after six years and he or she says to his Minister that he would be willing to go on. The Minister replies that he may, but that the job will be put out for tender, so others can turn in their bits and as a consequence the current judge has to turn in his bit too if he wants to be re-appointed. That means that the judge is going to be subject to a review whether it is from peers or not remains open. In all honesty, I feel uneasy with this practice. In my opinion, it is not compatible with the judge's independence, but I am curious to know what Paul Mahoney, President of the Civil Service Tribunal of the EU, thinks about the issue.

PAUL MAHONEY
The appointment process of judges in general is regarded as constituting one of the main weaknesses of international courts in relation to their judicial independence. Criticisms are, for example, directed at the political colouring of the procedures for selecting candidates, at the lack of independent control of the qualifications of the candidates nominated by governments and – coming to the point alluded to by Professor Baudenbacher – at the relative precarity of the appointment.[6]

---

6   See Paul Mahoney, "The International Judiciary – Independence and Accountability", 7 The Law and Practice of International Courts and Tribunals 313, at 324–330 (2008).

Judges are appointed for limited-duration terms: six years, renewable, in most cases, which inevitably means that judges are very often looking to their re-appointment or to employment in the national public sector on expiry of their international term of office. In either event they will need to gain the support of their own government or, for international re-appointment, even that of other governments, because in some international systems, such as the UN system, there is a competitive election between States for a limited number of seats. As far as the Strasbourg Court is concerned, most of you are probably aware that there is a proposal under Protocol No. 14 to the ECHR, which has not yet come into force, to institute a system of one single, nonrenewable term of nine years – precisely to avoid the undesirable pressures inherent in renewable terms of office. On my small Tribunal there are only seven judges – unlike the main Court of Justice and the Court of First Instance in Luxembourg, there is not one judge for every Member State – and the terms are limited to six years. If a judge on the EU Civil Service Tribunal wishes to continue, he or she has to stand again and face competition. This has already happened. Three of the judges initially appointed after an open, competitive recruitment process when the Tribunal was set up in 2005, received truncated terms of three years; they were obliged to re-apply in 2008 and to go through the interview process in competition with other candidates before they were re-appointed for a second term.

In short, I agree with Professor Baudenbacher that the practice of re-appointment of sitting judges in international courts represents a serious and genuine problem. In particular, it carries the potential of undermining the independence of both the individual judge and the relevant court as an institution.

CARL BAUDENBACHER

Thank you. I would like to comment on the two other issues raised by Mr. Tschäni. Regarding the comment that the Federal Supreme Court of Switzerland ought to follow only old case law. I can see the logic of what you are saying clearly. But there is one exception to that rule. I am talking about EC law, which has been autonomously implemented in Switzerland, without there being a legal obligation, without there being a treaty. In a famous case[7], the Federal Supreme Court has held, that such autonomously implemented law must be interpreted in conformity with the newest ECJ case law. That is a clear dynamic element.

The second remark I want to make: Even if the Federal Supreme Court of Switzerland refuses to follow new ECJ case law, that does not guarantee that Switzerland is not going to be in political trouble. Let me give you a very famous example. Switzerland as Liechtenstein has a social security system under which they pay out rather high helplessness allowances to elderly people who are in need of help because they cannot get dressed anymore or they cannot go to the bathroom without help. These are payments that are non-contributory. And all the Member States have norms which state,

---

7   BGE 129 III 335.

that these payments are only made to residents, not the people who have worked in the country and then live abroad. Now, the Swiss Supreme Court ruled that it would not follow ECJ case law and would not open up these payments for people living in France or in Italy, for instance, reasoning that this would be new ECJ case law. Then the following happened:

It turns out, that same situation existed in Liechtenstein. The Commission, which was not very amused about the Federal Supreme Court findings, decided to seize the opportunity and contacted the EFTA Surveillance Authority. Some time later, the EFTA Surveillance Authority sued Liechtenstein before the EFTA Court. The EFTA Court decided against Liechtenstein and now the Commission is taking exactly this judgement and will harass the Swiss. Not for the time being. The Commission is smart enough to wait until all this discussion on the prolongation of free movement of persons is finished and on the extension of the bilateral agreement to Romania and Bulgaria and once this is done the Commission will present this bill to the Swiss.

MARK VILLIGER

A few remarks on the point of view of the European Court of Human Rights on judicial dialogue. The first one: Judges of the Strasbourg Court are appointed in respect of 47 states, which implies a priori that they are naturally open for judicial dialogue. They have learned to discuss, to deal with each other and to try and understand other cultures. That is the daily routine of Strasbourg, that is an essential part of the Court's work.

The second point: Judicial dialogue consists, among many other things, in the willingness of talking to others and listening. Like me, today. Unfortunately the Strasbourg Court, drowning in work, does not have the means to let judges go as often as they wish and should to other events and explain and listen. The judges are considered to be best in Strasbourg, deciding cases.

The third point which you also have mentioned is that our Court has a very efficient research department. This really makes a world of difference. To be shown what other courts on the national and international level have said on the same matter is extremely helpful. Not just to bolster, to boost our judgment, but to assist in finding the right decision in the right case.

The fourth point I wish to make is that the dialogue between Strasbourg and the national courts is special because it also takes place in the context of implementing the judgments of the Court. Within this context, the Court may well explain its judgments. But at the end of the day, the national authorities are bound by the judgment. The dialogue which you, President Baudenbacher, enjoy with the European Court of Justice is far more free.

A very last point regarding the election of judges. The Council of Europe and in particularly its Parliamentary Assembly insist that there are procedures whereby the national authorities prepare lists with three candidates for the post of judge. Now, I see your point completely, but there are also positive sides. What the Parliamentary Assembly wants to avoid is that a political friend of some national authority or minister is appointed candidate.

HJALTE RASMUSSEN

In my opinion, judicial dialogue is fascinating but enormously problematic. You have dealt in detail with your court taking over the *Francovich* case law from the ECJ and I wonder what was the communal memory behind *Francovich*, why was it decided at all? It was not prescribed by the treaty, it was a judicial invention. And where did this invention come from?

Mancini once said that what the Court in Luxembourg does is determined by a genetic code transmitted to the Court by the founding fathers.[8] How can you have a dialogue with a genetic code?

CARL BAUDENBACHER

Obviously, we did not dialogue with a genetic code, but with *Francovich*. It was existing case law and if I tried to explain that without at least this constitutional principle in the EEA law, the EEA Agreement would not have flown. It was that simple. There would not have been sufficient pressure on the Member States to comply. That was decisive. I may say here that the judgment was taken by a two against one vote because the overruled judge went public about it. The then Norwegian President of the Court had the delicacy of going before the Nordic Law Conference the year after and speaking up against the judgment in which he actually was the Judge Rapporteure. So it became very clear that the Icelander and I were the guilty people. But I have no bad feelings about that. I stand by it.

One last question and then we have to come to an end.

SANDRINE GIROUD-ROTH

Thank you. You mentioned a few times the Lugano Convention and the one way street of homogeneity, meaning the ECJ not mentioning the Contracting States' case law but the other way around. And I was wondering what your opinion on the new Lugano Convention is, since Protocol 1 states an equal and reciprocal obligation. Considering that, do you believe that the ECJ will ever mention Contracting States' case law?

CARL BAUDENBACHER

That is a very good point. In fact, when the new Lugano Convention was being negotiated, the EFTA States and in particular Switzerland insisted on a new formulation.

---

8 Mancini/Keeling, MLR 57(1994), 186.

And now this obligation, also on the ECJ, to make reference is no more just in a declaration, it is in a protocol which means it is part of the agreement itself.

There is a second novelty in that the ECJ is now also competent to give interpretation to the Lugano Convention, not only to the Brussels regulation as was previously the case. Whether this is going to work out in practice remains to be seen.

First commentators, for instance Professor Christian Kohler, the Director General of the Research Department at the ECJ, Professor at the Saarland University, has written on that subject. In his opinion one solution could consist in that the ECJ will continue not to make reference, but instead the Advocates General will. You know, the way judges function is sometimes funny. And the ECJ would then make reference to the paragraph in which the Advocate General has mentioned the Swiss or the Norwegian or Icelandic Supreme Court. I think we could go on forever but we have to stop here.

Focus:
Proportionality and the Margin of Appreciation: National Standards v. Harmonization by International Courts

Introduction

CARL BAUDENBACHER

Let us start with the third panel of this conference on the issue of proportionality and the margin of appreciation.

On March 7, 1994 the then California Governor, Pete Wilson, signed into a law a legislation referred to as "three strikes and you're out law", a criminal sentencing measure. This was then re-affirmed by the Californian voters. I would say that such legislation would hardly be thinkable in Europe because it would be deemed to be unproportionate in itself. The proportionality test – a typical European accomplishment – bears an inherent tension between, on the one hand, the obligation of a court to assess the suitability and the necessity of a measure which restricts a right or a freedom, and on the other hand, a margin of discretion offered to the Member States. In recent years, European courts have been under even closer observation by national media and politicians on whether they give sufficient leeway to the Member States. There may be various reasons for that, but one of the biggest ones may be a general fear of losing sovereignty to organisations such as the European Union or the WTO or even the EEA, which are perceived as rather abstract bureaucratic institutions that are out of touch with ordinary people.

Politicians – who are so-called "vote-maximizers" – have discovered that court bashing is a popular thing among potential voters. Even judge bashing has become an issue. I made that experience myself. At the time when the Norwegian *Gaming Machine* case[1] was brought before the EFTA Court, a very respected Norwegian newspaper published an article in which it speculated on how the three EFTA Court judges would vote in this case and sure enough I was "kindly" described as a judicial activist, because I would stand for free market principles. Now, if standing for free market principles in a set up which is deemed to realize an internal market makes you a judicial activist, I am proud to be one.

Right now there are two cases pending[2] before the EFTA Court, concerning the specific characteristic of national health systems, namely, whether you can claim to get socalled experimental treatment abroad, covered by the national social security system. In these cases the governments claim a wider margin of discretion than under a normal proportionality test. The same has been claimed in another sensitive field, namely, in the field of national gambling and betting legislation. Again, the argument was, that

---

1   Case E-1/06 – *EFTA Surveillance Authority v. The Kingdome of Norway* ("Gaming Machines").
2   Joined Cases E-11/07 and E-1/08 – *Olga Rindal and Therese Slinning v. Norwegian State*.

this field was politically very sensitive. The European courts should not look deeply into that, they should leave a margin of discretion.

This calls for numerous questions. I will just mention a few. First of all, what are the reasons of the closer observation of international and European courts? How far can international and supranational courts go? To what extent can and shall judges interfere with national policy choices? Where should the line for the margin of appreciation be? Should the margin be bigger in politically delicate cases? Do international judges have to restrain from a strict proportionality test in order to see their decisions being accepted in the Member States? Are there other factors which may influence acceptance? Is there a difference between public opinion and publicized opinion?

In my own court, the EFTA Court, I have also observed that public morals, meaning moral convictions in a society, are being used by the Member States under the heading of public policy as one kind of reason of overriding general interest. I may also recall the *Omega* case[3] on certain gaming facilities in Germany, in which a game was played in a so-called laser dome. The goal of the game was for a player to hit sensory tags, placed on the jackets worn by the other participants. To make a long story short, it was a killing simulation. The German authorities prohibited this kind of game and thus restricted the freedom to provide services under the public morals defence. On the one hand, the ECJ held: *"[...]the specific circumstances which may justify recourse to the concept of public policy may vary from one country to another and from one era to another. The competent national authorities must therefore be allowed a margin of discretion within the limits imposed by the Treaty,"*[4] referring at the same time to the *Van Duyn* case[5]. The ECJ also mentioned that different courts in Germany had agreed on the meaning of the fundamental value enshrined in the national constitution as human dignity. On the other hand, the ECJ held: *"[...] the concept of "public policy" in the Community context, particularly as justification for a derogation from the fundamental principle of the freedom to provide services, must be interpreted strictly, so that its scope cannot be determined unilaterally by each Member State without any control by the Community institutions. Thus, public policy may be relied on only if there is a genuine and sufficiently serious threat to a fundamental interest of society."*[6]

The *Omega* case involved a fundamental right, human dignity, which referring to the ECJ is also protected in Community law. The Court held it immaterial, the fact that in Germany human dignity has a special status as an independent fundamental right

---

3   Case C-36/02 – *Omega Spielhallen- und Automatenaufstellungs-GmbH v. Oberbürgermeisterin der Bundesstadt Bonn*, ECR 2004, I-09609.
4   Case C-36/02 – *Omega Spielhallen- und Automatenaufstellungs-GmbH v. Oberbürgermeisterin der Bundesstadt Bonn*, ECR 2004, I-09609, par. 31.
5   Case C-41/74 – *Yvonne van Duyn v. Home Office*, ECR 1974, 01337.
6   Case C-36/02 – *Omega Spielhallen- und Automatenaufstellungs-GmbH v. Oberbürgermeisterin der Bundesstadt Bonn*, ECR 2004, I-09609, par. 30.

under its national constitution. A similar Community protected right was not pleaded in the gambling cases.

I was thus wondering, in what consist legally relevant differences from one Member State to another with regard to public morals? How do such differences directly influence national policies, for instance anti addiction policies? In the context of WTO law, I believe that the Appellate Body will probably have to answer more and more questions in that direction, too.

Let me then just briefly introduce the three gentlemen here on the panel. I would suggest that we start with Judge Villiger. Professor Villiger is a judge on the European Court of Human Rights (ECrtHR) and he is in the same situation as I am. We are both Swiss nationals but we have been nominated by the Principality of Liechtenstein and been appointed by common accord of the respective governments. He has been with the European Court for many years as a member of the registry and he is extremely familiar with the case law of the Court. And since it is your Court which has developed the famous margin of appreciation doctrine, we are particularly happy that you agreed to sit on this panel.

Then the gentleman on my right hand is Mr. Vlaemminck, a well-known attorney from Brussels. I have asked him to join us in this conference because he has pleaded two huge cases before my court and I have learned that he is the number one specialist in gambling and betting law, usually representing the governments in these cases. I think he had his hands in all of the cases decided by the ECJ, since the *Schindler* case[7] in 1994.

And on my left hand there is Professor Hjalte Rasmussen from the University of Copenhagen School of Law. He has been a well known critic of the European Court of Justice for many years, very outspoken and most entertaining. We met for the first time last year in Salzburg and at the end of a dinner, with a little bit of wine, we said to each other: "It's a pity that we didn't get to know each other earlier." Better now than never.

---

7   Case C-275/92 – *Her Majesty's Customs and Excise v. Gerhart Schindler and Jörg Schindler*, ECR 1994, I-01039.

Proportionality and the Margin of Appreciation: National Standard Harmonisation by International Courts

MARK VILLIGER [1]

The topic of this panel is proportionality and the margin of appreciation viewed within the framework of national standards and the harmonisation by international courts. I shall say some words on this topic from the point of view of the European Convention on Human Rights (ECHR) and its interpretation by the Strasbourg Court.

I may at the same time use the occasion to convey to you the good wishes of the European Court of Human Rights and its President for the success of the conference and I should also add that the views expressed here are entirely my own.

When looking at the topic, two questions arise. First, how is it possible to harmonise discretion, the margin of appreciation? After all, discretion implies according to the dictionary the freedom to decide on one's own. And second, how should an international court go about to reach this aim?

Let me start by decomposing the topic, by breaking it down into its various parts. According to the Strasbourg case law, issues of proportionality and margin of discretion or appreciation arise mainly in the context of Articles 8 to 11 concerning the right to respect for private and family life, freedom of expression and so on. You will find the texts of these provisions on the hand out in my document which is in your file. Of course, the principle of proportionality and the margin of appreciation are also embedded in other guarantees, for instance, the right to property. But I shall concentrate for the sake of clarity on Articles 8 to 11.

Now Articles 8 to 11 each contain the same structure. In their first paragraphs the provisions enshrine certain rights, whereas their second paragraphs list these three conditions for the possible justification of an interference with these rights. The three conditions are the same in all four articles, though they are formulated slightly differently. Thus, to justify an interference, for instance, with the freedom of expression in Article 10, its paragraph two stipulates first that the measure must be lawful, prescribed by law; and second, that it must correspond to the public interest. In the descriptive language of paragraph 2 it must be in the interests of national security and so on.

---

1   Prof. Dr. Mark Villiger, Judge at the European Court of Human Rights in respect of the Principality of Liechtenstein, "Titularprofessor" at the University of Zurich.

Third, the interference which is to be justified with the freedom of expression must be necessary in a democratic society. It is here, in respect of this third condition, that proportionality and the margin of appreciation come to play.

The requirement "necessary in a democratic society" has been interpreted by the Strasbourg Court as meaning, on the one hand, that the interference with the individual's rights must reflect a pressing social need and must generally be proportionate. On the other hand, when examining proportionality, the domestic authorities and in particular the domestic courts enjoy a certain margin of appreciation which may vary from one case to another.

That the interference must reflect a pressing social need, implies that the grounds of public interest invoked must be convincing and must be of a certain urgency. If a critical newspaper is banned, for instance, on grounds of national security, to take an example under Article 10, then this ground must truly apply. This ground cannot be put forward as a fig leaf which hides other, in particular, arbitrary reasons for banning the newspaper, for example, its criticism of the government.

Next, the interference must be proportional. The public interest in interfering with a particular basic right in question must be balanced with the interests of the individual. For instance, when prohibiting the newspaper on grounds of national security, the domestic courts must strike a fair balance between the interest of the public in order and security and the individual's rights in its rights. To take our example, on the one hand: how far did the newspaper endanger national security, and how far did it leak example military secrets. And on the other: the interests of the newspaper in its own right to freedom of the press.

Naturally, weighing these different interests is a balancing exercise. And the Strasbourg Court leaves to the domestic authorities a margin of appreciation to undertake this balancing exercise. However, even in this area the domestic courts are not completely free. In particular, they are not entitled arbitrarily to undertake the balancing exercise. The Strasbourg Court is called upon to examine extent and limits of this margin of appreciation and how it was exercised. Still, bearing in mind the liberty which authorities actually enjoy, the Court limits its control to that of, I quote, a European supervision, end of quote.

Let me here dwell briefly on the questions where the concept of the margin of appreciation stems from and why the Strasbourg Court employs it.

The notion of margin of appreciation originally derives from national administrative law. Administrative authorities are often called upon to take decisions which permit a certain discretion allowed by law. In most systems a distinction is made between a full review of administrative decisions interpreting undefined terms of law and a limited review of decisions taken in the exercise of a discretion allowed by law. In the latter case, all that is reviewed by the higher instance of the administrative authorities is whether discretion was excessive and was exercised in accordance with the law. The latter method lies at the basis of the method employed by the Strasbourg Court under the Convention.

The Strasbourg Court employs the margin of appreciation, *inter alia*, as it re-enforces the principle of subsidiarity which lies at the basis of the entire European Convention on Human Rights.

The principle of subsidiarity, which is indirectly mentioned in Article 1 of the Convention, implies that in a given community it falls in the first place to smaller, lower social units to assume responsibility for functions of the society; and the larger, higher units should only take over in so far as the smaller unit is unable to do so. Viewed from the point of view of the Convention on Human Rights, subsidiarity implies that the protection of human rights falls first of all to the member states and their courts and authorities. And only to the extent that they do not protect human rights, will the Court step in.

The principle of subsidiarity finds an important, even central application in the margin of appreciation. A further emanation is, for instance, the necessity of the exhaustion of domestic remedies before filing an application with the Court.

So it is on account of the principle of subsidiarity that domestic courts have an area, in particular under Articles 8 to 11, where they may themselves determine whether or not an interference is required, in particular when undertaking the balancing exercise of the various elements is concerned.

Now, it is in the nature of things that this margin of appreciation of domestic judges is highly variable. But the variability, the fluctuating nature of the margin of appreciation does not stop there. For the Strasbourg Court, when examining the exercise of the margin of appreciation by the domestic judges, itself enjoys a margin of appreciation. So we are faced here with an area of judicial activity of domestic courts, where domestic judges have a certain discretion, but also the Strasbourg Court when examining whether a domestic judge has overstepped his or her discretion.

It is here where the important question is raised and indeed the criticism sets in. Is it possible to predict, to foresee how the European Court will assess in future the margin of appreciation as employed by the national courts?

The Strasbourg Court is fully aware of these difficulties and has from the outset formulated conditions and principles aiming at contributing towards predictability, foreseeability and rationality in this area.

Let me mention three conditions or principles. One concerns the Court's case law which attributes to different guarantees in the Convention, different limits of the margin of appreciation. The second principle relates to certain public interests where the Court *a priori* envisages a large margin of appreciation, for instance, as regards morals and religion. The third principle concerns the means which the Court envisages to prevent arbitrariness. Let me deal with these three different principles in turn.

As to the first principle or condition. The limits set up by the Court in its case law on the margin of appreciation vary within the Articles 8 to 11, from one article to another. The most limited, the narrowest margin of appreciation would probably be left to a domestic judge balancing interferences under Article 8 of the Convention with a person's private life. And here in particular with that person's right to physical and personal integrity or that person's sexual determination. Here must be a quite overriding public interest which outweighs the individual's rights.

At the other side of the spectrum, the widest margin of appreciation could probably fall to authorities determining rights of coalition as in Article 11 of the Convention, among them, for instance, the right to found a trade union, to conduct collective bargaining and in particular the right to strike.

But even within a Convention provision, the margin of appreciation varies according to the Court's case law. Take Article 10 concerning the right of freedom of expression. The latter, in particular a single person's and individual's freedom of expression, is one of the most important human rights of all. Without the freedom of expression, one cannot complain about other human rights' violations for example. And yet nuances can be seen, particularly as regards the authorities' discretion when balancing interferences with this right.

I will mention two sides of the spectrum. On one hand, one could say that the straightforward expression of a personal opinion, political or otherwise, implies a very narrow margin of appreciation for national courts. For the national courts, the personal opinion of the individual must weigh heavily in the balance. Conversely according to the Strasbourg case law, economic speech, for instance, by means of economic publications, entails a larger margin of appreciation for the national courts. The example of unfair competition is illustrated in this respect by a Swiss case, which, although not the youngest, is a very illustrative one. It is that of *Hertel v. Switzerland*.

The applicant Hertel was an engineer who believed that microwave ovens were carcinogenic. He frequently published studies along these lines. Often his studies were accompanied by a picture of a skeleton with a scythe, which is the symbol of death. This upset the Swiss association of producers of small electrical household equipment, which sued the applicant on account of unfair competition. They won and the applicant was prohibited from criticising microwave ovens, mainly as his conclusions were not scientifically proven. In Strasbourg the Court found a breach of the freedom of expression under Article 10 of the Convention. While it considered that in the area of true unfair competition States had a considerable margin of appreciation – for instance, no issue arises if a State prohibits publicity saying that this car is better than another car – the matter is different where a person is in fact putting forward its own personal point of view, even if this personal opinion does not find widespread scientific support. Here the domestic authorities have less leeway when balancing interferences with the freedom of expression.

There is an equally illustrative sequel to the case of *Hertel v. Switzerland*, a Part Two, so to say. After he won in Strasbourg, the applicant again published his theories that microwave ovens could be deadly. Again proceedings were brought against him. This time the Swiss Federal Court in view of the Strasbourg judgment authorised the publications though it obliged the applicant in a footnote of each published study to add that the views he was expressing were not scientifically proven. A second time the applicant applied to the Strasbourg Court, which this time found that the interference with the applicant's free speech was limited and lay within the authority's margin of appreciation.

So, I can summarise that the Court has carved out guarantees which allow for a limited margin of appreciation and others where the authorities enjoy a wider one.

This, I put to you as my first reply to the question in the title of the conference. It is with this case law, to which the European Court adheres faithfully, that it aims at harmonising different national standards.

The second principle whereby the Court provides for predictability and foresee ability concerns certain public interests in respect of which the Court *a priori* envisages a large margin of appreciation. These public interests concern, summarily speaking, the protection of morals and of religious feelings. Here, two classic cases in the Court's case law may be mentioned.

One is the case *Müller v. Switzerland* concerning a well-known Swiss artist, Felix Müller. His paintings depicting, *inter alia*, sodomy and blasphemy were exhibited in Fribourg in Switzerland where they shocked an underage girl to such an extent that her father complained to the Fribourg authorities. The authorities prohibited the exhibition but also confiscated the pictures. Upon application, Strasbourg considered that the authorities enjoyed considerable discretion, a large margin of appreciation, when deciding whether the paintings breached local morals and Strasbourg accepted the prohibition of the exhibition. However, it found that the margin of appreciation was far more limited in respect to the confiscations. Indeed, the applicant had been asked to display his paintings in many museums all over the world. Here the artist's interests and his freedom of expression outweighed the interests of the Fribourg population for Müller not to exhibit the paintings in London, Tokyo and New York.

The other classic case, *Preminger v. Austria*, concerned a film, "The Council of Heaven" ("Das Liebes-Konzil"), which was to be screened in Innsbruck in Austria. The story depicts God the Father as a tottering old man, Jesus as a cretin and Mary as a loose woman. The film was prohibited and a complaint duly filed in Strasbourg. The Court found that it did not breach the local domestic authorities' margin of appreciation if they considered the film as an abusive attack on the Roman Catholic religion according to the conception of the public.

So, the second condition whereby the Court assures predictability and foresee ability, is ensured by providing for certain public interests where the margin of discretion is comparatively large.

When examining the third manner in which the Court controls the margin of appreciation, the underlying consideration is that the freedom which the national judge enjoys is not unlimited or unfettered. The discretion which a judge enjoys is not tantamount to arbitrariness, quite the contrary.

How does this translate into the Court's daily practice? What does this mean for the national authorities? The lesson is that they are required to motivate their judgments even when, actually particularly when, they are enjoying discretion. The better the authorities explain how they employ their discretion, their appreciation – for instance why they prohibited the applicant from choosing a particular name, from frequenting a church, from demonstrating outside a government building, from joining a trade union –, the better they motivate their decision, the more the reasons given are in themselves consistent and convincing, the more it transpires that the margin of appreciation was not employed in an arbitrary manner, the less the Strasbourg Court can interfere with this reasoning and the less it will find other, better reasons in order to reach a different solution. In other words, good, thorough, convincing reason ties to some extent, I would even say to a considerable extent, the Strasbourg Court's hands.

But then the opposite must equally hold true. The less the domestic authorities motivate their decisions, the larger will be the freedom which the Strasbourg Court will enjoy to reach a different conclusion and, in particular, to find that the decision taken breached the Convention.

So, I submit that the third reply to the question in the title of the conference is: the Court harmonises differing national standards by requiring domestic courts fully to motivate any discretion which they have employed when interfering with fundamental rights.

If we stand back and look at the results, are we able to draw further conclusions? I would submit that this is possible. On the one hand, I believe I have been able to reply, at least to some extent, to the often strong criticism directed against the Strasbourg Court, namely that all is flux and nothing is certain. The Strasbourg judges themselves have thoroughly considered the problem over many decades and have come up with the case law mentioned which aims at harmonising the discretion employed by the domestic judges.

On the other hand, I am the first to admit that this is not an area of fast and easy recipes for the domestic courts. Those expecting a doctrine on the margin of appreciation which can be applied as a sort of matrix to each case as it comes up will be disappointed. Domestic courts are not machines, they are called upon closely to examine and appreciate individual circumstances of the cases presented to them and to give reasons for every step in their reasoning, and all the while to consider the case law of the Strasbourg Court concerning the varying margin of appreciation of different rights in Articles 8 to 11. This is not an easy task. Of course the Strasbourg case law is made by judges for judges, by professionals for professionals.

The Strasbourg Court has a further obligation in all of this. It must never forget the principle of subsidiarity. The European States did not intend the Strasbourg Court to act as a first instance body. They wish it to be the last instance. It is mainly up to the domestic courts at the front, as it were, to deal with the situation.

In the light of all of these considerations it is all the more important that the Strasbourg Court entertains an ongoing communication with their counterparts, the domestic judicial professionals, to listen to their difficulties when applying the Strasbourg case law, when dealing with this margin of appreciation. I see that the present conference falls into this wider framework of communication between the European and the international and national judiciary. So I would thank you warmly for having given me the opportunity to explain to you the European side.

Discretionary Power of States in the ECJ & EFTA Court: The Difficult Case of Gambling Services

PHILIPPE VLAEMMINCK[1]

First of all, I would like to clarify that even though you presented me as a lawyer representing the Belgian government in most of the gambling cases, today I am sitting here with the sole purpose of expressing my very own views.

You also presented me as an expert in gambling laws and I would just like to add, that I entered that field by accident. Starting in this area as a European lawyer in 1992, when the first case on gambling came before the ECJ, the *Schindler* case[2], I was really not expecting this to go beyond the one case and I certainly did not see coming that gambling would become a huge political problem in the European Union. Since then, however, I have been attracting many of these controversial cases, so much so that I kind of felt obliged to continue working in this field. However, even though here I am being presented as a gambling lawyer, let me tell you, that in other situations I am presented as a banana lawyer, since I also handled a WTO case in bananas and, another very controversial case, the *Léon Van Parys*[3] case before the ECJ.

Still, there are similarities between both areas. In both of them the discussion at the end of the day is about "the discretion" available to the ones who have to regulate it: the Member States regarding the gambling and the European Commission and the Council when it comes to bananas. I am sure that Dr. Jacques Bourgeois will come back on this controversial question since there was a discussion about the questions, as to what extent the European Union was obliged to implement the WTO dispute settlement recommendations and what the latitude given to the Community was.

But coming back to gambling. The peculiar aspects of gambling are mainly driven by the fact that basically nobody would believe that gambling had anything to do with European law. When I first mentioned to a civil servant in Belgium – around 1988 – that it could well be that lotteries would become a European problem, he laughed it away and said: *"No, because it is not an economic activity. It has nothing to do with economics."* The same question was raised when in 1997 I spoke in Portugal at a conference, saying that it could well be that the United States would face a WTO dispute about gambling.

---

1 Attorney at Law, Head of the Law office Vlaemminck & Partners, Brussels.
2 ECJ, *Schindler*, 24 March 1994, C-275/92, ECR [1994]-1039.
3 ECJ, *Léon Van Parys v. BIRB*, 1 March 2005, C-377/02, ECR [2005]-1465.

A US civil servant responded: *"No way, because this is a question of morality and order."* Both civil servants were convinced, that an interference in those policy areas, which are rightly considered to be sensitive, would not be possible.

Today, we see it in a very different light. There has been a considerable number of cases. Just to give you an overview, up until now the ECJ decided 14 cases[4], the EFTA Court another two and finally there is the dispute in the WTO which is still a matter of debate[5]. I would even say, looking at what is coming up in the ECJ – there are a lot of new referrals – that we do not know what will be the end of it[6]. The Swedish courts just referred another case[7] and in the meantime there is also a debate between the Community and the United States following a complaint by the Remote Gambling Association in the UK under the Trade Barriers Regulation about the question of the way the United States has implemented the WTO dispute settlement recommendations[8]. Although the Commission has concluded that there might be a violation of WTO law by the USA for past trade, it is unlikely that another WTO case on gambling services will be initiated.

Is there a need in this area to find a solution? The ECJ is quite fed up with the enormous number of cases it is facing, which is understandable since all of them are mainly driven by the lack of a political consensus, the lack of willingness of the Member States and the Commission to come to a regulatory framework[9]. The European Court of Justice does not want to replace the politicians, but at the same time it is faced with a situation in which it actually has not much of an alternative.

---

4   ECJ, *Schindler*, 24 March 1994, C-275/92, ECR [1994]-1039; ECJ, *Läärä*, 21 September 1999, C-124/97, ECR [1999]-6067; ECJ, *Zenatti*, 21 October 1999, C-67/98, ECR [1999]-7289; ECJ, *Gambelli*, 6 November 2003, C-243/01, ECR [2003]-13031; ECJ, *Lindman*, 13 November 2003, C-42/02, ECR [2003]-13519; ECJ, *Anomar*, 11 September 2003, C-6/01, ECR [2003]-8621; ECJ, *Placanica and others*, 6 March 2007, joined cases C-338/04, C-359/04 and C-360/04, ECR [2007]-1891; ECJ, *Commission v Italy*, 13 September 2007, C-260/04, ECR [2007]-7083; ECJ, *Centro Europa*, 31 January 2008, C-380/05, ECR [2008]-349; ECJ, *Unibet*, 13 March 2007, C-432/05, ECR [2007]-2271; ECJ, *KommAustria*, 18 October 2007, C-195/06, ECR [2007]-8817.
5   Appellate Body Report, *United States – Measures Affecting the Cross-Border Supply of Gambling and Betting Services*, November 10, 2004, WT/DS285/AB/R.
6   ECJ, *Winner Wetten*, C-409/06; ECJ, *Liga Portuguesa de Futebol Profissional*, C-42/07; ECJ, *Markus Stoss and others*, joined cases C-316/07 and others; ECJ, *Carmen Media Group*, C-46/08; ECJ, *Engelmann*, C-64/08; ECJ, *Club Hotel Loutraki*, C-145/08; ECJ, *Betfair*, C-203/08; ECJ, *Zeturf*, C-212/08; ECJ, *Dutch Ladbrokes*, C-258/08; ECJ, *Langer*, C-235/08.
7   ECJ, Sjöberg e.a. C-447/08 & 449/08.
8   Commission Notice of 11 March 2008 of initiation of an examination procedure concerning obstacles to trade within the meaning of Council Regulation (EC) No 3286/94 consisting of the US ban on foreign internet gambling and its enforcement, OJ 2008, C 65/5.
9   It has to be mentioned that in the meantime the Member States have been discussing under the French Presidency the issue of gambling services in the Services & Establishment Working Group. During the Competitiveness Council of December 2008, the Council did call, along the lines of art. 208 EC, upon the Commission to participate actively in the debate – See Progress Report of the French Presidency, "Gambling and betting: legal framework and policies in the Member States of the EU", dated 27 November 2008, 16022/08. In a resolution of the European Parliament adopted with a very large majority the Parliament made the same call – see EP resolution of 10 March 2009 on the integrity of online gambling, 2008/2215(INI).

If we see what happens in the Member States, it is quite clear that there is a need for the European courts to go further in defining and balancing the question of proportionality assessment. The most recent gambling case before the European Court of Justice, in which we have no judgment yet but instead the Advocate General's opinion[10], is the *Liga Portuguesa de Futebol Profissional* case. During the hearing the Judge Rapporteur, Konrad Hermann Theodor Schiemann, did not only question the parties involved but questioned all the Member States on the extent that the Court could take over the proportionality assessment from the national courts. Whether it was permissible to do so in the absence of common understanding – in the absence of a true judicial dialogue – is the actual question.

We also see that at a national level. Let us take a look at Germany, for instance: If I remember correctly, there were more than 100 cases before German courts, relating to the question of restrictions on gambling, in which you see a variety of decisions which almost exceeds the number of German courts. This actually proves that the answers currently given by the European Court of Justice as well as by the EFTA Court are far from providing legal security. Therefore, there is obviously a need for ways to cooperate in order to resolve the problems of proportionality assessment and discretionary power of the Member States.

Let me explain to you the reason why this is so difficult in gambling. In the first case, the *Schindler* case, the discussion was about whether the European Court of Justice had any competence in this matter. Many Member States were saying, that based upon the fundamental principles of civil law, the Court could not have any competence. They were referring to the principle that contracts of chance were illegal as they were violating principles of the public order as mentioned in civil law. The Member States at the time made many references to the *Banque Alsacienne versus Koestler* case[11], in which somebody speculating on the financial markets refused to pay back his bank by invoking the exception of gambling. The case was referred to the ECJ. It held that, notwithstanding the question of freedom of services, it could agree that the exception of gambling could be validly invoked.

In *Schindler* the following questions were raised: Does the Court have competence in this matter? Is a lottery an economic activity? The Court in *Schindler* was very reluctant to get to the bottom line of the proportionality, which is one of the main reasons why it has been strongly criticised by legal writers. The Court's reasoning was relying entirely upon the Member States' argumentation that one cannot disregard moral, religious and cultural aspects. A lottery is a form of gambling and therefore, there is a high risk of crime and fraud. Additionally, there are risks for social disorder and individual problems, like addiction. And finally, although it is not an objective on its own, there is a significant contribution to the financing of good causes. This last element is indeed

---

10 Opinion of AG Bot in the case *Liga Portuguesa de Futebol Profissional*, C-42/07, 14 October 2008.
11 ECJ, *Banque Alsacienne v Koestler*, 24 October 1978, 15/78, ECR [1978]-1971.

making this a very sensitive question. Everybody knows that in all the states, lotteries contribute to a large extend to the funding of good causes like for instance culture, sport, development aid, etc. Just to give an example, the UK national lottery will fund the London Olympic Games and therefore it is absolutely essential that the monopoly of lotteries in the UK remains in force. Although the UK is one of the Member States favouring a more market driven approach of gambling services.

These are the reasons why it is such a sensitive area and why the Court immediately added in paragraph 61 of *Schindler*, which says that there has to be a sufficient degree of latitude to determine what is required to protect the players. The strange thing was that the Court did not even go beyond that point and did not even say that the referring English court had to make a further assessment as to whether the restrictions are proportionate. The ECJ just stated that it seemed useful to have these restrictions and therefore, it accepted them as such, without indeed asking the national court to make any further assessment.

The case that followed was about slot machines in Finland[12]. In this slot machine case the Court reiterated what had been said five years earlier in *Schindler*, by accepting all of the four elements that were driving the Member States policies. However, this time the Court added that it would be necessary to see whether those reasons guaranteed the achievement of the aims pursued, without going beyond what was necessary in order to achieve them. That was a first step towards a proper proportionality assessment by the national courts. Further on, the Court went on by declaring that it was up to the Member States to determine the extent of protection they want to grant to their citizens. Additionally, it held that the fact that a Member State had opted for a system of protection, which was different from the one adopted by another Member State, could not affect this assessment.

The Court concluded that the individual Member States had the competence to make the actual assessment and that there was a large latitude that had to be taken into consideration. At the end of the judgment the Court provided a short guideline of how to make the proportionality assessment by mentioning that the only thing a Member State had to do, is to find out whether the measure was disproportionate.

Summarising those two cases, we see a very lenient approach towards the policy of the Member States in these first gambling cases. Nobody was expecting that this would go beyond that, probably because gambling services at the time were only an issue of land based activities. The reason Member States have such an extensive amount of problems today is largely due to the fact that nowadays the internet is playing a very important role in the gambling sector. Gambling, unfortunately, became the second biggest economic internet activity after pornography.

---

12   ECJ, *Läärä*, 21 September 1999, C-124/97, ECR [1999]-6067.

Now, let me immediately come to the *Lindman* case[13]. *Lindman* has been quoted also in the current hearing of the *Liga Portuguesa de Futebol* case, by the Judge Rapporteur, Schiemann, because it was the first gambling case, in which the Court took over the proportionality assessment. *Lindman* was about a player from Finland who gambled abroad, brought back the winnings to his own jurisdiction and was taxed on them. Had he won in the Finnish lottery, he would have been exempt from taxation. Clearly, it was a matter of discriminatory taxation. Notwithstanding that, the Finnish government was saying that taxing earnings on foreign lotteries was part of the need to keep the gambling environment limited. They needed to have a certain form of control. The Court denied that, by stating in its reasoning that the file transmitted to the Court by the referring court, disclosed no statistical or other evidence, which would lead to a conclusion regarding the gravity of risk connected to playing games of chance. It was very important that the Court mentioned the need for evidence of the risk.

In later cases the Court walked away from *Lindman*, but at least it provided the governments of the Member States with more substantial guidelines. In *Zenatti* there was a first step into that direction by saying that it could accept the four reasons the Member States invoked, but those reasons all together had to prove a concern to bring about a genuine diminution in gambling opportunities. As far as the financing of the good causes was concerned, they could only constitute an incidental beneficial consequence.

We come then to the *Gambelli* case which has been quoted as being the most controversial of all. In the *Gambelli* case the Court went into a partial assessment of proportionality on its own and a partial referral to the national courts, which made it even more difficult. Indeed the Court held in paragraph 69 of the judgment that as far as the authorities incited and encouraged consumers to participate in gambling, they could not invoke public order. With this statement the Court did set a borderline. By encouraging people to play – and in the case of *Gambelli* the Italian legislature had indeed confirmed that they wanted to expand gambling because it raised more money for the state – the state would forfeit his rights to invoke public order and therefore to limit the access to the market. Additionally they referred an other aspect back to the national courts, namely the applicability of criminal sanctions to people who are offering (from the UK) betting services on the Italian market without a licence.

This caused an ongoing debate in many Member States about whether the restrictive environment created by the states can go as far as applying criminal sanctions to people who have no licences to operate gambling activities.

Gambelli was the case which actually led to these 100 cases in Germany. In one case the judge said that all restrictions have indeed to be banned and the market must be opened. However, other judges held that the market must be kept closed. It ended up

---

13 ECJ, *Lindman*, 13 November 2003, C-42/02, ECR [2003]-13519.

in one of the most important, most productive and constructive judgments, which was the given on 28 March 2006 by the Bundesverfassungsgericht. I believe that part of the solution in gambling cases can be resolved by applying the same reasoning, the German Constitutional Court came up with in this case.

I also want to make reference to your own cases in the EFTA Court. I think the contribution of the EFTA Court – we can actually say today that in the *Portuguese* case the contribution of the EFTA Court was largely quoted by the Member States – was a step forward. The main contribution – although there was a clear intention to apply the homogeneity principle – was that one of the benchmarks the European Court has provided the Member States with in *Placanica*, was applied in a broader way. The theory of controlled expansion of gambling opportunities accepted by the European Court of Justice in order to improve the fight against crime, in the Norwegian cases was applied also to policies aiming at protecting the consumer. By doing so, the EFTA Court substantially clarified the situation.

Finally, coming to the WTO. Where is the important difference between the WTO assessment and the assessment made by the European courts? In my opinion, the biggest difference is the way that the public order and public morality question was initially assessed. While the European Court admitted that based on sociocultural and historical differences, questions of public morality and public order in gambling were a matter of national assessment and individual views, the WTO Panel in the *US-cross border supply of gambling services* case accepted that public morality could be invoked because there was a general understanding that in most of the states around the world gambling had a certain connection with morality. This was heavily criticised in the legal literature. It is not acceptable to make an assessment of morality based upon common standards in the world, as you have to base the morality concept on individual standards.

The Appellate Body overruled the assessment made by the panel to a certain extend. While the panel clearly said the United States should have negotiated with Antigua, the Appellate Body held that the assessment on public order was an individual assessment that the United States could make independently.

Let me turn immediately to the point where we are today. The courts have been saying there is a wide margin of discretion. They have also been saying that there are certain guidelines for the public order assessments. Notwithstanding that, today we are in a situation in which there are 27 cases in the European Court, out of which 14 have already been decided and 13 are still pending.

In the *Liga Portuguesa de Futebol* case, Judge Rapporteur Schiemann really tried to break through by having a debate with all the Member States. But still we do not know where it will go. So the question remains: What can an international court do in that regard to find a proper solution? These are sensitive areas. Areas, in which the consequent application of the fundamental freedoms could lead to chaotic situations in some

Member States. The courts have accepted that there is a reason for invoking public order. But at the same time we know that the practical assessment is not there.

I want to end my presentation by referring to the decision of the Bundesverfassungsgericht from 2006 and thereby addressing two questions.

One is, can we indeed apply a kind of precautionary principle in the gambling cases? Can we refer to the status of knowledge in addiction to avoid opening up the markets in case of uncertainty of the risks of addiction of certain forms of gambling? The Bundesverfassungsgericht has, in its decision, referred four times to this question: the present state of knowledge, the present stage of research. They have done it several times by saying they could accept restrictions because the present state of research did not prove that there was no risk for addiction in certain areas. In my view, that is the first element that could be taken into consideration in proportionality assessment, also in areas which are very sensitive.

The second point is that the Bundesverfassungsgericht argued that while, in principle, it is acceptable that the states have been organising gambling and have implemented the restrictions – because it was contributing to the aims that they were pursuing – in practice, they were no longer fulfilling these criteria. The Bundesverfassungsgericht made the assessment, but provided a way out for the states. In order to cope with the problem resulting out of the assessment, the Court mentioned that since the states had a discretion competence for organising gambling services such discretion should also be available for the state to find a solution as soon as the court finds that in practise the concerned state is no longer in line with its own criteria. The Bundesverfassungsgericht actually granted the states a transition period for more than a year. According to the Court, in an area where the state has a wide margin of discretion to establish restrictions – to the extent that the state is found to be in breach of law by the way that it has been implementing the restrictions – the Court can grant the state time to find a solution.

To conclude: In very sensitive areas, where a lot of discretion must be left to the states by the different courts, maybe they can go further in their guidance and at the same time leave a larger latitude in the way that it has to be implemented by the states. I think this is also compatible with the way that the ECJ has been looking to the questions of implementation of WTO decisions by the European institutions.

Why Deprive the European Judges their National Brethren of their Treaty-Given Competence to Perform Proportionality-Review?

HJALTE RASMUSSEN [1]

A. Introduction: One of Activism's Paradoxes

The European Court of Justice's "activism" is shorthand for the EU's top court's firmly established strategy to rigorously deepen European political integration. By judicial fiat it incessantly generated groundbreaking new constitutional law[2], a tactic the judges or their majorities piously hoped would help create a centralized federal union.

Poetically, former EC-judge Federico Mancini explained what he and his Brethren perceived as the origins of this endeavour. He said that it all could be traced back to *"a genetic code transmitted to the court by the Founding Fathers, who entrusted to it the task of ensuring that the law is observed in the application of the Treaty whose primary objective is an ever closer union among the peoples of Europe"*[3].

Hyperbole aside, Mancini's central idea in this was a perception of the judges as essentially messenger boys. The celestial promised land of a federalized Europe was not of their invention. They were serving a higher cause or authority whose command they had to obey regardless of that the treaties took care never to entrench the ever-closer-union objective in terms of binding law. And irrespective of that both the constitutional details and broad outlines of the allegedly promised union were unknown to all men. Indeed, obviously in want of any legally binding identification of the Preamble's sort of federal union and/or a road map telling how to accomplish it, the Court's philosophy seems to have been that, then, neither could the judges be blamed for serving it without cognizance. In some way, the scene was thus set for the European judges acting like a "Homeric King who receives divine revelations from Zeus (*themistes*) and makes them the basis of his judgment"[4]. Professor Martin Shapiro of Berkeley likened

---

1 Professor at the University of Copenhagen.
2 The expression is borrowed from the EC Court's President, Vassilos Skouris; in 2005-speech entitled: "Self-Conception, Challenges and Perspectives of the EU Courts", published in The Future of the European Judicial System in a Comparative Perspective, 6 European Constitutional Law Network Series, pp. 19–31, at 24–25 Nomos, 2006; papers from a conference held in September 2005.
3 Mancini et al, Democracy and the European Court of Justice, (1994) 57 M.L.R. pp. 175.
4 The citation is from the Danish Professor Alf Ross, On Law and Justice, Stevens, London 1958 and University of California Press, Berkeley 1959, p. 229.

this when he observed that the European judges have for decades feigned to be the disembodied voice of constitutional theology[5].

Judges expounding on a quasi-religious doctrine are presumably not among the first to be concerned with how well or poorly the real world's actors will receive their right reason. Nor, at least, to convey to the outer world that they might none the less be concerned. If the European Brethren in judicial conference do actually raise and deliberate the societal acceptability of their preferred pronouncements[6], they take care not to inform the public about it.

In a recent Editorial Comment, Common Market Law Review noted that judicial reality corroborates the no-concern assumption. As it were, the leader rather sharply criticized the Court on two counts. First, that many of its jurisprudences were in lack of a sufficient legal basis when they eroded competencies reserved for themselves by the Member States. Second, the Editor emphasized that the judicial outcomes of too many important judgments have in recent years been incompletely and inadequately motivated. Even incomprehensively, one might add. Spectacularly, the Leader concluded that the Court ought to soldier a good deal more to make its judgments acceptable to those who are supposed to enforce them[7].

It can be taken that one of the concerns triggering the Editorial Comment was this: It does not come without costs and untended side effects to systematically gloss over the legal and political digestability of judicial output. The *Activism's paradox* of this Paper's "Introduction" points to but one of these many unintended side effects. It draws attention to a phenomenon which in recent years has become increasingly notorious about the preliminary cooperation procedures involving national and European judges under Article 234.

Article 234 fundamentally vests with the national courts an exclusive competence to apply the Union's laws while granting to the EC Court a last-resort monopoly to interpret them. This division of powers makes both sides powerless without the other's active and trustful participation in furthering the goals of Article 234. In fact, for almost half a century the vitality of the Court's union-building activism was made possible because of the mutual trust with which the judges on the two sides approached their preliminary cooperation. Both sides' recognition that the other judicial partner rigorously observes the limits to its competences conditions that this trust is not forfeited.

---

5   Martin Shapiro, Commentary, in: 53, Southern Californian Law Review (1980), pp. 537–542.
6   I dealt at length with the acceptability-of-judgments issue in my 1986-book entitled On Law and Policy in the European Court of Justice, Nijhoff, Dordrecht. And more recently in anthology entitled The Role of International Courts, Baudenbacher and Busek (eds), Acceptance and Criticism of International Courts' Rulings, at pages 231–249.
7   CMLRev. 45: 1571-1578, 2008.

However, when the Court of Justice embarked on its sovereignty-consuming jurisprudential activism the trustfulness of the cooperation was prone to become a victim. The more obvious it became that the Court was aiming at setting up a superior courtroom government, the easier it seemed to predict that acceptance of many judgments would be endangered[8]. Whence, full compliance with them was also to be threatened. Arguably with good reason, many national judges then began to perceive an array of the Court's jurisprudences as mocking both of many Century-old golden European canons of interpretation but also of violating their own prerogatives under Article 234's division-of-powers scheme. Some may even have viewed the European case laws as unconstitutional.

In face of this, a number of national judiciaries, including not so few of the highest, reacted by drawing in their horns. Not only did they begin to think twice before they would trigger new preliminary questions. A pattern of non-loyal executions of the Community's laws as expounded by the European Court also emerged, matured and took root. A vicious circle had begun.

It can, next, be taken that the emergence of these unintended side effects did not go unnoticed by the European judges. In response, they probably realized that they had to make hard choices. One course of action would consist in transforming itself into a court of both interpretation and application of Community law. This would have to happen in blatant violation of Article 234's division of powers. Inside this option was a choice between playing with open cards or concealing as much as possible that the Court preferred to act regardless of Article 234's stipulations. The latter was what the Court arguably decided to do by deploying a tactic consisting in intertwining law and fact in an inextricable manner so as to leave in reality the national judge with one option: Namely to apply Community law as the Court had prescribed how it ought to be applied.

It is possible that the "genetic code" manipulated the European judges to think that this action was justifiable and legitimate because it was all done in order to ensure that the same European law applied Community wide. In the judges' eyes this was making the Community legal order appear more attractive. Be this as it may, what in the eyes of one beholder is attractive may be wholly unacceptable to another. As it were, grievances began to grow in face of what the national side of the equation often understood as an unconstitutional appropriation of powers which the treaty vested exclusively in them.

The vicious circle would not stop here. In turn, in fact, the Court realized that it required more than the said intertwinement of law and fact to accomplish a unified application of the Community's laws. At the latest by the mid-1990 it was emerging clearly that the Court had decided to trespass further onto the prerogatives of their

---

8   Compare work mentioned in fn. 5.

national Brethren. By then, ample evidence was at hand to demonstrate that the Court was also taking over the performance of what remained of national judicial sovereignty under Article 234.

This last victim of the Court's quest for EU-law's efficiency and uniform application throughout was the performing of proportionality-review. This, the Court preferred not to leave in the hands of those whose first choice might be to seek to mould – within the ambit of law's margins of discretions – the outcomes of the cases so as to ensure results least disruptive to local social, cultural, environmental, labour relations (etc.) traditions. In policy terms, because of its political sensibility, this trespassing onto the last bit of the national court's prerogative and discretion was uniquely contestable and trust-destructive. It was arguably far more so than the Court's acquisition of the competence to apply a Community law which itself by and large left merely one resolution open to the conflict only (although the latter was of course no less illegal).

Once again, this ultimate competence appropriation may have occurred as necessary and legitimate in the eyes of the European judges. They were after all serving the highest cause possible by whose command both they and their national judicial partners had to obey. In spite of this, viewed from the latters' perspective, the Court's move was still a contestable one. Arguably, it would fly in the face of many national judges as an illegal dismantling of their most precious responsibility. To many of them, proportionality reviewing was the perhaps most important element of their essential function, namely that of smoothening to the extent possible European Law's infiltration into the national legal orders including, as noted, their local social, cultural, environmental, labour relations (etc.) fabric and traditions.

Viewed in this light, proportionality-reviewing is a confrontation avoiding mechanism which no less than the Court's uniformity obsession ought to be axiomatic to the Union's constitutional theology. Yet, viewed from the EC's judicial temple complex in Luxemburg, confrontation seems to be a preferable mode to competence respectful cooperation. Seen from this elevated view point, the superior values of more and, notably, more uniform European Community (constitutional) law are not negotiable. The treaty stipulations do not belong to these values.

Many high national judicial voices have decried this lamentable state of affairs. To give voice in his native language to but one of them within the contexts of this paper, Mr. Pontoppidan – when he was Chief Justice of the Danish Supreme Court – gravely observed that "[d]en stedfundne udvikling [i EF-domstolens praksis] er ikke forløbet uden indsigelser. Ikke mindst i de senere år har ganske kraftige modstrømninger manifesteret sig [...]. Uanset om man som det til en vis grad er tilfældet for mit vedkommende deler de betænkeligheder, der er kommet til udtryk, er der ikke tvivl om, at udviklingen stiller danske jurister og ikke mindst danske dommere over for store udfordringer i de kommende år".[9]

In short, he said that he embraced with sympathy the great concerns and powerful countervailing reactions which many of the European Court's case laws and their manifest federalizing thrusts had provoked in recent years. Coping with the Court's judicial constitutional innovations was prone, in his view, to pose manifest challenges for Danish judges, both at present and in coming years. During his time in office, Mr. Pontoppidan led to court to earn a solid reputation for demonstrating, to put it diplomatically, lukewarm willingness only to cooperate with the European Court. That a link exists between "the Community judicial activism and national judicial hostility (hampering the enforcement of the Court's judicial directives)", was understood long ago[10].

B. Contextualizing this Article's Main Theme

The terrain of interest of this article is thus located in the intersection between the Court's discretion to say what EU-law means, a competence which on bottom line is exclusive. And the national courts' treaty-granted exclusive competence to apply the Union's laws as interpreted by the Court. An area where two exclusive and competing competencies interact was probably predestined to become a minefield.

As it happened, it emerges from well over thirty years of EC-jurisprudence that the Court has deployed its interpretative discretion to spectacularly curtail the national courts' Article 234-given monopoly of application of EU-law. As noted, it seems safe to assume that, hereby, the Court's "genetic code" dictated the course of events. This implies that personal ideologies instead of the messenger boy's loyalty to the original intentions of Article 234's draftsmen had taken hold of the steering wheel. To the treaty's quest for uniformity of EU-law interpretation, the European judges added on their own motion a strategy of uniformity of application[11]. This construction of Article 234 stands in flagrant contrast to the approach adopted by the drafters of Article 234.

As it were, the Founding Fathers drew their major inspiration from values and considerations that are associated with what today is commonly referred to as subsidiarity[12]. This translates *inter alia* into the decision maker's closeness to the local facts and policies of the cases. These encapsulate interests and values whose unfettered survival

---

9   The President's observation came in the form of a comment to two interesting articles authored by a former and a present EC-judge: T. Koopmans, "Sources of Law: the New Pluralism", Festskrift til Ole Due, København 1994, pp. 189–246; and F.Mancini (et al) "From CILFIT to ERT: The Constitutional Challenge Facing the European Court", Yearbook of European Law, 1991, 1-13.
10   J. Weiler, "The Community System: The Dual Character of Supranationalism", Yearbook of European Law I, 1981, at p. 302.
11   H.Rasmussen, "Why is Article 173(2) interpreted against Private Plaintiffs?" In: 5 ELR, 1980, pp. 112–127.
12   Nice-treaty Article 5, (draft, Function) Lisbon-treaty Article 5.

comes under threat when one of the Unions laws and some national legal prescription simultaneously claim to apply to the particular facts of a case.

The draftmen's legal conviction emerges clearly from the two last paragraphs of Article 234. This obviously was that the judges of the Member States are in general better equipped than their European Brethren to have the last word, especially where this implies to render final judgment about how much of the one law or the other should be permitted to survive the clash between them. In this process, the Court again and again paid lip service to Article 234's fundamental rule that it is for the national courts to apply EU-law – its own role being confined to interpreting this law. In *Omega* it acknowledged, for example, that "the specific circumstances [where, e.g., a national statute provides for the protection of human dignity; author] which may justify recourse to the concept of public policy may vary from one country to another and from one era to another. The competent national authorities must therefore [subsidiarity dictates; author] be allowed a margin of discretion."[13]

Article 234's scheme of division of powers was thus designed so as to give unto Caesar the things that are Caesar's – but not more. As the Court saw things, it was a risk that national rule application, and the discretion that goes with it, would not be inspired by anything like the Court's obsession with uniformity. In order to minimize this risk's negative fall outs, the Court all too often ended by sacrificing law and legal principles.

Needless to argue that any national exercise of a discretion of application must take place within the limits imposed by the treaty goes without saying. Thus, in dispute is where these limits are to be located: Where the treaty placed them or where the Court subsequently removed them. Admittedly, a high level of uniformity-ideology run legalization may appear to be attractive to some observers because the judicial outcomes may be dear to them. This cannot, however, belittle the fact that EC-judicial rule-application in preliminary cases takes place *ultra vires*. It is from a legal point of view to be deplored that even the *ultra vires* barrier did not stop the EU's High Guardian of law and legality. Neither did, apparently, the immanent risk that several national courts would begin reconsidering their position on the desirability of Article 234-"cooperation" stifle the Court's hegemonic instincts, including its appropriation of the proportionality testing power.

I. Afraid of its own Shadow

The issues (just discussed) are big and serious. They make it compelling to ask, as this article does in what follows, why the Court steadfastly pursued a proportionality strategy that was both unconstitutional and likely to provoke national wrath and opposi-

---

13   Case C-36/02, *Omega* [2004] ECR I-9609.

tion? And to, in turn, diminish national courts disinterested willingness to cooperate with the Court under Article 234? And thereby launch a process of dessication of the source nurturing its groundbreaking constitution making pro communitatæ?

So, why did the Court regularly trespass onto the powers which the treaty had so unambiguously vested in the national courts? Considering that the Court has never offered an intelligible answer to this question, the Court's observers are left to speculate.

It can hereby first be taken that the Court was well aware of that many of its activisms on behalf of the ever closer, legally uniform union were provocative. They caused national opposition, widespread animosity and perhaps even hostility to grow. Second, it must be taken that the Court did not grab the proportionality testing competence without some compelling reason to guide its action. It requires, it must be assumed, long and intense analysis and calculations of the risks inherent in such a move before it will be launched. All other things equal, many national judges can be taken to be predisposed to favour localism as soon as this can be done within the limits of the treaty. Yet, uniformitarianism is only in the Court's vision one of these limits.

In this conjecture, a credible hypothesis is that the Court had become afraid of its own shadow. The shadows cast by many of its most groundbreaking constitutional lawmaking judgments had, as noted, encouraged widespread national judicial doubts, scepticism and sometimes even opposition *viz.* hostility. On this backdrop, to make national judges responsible for any final proportionality testing would be reminiscent of letting goats guard cabbages.

Imbued with the ideology that former Italian EC-judge Mancini so eloquently gave name to [14], the Court seems to have found itself in a Catch 22 situation. Either it ensured uniformity and thereby violated the treaty, and notably Article 234, by depriving the national judges of their treaty-given power of proportionality testing. Or it abided by the constitutional commands of that provision at the price of an almost certain loss of a Community wide one hundred per cent uniform application of EU-law. In face of this, the Court preferred in three out of every four situations where a proportionality test was part of the dispute's resolution, to disregard the impositions of the treaty [15].

II. Paradox Continued

The overriding goal behind all this was to boost EU-law's *effet utile*, a concept which is a brainchild of Mancini's genetic code [16]. Incantations of *effet utile* normally occur in its judicial reasoning when the Court is about to draw a legal conclusion that the other-

---

14 See quotes in the first part of this article.
15 The three-to-four measurement is made at arm's length.
16 Mentioned in the opening sentences of this article.

wise available argumentation and normal methods of interpretation cannot justify or at least not in its entirety. Technically, "effet utile" identifies an activity that consists in filling in of lacuna of the EU's legal system or of interpretations or reconstructions of its individual legal texts. Yet, the typical situation is one where the legal reasoning needs an ideological vitalization that only an injection of some amount of ever-closer-union serum can provide it with. In one of its variations *effet utile* means making new constitutional law which is designed to strengthen Member States' EU-law compliance, especially by making less than a hundred per cent perfect enforcement cumbersome or costly.

Tracking *effet utile*'s history brings us back to the 1960 judgments in *van Gend en Loos*[17] and *Costa v. ENEL*[18] in which the Court gave life to the concepts of EU-law's direct effects and supremacy. Thereby it undoubtedly acted statesmanlike and with great wisdom and vision – but quite probably also unconstitutionally. In the following decades it added many other legal instruments and general legal principles, all unknown to the treaty, to the armoury that should ensure more *effet utile*. Taking over from the national courts the exclusive competence to apply Community law was only one such step.

A big problem was, of course, that many of these visionary and (perhaps) necessary constitutional innovations were in want of a proper legal basis. What carried the day were instead the judges' personal convictions. Or, in Judge Mancini's often quoted descriptions of the judges' job-performance: "[t]he combination of being, as it were, out of sight and out of mind by virtue of its location in the fairytale Grand Duché of Luxemburg and the benign neglect of the media has certainly contributed to its ability to create a sense of belonging on the part of the independent minded members of the Court and, when necessary, to convert them to confined Europeanists"[19].

However, "[w]hen judges get carried away by their personal convictions (…) they create uncertainty. If those convictions are held on issues which are political (…), then they arose animosity as well as support. And if the issues are serious and large (…) judicial pronouncements begin to loose their authority and legitimacy"[20].

Needless to argue that when rendering hundreds of judgments dealing with matters of serious and large political importance, the European judges relied more on their personal convictions than on (what another famous EC-judge, Pierre Pescatore) once labelled the "legal niceties of the cases"[21]. Many of the groundbreaking constitutional innovations were more carried by liturgy and methaphysics than by judicial work built on European judicial traditions.

---

17   Case 26/62 [1962] ECR 1.
18   Case 6/64 [1964] ECR 585.
19   In: The Making of a Constitution for Europe, 1989, 26 CMLRev, pp. 595–614 (at p. 597).
20   J. A. G. Griffith, "Politics of the Judiciary" 1981, Fontana Paperbacks.
21   In: "The Doctrine of Direct Effect: An Infant Disease of Community Law",1983, 8 ELRev, p. 155.

Fighting thus for a cause that in its view was right, the Court's judgments began to loose both authority and legitimacy. However, "[f]or legal institutions, no attribute is more important than legitimacy. Legitimacy allows courts the latitude necessary to make decisions contrary to the perceived immediate interest of their constituents. Since courts typically have neither "the purse nor the sword", this moral authority is essential to judicial effectiveness."[22]

In the wake of this, views as those of the Danish Chief Justice (cited above) boldly claimed that they were right as well and submitted that they often had EU-law on their side. As it were, the growing loss of legitimacy laid the foundations for a noteworthy decline in national judicial institutions' loyal implementation, more specifically, of the stipulations of Article 234 on one hand and, on the other, of wider fields of EU-law in general.

When it became aware of all this, presumably a decade ago or so, the Court had to choose between two strategies. One was to raise further the stakes by monopolizing in its own hands the application of EU-law in all important preliminary cases. The other was to loosen its suffocating and harmful *effet-utile* grip on Member States' compliance – notably by granting (as it said in the *Omega* case) "the competent national authorities a larger margin of (subsidiarity) discretion"[23].

However tempting it might have been to (at least some members of) the Court, there is nothing really in its case laws of the first years of this Century to suggest that it considers to follow the path laid out in *Omega*. In *Église de scientologie* the Court, for example, said that "the concept of "public policy" in the Community context, particularly for a derogation from the fundamental principle of freedom to provide services, must be interpreted strictly, so that its scope cannot be determined unilaterally by each Member State without the control of the Community institutions [here the Court referred to *van Duyn*; added by the author]. Thus, public policy may be relied on if there is a genuine and sufficiently serious threat to a fundamental interest of society."[24] An entirely different approach, here advocated, would have been to encourage "the hundred flowers to grow and blossom" – subject to the within-the-limits of the treaties proviso, of course.

It was dicta such as the one in *Église de scientology* which prompted me to suggest above that the Court had become afraid of its own shadow. It was apparently seeing foes where there was no one. Too suspicious, to it the fantasy was depicting reality that if it gave the tip of finger of real influence to the national courts they would take the whole arm – thereby destroying union. Isolated in its palaces in Luxemburg, obsessed

---

22 J.L. Gibson/ G.A. Caldeira: The Legitimacy of Transnational Legal Institutions: Compliance, Support and the European Court of Justice, American Journal of Political Science, vol. 30, 1995, pp. 459–489 (at p. 460).
23 *Omega*, cited in text over fn. 7.
24 Case C-54/99 [2000] ECR I-1335.

with uniformity, internally presumably deeply divided and therefore fearful of dialogue, it was easier to treat the national courts as if they were incapable of managing their own mandate under Article 234. Horror! if legitimate local interests and values were promoted – even within the applicable EU norms.

This judicial approach can hardly be blamed for being overly concerned with the acceptability of its outputs. In fact, it does not require an Einstein to prophecy to which extremes the Court's cementation of its violations of the national courts' Article 234-given monopoly of law-application might inspire the latter. In fact, new declines in the necessary trustfulness and atmosphere of fighting for a common cause of the preliminary cooperation will in all likelihood generate but two losers. The first will be the overall quality of the Community legal system. The other victim is likely to be the European Court's authority and legitimacy. Whence, the already calamitous vicious circle is not prone to stop any time soon.

To illustrate, in *Laval* the Court decided that some Swedish trade union's strike action (that was legal under national constitutional law) placed a disproportional burden on a Latvian company's EU-given right to free establishment and freedom to provide services[25]. It hereby deprived the submitting Swedish court of its treaty-given competence to do the proportionality testing. By contrast, in *Viking* the Court obligingly deferred and invited the submitting English court to review the disputed measure's proportionality[26].

This deference is a textbook example of compliance with the commands of Article 234. The absence in the Court's *Viking* files of crucially necessary information about the availability, for the involved Swedish and other trade unions, of alternative courses of action (than the one under scrutiny) may well have triggered the deference in this case[27] which its Advocate General had also favoured. An additional rationale might be that the psychological barrier to its compliance with Article 234 was in the particular circumstances of this case lowered. As it were, it was not a Swedish court that would eventually have to perform the proportionality balancing but a court of another Member State which, everything equal, probably would be less ideologically and emotionally inclined to safeguard local instead of EU-law interests. The stakes were reversed in *Laval*.

---

25   Grand Chamber, in Case I-341/05, of 18 December 2007.
26   Grand Chamber, in Case I-438/05, of 11 December 2007.
27   See notably premises 87 to 88.

Discussion

CARL BAUDENBACHER
Thank you very much, Professor Rasmussen. It is always good to have you on such a panel, since it is important to get different points of view.

Now, I am in a sensitive situation. I will just say the following. First of all, I think the criticism of a court like the European Court of Justice is something Americans have been familiar with for decades, with regard to their Supreme Court. I may remind you of President Roosevelt's plan to pack the Supreme Court because at the time it was not willing to implement the New Deal legislation. I also remember that once Congress was so mad at the Supreme Court that they decided on a general increase of the pay for all of the federal judges but in the case of the Supreme Court they limited this increase.

In the last issue of the Fordham International Law Journal is an article by Anthony Arnull on possible reactions of Member States towards the ECJ and Member States feeling the ECJ was going too far.[1] The author mentioned a lot of possible actions but not the most obvious one: Making re-appointment difficult.

When new ECJ judges are being sworn in, what interests me most is the reading out of the CV of the new judge. Oftentimes, you will see that judges from certain Member States come from the Prime Minister's office. Would you think that is an ideal solution? These judges are deemed to be loyal to their capitals at the end of the day. Is this a solution to remedy what you criticise here as judicial activism of the court?

HJALTE RASMUSSEN
I have somewhere a list of ten possible actions, out of which one is to look more keenly at who gets appointed as a judge.

CARL BAUDENBACHER
Your country is already doing that.

HJALTE RASMUSSEN
Once upon a time – I frankly admit to you, but I will not be quoted for saying it – I suggested to my government they should appoint me to the court.

---

1   Anthony Arnull, Me and my shadow: the European Court of Justice and the disintegration of EU law, 31 Fordham International Law Journal (2008), 1174–1211.

CARL BAUDENBACHER
Is that the reason why you are so critical now?

HJALTE RASMUSSEN
No, no, I have been critical for ten years. But as you may guess, they were not very thrilled about the offer I made them.

CARL BAUDENBACHER
The former President of Germany and at the same time the former President of the German Constitutional Court has beaten up the ECJ in a recent article in the Frankfurter Allgemeine Zeitung[2], which I consider highly irresponsible. It is not understandable that a man of his standing takes the low road in such a way, calling upon the German Constitutional Court to refuse to follow the ECJ in the future. This is unheard of and I doubt whether it is the ECJ, who occasionally may be wrong, undermining the legitimacy of the European project or the politicians who for short time interests are bashing the court regularly.

I would remind you of the former Austrian Chancellor, Wolfgang Schüssel, who had known since Austria adhered to the European Economic Area, that their admission system with regard to medical schools would not hold water. He did not do anything about it. At the end of the day, after approximately ten years, they lost the case and then they started bashing. That is hypocritical.

ULRICH HALTERN
Philippe Vlaemminck, full disclosure: I am one of the seven members of the German expert advisory board on gambling addiction that was established after the groundbreaking decision of the German Federal Constitutional Court[3]. I was not appointed because I am an expert in gambling law but it seems I was among the few German law professors who were not bribed by the gambling industry. So maybe that was what made you an expert in gambling law too. It is nice to talk to somebody who cannot be bribed.

One short comment and two questions to your speech. If I understand correctly, we should look at the proportionality principle as employed by the European Court of Justice in a way that makes it possible to have a unified theory of proportionality. Proportionality in Luxembourg is complicated, and it is certainly very different from, say, proportionality in Karlsruhe. The Luxembourg Court filters issues of competence, the grade of harmonisation, institutional questions etc. through the funnel of proportionality. A lot of seemingly extra-legal considerations flow into the Court's findings on proportionality. If there is any truth to this observation, why bother to look for a

---

2 http://www.cep.eu/fileadmin/user_upload/Pressemappe/CEP_in_den_Medien/Herzog-EuGH-Webseite.pdf.
3 BvR 1054/01, March 28, 2006, BVerfGE 115, 276.

unified theory of proportionality? Wouldn't proportionality be a function of sector-specific particularities? Proportionality, then, is not a singular, but a plural, and it is functionally diverse.

First question, I am very interested in the split within the Commission between the legal service on the one hand and Commissioner McCreevy's DG MARKT on the other. That split became blatantly apparent in the legal service's brief in the *Stoss* case[4]. Do you have any information on the background?

Second question, what do you think is going to happen? Your slides on the *Liga Portuguesa* case suggested that the European Court may be tightening the screw a little. Is that your hunch?

Hjalte, as you well know I am a great admirer of your work. You did groundbreaking research on the European Court of Justice, and your 1986 book is mandatory reading in my classes.[5] It is the methodological foundation on which I stand, and I believe that holds true for most of our best EU scholarship. However, the way you handle your methodology, and your brilliant insights, seems – let me put it diplomatically – biased. The picture of the Court that you draw is more of a caricature than a fair representation.

First of all, you may be aiming at the wrong target. The quotations you use, by Shapiro and by Weiler, are not directed at the Court. They are directed at EU scholarship. They are, in other words, directed at us. Shapiro said that what we do, as scholars, with court decisions is reading them as gospel. So he is criticising not the Court, but you and me. Well, not you, obviously, because if there is one person in the world who is not guilty of reading court decisions as gospel, that would be you. In any case, Shapiro is not accusing the Court of handing down the Commandments, and I believe it is problematic to put words into his mouth. To be sure, there is something profoundly disturbing about legal scholarship that finds itself incapable of achieving a critical stance towards court decisions. German academia struggles with the same problem with regard to decisions by the Federal Constitutional Court. However, hasn't scholarship changed over the last 30 years? Do we really believe everything the Court says? Are we still unthinking disciples? Isn't it rather the other way round – are we not exceedingly critical towards jurisprudence from Luxembourg? Take the torrent of acerbic criticism that has met the Court's Union citizenship jurisprudence, the *Mangold* decision, and many more. It seems to me the tide has long turned, and bashing academia is like bashing an imaginary villain you are creating yourself for the sake of bashing it. Perhaps it is time to realize that your powerful criticism has had many more followers than you yourself are willing to realize.

---

4 Case C-316/07 – *Markus Stoss*; the Legal Service's brief is printed in ZfWG 2008, 94.
5 *Hjalte Rasmussen*, On Law and Policy in the European Court of Justice: A Comparative Study in Judicial Policymaking, Dordrecht 1986.

As to the substance of your talk, I am not sure how much of it is owed to maximize its effect on us and to your willingness to be challenging to the brink of being polemical. You identify, as your villain, the Court, and go about destroying its credibility and legitimacy. But is the Court really the villain (supposing there is one)? Let's look at it from a different angle, for instance from a perspective that, among others, Alec Stone Sweet has elaborated.[6] The Treaty, like any constitution, may be analyzed as an incomplete or relational contract. Much is left general and vague, probably deliberately so in order to facilitate agreement between the Member States. But then, vagueness is normative uncertainty, which in itself is a threat to the rationale of contracting in the first place. Member States have reacted by establishing procedures for "completing" the contract over time. The prime procedure, of course, is the establishment of the ECJ as an institutional response to normative uncertainty. It is the Court's duty, then, to clarify over time the meaning of the Treaty, to see to it that Member States honour their obligations, and to punish them in case of non-compliance. The punchline is that what the Court does is precisely what it was set up to do. It was the Member States who delegated serious and difficult decisions to the Court – all those decisions they themselves could not settle on. They set out basic goals and objectives – among them the creation of the Common Market – and left the Court to put flesh to the bare bones of constitutional talk. Is it not disingenuous, then, to scold the Court for something the Member States themselves wanted it to do? Perhaps we should focus more on the Member States who celebrate themselves each time they create another incomplete agreement, and then accuse the Court of illegitimacy each time it cleans up after the party?

Furthermore, I do not share your charge that the Court is insensitive to criticism or even to hostility; quite the opposite. I believe the Court is extremely sensitive towards political and national court resistance. As we all know, effectiveness of EU law critically depends on a working partnership between the ECJ and national courts, its primary interlocutors. That relationship has been extremely complex and shifty, characterized by cooperation as well as conflict. It is possible to focus on either of those, cooperation or conflict. You have chosen to focus on conflict. In either case, however, there is no denying the fact that there has been the rich judicial dialogue Carl has reminded us of. Judicial dialogue, be it of a cooperative or a conflicting kind, presupposes listening to your interlocutor. One may or may not share the opinion of the interlocutor – but one has to acknowledge it. The Court often does not share Member State courts' opinions; Member State courts often do not share the Court's opinion. Yet, they listen to each other. Furthermore, the ECJ needs the voluntary cooperation of national courts under Article 234 EC. It is forced to convince them in order to keep up a working partnership. The Court needs references from the lower national courts to be able to do what it is doing. National courts can always balk, and withdraw their cooperation. Without the national courts, the ECJ is nothing. We have a plethora of examples of ECJ decisions directly reacting to national court resistance. The saga on horizontal direct ef-

---

6   Alec Stone Sweet, The Judicial Construction of Europe, Oxford UP 2004.

fect of directives is just one such example. *CILFIT*[7] is another, and you yourself have written a seminal article acknowledging this.[8] I am surprised to hear you retracting your own insights. What's more, we would need a cogent explanation of why it is that Member States have never amended the Treaty, or consented on secondary legislation, to keep the Court at bay if it were true that they do not like what the Court is doing. Absent such an explanation, I believe the story is more complex than you tell it.

CARL BAUDENBACHER
Thank you.

MARK VILLIGER
Let me briefly explain the point of view of the European Court of Human Rights (ECrtHR). I can confirm that we get the same criticism from many other persons, and that, incidentally, the views expressed by Professor Rasmussen are the views of many Danes in Denmark. But not everybody thinks like that about European integration. NGO's think completely differently. Or take the following example:

Some months ago, Chancellor Merkel was in Strasbourg, visiting the ECrtHR. And what did she tell us? In German: *"Mischt euch ein"*. In English we could say: *"Interfere!"* We hear completely different voices, melodies, as it were, from the different corners in Europe. I think that is what all the European Courts are facing. In the European orchestra your voice, Professor, is one of the many instruments contributing to the European Anthem and then there are other voices and if we want to do it right, we have to listen to all of them and try to get the common sound. My advice would be, it is all fine to spend a lot of energy to criticise the court's decisions afterwards. But why not invest this energy beforehand when the domestic courts are preparing and drafting their judgments? That would make things much easier for the European courts.

CARL BAUDENBACHER
If I may just add one thing. We see a well-known pattern in the Member State's behaviour. Governments know exactly that they have no chance to prevail, even under conservative interpretation of the treaty or of the agreement. And they prefer to be sentenced in order to show a clean vest at home. That is double standard. And that undermines the standing of the courts in the view of the public. Please, Mr. Vlaemminck.

PHILIPPE VLAEMMINCK
I think, I can respond to the question and at the same time respond to my colleague here on the panel. Let me first start by saying that I am a fan of the international courts, which means that I think they are much more reliable than some of the so-called political institutions. This means that talking to the European Parliament is much more

---
7   Case C-283/81 – CILFIT, ECR 1982, I-03415.
8   Hjalte Rasmussen, The European Court's Acte Clair Strategy in CILFIT, Eur.L.Rev. 9 (1984), 242.

unpredictable than talking to the Court. I would say that debates at the ECJ, at the EFTA Court and even the at the WTO panels and Appellate Body are indeed debates which always go to the fundamental questions which are at stake. To your benefit, Mr. Chairman, I think the cases we handled before the EFTA Court have indeed proven that a lot of Member States had a very interactive dialogue, discussing with the Court the way that things should be discussed. In my experience, both courts have always taken a very cautious view on balancing the interests of the states and the politically sensitive versus the legal context. The role of the Court is to guarantee that the treaty stays where it is.

I think it was Advocate General Albers, who said that the ECJ is actually doing what the Member States agreed on to do. And I agree. He said that at the Conference on the Future of Europe.

Professor Lenas made the same quote in Trier by saying that a certain activism of the ECJ is due to the inactivity of the politicians. It is very often because the politicians do not take up their responsibilities in regulating something that the Court has to intervene. I would go as far as to say that the Court does not like to be the arbitrator in absence of political agreement. The gambling cases are very clear evidence of that. Indeed, the Commission does not want to take any initiative because Mr. McCreevy is frustrated that the Member States and the European Parliament did not accept that the Service Directive[9] would cover gambling. Since that very moment, he has decided that he would no longer make any proposal. The only thing he is doing, is initiating infringement cases.

As a result we have now 11 Member States, which are facing an infringement case in courts. Rather than saying there is a problem of law, I would suggest that there is a problem of politics. If there are 11 Member States referring the same question to the courts, it is a clear sign that the problem is political, which shows that there is a firm need of harmonisation.

What is happening now is that the Member States themselves, facing this enormous amount of cases, have decided to set up a forum for debate. This means the French Presidency has initiated the Council Working Group on establishment and services to discuss the matter of gambling. The Commission is vigorously opposed because Mr. McCreevy does not want it. And you get the stupid situation where the representative of the Commission is sitting there not saying anything in those meetings, because the Commissioner does not want him to. Now, in that situation, the Court has no other alternative, than making the decision. The Court is in fact obliged when there is a referral to provide an answer. And they are not very happy with that. And I think

---

9   Directive 2006/123/EC of the European Parliament and of the Council of 12 December 2006 on services in the internal market.

very recently we saw it. I did not quote the – momentarily pending – *Winner-Wetten*[10] case because there was no time, but it is indeed a case which ECJ is being asked if, the transition time that the Bundesverfassungsgericht has granted the Bundesländer is acceptable, considering that under European Law you have truly the direct effect of these principles which are at stake.

I have to say, the European Court is very reluctant in answering that question, because it is a discussion between the Federal Constitutional Court's view on German Constitutional Law and the way that a preliminary ruling has to be granted. And actually this week we received a correspondence between the ECJ and the referring court where the ECJ was saying: *"Do you think it is important to answer the question, since the transition period was already over?"*. And unfortunately the Verwaltungsgericht Köln said: *"Yes, it is important that you answer the question."* So, the European Court has no alternative. The referring judges want a answer to their question. And whether that is activism or not, we need to have a kind of legal security that the politicians are not willing or able to grant us.

Of course, sometimes I am disappointed because I would like the judgement to be different. But I think, in general the courts do it in a cautious way, taking into consideration the political consequences that the judgement can have. It does not always turn out the way we want to, but if the treaty is there, if it is working, I think it is because there is such respect for the balancing of interests. All in all, I am a fan of the international courts.

HJALTE RASMUSSEN
You stressed two points I want to address. The one statement is that the courts always calculate the risk and possible consequences of a new judicial move, which may be true in some cases, but in many other instances they obviously do not make that calculation and an extremely illustrative example was the *Metock* case.[11] It was completely unnecessary to overrule itself, unless you were considering to safeguard the interests of organised crime.

Now I would like to stress another point. You said that the court only does the job that the politicians should have done, if I understood you correctly. That is true to a certain extent but not completely. There are many examples in which the ECJ created legal institutions that the Member States or the politicians had no obligation whatsoever to create. Let us just take the most important EC Law principles as an example: direct effect, supremacy and state liability. There was no obligation anywhere in the EC treaty to make these principles part of Union Law. The Court made it nonetheless and it made it on its own discretion.

---

10   Case C-409/06 – *Winner Wetten*.
11   Case C-127/08 – *Metock and Others v. Minister of Justice, Equality and Law Reform*.

So the old story about the Court doing the job that politicians should have done is partly very true. Carl is correct, Wolfgang Schüssel was dishonest when he took the Danish Prime Minister by the hand and told the press that they had to revolt against that ECJ.

Then a brief remark regarding what Professor Haltern said regarding Shapiro and Weiler. Yes it is true, they were criticising us, but what we, the academics, were doing, was to recite what the Court had said in the first place. *"We are the biggest and most beautiful, you have to comply unconditionally. It will be doomsday if you don't. And it will be the detriment of us all."* With this attitude they persuaded many academics to stop questioning the ECJ's judgements.

CARL BAUDENBACHER
We probably should get back to the proportionality and margin of discretion issue. Professor Ulrich Haltern said, and I absolutely agree, that there cannot be a general test. It must be differentiated depending on the subject matter which is involved.

Would somebody like to take the floor on this? Yes, Mr. Planzer.

SIMON PLANZER
I would like to very briefly comment and at the same time pass a question to you on the aspect of public morals. Judge Villiger mentioned that when it comes to public morals, usually, Member States enjoy a large margin of appreciation. I would like to question that for the following reason. I do not think that the courts put enough importance in their gambling case law, particularly on the importance of the protection of the individual. The Member States like to rely on public morals as a justification but the question is, do they actually implement what they claim to do. Of course, it is difficult for an international court to assess, but I would at least expect that an international or supranational court tries to define what is expected and then leave it to the national court to assess whether this is the case. And in that regard I see the importance of the *Ladbrokes* decision[12] of the EFTA Court, which is probably the most important decision in that regard, in that it finally gave a meaning to what consistent and coherent policy means.

Just to give you a short example, in Norway, after it won the case EFTA *Surveillance Authority v The Kingdome of Norway*[13], a fight broke out between some communes who did not want to allow more gaming machines on their territory and the state monopolist which wanted to expand with gaming machines. However, the official position of Norway was that they wanted to restrict gaming, so this was perceived as a bit bizarre and the Minister of Economics was actually quoted by saying that if the communes

---

12 Case E-3/06, *Ladbrokes Ltd. and The Government of Norway, Ministry of Culture and Church Affairs*, [2006].
13 Case E-1/06, *EFTA Surveillance Authority v. The Kingdome of Norway*, [2006].

would not comply with what the public monopolists wanted, it would have an impact on what they would receive as revenues out of it.

This is not exactly consistent and that is why I am very critical of the approach that if the facts of a case touch on public morals, international courts should not interfere and maybe, I might invite the Strasbourg Court to revise this approach and to give further guidance, but then leave it to the national courts to assess whether this is fulfilled or not. Would you like to comment on such an approach?

PHILIPPE VLAEMMINCK
It is difficult to disagree with what you said. The current situation is proving indeed that the matter of coherence and consistent policy, which has been mostly added in the *Ladbrokes* case by the EFTA Court, is an important benchmark for the assessment the national judge has to make. It is an extremely important aspect that the Court goes as far as possible in providing guidelines on how the interpretation of European law has to be applied.

I would even go one step further. Germany's Federal Constitutional Court, in my view, did it the right way. By first accepting that the decision, regarding if something belongs to public morals or public order, is a matter that belongs to the Member State's discretion. This means it is very different from Member State to Member State. In this regard I remember a discussion we had in the EFTA Court: Can you compare the level of advertising in Italy with the level of advertising in Finland? No, because your benchmark has to be Italy versus Italy. Advertising for gambling in Italy is just as advertising in general in Italy and I think everybody who has arrived in Rome will know that advertising in Italy is a little bit more present than, for instance, when you arrive in Finland. There is a different perception of the same question, so your benchmark has to be to a certain extent national. You have to accept that the basic discretion in sensitive areas belongs to the state.

The second step is in fact finding out whether that state is abiding by its own views. The ECJ has been very cautious in saying that it must bring about an aim or a concern. The practice of the Member State's policy must be that you are in line with what you initially have been saying.

CARL BAUDENBACHER
Thank you to the three speakers and thank you for your participation in the discussion.

Focus:
Arbitration and Adjudication

Introduction

GABRIELLE KAUFMANN-KOHLER [1]

I am very pleased to open this afternoon's session. It is my pleasure to be here and I thank the organisers for the invitation. I am also very pleased that the students of the new Geneva Master in International Dispute Settlement are all here to attend this conference.

We will speak about arbitration and adjudication, and the choice between the two. Why do you arbitrate? Why do you not arbitrate and rather go to court? Actually, there are a number of topics we discussed this morning that we could pursue in the present context. For instance, we spoke about *judicial* dialogue. We could also think about dialogue between arbitration and international courts or between arbitration and arbitration. It may be interesting to come back to these topics later in the discussion.

In the meantime, I suggest that we proceed in the following fashion: We will first have Professor Alan Rau discuss the aspects of courts and adjudication from the point of view of commercial arbitration. Then, we will go over to Professor Christoph Schreuer who will discuss the same topics but from the viewpoint of investment arbitration, after which Professor Baudenbacher will talk about arbitration in public international disputes. The last speaker will be Professor Thomas Cottier, who will be addressing issues of arbitration and adjudication in the World Trade Organization. We will start with arbitration between private parties, then go over to arbitration between one private party and one state, and end with arbitration between two states.

I do not need to introduce any of the speakers. Let me just remind you that Alan Rau is a Professor at the University of Texas in Austin. He is one of the most authoritative writers on international arbitration in the US. There are two US writers whose writings I never miss and he is one of them.

---

1   Professor at the University of Geneva, Director of the Geneva Master in International Dispute Settlement, Attorney at law and Partner with Levy Kaufmann-Kohler, Geneva, Honorary President and former Chair of ASA, Member of ICCA, the ICC Court of International Arbitration and of the Board of the AAA.

Underlying Tensions in the Field of Arbitration

ALAN RAU[1]

A. The Choice of Arbitration: "The Parties' Dream"[2]

Some background first. In any given legal system, in a domestic case for example, parties make a choice to use or not to use arbitration purely as a tactical decision: Do they want to avoid a jury, if this is the United States? Do they want to insulate the decision from rules of law? Or do they want to submit to a more formal adjudication of their legal rights?

In international transactions, by contrast, arbitration is not so much chosen by the parties as a tactical decision, it is instead merely imposed by necessity. It is imposed because in litigation arising out of international transactions there is very little protection against parallel litigation going on simultaneously. A party will want to avoid, if possible, litigating in the courts of his opponent. This might be simply because of unfamiliarity or trying to avoid a home court advantage; more seriously, one might legitimately have some serious doubts about the fairness of the justice available in a particular court system.

A rather more primitive form of risk management might be to provide by contract for a choice of forum, a choice of public courts in which to hear a dispute. Choice of forum clauses, however, as you know, are not foolproof. They are often not enforced, they are often not honoured, and the resulting judgment itself may not be honoured. Until the Hague Convention is widely ratified that is not likely to be a serious alternative.

So by comparison arbitration is way ahead, both in the enforcement of agreements and the enforcement of awards. And so it is almost an inevitable alternative form in international transactions.

---

1 Burg Family Professor of Law at the University of Texas School of Law, Austin, Panelist on the Commercial and International Panels of the American Arbitration Association.
2 See Henry Hart & Albert Sacks, *The Legal Process* 310 (1994):
   Within broad limits private parties who submit an existing dispute to arbitration may write their own ticket about the terms of submission, if they can agree to a ticket. [The authors refer to an old story about a person who, in a dream, was threatened by an ominous character and who asked, tremulously, "Wh- what are you going to do now?"– only to receive the answer, "How do I know? This is *your* dream."] The arbitration of an existing dispute is the parties' dream, and they can make it what they want it to be.

B. Private Fora and Official "Public" Fora

Now, that leads to the next question which is the important one of the interaction between this alternative system of justice, and public forums and public courts. And the story that is usually told at conferences like this is this cheerful story of homogenisation, of congruence, of uniformity in national legislation in the widespread adoption by states of a common regime governing arbitration, which is more or less uniform across international borders. That is an important part of the story (although it is not that part of the story that particularly interests me). This process of gradual harmonisation of national legislation is exemplified by legislation like the UNCITRAL Model Law, which was adopted by UNCITRAL in 1985. It was intended for states that have an antiquated or an obsolete arbitration regime but it has been adopted by many nations (such as Australia and Germany) which had well developed arbitration regimes, as well (for reasons which I cannot possibly understand or justify) as many states in the United States.

What is typical of modern legislation and arbitration, exemplified by the Model Law is a hands-off approach to arbitration. The interconnectedness of national markets – what we call "globalization" – has been accompanied by a strong resurgence of neo-liberal ideology, a growing acceptance of the principle of party autonomy. And competition for the invisible export of arbitration services has led to the liberation of the arbitral process from the idiosyncrasies and parochial burdens of many domestic legal systems.

So under most modern legislations, the possibility of a state's intervening is limited to simply setting up the process, making sure that any necessary discovery or evidence is presented, the possibility of interim relief and then the enforcement of arbitration awards.[3] And the enforcement of arbitration awards by states under this modern legislation is typically routine.[4] A state court may decide not to enforce an award for very limited reasons such as lack of agreement or some due process violation. But the fact that an arbitrator may have made a mistake, even an important mistake or mistake of law, is not usually a ground for refusing to enforce an award. As Judge Posner said, the arbitrator's decision can be "wacky," but that does not prevent it from being enforced.[5]

Now, there are variations outside that main stream. In some states enforcement of awards is far more difficult and there are grounds for refusal to enforce awards which may appear somewhat more "parochial." At the opposite extreme, states like Belgium

---

3 See, e.g., the UNCITRAL Model Law, arts. 5 ("In matters governed by this Law, no court shall intervene except where so provided in this law"), 8 (court shall "refer the parties to arbitration"), 17H (recognition and enforcement of "an interim measure issued by the arbitral tribunal"), 17J ("court-ordered interim measures"), 27 ("court assistance in taking evidence").
4 See the UNCITRAL Model Law, art. 34 (limited grounds for setting aside arbitral award).
5 Wise v. Wachovia Securities, LLC, 450 F.3d 265, 269 (7th Cir. 2006).

or Switzerland have made it possible for the parties to avoid any judicial review whatsoever of arbitration awards.[6] But the most common model for enforcement is that awards are rubber stamped by national courts with very few grounds for refusal of enforcement – grounds like "lack of agreement" or "lack of a fair hearing" that are inevitable and that you might readily expect.

Now as I said, the usual upbeat view in most conferences that deal with arbitration is to present this image of an integrated, harmonious international system where there are shared norms and expectations across national borders, all in the interest of making it possible for parties to resort to arbitration in commercial disputes. That is part of the story but as I say that is not the part of the story that interests me the most. Because what interests me more, and I believe what is worth talking about, is the possibilities of tension. The continuing conflicts and divergences in rules governing arbitration are precisely the sort of thing that allows academics to have something to talk about. And I want to draw attention to three underlying tensions in particular that recur in the arbitration field. This will, regrettably, have to be a very brief survey – in the old Chinese phrase, "glimpsing flowers from horseback."

C. Underlying Tensions: Party Autonomy and Mandatory Rules

The first is the tension between party autonomy and mandatory rules of state law. Historically arbitration developed in the interest of self government by mercantile communities, allowing merchants to entrust difficult problems of trade, customs and usage to a decision by insiders. But that is an historical development which has very little resonance today, because it is very hard to find any purely private commercial disputes today where the state – some state somewhere – does not have a strong regulatory interest or concern. That is to say, there is a public interest (for example, the interest of regulating competition) that is represented by mandatory, regulatory, statutory law. And we have seen an increasing tendency to sweep all sorts of regulatory, mandatory, imperative laws into the domain of arbitration. The United States has probably gone further than most other jurisdictions because in the United States today there is no case, no kind of case no matter how great the public importance that is implicated, that the parties may not agree in advance of a dispute to submit to arbitration.

But even in other jurisdictions there is continuing palpable conflict between the notions of private autonomy represented by the arbitration agreement and the background mandatory law of a state. And I think we have seen an erosion of the idea – of the illusion, really – that state courts are the only appropriate fora for applying applicable norms and enforcing applicable norms. The ideology of arbitration, as I have said, has become an

---

6   See, e.g., Switz. Private International Law Act art. 192 ("exclusion agreements" which "exclude all setting aside proceedings" where neither party has a domicile or place of business in Switzerland).

ideology of deregulation, and privatisation, which it is thought through the notion of "autonomy" might allow parties to escape the application of mandatory rules.

Now, one of the things that makes arbitration so interesting is its dual nature. It is on the one hand a contractual process that parties choose and design and construct according to what they think serves their own interest. But it also looks very much like adjudication. We have the presentation of evidence. We have deliberation. We have adversarial proceedings and we have an award which is binding on the parties and has the force of law. There is always this tension between the contractual view of arbitration and the jurisdictional view. In the United States, as you might expect, the contractual view is by far the most dominant and most important.[7] But in any system of private dispute resolution, in any country, the arbitrator draws his or her powers only from the contracting parties. And so from the perspective of the arbitrator it is never possible for party autonomy to be "trumped." It is never possible for the party's choice of applicable rules to somehow be overridden. That is something of an overstatement but I think it is true in any interesting sense.

I may have to leave aside cases where the parties have tried to use the arbitration mechanism to facilitate involvement in what used to be called the white slave trade.[8] I am not entirely sure that one can still use that phrase, but in any event, outside of cases that are universally thought to be immoral, it's really not possible to trump exercises in party autonomy.

So, commentators often ask, just where does the allegiance of arbitrators lie? Does it lie with the parties that appointed them – are arbitrators "the servants of the parties" – or does it lie with the states? Is an arbitrator to be really concerned with keeping the deal going or is an arbitrator supposed to be a statesmanlike jurist "whose first dedication is to the law"?[9] Now, that strikes me as being the perfect false dichotomy and one should not have to make any such choice – but if I had to make the choice, I would choose the former because that is where the obligations of the parties lie. And in trying to discover what that obligation consists of – what task has been entrusted by the parties to the arbitrators – one has to remember also that the arbitrator (as Holmes' "bad man")[10] has to be aware above all else of the consequences of his award. He has to look and see what is likely to happen to his award and the threat of non-enforcement of the award for failure to comply with some mandatory rules of a state. The key point for the purposes of our discussion is that possibility is largely theoretical and unlikely to be seen in practice.

---

7 See, e.g., Alan Scott Rau, *Integrity in Private Judging*, 38 So. Tex. L. Rev. 485, 487 (1997).
8 See, e.g., Pierre Mayer, "Reflections on the International Arbitrator's Duty to Apply the Law," in Julian D.M. Lew & Loukas A. Mistelis (eds.), *Arbitration Insights* 289, 303 (2007); Pierre Mayer, "La regle morale dans l'arbitrage international," in *Etudes Offertes a Pierre Bellet* 379, 389-94 (1991).
9 E.g., Marc Blessing, *Mandatory Rules of Law versus Party Autonomy in International Arbitration*, 14(4) J. Int'l Arb. 23, 40 (1997); Andreas Lowenfeld, *The Mitsubishi Case: Another View*, 2 Arb. Int'l 178, 188 (1986).
10 See Oliver Wendell Holmes, Jr., "*The Path of the Law*," 10 Harv. L. Rev. 457, 459 (1897).

The Supreme Court of the United States in the famous *Mitsubishi* case said that if the arbitrator has "taken cognisance" of the particular mandatory law (it was the antitrust laws that were in particular involved there), if he has merely taken cognisance of that law, that will be enough to justify enforcement of the award.[11] That language has been taken quite literally by American lower courts.[12]

The decision in the *Thalès* case in the Court of Appeals of Paris in many ways goes even further because in the *Thalès* case the arbitrators awarded damages for breach of a licence without ever having considered the question of the possible invalidity of the licence under the treaty of Rome. They did not even consider it because the parties had never raised that point before them. Nevertheless the award of the arbitrators was enforced by the court. The court said it is only where the illegality jumps out at you, "knocks your eyes out" – only in such cases will enforcement not be justified. But those cases of course are difficult to find.[13]

At the law faculty of the University of Geneva, there are, or at least were until recently, signs in the common areas that said, "thank you for not smoking in this area, and if necessary – *le cas écheant* – for not throwing your cigarette butts on the floor." And that too was an injunction that did not lay claim to being taken very seriously. And I think the same thing can be said of the problem of mandatory rules of competition law, at least as far as the arbitrators are concerned.

D. Underlying Tensions: Efficiency and Autonomy

A second tension that underlies our present structure of arbitration has to do with the existence of true exercises of autonomy, that is to say the existence of consent. It is the most banal starting point possible to say that arbitrators only have power if there is consent to arbitration on the part of the parties. But really, just about anything, in theory, can raise the existence of whether there is consent or not. Was there an agreement? Was there an agreement arrived at to arbitrate this particular dispute? What if the agreement says that any claims have to be raised within six years? After seven years, can one say that anyone has really "consented" to arbitrate? Any possible limitation on the power of the arbitrators could be seen to raise the question of the existence of consent. What I would suggest is that consent is not an all or nothing problem, that

---

11 Mitsubishi Motors Corp. v. Soler Chrysler-Plymouth, Inc., 473 U.S. 614, 626 (1985).
12 E.g., Baxter Int'l, Inc. v. Abbott Laboratories, 315 F.3d 829 (7th Cir. 2003)("*whether* the tribunal's construction of [the license] has [the effect of commanding the parties to violate rules of positive law] was a question put to, and resolved by, the arbitrators," and as between the parties "their answer is conclusive").
13 SA Thales Air Defense v. GIE Euromissile, [2005] Rev. de l'Arb. 751 (Cour d'Appel de Paris, 2004). See also Tensacciai v. Terra Armata, [2006] Rev. de l'Arb. 763 (Trib. Fed. Switz. 2006)("the provisions of competition law, whatever they are, are not part of the essential and widely-shared values that make up the foundation of any legal order," so that a violation of these provisions is not "incompatible with public policy").

there are different degrees of consent and one has to make, in the interest of efficiency, one has to make some critical distinctions.[14]

So here is something I am very proud of.

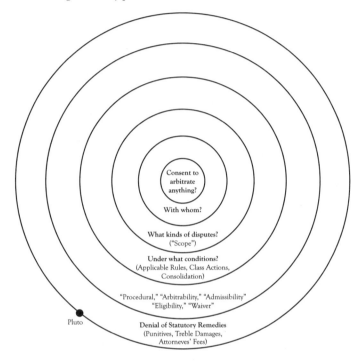

The core question one has to ask is was there any consent to arbitrate anything at all. That is, for example, was the document forged? Was someone a lunatic or an infant and thus incapable of consent? Was there in effect an agreement to *something*?

Now, if there is agreement to *something*, the case becomes a little bit more difficult. If there was no agreement to arbitrate anything, then the case becomes fairly easy. And I think if a party did not agree to arbitrate anything, then a court should be able immediately to enjoin the conduct of any arbitration because if the arbitrators proceed, they are strangers, they are officious intermeddlers, they have no standing to proceed.

But if there is an agreement to arbitrate *something*, the matter becomes very different. For example, the question will arise, *what sorts of agreements, what sorts of disputes* did you agree to arbitrate? The contract may have called for the arbitration of a dispute

---

14 More elaborate versions of this discussion can be found in Alan Scott Rau, *All You Need to Know About "Separability" in Seventeen Simple Propositions*, 14 Am. Rev. of Int'l Arb. 1 (2003); Alan Scott Rau, *Arbitral Jurisdiction and the Dimensions of Party "Consent"*, 24 Arbitration International 199 (2008).

arising out of the sale of oranges. What if a dispute arises in connection with the sale of a shipment of apples? Did you agree to arbitrate that at all? It seems to me that once the parties have agreed to arbitrate something, the arbitrator is not a stranger, is not an officious intermeddler and we ought to temper our insistence on consent in the interest of efficiency. That is to say very often the question, what is the scope of the agreement to arbitrate, that third circle there, will be very closely connected to the merits of the dispute. It makes some sense to have the same person, judge or arbitrator, decide both, the merits and the scope. Lord Hoffmann in the English Court of Appeal talked about the advantages of "one-stop adjudication."[15] That is to say, it is probably more sensible and efficient for the same party to decide both issues and if the parties wanted to submit the merits to arbitration, they probably also intended to submit the question of the scope of the arbitration to the same tribunal. We should attribute an intention to them which is consistent with the notion of reduced cost and efficiency. And one way of doing that is to allow the arbitrators to decide the question of the scope of arbitration. And that I think is precisely where American Law is going or indeed where American Law is.

One of the most common questions in arbitration these days is the question, *"with whom* am I obligated to arbitrate?" This is one of the most difficult topics in international arbitration because the globalisation of international trade has caused all sorts of complex webs of interwoven agreements to arise. And if everybody who is involved in a dispute can not be brought into the same proceeding, then, we are going to have duplicative proceedings; we are going to have inconsistent results. And so while consent and agreement is important, efficient dispute resolution is equally important. I think that in many circumstances, the question of whom are you obligated to arbitrate with is a question that might well be for the arbitrators also. At least this is true where a signatory to an agreement is being asked to arbitrate with someone else, with a non-signatory. The signatory has after all agreed to arbitrate something. Whether he has to arbitrate with this non-signatory is a question of the scope of his obligation, the dimensions of his obligation, the parameters of his obligation, but the arbitrator is not a complete stranger to him because the signatory has agreed to entrust this arbitrator with something. The argument is that "it is more foreseeable, and thus more reasonable, that a party who has actually agreed in writing to arbitrate claims with *someone* might be compelled to *broaden the scope of his agreement to include others.*"[16] As with other matters of scope, such a presumption brings all the advantages of efficiency with limited impingement on contractual autonomy. So if the question is, "is a signatory obligated to arbitrate," I think that looks very much like the third circle in my drawing, and I think that is something that could and should be left to the arbitrators them-

---

15 Harbour Assurance Co. (UK) Ltd. v. Kansa Gen. Int'l Ins. Co. Ltd., [1993] Q.B. 701, 724, 726 (C.A.) (Hoffmann, L.J.). See also Fiona Trust & Holding Corp. v. Prvalov, [2007] 1 All ER (Comm.) 891, 900 (C.A. 2007)("if businessmen go to the trouble of agreeing that their disputes be heard in the courts of a particular country or by a tribunal of their choice they do not expect that time and expense will be taken in lengthy argument about whether any particular cause of action comes within the meaning of the particular phrase they have chosen")(Longmore, L.J.).
16 Bridas SAPIC v. Government of Turkmenistan, 345 F.3d 347, 361 (5th Cir. 2003).

selves. If by contrast it is a *non-signatory* that is being asked to arbitrate, that is very different because the non-signatory by hypothesis may have agreed to nothing. So, it is an important distinction to ask whether the signatory or the non-signatory is the party who is trying to avoid arbitration.

That is a distinction which I think is quite familiar to the common law, although it is a distinction that has absolutely no resonance whatever in civil-law jurisdictions, as near as I can tell. But that is because the civil law inquiry is conventionally phrased, at the customary high level of abstraction, as one into the "transmission," or "transfer," or "extension," or "circulation" of the arbitration clause – without attention to the status of the party who is seeking to invoke it. But if someone has consented to arbitrate, if that core circle is satisfied, then our usual insistence on consent and agreement might well be tempered.

E. Underlying Tensions: Congruence and Conflict Among National Regimes

The third tension is conflict across national regimes and that is a function of the question, "which state (or more properly, the courts of which state) constitute the primary source of control of arbitration?" Is it the state where the arbitration takes place? Or is it some other state?

The usual territorial assumption is that the courts of the state where the arbitration takes place (or more properly, the state where the parties have indicated that the seat of the arbitration is to be) is the state that has the ultimate control over the fate of the arbitration award. The idea, by contrast, that an arbitration does not depend at all on the law of the state where the arbitration takes place – but that the arbitration is somehow independent, somehow untethered, somehow detached, that it exists in the sky without being dependent on the law of any particular state – is an idea that has had a lot of play in the Gallic imagination, if I can use that phrase: That is to say, it's an idea that the French seem to have adopted with enthusiasm. I can not tell you, in the time that I have left, the amount of problems this causes. Let me instead tell you a story:

There was an English arbitration. The award was handed down in England. And the English courts annulled the award on the ground of an "error of law" as they have the right to do: That is an unusual feature of English law but under the English Arbitration Act, the award can be overturned for error of law and that is what the English courts did. So, the parties went through a second arbitration. And as you might expect, the second arbitration came up with a different result. Meanwhile, the winner *in the first arbitration* took the award to France and the award was enforced in France on the French theory that an international award "is not attached to any state's legal order," and "does not depend on any state law in order to exist" – so, without regard to English arbitration law, if the award was otherwise unobjectionable, according to the notions of French courts, it can be enforced by them. And it was.[17] So this first award was enforceable in France – but of course, it was enforceable nowhere else in the world. The *second* award could not be enforced in France, because it was incompatible with the first, but it *could* be enforced *anywhere else* in the world.

Now, that absurdity is the result of refusing to give deference to the law of the state where the arbitration takes place. I think to some extent the problem is metaphysical, that is, it is an enslavement to an a priori intellectual scheme.[18] In addition, though, I think such decisions are explainable on the grounds of a simple distrust of the judiciary of other states: In another case, for example, a French court has enforced an award that had been vacated in Dubai on the grounds that the arbitrators had not taken an oath – which was a sufficient ground to overturn an award under the law of Dubai. The French courts deemed this not to be an acceptable reason and so enforced the award anyway, even though it had been vacated in Dubai. Perhaps this result was a response to the fact that the losing party in the arbitration – at whose behest the award has been overturned – was a state agency of Dubai.[19] Or perhaps it represents a judgment that some states like Dubai – neophytes in the recondite world of international arbitration – are not yet able to understand the proper standards for the review of awards. Or perhaps, as some French commentators have suggested, such a decision is justified on the grounds that it is in Dubai's own interest – that the state of Dubai needs to be protected against its own judiciary: Because if awards handed down in Dubai are regularly enforced in France, then Dubai will become a more popular location for arbitrations to take place. If they could only be freed from the parochialism of their own courts, it will be in their own interest that we are enforcing awards emanating from these states.[20]

If you think about this reasoning, it looks very much like the classic neo-colonialist move – in which we choose to ignore the policy decisions made by other countries, who do not quite understand, and we are doing it for their own interest. And they will thank us for it later. Now, if that is not colonialism, I do not know what is. I apologize for well exceeding the time allotted, but I have really been able merely to hint at the many tensions and conflicts that underlie what would otherwise be a perfectly seamless regime of arbitration.

---

17 Soc. PT Putrabali Adyamulia v. Soc. Rena Holding, [2007] Rev. de l'Arb. 507 (Cour de Cassation, 2007); cf. id. at 511 (rapport of President Jean-Pierre Ancel; "when the ground for annulment is "local," that is, closely linked to national legal concepts, it has no claim to be honored internationally").
18 "Their definitions surround them like a kennel contains a hound . . . like a thrown stone imagining it will not fall/their explanations work to keep the world fixed." Stephen Dobyns, "Sleeping Dogs," *Times Literary Supplement*, Feb. 3, 2006, p. 4.
19 *See* Direction générale de l'aviation civile de l'Emirat de Dubai v. Société international Bechtel, 2006 Rev. Arb. 695 (*Cour d'Appel de Paris*, Sept. 29, 2005); Thomas Clay, Note, [2007] J.D.I. 1236, 1248 (the fact that the courts of Dubai had annulled an award against the state's own civil aviation authority, and in favor of a foreign company, was "perhaps not totally irrelevant to a true understanding of the court's decision").
20 *See, e.g.*, Jan Paulsson, Note, 2007 Rev. Arb. 559, 564 (French jurisprudence tends to ensure "that the number of sites of arbitrations will be more widespread"; parties "may find it more acceptable to fix the situs in a country that is less experienced in arbitration, and which does not benefit from a serious tradition of judicial independence, if they can be assured that any award ultimately rendered will survive local abuses").

Investment Arbitration

CHRISTOPH SCHREUER [1]

A. The Function of Investment Arbitration

Much of what Professor Rau has said, also applies to investment arbitration, but there are some important differences. For one thing, investment arbitration is always mixed, meaning that there is a sovereign state on one side and a foreign investor on the other side. Typically the foreign investor is the claimant and the state is the respondent, although this is not necessarily so.

Investment arbitration is also international, more so than commercial arbitration in two ways. Most often it is based on a treaty. Also, in most cases public international law is applied. That is another distinctive feature of investment arbitration.

Why do we need investment arbitration in the first place? I think this is best explained by looking at what investment arbitration has replaced. Before investment arbitration the investor had essentially two means of recourse. One was diplomatic protection, that is, turning to the investor's state of nationality and asking for help. Diplomatic protection, of course, looks wonderful at first sight. The state takes care of you. But it has serious disadvantages. First of all, it is discretionary. The home state of the investor may but does not need to exercise diplomatic protection. The state may abandon diplomatic protection and it may waive the claim altogether. Diplomatic protection also has disadvantages for the states concerned. It can strain the relations of the two countries. This can be particularly disadvantageous for weaker states.

The other classical remedy for foreign investors was domestic courts, typically the courts of the host states. Rightly or wrongly, foreign investors have little confidence in the courts of the host state. In most cases I believe more rightly than wrongly. This is not necessarily parochial. I would not recommend choosing Austrian courts to a foreign investor in Austria. And the same applies to Switzerland, Germany and the United States, whatever.

Investment arbitration usually involves very large sums of money and often essential interests of the host states. It is simply asking too much of a host state court to be objec-

---

1 Prof. Dr. Christoph Schreuer, Professor at the University of Vienna.

tive in situations like that. If you need an illustration there is a famous case, the *Loewen* case.[2] If you want to know how this works in Mississippi all you need to do is to read that particular case. I will not go into details.

Investment arbitration nowadays is probably the most vibrant area of international law. There are numerous cases pending. My rough estimate is that there are probably around 200 investment cases pending at the moment. Another interesting feature of investment arbitration that distinguishes it from commercial arbitration is that it very often involves public interests. Think of a situation where a foreign investor arbitrates, say, with Argentina about the water supply of a large city. That has a commercial side, but I do not need to explain that there is also a public interest side. This is not a purely commercial case. That of course makes it rather more complex.

B. The Arbitration Agreement

Where does the arbitration agreement come from in investment arbitration? As you know, every arbitration is based on an agreement between the parties. Here we also find some peculiarities in investment arbitration. In some situations you have the classical arbitration agreement, a document signed by both sides that has an arbitration clause in it. This was the typical basis of investment arbitration for a long time.

Things have changed radically, especially over the last ten years or so. Nowadays the typical basis for investment arbitration is a treaty, often a bilateral investment treaty (BIT) between the host state and the state of the investor's nationality. Most BITs contain offers of investment arbitration to foreign investors provided they have the right nationality. In other words, the two countries, parties to these bilateral treaties, offer special conditions to the nationals of the respective other country including investment arbitration. The treaty clause is only an offer to eligible investors. How does the offer turn into an agreement? Often quite simply through the institution of proceedings. That is how the investor accepts the offer and perfects the investment arbitration agreement.

The third source, which is used less frequently, is domestic legislation. It works in a similar way. Many states offer investment arbitration through their investment codes or other pieces of domestic legislation to foreign eligible investors.

---

2   *Loewen Group, Inc. and Raymond L. Loewen* v. *United States of America*, Award, 26 June 2003, 42 ILM 811 (2003); 7 ICSID Reports 442.

C. The Subject Matter of Investment Arbitration

The subject matter of investment disputes has changed dramatically over time, especially in the last couple of years. If you look at older cases, expropriation was very much in the foreground. Nowadays relatively few decisions uphold claims of expropriation for the simple reason that practice has adopted a narrow concept of expropriation. It has become very difficult to prove an expropriation. There has to be a complete or substantial deprivation. So if there has just been some damage to the investment, that is not good enough to establish an expropriation.

Nowadays the most important standards come from treaties. Typical standards are: fair and equitable treatment, protection against arbitrary and discriminatory measures and full protection and security. These standards sound very abstract. And they are. But they are applied in practice and have been filled with some substance. If you think this is unworkable, just think of the American concept of due process. That is highly abstract and has been filled with life through the practice of the courts over the years.

D. Investment Arbitration and Domestic Courts

Let me say a few words about the relationship of investment arbitration to domestic courts. This is a particularly complex issue that has quite a few facets. The most prominent aspect of it, is the distinction between treaty claims and contract claims. This distinction has developed over the last seven or eight years. The problem behind it is, that many investment contracts that foreign investors enter into with host states or their instrumentalities contain domestic forum selection clauses, that is, the selection of domestic courts of the host state in case of disputes. Not a very wise move on the part of the investors.

At the same time you have a treaty. For instance, a bilateral investment treaty that promises international arbitration to foreign investors. Now which prevails? Is it international arbitration or is it the domestic court?

The investor almost invariably opts for international arbitration because it has more confidence in international tribunals. The host state insists on the use of its own domestic courts knowing pretty well that it has a much better chance of gaining the upper hand in its own courts. International tribunals have developed the distinction between treaty claims and contract claims in order to defend their jurisdiction. They said: the domestic forum selection clause only applies to breaches of the contract, but does not apply to treaty claims, that is, alleged violations of the treaties themselves. This is a bit of an oversimplification and I hope the Chair will forgive me for that.

Then, related to this, in many treaties you have so-called umbrella clauses. In an umbrella clause the host state promises to honour commitments, especially contractual commitments it has made. The prevailing but not the only reading is that this turns a breach of contract into a breach of treaty. It is a violation of the umbrella clause if you breach the contract. In this way you also gain access to the international tribunal. However, there are also other views. Some people say this only applies to certain types of contracts and other people say this only applies to certain types of violations. This is one of the most hotly disputed and contentious areas of international investment law.

To stay with the relationship of international investment arbitration and domestic courts, you will find that many treaties have so-called fork in the road clauses. Essentially, a fork in the road clause says that the foreign investor has a choice between domestic courts and international arbitration but once he has made the choice he cannot turn back. Or if you prefer it in Latin it is *una via selecta non datur recursus ad alteram*. Only for those of you who speak fluent Latin and please excuse my German pronunciation of it.

Even though investors often get involved into domestic litigation, fork in the road clauses have hardly ever worked. International tribunals have found that the domestic litigation concerned a different cause of action, in other words, that it was not the same dispute.

Another strange clause that you find in many treaties is a so-called 18 months in domestic courts clause. It says, yes you can go to international arbitration but before you are allowed to do that, you must have tried to settle your dispute in the domestic courts for 18 months. In practice this is a waste of time because no legal system can settle a complex dispute in 18 months, especially if you think of appeals procedures. And when you are talking about several hundred million Euro or Swiss Francs or Dollars, you will have an appeal, you can be sure of that. So, in a sense this just extends the dispute. Most investors who tried to get around the 18 month rule have managed to do so with the help of most favoured nation clauses.

In principle, an investor who goes to international arbitration does not need to exhaust local remedies. So the traditional rule of exhaustion of local remedies that you have in interstate disputes and in the human rights field is not applicable in investment arbitration. But there is an interesting phenomenon: the requirement to resort to domestic remedies is creeping back into practice. I have already mentioned the 18 month clause. In addition, it is generally agreed that in case of an alleged denial of justice, which is a specific tort under international law, you need to exhaust local remedies. That is still understandable. But then, recently some tribunals have argued that one cannot really speak of an expropriation, unless there has at least been a try at domestic courts: you must first have tried to get rid of the measure before you come to us for international adjudication. Or: before you complain about unfair and inequitable treatment you must at least have tried to get redress in the domestic courts. It is easy to see that this is a slippery slope. Once you ask an investor to try domestic remedies where is he supposed to stop trying? Why not go all the way to the Supreme Court? Then the requirement to exhaust domestic remedies is back.

Then you have the paradoxical situation that the decisions of domestic courts may well be scrutinised by the international tribunal. A domestic court may act in a way that violates the rights of a foreign investor, incurs the liability of the host state, leading to state responsibility. This may in turn be a violation of a bilateral investment treaty or another treaty and be subject to adjudication by international investment tribunals.

But there is also the opposite situation. In non-ICSID arbitration, the normal supervisory power of the domestic courts, that Professor Rau spoke about earlier, still applies. For instance, investment decisions in the framework of the North American Free Trade Agreement (NAFTA) are subject to the supervision and scrutiny of domestic courts. So in some situations domestic courts and investment tribunals supervise each other. This is strange because we are used to think in terms of hierarchies of courts and tribunals and not of mutual control.

E. Precedent in Investment Arbitration

One of the questions that was put to us by the organisers was: how do you ever reach a reasonable system of precedent when all of these investment tribunals are individually composed? If you look at lists of cases, you will find that every case has its own panel. Some arbitrators appear more often than others but in principle every tribunal is on its own. At the same time we have a rich case law, not all of which gets published but much of it or most of it does. The fact is that there is a system (it is not really a system but a phenomenon) of constant reference and deference to earlier decisions. But this practice is not entirely consistent. There is no doctrine of precedent in the classic common law sense. But tribunals have a tendency to look at earlier decisions and to follow them. Here again, you have different schools of thought. Some are of the opinion that every tribunal is on its own. I call that the condor approach, named after a remark by Professor Orrego Vicuña, who extolled the virtues of the condor, cycling freely above the Andes and said that is how an arbitrator should behave.

Then there is the flock of birds approach, just to stick to the metaphor. That approach is perhaps best epitomised by a formula that you will find in some recent decisions by investment tribunals, usually chaired by Professor Kaufmann-Kohler. I completely subscribe to that approach. This formula is as follows:

> *The Tribunal considers that it is not bound by previous decisions. At the same time, it is of the opinion that it must pay due consideration to earlier decisions of international tribunals. It believes that, subject to compelling contrary grounds, it has a duty to*

adopt solutions established in a series of consistent cases. It also believes that, subject to the specifics of a given treaty and of the circumstances of the actual case, it has a duty to seek to contribute to the harmonious development of investment law and thereby to meet the legitimate expectations of the community of States and investors towards certainty of the rule of law.[3]

So, yes, there is a system of precedent but it is relatively loose. It does not work at hundred percent and you can see that in some contentious areas. In some areas investment tribunals do contradict each other.

F. The Tribunal

What about the qualifications of investment arbitrators? This is a mixed group. Some reach this particular area from commercial arbitration, some from public international law. Sometimes you will find a former national judge. I think this mix of different qualifications is wholesome. Obviously, being a public international lawyer I feel that there should always be a public international lawyer on every panel. But that is not always the case and even then they usually do reasonably well. But of course we have to be honest: when it comes to the selection of arbitrators by the parties, they make their selections mostly on tactical grounds. This is a fact of life. The Counsel will look at lists of names and will think: who is going to be most useful to us. But then, of course, you always need a chair and it is very often the chair who plays a decisive role because the chair is not selected by one side but either by both or by an appointing authority.

G. Nationality

Nationality is an interesting issue. Nationality plays a very important role in investment arbitration for a number of reasons. First of all, a big part of investment arbitration is based on treaties, mostly bilateral treaties. So a claimant needs to have the right nationality. If you want to rely let us say on a bilateral investment treaty between Italy and the United Arab Emirates and the claimant wants to sue the United Arab Emirates, he needs to show that he is an Italian national. And if he cannot do that he is out.[4]

Another restriction, which is perhaps not so severe, is nationality under the ICSID Convention. If you want to operate under the ICSID Convention, the most popular system of investment arbitration, your state of nationality needs to be a party to that Convention. Some countries are not. I am not going to list them but there are some

---

3   See *Saipem S.p.A. v. People's Republic of Bangladesh*, Decision on Jurisdiction and Recommendation on Provisional Measures, 21 March 2007, 22 ICSID Review – FILJ 100 (2007).
4   See *Hussein Nuaman Soufraki v. United Arab Emirates*, Award, 7 July 2004, 12 ICSID Reports 158.

important countries that have not ratified the Convention. So that is another issue of nationality.

And then you have the diversity of nationality rule. An investor may not sue his home country. The whole idea is to attract foreign investment.

The problem already starts with natural persons. There are some cases where the nationality of natural persons is an issue. But the problem really becomes big when it comes to juridical persons, to corporations. What is the nationality of a corporation? There are rules about that. The problem with the nationality of corporations is that it is relatively easy to organize or manipulate it. In fact, nationality planning nowadays is a very important subject. And it is not illegitimate. For instance, many corporations like to incorporate in the Netherlands because the Netherlands have a very good system of bilateral investment treaties. So it is advantageous to be a Dutch corporation.

Some countries counteract these tendencies by inserting "denial of benefits" clauses in their treaties. They say: you can only claim to be a national of our country if you have genuine economic links, if you are owned (we are talking about corporations) by our nationals or if you do business in our country. Switzerland has such clauses in its treaties.

So the nationality requirements are often relatively easy to circumvent and this happens more and more. This is neither illegal nor invalid. There was a famous case, *Tokios Tokelès*, where a group of Ukrainians incorporated a company in Lithuania and the company then sued the Ukraine and prevailed on jurisdiction[5] though not on the merits.[6] Some people got very upset about this case. This is not their idea of protecting foreign investors.

There is a general paradox about this whole business of nationality. When it comes to access to investment arbitration, to jurisdiction, nationality is extremely important and a lot of ink is spilt and a lot of time is spent to prove a particular nationality. I have myself been involved in several cases where an enormous amount of effort went into proving or disproving a nationality.

When you come to the merits, strangely enough, distinctions on the basis of nationality become taboo. You are not allowed to discriminate on the basis of nationality. You will find national treatment clauses and most favoured nation clauses. Therefore, on substance you must not distinguish on the basis of nationality.

---

5 *Tokios Tokelès* v. *Ukraine*, Decision on Jurisdiction, 29 April 2004, 20 ICSID Review – FILJ 205 (2005); 11 ICSID Reports 313.
6 *Tokios Tokelès* v. *Ukraine*, Award, 26 July 2007, http://ita.law.uvic.ca/documents/TokiosAward.pdf.

Of course the human rights lawyers have found a solution to this. They say, human rights are enjoyed regardless of nationality. Perhaps in the long run, this will be the future of investment arbitration. But we are still a long distance from that.

Arbitration in Public International Disputes

CARL BAUDENBACHER
FRANK BREMER[1]

A. Introduction

Despite numerous obituaries that have been written in the past, most notably after the inauguration of the International Court of Justice (ICJ), public international arbitration or interstate arbitration has persisted as one of the pillars of dispute settlement between state entities. It is the objective of this article to give an overview of the historical origins of interstate arbitration and its defining characteristics as well as a brief outlook on its future prospects in international dispute settlement.

As a side note, the topic also merits special consideration from the authors' Swiss perspective. In its formative years, the idea of arbitration was strongly supported by the Swiss nationals Henry Dunant (1828–1910) and Johann Kaspar Bluntschli (1808–1881). Dunant, founder of the Red Cross, was convinced that the prevention of armed conflicts necessitated the establishment of an international court of arbitration with arbitrators selected from various nations. Through his many activities, he had ultimately become very influential for the groundbreaking Hague Conference of 1899 out of which the Permanent Court of Arbitration was born. Bluntschli, a founding member of the Institute of International Law and arguably the most famous 19th-century Swiss jurist, was much inspired by the successful conclusion of the *Alabama Claims* dispute between the United States and Great Britain (1872)[2] and, through his much-acclaimed works, greatly contributed not only to the development of international law but also to the emergence of peaceful interstate arbitration.

Furthermore, some of the most prominent arbitrators in the history of arbitration were of Swiss nationality. Jakob Staempfli (1820–1879), former President of the Swiss Confederation, was one of three neutral nominees in the seminal *Alabama Claims* case.[3] Max Huber (1874–1960), President of the Permanent Court of International Justice (PCIJ) from 1925 to 1927, acted as one of the arbitrators in the *Island of Palmas* case,[4]

---

1   Ass. iur. Frank Bremer, LL.M. (Liverpool), Research Associate at the Institute of European and International Business Law, University of St. Gallen. The authors acknowledge the valuable assistance of James Thurman in finalizing this paper.
2   *Alabama Arbitration* (United States v. Great Britain, 1872), reported in: J. B. MOORE, *History and Digest of the International Arbitrations to which the United States has been a Party*, London, 1898, Vol. I, p. 543. Award: *ibid.*, 653.
3   Ibid.
4   *Island of Palmas Arbitration* (Netherlands v. United States, 1928), 2 R.I.A.A., p. 829.

which was ultimately to become one of the most cited cases in international law books. In this connection, it may also be noted that many interstate arbitrations have taken place in Switzerland, such as the aforementioned *Alabama Claims* arbitration, the *Beagle Channel* arbitration between Chile and Argentina (1977)[5] and the *Taba* arbitration between Egypt and Israel (1988).[6]

Finally, in 1291, one of the earliest arbitration treaties was concluded in what would later become Switzerland. The Cantons of Uri, Schwyz and Nidwalden signed a permanent arbitration treaty which provided that:

> "If a disagreement has come between the confederates the most prudent will intervene by arbitration to end by the means which appear the most appropriate [...].[7]

The authors thus observe that the topic is not only of interest "ratione materiae" but also "ratione loci".

B. Arbitration – Scope of the Analysis

In international law, "Arbitration" (from Latin arbitrārī: to give judgment) can refer to two different situations. First, in its classical meaning, it can describe a form of dispute settlement between States. For this branch of arbitration the term "public international arbitration" or "interstate arbitration" has come to be accepted. Second, arbitration can relate to dispute settlement involving individuals or corporations as parties. This form of arbitration is usually called "private international arbitration" or "international commercial arbitration". Private international arbitration can be further subdivided into dispute settlement between States/State-owned corporations and private entities on the one hand and dispute settlement involving only private entities on the other hand. In the present article, only the first form of arbitration, public international arbitration or interstate arbitration will be considered.

C. Arbitration – Definition

Arbitration can be broadly defined as the resolution of a dispute between States through a legal decision of one or more umpires or of a tribunal, other than an international court, chosen by the parties.[8]

---

5   *Beagle Channel Arbitration* (Argentina v. Chile, 1977), 17 I.L.M., p. 631.
6   *Taba Arbitration* (Egypt v. Israel, 1988), 20 R.I.A.A., p. 12.
7   Arbitration Treaty reported in: EDOUARD LANGLADE, *De la clause compromissoire et des traités d'arbitrage permanent*, (1899), p. 33; translated in J. ALLAIN, *A Century of International Adjudication: The Rule of Law and it[s] Limits*, (2000), p. 15.
8   L. OPPENHEIM, *International Law*, Vol. II, *Disputes, War and Neutrality*, H. Lauterpacht, (1952), p. 22.

Arbitration is to be distinguished from dispute settlement by diplomatic means, such as negotiation, mediation, inquiry or conciliation[9] and from dispute settlement by international courts. Arbitration differs from diplomatic means of dispute settlement in so far as that the decision is binding and must be based on the law. This is not to say that diplomatic dispute settlement forbids the parties from allowing legal considerations. However, the parties are not obliged to do so and therefore, whenever they see fit, may decide to base their decision on political, economical or other non-legal grounds rather than on legal principles. The famous view of Aristotle that

> "An equitable and moderate man will have recourse to arbitration rather than to strict law [...] because an arbitrator may consider the equity of the case, whereas a judge is bound by the letter of the law."[10]

thus no longer holds true for the modern conception of arbitration.

Arbitration is set apart from judicial settlement by the fact that the State parties do not submit a dispute to a standing court but have to set up the decision-making institution themselves.[11] As a consequence, they enjoy considerably more influence on (a) the persons who are called upon to decide the dispute, (b) the procedural rules according to which the proceedings of the case are conducted, (c) the law or legal principles determinative for the decision, (d) the right of appeal, and finally (e) the enforcement of the arbitral award. The main distinctive element of arbitration vis-à-vis judicial settlement is thus epitomized in the notion of *party autonomy*.[12] Put differently, arbitration is a creature of the agreement of the parties – it is their dispute, and it is their way of resolving that dispute.[13] To borrow from Clausewitz, interstate arbitration, considered by many writers to be a hybrid oscillating between classic diplomacy and a court-like adjudication[14] can be described as the continuation of diplomatic dispute settlement by legal means.

Before going into the details of interstate arbitration, it is pertinent to look first at the historical roots of interstate arbitration in order to gain a better understanding of its relevance in international law.

---

9   For an overview of the different diplomatic means of dispute settlement, see, J. G. MERRILLS, *International Dispute Settlement*, (2005), pp. 1–87.
10 Reported in: CF. H. GROTIUS, *De Jure Belli ac Pacis*, Book III, Cap. XX, XLVIL, translated by A. C. CAMPBELL, *The Rights of War and Peace, Including the Law of Nature and of Nations*, (2007), p. 398 (quoting ARISTOTLE, Rhetoric I, 13).
11 Increasingly, many writers reject the idea of a strict distinction of arbitration and court adjudication but prefer to speak of fluid boundaries. See K. H. BÖCKSTIEGEL, States in the international arbitral process, in: J. D. M. Lew (Ed.), *Contemporary Problems in International Arbitration*, (1987), p. 41; One of the reasons is that, even in proceedings before the ICJ, States have the option to use ad-hoc chambers under Article 26 (2) of the ICJ Statute in which judges are to be appointed by the States themselves.
12 H. M. HOLTZMANN, Some Reflections on the Nature of Arbitration, in S. Muller, W. Mijs (Eds.), *The Flame Rekindled, New Hopes for international Arbitration*, (1994), p. 68.
13 G. GIBSON, *The Arbitrator's Companion*, (2001), p. 4.
14 J. H. W. VERZIJL, International Law in Historical Perspective, Part VIII: Interstate Disputes and Their Settlement, (1976), p. 163.

D. History of Arbitration

I. The Jay Treaty

The modern history of arbitration is generally considered to begin with the 1794 *Jay Treaty* between the United States and Great Britain.[15] The treaty is named after John Jay, the U.S. chief justice and envoy extraordinary, who signed the Treaty in London on behalf of the U.S. delegation.

In the *Jay Treaty* the U.S. and Great Britain established among other things three joint commissions. The mandate of the first arbitral commission (St. Croix River Commission) was to determine the exact location of the northwest boundary of the U.S. with Canada (British North America). The second arbitral commission (British Debts Commission) had the task to resolve claims by British merchants for outstanding debts incurred by U.S. citizens before conclusion of the Peace Treaty in 1783 that formally ended the War for Independence. The third commission (Maritime Claims Commission) had to settle complaints by U.S. citizens relating to irregular seizures of vessels and cargo under the colour or authority of the British government. This short description indicates that only the first commission constituted a classic interstate arbitration.

Besides averting an immediate war between the United States and Great Britain and strengthening the commercial relations between both parties, the *Jay Treaty* is credited with several important contributions to the development of international arbitration. The installation of arbitral commissions is viewed to have revived arbitration as an instrument of dispute settlement in modern times. Importantly, the decisions of the arbitral commissions were reasoned, final and, albeit often blended with diplomatic considerations, to a considerable degree based on law.[16]

This is clearly demonstrated by Art. 7 of the *Jay Treaty* which instructed the third Commission, the Maritime Claims Commission that it

> "[...] shall decide the Claims in question, according to the merits of the several Cases, and to Justice Equity and the Laws of Nations."

The commissions confirmed thus the essentially judicial character of modern arbitration. However, diplomatic negotiations still played an important role in the procedures which is also evidenced by the fact that the commissions consisted exclusively of citizens from the disputing parties. Nevertheless, the composition of the claims commissions can be seen as an important precursor of modern forms of arbitral tribunals. As a final important legacy of the Jay Treaty, the Maritime Claims Commission introduced

---

15 *Treaty of Amity, Commerce and Navigation* (United States of America v. United Kingdom), London, 19. November 1794, Consolidated Treaty Series, Vol. 52, pp. 245–272.
16 G. SCHWARZENBERGER, *Present-Day Relevance of the Jay Treaty Arbitrations*, 53 Notre Dame L. Rev., p. 716, (724).

the concept of *competence-competence* according to which a tribunal has the authority to rule on the scope of its own jurisdiction.

II. The Alabama Claims Arbitration

The procedure laid down in the *Jay Treaty* was successfully applied in the *Alabama Claims* arbitration of 1872.[17] The Alabama claims arose out of a diplomatic dispute between the United States and Great Britain in connection with the Civil War. The United States successfully demanded compensation from Britain for the damage caused by the British-built, Southern-operated *Alabama* war vessel, based upon the argument that the British Government, by aiding the creation and supply of a Confederate Navy, had contravened its neutrality laws. The British Government had received information that the *Alabama* had been commissioned not as formally declared by China but by the Confederates and, despite this warning, did not prevent the delivery of the vessel. During the Civil War the *Alabama* attacked and captured more than 60 Northern freight vessels leading to considerable damage to the Northern economy. The arbitration ultimately culminated in an award against Great Britain of US$ 15,500,000 in gold.

As the arbitrations under the Jay Treaty, the *Alabama Claims* arbitration is considered to have made important contributions to the development of modern arbitration and is even touted by some writers as the greatest arbitration in modern history.[18] First of all, following the experiences of this tribunal, the Tsar of Russia and the U.S. President Theodore Roosevelt found encouragement to seek means of making international arbitration more effective in the *Hague Peace Conferences* of 1899 and 1907. Furthermore, in contrast to the sometimes quasi-diplomatic arbitral commissions set up by the *Jay Treaty*, the *Alabama Claims* arbitration for the first time established a collegial tribunal of jurists in which national arbitrators appointed by the disputing parties represented only a minority.[19] The consequence was that the tribunal's independence was strengthened which marked a decisive shift towards the judicialization of arbitration. In legal terms, the Alabama case confirmed what was already established by the Maritime Claims Commission, namely that, in the absence of any agreement to the contrary, an international tribunal has the right to determine its own jurisdiction and, for this purpose, to interpret the instruments which govern that jurisdiction.[20] Another important finding was that a State is barred from pleading a provision of its internal law or an act of its executive power as a defense to a charge that it has violated

---

17 *Supra* note 1.
18 See C. H. BROWER II, *The Functions and Limits of Arbitration and Judicial Settlement under Private and Public International Law*, 18 Duke J. of Comp. & Int'l L., p. 260.
19 See T. BINGHAM, Alabama Arbitration, in R. Wolfrum (Ed.), *The Max Planck Encyclopedia of Public International Law*, (2008), online edition, [www.mpepil.com], para. 10, visited on 2 April 2009.
20 See also *Nottebohm Case* (Liechtenstein v. Guatemala, 1953), I.C.J. Rep. 1953, p. 111 (119).

international law.[21] Finally, the tribunal granted arbitrators the right to state separate or dissenting opinions.

III. Further Arbitrations

After enjoying considerable success, these early arbitrations were followed by nearly 100 further arbitration procedures before the end of the 19th century.[22] As no exhaustive coverage can be attempted, suffice it to mention only two examples of this long list, the *Bering Sea* between Great Britain and the United States (1893)[23] and the *Venezuela – British Guiana Boundary* arbitration (1899).[24]

The subject of the *Bering Sea* arbitration was a fishery dispute between the United States and Great Britain concerning the capture of three British sealers by the United States who were condemned by a judge on the ground that they had been sealing within the limits of Alaska territory. The U.S. Government took the view that the seals in the Bering Sea were, practically, domesticated animals, and thus entitled to protection of the Government of the United States. In addition, it argued that the United States had the exclusive rights of fishing in the Bering Sea. The arbitrators came to the conclusion that the seals were *fera natura*, and that the U.S. had no exclusive right to fishing in the Bering Sea.

The *British Guiana and Venezuela Boundary* dispute concerned one of Latin America's most persistent border disputes. In 1835 the British government asked the German explorer Robert Hermann Schomburgk to map British Guiana and mark its boundaries. Venezuela filed protests against the boundaries. Negotiations between Britain and Venezuela over the boundary began, but no agreement could be reached. Venezuela finally broke diplomatic relations with Britain in 1887 and appealed to the United States for help. The British at first rejected the U.S. Government's suggestion to submit to arbitration, but when President Grover Cleveland threatened to intervene, Britain agreed to let an international tribunal arbitrate the boundary in 1897. The arbitral commission finally rendered a decision in which it directed that the border follow the Schomburgk Line preserving the 1835 demarcation. Although deeply disappointed with the commission's finding, the Venezuelans ratified the ruling.

---

21 See also *Fisheries Case* (United Kingdom v. Norway, 1951), I.C.J. Rep. 1951, p. 116 (181).
22 It is suggested that between 1794 and 1899, States have entered into 239 arbitration agreements. See A.M. STUYT, *Survey of International Arbitration 1794–1989*, (1990).
23 *Bering Sea Arbitration* (Great Britain v. United States, 1893), 6 A.J.I.L., p. 233.
24 *Venezuela – British Guiana Boundary arbitration* (1899), 44 A.J.I.L., p. 682.

IV. The Hague Peace Conferences of 1899 and 1907

The high number of successful arbitrations in the 19th century led to the *First Hague Convention for the Pacific Settlement of Disputes* in 1899. As a general statement concerning the importance, Article 16 of the Convention laid down that:

> "In questions of a legal nature, and especially in the interpretation or application of international conventions, arbitration is recognized by the signatory Powers as the most effective, and at the same time the most equitable, means of settling disputes which diplomacy has failed to settle."

Article 15 of the Convention confirmed the juridical character of arbitration, stating that:

> "International arbitration has for its object the settlement of differences between States by judges of their own choice, and on the basis of respect for law."

This definition was repeated in Article 37 (1) of the 1907 *Hague Convention for the Pacific Settlement of Disputes* and became the accepted definition of arbitration in international law. The Hague Conventions thus defined arbitration as based on the application of legal principles and, hence, as a judicial form of dispute settlement.

The judicial character was further emphasized by Article 37 (2) of the 1907 Convention which provided that States were obliged to accept the terms of the award:

> "Recourse to arbitration implies an engagement to submit in good faith to the Award."[25]

Thus, arbitral awards were considered to be legally binding decisions.

Nevertheless, the wording recognized an inherent limitation to arbitration, insofar as so-called "non-justiciable" disputes regarding "conflicting interests" or "differences of a political nature" not based on legal propositions were excluded and had to be dealt with exclusively by diplomatic means.[26]

The Conventions established the misleadingly termed *Permanent Court of Arbitration* (PCA). It was not a court in the proper meaning of the word but a list of persons eligible for taking up the function of an arbitrator. The PCA served thus rather as an agency to facilitate the establishment of arbitral courts. The major importance of the 1899 and 1907 Hague Conventions derives from its specified rules of procedure which

---

25 Article 18 of the 1899 Convention declared that *"The Arbitration Convention implies the engagement to submit loyally to the Award."*
26 H. LAUTERPACHT, *The Function of Law in the International Community*, (2000), p. 29.

are designed to govern arbitral proceedings if the States have made no provisions to the contrary. Therefore, arbitral tribunals today still rely on them as authority for procedural questions or view some of them as expressive of customary international law.[27]

Despite having achieved substantial progress, the Conferences could not entirely satisfy the hopes of their initiators. Germany, in particular, opposed obligatory arbitration as an unacceptable restraint on its national sovereignty, instead preferring bilateral undertakings between States.[28] As a result, the *Hague Conventions* had to leave it to States whether or not to take recourse to arbitration for the settlement of disputes.[29] Furthermore, States could not agree on establishing a truly permanent tribunal. The main stumbling block proved to be the inability of States to find a satisfactory method of electing arbitrators.[30] The goal of establishing a court which, by holding continuous and connected sessions, would gradually build up a consistent body of international law was thus thwarted. Finally, no common position was found on challenging the validity of an arbitral award. States were most notably at loggerheads as to the competent authority to adjudicate on this question.[31] The result was that revision, for which States, in any event, had to make an express reservation, was confined exclusively to the discovery of new facts (novum).[32] Even though States were thus barred from basing nullity on other grounds, reluctance to respect unfavorable decisions would often persuade them to show disregard for any such restriction.

Between 1900 and 1932, some twenty disputes went through the PCA procedure.[33] However, with the creation of the Permanent Court of International Justice (PCIJ), the number of cases registered with the PCA decreased significantly. In the period between the two World Wars only six arbitral tribunals were constituted under the auspices of the PCA.[34] With the installation of the PCIJ, the PCA thus lost its relevance as an institution of international dispute settlement to a considerable degree. Nevertheless, in more recent times the PCA has again begun to play a more important role in international dispute settlement, acting, for example, as registry in the *Erit-*

---

27 ARON BROCHES in: *Contemporary International Law Issues: Opportunities at a Time of Momentous Change: Proceedings of the Second Joint Conference Held in The Hague, The Netherlands, July 22–24, 1993*, (1994), p. 93.
28 See J. ALLAIN, *A Century of International Adjudication – The Rule of Law and its Limits*, (2000), p. 26.
29 See Art. 38 of the Hague Convention of 1907: "Consequently, it would be desirable that, in disputes about the above-mentioned questions, the Contracting Powers should, if the case arose, have recourse to arbitration, in so far as circumstances permit."
30 See M. POMERANCE, *The United States and the World Court as a "Supreme Court of the Nations": Dreams, Illusions and Disillusion*, (1996), p. 56.
31 K. OELLERS-FRAHM, *Judicial and Arbitral Decisions, Validity and Nullity*, in R. Wolfrum (Ed.), The Max Planck Encyclopedia of Public International Law, (2008), online edition, [www.mpepil.com], visited on 2 April 2009.
32 See Article 55 (1899) and Article 83 (1907) of the Hague Conventions.
33 See generally D. Johnson, *International Arbitration back in Favour?*, 34 Y.B.W.A. 1980, p. 305.
34 N. L. WALLACE-BRUCE, *The Settlement of International Disputes – The Contribution of Australia and New Zealand*, p. 58.

rea/Yemen arbitration (1996–1999)³⁵ and as registry for the *Eritrea/Ethiopia* Boundary Commission (2000–2008)³⁶ and the *Eritrea/Ethiopia* Claims Commission (2000-case still pending).³⁷

V. Interstate Arbitration between the World Wars

Although the relevance of the PCA was in sharp decline following the establishment of the PCIJ, States still conducted some 50 interstate arbitrations outside the framework of the PCA during the existence of the PCIJ.³⁸ This is all the more remarkable as the PCIJ only dealt with 29 contentious interstate cases between 1922 and 1940. Among the most important arbitrations in the interwar period are the *Tinoco* Arbitration between Costa Rica and Great Britain (1923)³⁹, the *Isle of Palmas* case between the United States and the Netherlands (1928)⁴⁰, and the *Naulilaa* Arbitration between Portugal and Germany (1928).⁴¹

The provisions in the two *Hague Conventions* on arbitration had a positive influence on new arbitration agreements, in particular, with respect to the inclusion of arbitral clauses in bilateral treaties. The important role of arbitration was subsequently acknowledged when it became part of the peacekeeping system of the *League of Nations*. In Article 12 of the *Covenant of the League of Nations*, the Member States agreed that a "dispute likely to lead to a rupture" had to be submitted either to arbitration, judicial settlement or to enquiry by the *League Council*. Although States were, thus, strictly speaking, not obliged to submit a dispute to an arbitral tribunal or an international court, absent such a judicial settlement, they had to bring any dispute before the organs of the League.

In order to close the gap left by the Covenant with regard to recourse to force by States should economic sanctions fail, the Assembly of the League of Nations adopted the so-called *Geneva Protocol* in 1924.⁴² Arbitration was envisaged as an important part of the Protocol, requiring judicial settlement or arbitration of all disputes (Article 4) and defining the aggressor as a nation violating the undertakings contained in the Covenant (Article 10) against whom all League Members had to provide support to each other. Consequently, unwillingness to submit a case to arbitration could, in theory, lead to a

---

35 *Eritrea-Yemen Arbitration* (1998), 114 I.L.R., p. 1 (Phase One: Territorial Sovereignty and Scope of the Dispute); 119 I.L.R., p. 417 (Phase Two: Maritime Delimitation).
36 *Eritrea-Ethiopia Boundary Commission* (Decision regarding Delimitation of the Border between Eritrea and Ethiopia, 2002), 41 I.L.M. p. 1057.
37 *Eritrea-Ethiopia Claims Commission* (Partial Award, Ius Ad Bellum, 2005), 45 I.L.M. p. 430.
38 C. H. BROWER, Arbitration, in R. Wolfrum (Ed.), *The Max Planck Encyclopedia of Public International Law*, (2008), online edition, [www.mpepil.com], visited on 2 April 2009.
39 *Tinoco Arbitration* (Costa Rica v. Great Britain, 1923), 1 R.I.I.A., p. 369.
40 *Isle of Palmas Arbitration* (United States v. Netherlands, 1928), 2 R.I.I.A., p. 829.
41 *Naulilaa Arbitration* (Portugal v. Germany, 1928), 2 R.I.I.A., p. 1013.
42 *Protocol for the Pacific Settlement of International Disputes*, J.O.R.F. 1924, Suppl. Spéc. No. 23, p. 502; Survey of International Affairs (1924), p. 36.

condemnation as aggressor and severe international sanctions. However, as the Protocol failed to be adopted by the Member States, it never came into effect.

The failure to come to an agreement was partly overcome by the *Locarno Treaties* of 1925. Germany, for its part, signed arbitration conventions with France and Belgium and arbitration treaties with Poland and Czechoslovakia. The treaties set out that controversies with regard to which the parties are in dispute as to their respective rights shall be submitted either to an arbitral tribunal or to the PCIJ. Non-legal issues where covered inasmuch as following the failure of conciliation, the Parties were obliged to continue the "pacific procedure" of dispute settlement before the Council.[43]

Eventually, the 1928 *Geneva General Act for the Settlement of Disputes* (General Act)[44], which is still in principle in force, obliged States to submit legal disputes to the decision of the PCIJ or, if they so agreed, to an arbitral tribunal. In contrast, obligatory conciliation was reserved for disputes of a non-justiciable nature. However, in case the parties did not reach an agreement, such a dispute could be submitted to an arbitral tribunal by either party (Article 27). Consequently, whereas legal disputes were to be brought exclusively before the PCIJ, non-legal (or "political") disputes were reserved for arbitration.[45] Interestingly, arbitration, generally conceived as a means for resolving legal disputes, was now remodeled as a means for non-legal dispute resolution. The Geneva Act can be regarded as an important step forward because it marked the first inclusion of compulsory recourse to dispute settlement in a multilateral treaty. However, the efficacy of the Treaty suffered considerably from the fact that it was ratified by only 23 States, accompanied with a high number of reservations and later denounced by important Members such as Spain (1939) or Great Britain (1974).[46]

VI. Interstate Arbitration since 1945

After the Second World War, the tendency to incorporate arbitral clauses for the settlement of disputes continued, the most prominent example being the *Charter of the United Nations* (UN Charter). Article 33 (1) states:

> *"The parties to any dispute, the continuance of which is likely to endanger the maintenance of international peace and security, shall, first of all, seek a solution by negotiation, enquiry, mediation, conciliation,* **arbitration***, judicial settlement, resort to regional agencies or arrangements, or other peaceful means of their own choice."*

---

43 H. LAUTERPACHT, *The Function of Law in the International Community*, (2000), p. 39.
44 League of Nations, *Treaty Series*, Vol. XCIII, p. 343; The General Act was revised in 1949 to reflect the new United Nations system.
45 Verzijl, International Law – In Historical Perspective, p. 89.
46 The General Act was revised in 1949 by the General Assembly. However, the success was even more limited as only 7 States acceded.

Acting on the principle laid down in Article 2 (3) of the UN Charter to settle international disputes by peaceful means, the *Council of Europe* adopted the *European Convention for the Peaceful Settlement of Disputes* (ECPSD) in 1957. The ECPSD was intended to provide a regional dispute settlement mechanism for Europe. In addition to provisions for judicial settlement and conciliation, it established a procedure for arbitration. Just as in the *General Act*, arbitration is limited to the resolution of non-legal disputes.[47] However, there is widespread criticism regarding the use of arbitration as a compulsory means for the settlement of political disputes.[48] It appears, in particular, contradictory to stipulate respect for principles of international law when settling non-legal disputes.[49] The ECPSD has not lived up to the expectations of the *Council of Europe*. As of April 2009, only 14 States have acceded to the Treaty (among them Switzerland and Germany), and since its entering into force it has never been used to settle a dispute. The main reason for the failure of the ECPSD may be attributed to the fact, that by attempting to submit legal and non-legal disputes alike to binding settlement – as had been already done in the Locarno Treaties and in the General Act – it has arguably overstepped the bounds of what would have been tolerable for States. On the other hand, by permitting States to opt out of the conciliation and arbitration procedures[50] and by providing for an overly broadly worded reservation clause,[51] States may view accession to the treaty as having little value to future dispute settlement.

It is to be observed that the same fate as that of the ECPSD seems to await its more recent companion, the *Convention on Conciliation and Arbitration within the OSCE*.[52] The Treaty entered into force in 1994 and, as of April 2009, has 33 Member States. However, there has yet to be a case brought under the Treaty condemning it, at least until now, to a dead letter.

The International Law Commission's (ILC) *Model Rules on Arbitral Procedure (Model Rules)* of 1958,[53] a downgraded version of the 1953 ILC *Draft Convention on Arbitral Procedure* for interstate disputes, did not fare much better than the above conventions. The ILC Model Rules lack legally binding character as they were, by General Assembly Resolution, merely brought to the attention of Member States

---

47 Article 19 in connection with Article 1 ECPSD.
48 L. CAFLISCH, European Convention for the Peaceful Settlement of Disputes (1957), in R. Wolfrum (Ed.), *The Max Planck Encyclopedia of Public International Law*, (2008), online edition, [www.mpepil.com], para. 13, visited on 6 April 2009.
49 See Article 26 ECPSD: "If nothing is laid down in the special agreement or no special agreement has been made, the Tribunal shall decide *ex aequo et bono*, having regard to the general principles of international law, while respecting the contractual obligations and the final decisions of international tribunals which are binding on the parties."
50 Art. 34 ECPSD.
51 Art. 35 ECPSD.
52 *Convention on Conciliation and Arbitration within the OSCE*, (1993) 32 I.L.M. p. 557.
53 Y.I.L.C., 1958 II, p. 83.

> "[...] for their consideration and use, in such cases and to such extent as they consider appropriate, in drawing up treaties of arbitration or compromis[54]."

with the invitation

> "[...] to send to the Secretary General any comments they may wish to make on the draft, and in particular on their experience in the drawing up of arbitral agreements [...] with a view to facilitating a review of the matter by the United Nations in an appropriate time."[55]

The ILC Model Rules are based on the concept that the undertaking to submit to arbitration amounts to an international obligation equivalent to a treaty obligation. States are thus required to take all the steps necessary to enable arbitration and to refrain from any action which could impede or frustrate the objective of the arbitral proceedings. However, by turning arbitration into a quasi-compulsory jurisdictional procedure which severely curtailed the procedural autonomy of the parties, States have avoided an explicit reference to the Model Rules. Instead, they have tended to give preference to the rules of arbitration enshrined in the Hague Conventions. However, in some instances tribunals have made use of the ILC Model Rules as authoritative source, and sometimes even considered parts of them as indicative of customary international law.[56]

Further impetus for interstate arbitration came eventually from the unlikely source of the *United Nations Commission on International Trade Law* (UNCITRAL) *Arbitration Rules* which were formally approved by the General Assembly in 1976.[57] Despite the fact that the UNCITRAL Arbitration Rules were designed for international commercial arbitration between private parties, they have been influential in interstate disputes in a twofold way. First, they were adopted as procedural rules in some interstate disputes, for example the *Iran–United States Claims Tribunal*. In Article III (2) of the *Claims Settlement Declaration* of 19 January 1981[58] the parties agreed that:

> "Members of the Tribunal shall be appointed and the Tribunal shall conduct its business in accordance with the arbitration rules of the United Nations Commission on International Trade Law (UNCITRAL) except to the extent modified by the Parties or by the Tribunal to ensure that this Agreement can be carried out."

---

54 As to the term "compromis", see below.
55 Resolution 1262 (XIII) of 14 November 1958.
56 *Dubai/Sharjah Boundary Arbitration (1981)*, 91 I.L.R., p. 543. However, it should be noted that the dispute relates to internal borders within the United Arab Emirates and is thus not a proper interstate case.
57 Commission on International Trade Law, UNCITRAL Arbitration Rules, U.N. Doc. A/31/17, U.N. Sales No. E.77.U.6. (1976).
58 Declaration of the Government of the Democratic and Popular Republic of Algeria concerning the Settlement of Claims by the Government of the USA and the Government of the Islamic Republic of Iran, *Iran – United States Claims Tribunals Reports*, Vol. 1, pp. 9–12.

Second, they provided a major stimulus for the drawing-up of a new arbitration procedure which was better fitted to the needs of State parties. Thus, the UNCITRAL Arbitration Rules served as a major source of inspiration for the PCA when setting up, inter alia, the 1992 *Optional Rules for Arbitrating Disputes between Two States*[59] or the 2001 *Optional Rules for Arbitration of Disputes Relating to Natural Resources and/or the Environment*.[60] The special attraction of the UNCITRAL Arbitration Rules for States lies in their framework character which leaves sufficient flexibility for the adaptation to the specific characteristics of each case. However, the same regulatory openness prevents it from contributing to the standardization of arbitration procedure in international law.

Turning to interstate arbitration cases since the end of the Second World War, the decline already visible during the existence of the PCIJ gathered further momentum. While Stuyt's *Survey of International Arbitrations 1794–1998* counts approximately 178 interstate arbitrations between 1900 and 1945, it lists only 43 arbitrations for the same number of years afterwards.[61] At first glance, this decrease is in stark contrast to the significant increase in the number of States since the Second World War. Moreover, it seems also at odds with the high number of arbitration clauses inserted into bilateral and multilateral treaties. However, it is not difficult to see that the dwindling importance of interstate arbitration is directly related to the growing number of international courts. It is thus observed that the general proliferation of judicial organs on the international and regional level indicates a general transition from arbitration to judicial settlement as the preferred form for the resolution of international disputes among States.

Against this rather sober background, it is important to stress that nevertheless some important arbitration procedures were successfully brought to a close since the Second World War. One broad category is formed by border disputes. Examples are the *Lac Lanoux* case between France and Spain (1957),[62] the *Western Boundary* dispute between India and Pakistan (*Rann of Kutch*, 1968),[63] the famous *Continental Shelf Delimitation* case between Great Britain and France (1977),[64] the *Guinea/Guinea-Bissau* case (1985),[65] the *Taba* case,[66] the *St. Pierre and Miquelon* arbitration between Canada and France (1992),[67] the *Yemen and Eritrea* case (1999),[68] and finally the *Barbados v. Trinidad and Tobago* case (2006).[69] Boundary cases referred to arbitration accounted for

---

59   32 I.L.M., p. 572.
60   41 I.L.M., p. 202.
61   A.M. STUYT, *Survey of International Arbitration 1794–1989*, (1990).
62   *Lac Lanoux Arbitration* (France v. Spain, 1957), 24 I.L.R., p. 101.
63   *India-Pakistan Western Boundary Arbitration*, (India v. Pakistan, 1968), 50 I.L.R., p. 2.
64   *Continental Shelf Delimitation Arbitration* (Great Britain v. France, 1977), 54 I.L.R., p. 6. Although the arbitral award was rendered in 1977, it was not accepted by the parties until 1984 under diplomatic mediation by the Vatican.
65   *Guinea-Guinea-Bissau Arbitration* (1985), 25 I.L.M., p. 252.
66   *Supra* note 5.
67   *St. Pierre and Miquelon Arbitration* (Canada v. France, 1992), 31 I.L.M., p. 1145 (1992).
68   *Yemen-Eritrea Arbitration*, (1999), 40 I.L.M., p. 983.
69   *Barbados-Trinidad and Tobago*, (2006), 45 I.L.M., p. 798.

about a quarter of all arbitrations since the Second World War.[70] The relatively high percentage can be partly attributed to the numerous border disputes that resulted from the emergence of new States in the post-Colonial world order and the breakdown of many Eastern Bloc communist States. Considering that with the passage of time such conflicts become naturally less frequent, the importance of this category of arbitration cases is bound to diminish.[71]

The majority of cases, however, dealt with arbitrations of commercial disputes among States. Examples are the *Diverted Cargoes* (1955),[72] and the *Ambatielos* arbitration (1956)[73] between Greece and the United Kingdom, the *Lighthouse* arbitration between France and Greece (1956),[74] the *Gut Dam* arbitration between Canada and the United States (1965),[75] and also, albeit somewhat ambiguous, the United Nations Compensation Commission (UNCC) created after the First Gulf War by the Security Council[76] and concluded in 2007.[77] Although the UNCC dealt, in addition to State claims, also with individual and corporate claims, the latter claims also had to be filed by States through so-called "consolidated claims".[78]

In the present context, special reference is lastly to be made to the *Iran-United States Claims Tribunal* which is widely regarded as the most influential case of interstate arbitration in commercial matters.[79] The Tribunal was instituted by the 1981 Algiers Accord[80] and designed for the settlement of claims resulting from the diplomatic hostage crisis between Iran and the United States. The Tribunal's jurisdiction is not confined to State claims but extends also to claims of nationals of the United States against Iran and vice versa. Inadmissible are, however, claims brought by a national of one State against the national of the other. It was agreed that claims exceeding US$ 250,000 must be brought before the Tribunal by the national claimants with all other claims

---

70 C. GRAY & B. KINGSBURY, Developments in Dispute Settlement: Interstate Arbitration Since 1945, in 63 BRIT. Y.B. INT'L L. 97, (1992), p. 108.
71 However, one should take a cautious stance as to any predictions as some new disputes amenable to arbitration appear on the horizon. For example, arbitration could become a vital instrument under the United Nations Convention on the Law of the Sea and its Annexes for the settlement of the conflicting sovereignty claims regarding the Arctic region.
72 *Matter of the Diverted Cargoes Arbitration* (Greece v. Great Britain, 1955), 22 I.L.R., p. 820.
73 *Ambatielos Arbitration* (Greece v. Great Britain, 1956), 23 I.L.R., p. 106.
74 *Lighthouse Arbitration* (France v. Greece, 1956) 23 I.L.R., p. 299.
75 *Gut Dam Arbitration* (Canada v. United States, 1965), 8 I.L.M., p. 118.
76 United Nations Security Council Regulation 687 of 9 April 1991 (S/RES/986).
77 The nature of the Commission is not entirely clear. According to the Secretary-General's report, the Commission is neither a court nor a tribunal but "a political organ that performs an essentially fact-finding function of examining claims, verifying their validity, evaluating losses, assessing payments and resolving disputed claims. It is only in this last respect that a quasi-judicial function may be involved." See UN Doc. S/22559, 2 May 1991, para. 21.
78 For an introduction into the structure of the UNCC, see: M. Frigessi di Rattalma & T. Treves (Ed.), The United Nations Compensation Commission – A Handbook (1999), pp. 2 et seq.
79 A detailed analysis of the arbitration proceedings is provided by C. Pinto, Iran-United States Claims Tribunal, in R. Wolfrum (Ed.), *The Max Planck Encyclopedia of Public International Law*, (2008), online edition, [www.mpepil.com], visited on 8 April 2009.
80 20 I.L.M., p. 223.

represented by the respective Governments. Those claims directly submitted by nationals do not constitute interstate arbitration but fall rather under the category of private international arbitration. The Tribunal has made not only many significant contributions to the interpretation and application of public international law, but, importantly, also heralded what is often called the "privatization" of international law.[81] Whereas in former times, many interstate arbitrations essentially concerned individual claims based on diplomatic protection, those claims have now by and large been taken over by international commercial arbitration.[82] It can be consequently concluded that the demise of interstate arbitration observed after the Second World War is also linked to the rise and growing popularity of international commercial arbitration.

Finally, as was already mentioned, given the predominantly commercial character of the dispute, it does not come as a surprise that the *Iran-United States Claims Tribunal* has operated from the beginning under the UNCITRAL Arbitration Rules, albeit with some modifications. In this respect, the *Iran-United States Claims Tribunal* provides clear indication that interstate arbitration is not only being increasingly substituted by international commercial arbitration but is also undergoing a significant process of procedural convergence. The old perception that interstate and international commercial arbitration are fundamentally different thus loses more and more validity.[83]

E. Characteristics of Arbitration

I. Compromis

According to international law, no State, without its prior consent, is obliged to submit disputes with other States to any kind of settlement.[84] Interstate arbitration therefore requires the conclusion of an arbitration treaty which contains the commitment of the disputing States to submit a case to an arbitral tribunal. An arbitration treaty constitutes an international law treaty to which the traditional rules of treaty law apply.

In international law parlance, an arbitration treaty is commonly referred to as a *"compromis"* or *"special agreement"*. Two different forms of *compromis* can be distinguished. States can agree to submit future disputes to arbitration. This type of *compromis* has come to be termed a *"general"* or *"abstract"* compromis. If a dispute arises and no such

---

81 J. WERNER, Interstate political Arbitration: What lies next?, *Journal of International Arbitration*, Vol. 9 No. 1 (1992), p. 73.
82 However, in politically sensitive cases, interstate arbitration has not lost its importance as the establishment of the United Nations Compensation Commission has shown.
83 H. M. HOLTZMANN, Some Reflections on the Nature of Arbitration, in S. Muller, W. Mijs (Eds.), *The Flame Rekindled, New Hopes for International Arbitration*, (1994), p. 71; Reference is made in particular to the adoption on the part of the PCA of the *Optional Rules for Arbitrating Disputes Between Two States* (1992), which were modeled after the UNCITRAL Arbitration Rules, See *supra* note 56.
84 L. OPPENHEIM, *International Law*, *supra* note 7, p. 22. The term "compulsory" or "obligatory" arbitration is thus, strictly speaking, a contradiction in terms.

undertaking has been previously entered into, States can also agree on an *"ad hoc" compromis* and submit the existing dispute to arbitration.[85] The *compromis* is often part of bilateral or multilateral treaties that include a variety of other provisions. In this case the *compromis* is generally called *"compromissory clause"*.

A compromissory clause can be either self-executing or a mere *pactum de contrahendo*. In the first alternative, either party may initiate the arbitration procedure without having to seek the consent of the other party, provided the dispute falls under the terms of the compromissory clause. If, however, the compromissory clause only amounts to a *pactum de contrahendo*, the parties still have to reach an agreement as to the modalities of the arbitration. In other words, such a compromissory clause constitutes nothing more than an obligation to conclude a *compromis*. An example can be found in the German-Austrian-Hungarian Trade Treaty of 6 December 1891 which provided:

> "Should the need arise and subject to special agreement, the contracting parties [...] shall submit for settlement by arbitration any differences of opinion as to the interpretation or application of this treaty."[86]

A *compromis* has to provide for a minimum set of rules with regard to the arbitration procedure. In this respect, some direction can be gleaned from Article 2 (1) of the ILC Model Rules on Arbitral Procedure, although they lack binding character. As core elements, a *compromis* must include provisions regarding (a) the undertaking to arbitrate according to which the dispute is to be submitted to the arbitrators; (b) the subject matter of the dispute; and (c) the method of constituting the tribunal and the number of arbitrators. These basic requirements will be explored in more detail below.

There are, of course, further optional provisions on which States can, and most of the times do, agree in order to guarantee the smooth functioning of the arbitration procedures. As envisaged by Article 2 (2) of the ILC Model Rules, provisions are often made with respect to (d) the rules of law and the principles to be applied by the tribunal; (e) the majority required for an award; (f) the time limit within which the award shall be rendered; or (g) the language to be employed in the course of the proceedings. Finally, ancillary provisions can also be made as to the right of the tribunal members to attach dissenting or individual opinions to the award.

---

[85] H. THIRLWAY, Compromis, in R. Wolfrum (Ed.), *The Max Planck Encyclopedia of Public International Law*, (2008), online edition, [www.mpepil.com], para. 2, visited on 31 March 2009.
[86] Text reprinted in: K. STRUPP, *Die wichtigsten Arten der völkerrechtlichen Schiedsgerichtsverträge*, (1917), p. 30.

II. Constitution of the Tribunal

The parties have to reach agreement as to who is to render the arbitral award. They may either entrust a single person or a collegiate body with that task.

In former times, arbitral tribunals consisted traditionally of an equal number of national arbitrators nominated by the parties. In case the national arbitrators failed to reach a decision, a "disinterested third party" was called upon to give a decision as a neutral umpire. This kind of tribunal can be traced back to the 1814 *Treaty of Ghent*[87] under which Great Britain and the United States, in addition to ending the Anglo-American War of 1812, referred certain boundary disputes to arbitration commissions. The commissions established under the Treaty consisted of 2 commissioners, one appointed by each State. A case was to be referred to a Head of State as a disinterested third party in the event of disagreement.

In modern times, arbitral tribunals tend to consist of an uneven number of persons, generally three or five. Typically, the umpire and often also the majority of the tribunal members have a nationality different from the disputing parties and the power to decide by majority vote. This modern type was first introduced in the 1872 *Alabama Claims* case which was discussed above.[88] In practice, both five-member and three-member tribunals can be found, although it has been observed that three-member tribunals have become the norm.[89] The selection of non-national tribunal members is to guarantee that the dispute is settled impartially and solely on grounds of law. This is because experience has clearly shown that national arbitrators typically tend to show some affinity to the legal views of "their" party. The State parties normally appoint either one (three member tribunal) or two member(s) (five member tribunal) of the tribunal and leave it then to the party-appointed members to designate the umpire. An example of a nine-member tribunal is provided by Article III (1) of the *Claims Settlement Declaration*:[90]

> "*The Tribunal shall consist of nine members or such larger multiple of three as Iran and the United States may agree are necessary to conduct its business expeditiously. Within ninety days after the entry into force of this Agreement, each government shall appoint one-third of the members. Within thirty days after their appointment, the members so appointed shall by mutual agreement select the remaining third of the members and appoint one of the remaining third President of the Tribunal.*"

---

87 Treaty of Ghent, 24 December 1814, 63 C.T.S., p. 421; H. MILLER, Treaties and Other International Acts of the United States of America, Vol. 2, (1931), p. 574.
88 See *supra* note 1.
89 C. H. BROWER, Arbitration, in R. Wolfrum (Ed.), *The Max Planck Encyclopedia of Public International Law*, 2008, online edition, [www.mpepil.com], para. 49, visited on 2 April 2009.
90 See *supra* note 57. Sometimes, it is provided that the umpire has to be agreed on by both State parties together.

This procedure is a further safeguard to the impartiality of the tribunal. As the outcome of arbitration in many cases hinges on the decision of the neutral members, it is not surprising that their appointment is often a point of contention. In order to avoid lengthy discussion or even an impasse, arbitration treaties normally provide that in the event of disagreement, the neutral members are to be appointed by the President of the ICJ or by some other disinterested party.[91]

It is possible for States to attempt to undermine the arbitration proceedings by refusing to appoint their members of the tribunal. This problem was famously addressed in the *Peace Treaties* case.[92] The *Peace Treaties* with Bulgaria, Hungary and Rumania each contained a compromissory clause whereby disputes arising out of the interpretation and execution of the Treaty had to be referred to an arbitral commission.[93] However, after Great Britain and the United States complained about human rights violations, Bulgaria, Hungary and Romania refused to designate their representatives to the commission. In an advisory opinion, the ICJ held that the compromissory clause obligated either party

> "[…] to co-operate in constituting the Commission, in particular by appointing its representative."[94]

It is thus now established that the conclusion of an arbitration treaty entails the obligation to take all necessary steps required to set up the arbitral tribunal. Non-compliance with this obligation constitutes a treaty violation. However, absent an alternative procedure to determine the members of the tribunal, it is impossible to compel the composition of a tribunal. As the ICJ further set out,

> "[…] the breach of a treaty obligation cannot be remedied by creating a Commission which is not the kind of Commission contemplated by the Treaties. It is the duty of the Court to interpret the Treaties, not to revise them."[95]

It follows that refusal to co-operate can still prove a successful course of action in order to avoid the rendering of an unfavourable arbitral.

States may also agree to refer a dispute to a sole arbitrator. In the past, disputes were

---

91 See *Rann of Kutch Arbitration*, *supra* note 62, where the umpire was selected by the UN Secretary General.
92 Advisory Opinion of the Court on the Interpretation of Peace Treaties with Bulgaria, Hungary and Romania, (1950), *I.C.J. Reports* 1950, p. 65 (First Phase), p. 221 (Second Phase).
93 Paris Treaty of Peace with Bulgaria, 1947, 41 U.N.T.S., p. 50, 84 (Article 36); Paris Treaty of Peace with Hungary, 1947, *ibid.*, p. 168, 210 (Article 40); Paris Treaty of Peace with Romania, 1947, 42 U.N.T.S., p. 34, 72 (Article 38).
94 *Supra* note 91, at p. 77 (First Phase).
95 *Ibid.* p. 229 (Second Phase); See also the dissenting opinion of Judge Read suggesting that "[…] no party to a treaty can destroy the effect of the treaty itself by its own default or by its failure to exercise a right or a privilege.", *Ibid.* p. 241 (Second Phase).

often submitted to foreign Heads of State or Government and even the Pope. The underlying reason was that the dignity of States prevented them from letting their affairs be decided by persons of lesser rank.[96] Furthermore, considering that the success of many arbitral procedures rested in those times on the arbitrators' diplomatic skills rather than on their legal education, Heads of States or Government were particularly qualified for that office. Even today, their involvement is not without benefit; for example, by choosing a strong and respected personality, the willingness of the parties to accept the decision can be significantly increased. Although arbitration by foreign Heads of State or Government has now become rather an oddity, it has not altogether disappeared. The arbitral decision of the King of Italy in the *Clipperton Island* case between France and Mexico (1931)[97] and the *Palena* arbitration between Argentina and Chile (1966)[98] may serve as examples.[99] The most recent example which arguably falls into this category is the first *Rainbow Warrior* case between New Zealand and France (1986).[100] After French agents sank the vessel *Rainbow Warrior* in the harbour of Auckland (New Zealand), the Secretary-General of the United Nations was asked to act as arbitrator and decide the legal consequences of this attack. In his "equitable and principled" ruling, France was ordered to pay financial compensation (US$ 7 Million), convey a formal and unqualified apology to New Zealand, transfer the agents to a French military facility on an isolated island outside Europe for a period of three years and discontinue opposition to New Zealand's imports in the European Community.

Should neither a collegiate nor a sovereign arbitrator be deemed suitable for the purposes of the parties, a dispute may also be referred to an individual person with special qualities. In this respect, reference can be made to the Permanent Court of Arbitration and its list of arbitrators. This form of arbitration offers certain advantages both over collegiate arbitration bodies as well as over sovereign arbitration. A single arbitrator can be quicker and less expensive than an arbitral commission and, unlike arbitration by sovereigns, guarantees unquestionable legal expertise. Early examples of this kind of arbitration are the *Tinoco* arbitration between Great Britain and Costa Rica (1923)[101] and the *Island of Palmas* arbitration between the Netherlands and the United States (1928).[102] However, it is clear that this alternative is not suitable in larger cases which require extensive and time-consuming factual and judicial examination.

---

96 See for example, Papal Award by Pope Alexander VI issued on 4 May 1493 deciding on conflicting territorial claims of the King of Spain and Portugal; VANDER LINDEN, Alexander VI and the Demarcation of the Maritime and Colonial Domains of Spain and Portugal, 1493-1494, 22 (1916) *American Historical Review*, p. 1. However, in modern international law phraseology, the Pope acted as *amiable compositeur* rather than as an arbitrator. In more recent times, the Pope was called upon as mediator in the *Beagle Channel* case (*supra* note 4) after Argentina had rejected the arbitral award. The proposal by the Pope led to an agreement in 1984 (24 I.L.M. 10 (1985)).
97 *Clipperton Island Arbitration* (France v. Mexico, 1931), 26 A.J.I.L., p. 390.
98 *Palena Arbitration* (Argentina v. Chile, 1966), 38 I.L.R., p. 10.
99 However, the British Government which was asked to intervene as an arbitrator, delegated its duties to a Court of Arbitration composed of three members, one jurist and two geographical experts.
100 *Rainbow Warrior Arbitration* (I) (New Zealand v. France, 1986), 74 I.L.R., p. 241.
101 *Tinoco Claims Arbitration*, *supra* note 38.
102 *Supra* note 3.

As to the qualifications of an arbitrator, it is often provided that he or she must be qualified to hold the highest judge's office, or that he or she must have special knowledge of international law. A neat illustration of this requirement can be found in Article 44 of the 1907 Convention which provides the qualities Members of the Permanent Court should possess:

> "Each Contracting Power selects four persons at the most, of known competency in questions of international law, of the highest moral reputation, and disposed to accept the duties of Arbitrator."

Only in cases that require special expertise arbitrators may be expected to have expert knowledge in a special field.

III. Jurisdiction

The subject-matter jurisdiction refers to the power or authority of a tribunal to hear and to dispose of a particular type of case. This form of jurisdiction thus determines the boundaries within which a tribunal may exercise its legal powers. When the tribunal defines its jurisdiction too broadly, the award may be challenged on the ground of *nullity*. An arbitral award outside the jurisdiction of a tribunal is not binding for the parties. It is therefore of utmost importance that the parties make sure that the *compromis* contains precise provisions delineating the matter under dispute. As a general rule, jurisdictional questions have to be dealt with by the tribunal very carefully and with the aim of reconciling the interests of the concerned parties. Otherwise, the likelihood of acceptance by the parties, although legally required, will be sharply reduced.

If the parties are in agreement that a dispute exists, but are unable to find common ground as to its exact scope, they may conclude a so-called "framework-agreement".[103] Under such an agreement, the parties are required to concretize the dispute unilaterally through their pleadings. As was already established by the Maritime Commission established under the *Jay Treaty* and confirmed in the *Alabama Claims* arbitration, a tribunal has the competence to pronounce on the scope of its own jurisdiction. However, if, *before* the establishment of the arbitral tribunal, the parties disagree as to the jurisdiction of the tribunal, such a preliminary question may also be brought before another judicial body, for example the ICJ, provided that the parties have so agreed.[104] In any event, a party, which, on the ground of a lack of jurisdiction, refuses to submit to arbitration, acts in bad faith if it does not allow for legal review of its claim.

The jurisdiction of a tribunal may be repudiated on different grounds. Typical chal-

---

103 P. TOMKA, The Special Agreement, in: N. Andō, E. McWhinney, R. Wolfrum (Eds.), *Liber Amicorum Judge Shigeru Oda*, (2002), p. 553.
104 See Article 1 (1) of the ILC Model Rules.

lenges relate to questions such as (a) whether there is a valid arbitration agreement, (b) whether the tribunal is properly constituted, (c) whether a dispute actually exists between the parties, or, most importantly, (d) whether the existing dispute is wholly or partly within the scope of the obligation to go to arbitration. A tribunal may rule on the plea of no jurisdiction either as a preliminary question or in the award on the merits. A preliminary award on jurisdiction is particularly advisable when the full participation of the parties in the arbitration procedures would otherwise be in doubt. Normally, jurisdictional objections are raised by the parties. However, it should be noted that, absent such jurisdictional objections, the tribunal is entitled to examine its jurisdiction *sua sponte*.[105]

Commonly, States tend to define the subject matter of the dispute, i.e. the question that is put to arbitration, rather narrowly so as to prevent the tribunal from making too far-reaching decisions on issues of national interest. However, the more restricted the jurisdiction of the tribunal, the less likely it is that the arbitral award can fully solve the dispute between the States. Moreover, when States fail to define the question to be dealt with by the tribunal with sufficient clarity, this will precipitate additional disputes about the scope of jurisdiction and thus prevent the tribunal from executing its proper task.

Considerably fewer problems arise with respect to the jurisdiction *ratione personae*. In general, personal jurisdiction extends to the parties of the arbitration agreement. Standing before the tribunal is consequently restricted to the parties to the agreement. It follows that third party interventions are, as a general rule, not permissible. Just as third parties do not enjoy standing, the arbitral award has binding force only for the parties to the agreement. As the parties are clearly defined by the arbitration agreements, disputes, regarding the jurisdiction ratione personae, will only rarely arise.

IV. Procedure

At the outset, it is thus to be noted that, until now, international law has not brought about any standardized and binding rules of arbitral procedure valid in interstate arbitrations. It has been observed that the typical method for forming general rules by way of customary international law has fallen short of producing a generally recognized procedural framework.[106] Moreover, as discussed above, neither the procedural rules of the Hague Conventions nor the ILC Model Rules on Arbitral Procedure were bestowed with mandatory character, let alone have gained universal acceptance among States.

---

105 N. D. PALMETER, P. C. MAVROIDIS, *Dispute settlement in the World Trade Organization: Practice and Procedure*, (2004), p. 40; With respect to the ICJ see C. F. AMERASINGHE, *Jurisdiction of International Tribunals*, (2003), p. 138. Quite another question is whether the tribunal is obliged to consider jurisdictional issue *sua sponte*.
106 M. RUBINO-SAMMARTANO, *International Arbitration – Law and Practice*, (2001), p. 145.

That being said, there are, of course, instances in which States have incorporated by reference some standard procedural rules into their procedural framework.[107]

Due to the lack of standardized procedures, only a few general remarks are pertinent. Echoing the general mantra of arbitration, it is for the parties to decide on the procedural arrangements. If the parties do not provide for procedural rules, it is generally acknowledged that the task falls within the competence of the tribunal itself.[108] However, despite this far-reaching autonomy, the procedural rules must ensure that the parties be treated fairly and equally. A violation of this basic principle would, in any event, undermine the judicial character of the proceedings and thus vitiate the final arbitral award.

The proceedings are usually divided into a written and an oral stage. If specific provisions on procedure are omitted by the parties, the tribunal often starts with preliminary hearings concerning procedural questions which will subsequently lead to procedural orders of the tribunal. If the dispute presents separable legal issues, for example in a case where jurisdiction, responsibility, and remedies are at issue, they may be dealt with in different phases. The parties have the opportunity to present their case both in written submissions and oral hearings. As in domestic law, the written submissions normally carry greater weight for the outcome of the proceedings.

Regarding evidentiary rules, a tribunal enjoys broad discretion in determining the weight of evidence. There is typically a preference for documentary proof over oral authority. A sensitive issue is how the tribunal is to obtain the necessary evidence. In view of State sovereignty, tribunals do not have firm powers to force the parties to produce evidence. However, failure to cooperate with the tribunal may be taken into account when evaluating the evidence. Article 18 (2) of the ILC Model Rules on Arbitral Procedure, for instance, lays down that:

> "*The parties shall cooperate with the tribunal in dealing with the evidence and in the other measures contemplated by paragraph 1. The tribunal shall take note of the failure of any party to comply with the obligations of this paragraph.*"

The burden of proof lies with the claimant who has to establish beyond a reasonable doubt all facts that support the claim. In interstate arbitration, a particular problem arises when the parties submit parallel claims to identical rights as is often the case in disputes regarding sovereignty over territory. Unless the *compromis* makes express provisions for this situation, both parties are to be given the same standing.

---

107 See *Delimitation of the Maritime Boundary Arbitration* (Guinea v. Guinea Bissau, 1985), 25 I.L.M., p. 251 where the parties agreed to apply some provisions of the ICJ's Rules of Court.

108 See H. THIRLWAY, Compromis, in: R. Wolfrum (Ed.), *The Max Planck Encyclopedia of Public International Law*, (2008), online edition, [www.mpepil.com], para. 19, visited on 15 April 2009.

Time-limits can also be found in interstate arbitration proceedings. However, they are not as frequent as in international commercial arbitration or domestic law and often more generous.[109] The ILC Model Rules on Arbitral Procedure again give an instructive example. Article 15 (3) provides that:

> "The time limits fixed by the compromis may be extended by mutual agreement between the parties, or by the tribunal when it deems such extension necessary to enable it to reach a just decision."

If nothing is provided to the contrary, each Party bears its own cost in preparing and presenting its case before the tribunal. The costs of the tribunal are to be shared between the parties in equal proportion. However, in some circumstances, the tribunal may decide that a higher proportion of costs is to be paid by one of the parties. Such a case could arise where additional costs have been occasioned by the refusal of one party to cooperate with the tribunal.

Many arbitration treaties explicitly require that all written and oral pleadings, documents, and evidence submitted in the arbitration remain confidential unless otherwise agreed by the parties. That makes arbitration a useful and convenient way to settle disputes where cases touch on politically sensitive issues which the parties do not wish to become known to the public. It is thus conceivable that even the existence of an arbitration procedure may be kept secret by the parties.

A party may seek to remove an arbitrator in the course of arbitration. International law provides neither rules regarding the grounds on which disqualification can be based, nor rules regarding the procedure to be adhered to by the parties. However, as was established in the *Iran-U.S. Claims Tribunal*, States do not have the power to remove a member of the tribunal unilaterally. The contention of Iran "that every sovereign State has to act in accordance with its interests in removing an arbitrator" was thus firmly rejected by the Tribunal.[110] If no provisions have been made by the parties, removal of an arbitrator from office is conditioned on the approval by the other party.[111] As arbitration is predicated on the principle of party-autonomy, the parties must have the freedom to change the composition of the tribunal any time they see fit. Interestingly, the ILC Model Rules on Arbitral Procedure also include provisions concerning the problem of disqualification. Regarding the competence to decide on the disqualification that has been proposed by one party, Article 6 (1) of the Model Rules lays down that the decision shall be taken by the undisputed members of the tribunal. In case the disqualification concerns a sole arbitrator or the president of the tribunal, Article 6 (2) of the Model Rules refers the question of disqualification, in the absence of agreement

---

109 J. COLLIER, V. LOWE, The Settlement of Disputes in International Law: Institutions and Procedures, (2000), p. 218.
110 Majority Decision by the Full Tribunal, *Re Judge N. Mångard* (15 January 1982), 68 I.L.R., p. 513, (p. 518).
111 C. N. BROWER, J. D. BRUESCHKE, *The Iran-United States Claims Tribunal*, (1998), p. 165 (fn. 774).

between the parties and on the application of one of them, to the International Court of Justice. However, one must recall that the Model Rules have not been vested with binding force. In any event, if an arbitrator, unfit for the office, participates in the proceedings, the aggrieved party may refuse acceptance of the arbitral award on the ground of nullity. There is thus a strong incentive for the parties to settle any controversy before the rendering of the award.

Further problems arise where arbitrators have been withdrawn from the tribunal. According to the prevailing view, the tribunal is allowed to proceed with the handling of the case without the missing arbitrator.[112] If one were to hold otherwise, the parties would possess a convenient instrument to frustrate the success of the proceedings. It is also worth noting that a similar problem occurs if one of the parties decides to boycott the proceedings.[113] However, it must not be overlooked that parties who behave uncooperatively in the proceedings are also likely to disregard an unfavourable arbitral award of the tribunal.

F. Applicable Law

In addition to procedural issues, of equal importance is the question of the applicable law. Frequently, the parties expressly stipulate the application of international law. But even in default of explicit provisions, the parties are generally presumed to have tacitly consented to the application of international law.[114] This is justified on the ground that the legal relationships between State parties are governed by international law which reflects most adequately the peculiarities of State sovereignty.[115] Even where the parties provide for the applicable law, the respective clauses are often framed in rather broad terms which leave ample scope for interpretation. The rather vaguely phrased Article 37 of the 1907 Hague Convention may be considered an archetype in this regard. According to this provision, disputes are to be settled "on the basis of respect for law". The wording does not exclude the possibility that the tribunal arrives at its decision by recourse to other sources of law. Nevertheless, the point of departure in arbitration proceedings conducted under such or similar instructions must be assumed to be international law. Incidentally, it is observed that, Article 37 of the 1907 Hague Convention, at first glance, would suggest that an arbitrator merely has to take the law into account. Such a view is even more compelling when the provision is compared with the more narrowly worded Article 38 of the ICJ Statute which requires disputes

---

112 H. VON MANGOLDT, Arbitration and Conciliation, in H. Mosler and R. Bernhardt (Eds.), *Judicial Settlement of International Disputes*, (1974), p. 517 (at p. 532, 533).
113 Article 28 (2) of the *Optional Rules For Arbitrating Disputes Between Two States* of the Permanent Court of Arbitration provides, for example, that "If one of the parties, duly notified under these Rules, fails to appear at a hearing, without showing sufficient cause for such failure, the arbitral tribunal may proceed with the arbitration."
114 M. RUBINO-SAMMARTANO, *International Arbitration – Law and Practice*, (2001), p. 157.
115 Cf. H. VON MANGOLDT, Arbitration and Conciliation, in H. Mosler and R. Bernhardt (Eds.), *Judicial Settlement of International Disputes*, (1974), p. 517 (at p. 533).

to be decided "in accordance with" international law.[116] However, as a general rule, arbitration must not be understood as implying a more flexible application of law as this would be contrary to its character as a legal form of dispute settlement.[117]

As the parties are at liberty to determine the law on which the tribunal is to base its decision, States may also direct the tribunal to apply domestic law. This modus operandi is particularly suitable when international law has not yet developed a coherent set of rules governing the issue in dispute. A case often cited in this connection, is the *Trail Smelter* Arbitration.[118] The parties reached agreement in Article 4 of the *compromis* to the effect that:

> *"The Tribunal shall apply the law and practice followed in dealing with cognate questions in the USA as well as in international law and practice."*

The *Trail Smelter* case concerned the issue of transboundary air pollution, i.e. pollution that is caused in one State and has adverse effects in another State. At that time, the international law on environmental issues was still in its infancy and was consequently not considered sufficiently developed to constitute an exclusive legal basis for the decision.[119] In the case, after reviewing domestic and international law, the tribunal held subsequently that no State has the right to use or permit the use of its territory in such a manner that emissions cause injury to the territory of another State or to properties or persons therein provided the case is of serious consequence.[120]

To impart further discretion to the tribunal, it can be asked to base the decision on "equitable principles" or, more cautiously, to take such consideration into account when applying the law. As a consequence, the outcome of arbitration will not depend so much on what is provided by international law but rather on what is "fair" and "reasonable". Although determining equity as the basis for arbitral decision making certainly blurs the distinction between judicial and diplomatic dispute settlement, it does not remove the judicial character. This is borne out by the fact that, in contrast to diplomacy, the arbitral tribunal is still empowered to give a binding and final decision which constitutes a defining element of judicial activity.[121] This view is corroborated by Article 38 (2) of the ICJ Statute which sets out that, if the parties agree thereto, the ICJ has the power to decide a case even *ex aequo et bono*. It goes without saying

---

116 Cf. C. H. BROWER, Arbitration, in R. Wolfrum (Ed.), *The Max Planck Encyclopedia of Public International Law*, (2008), online edition, [www.mpepil.com], visited on 16 April 2009, para. 65.
117 This view is supported by the fact that the drafting history does not give clear indication as to the meaning of Art. 37 of the 1907 Hague Convention, See H. LAMMASCH, *Die Lehre von der Schiedsgerichtsbarkeit in ihrem ganzen Umfange*, (1914), p. 176.
118 *Trail Smelter Arbitration* (United States v. Canada, 1938 and 1941), 3 R.I.A.A., p. 1905.
119 Another case often referred to is the *Gut Dam Arbitration* where the tribunal was asked to apply the "substantive law in force in Canada and in the United States of America [...] In this article the law in force in Canada and the United States of America respectively includes international law" (17 UST 1567 (1966), Art. 2 (2)).
120 *Ibid.* p. 1907.
121 H. LAUTERPACHT, *The Function of Law in the International Community*, (2000), p. 326.

that the judicial character of the ICJ has not been called into question on account of this provision. It is of further importance that, as a general proposition, equity is not to be conceived as an extralegal concept in international law. In fact, the ICJ has stated that "It is not a matter of finding simply an equitable solution, but an equitable solution derived from the applicable law."[122] It is therefore noted that equity (*infra legem*), instead of absolving the tribunal from the duty to apply the law, rather requires, by way of interpreting it, its application. However, the last line of argument cannot be upheld where the parties seek equity *contra legem*.[123] In this respect, tribunals can encounter considerable difficulties in determining what kind of equity was envisaged by the parties. Allowing for considerations of equity is suitable for territorial disputes between States in particular, the reason being that those conflicts often imply highly political issues at the heart of national interests which could not be properly addressed by mere invocation of legal rules. A case that is illustrative in this respect is the aforementioned *Rann of Kutch* arbitration[124] which concerned the allocation of certain parcels of land to Pakistan. According to the prevailing opinion of the Chairman:

> "[...] it would be inequitable to recognise these inlets as foreign territory. It would be conducive to friction and conflict. The paramount consideration of promoting peace and stability in this region compels the recognition and confirmation that this territory, which is wholly surrounded by Pakistan territory, also be regarded as such."[125]

However, without further authorisation by the parties, arbitrators are not entitled to decide a dispute on equitable grounds even if the application of legal rules is detrimental to achieving satisfactory results.

Very rarely, tribunals are also asked to develop new rules governing certain aspects of the international relations between disputing parties. They are thereby put in a position of exercising quasi-judicial functions. In the absence of hard and fast rules of international law, the tribunals will almost certainly have recourse to equitable considerations as they are, in any event, not allowed to indulge in arbitrary decision-making. Examples of such proactively operating tribunals are the *North Atlantic Coast Fisheries* arbitration between Great Britain and the United States (1910)[126] and the *Free Zones* arbitration between France and Switzerland (1933).[127] However, it must be emphasized that rules regulating interstate affairs are typically laid down by treaty negotiations between the parties. As a result, pseudo-legislative activity of the latter kind takes place only exceptionally.

---

122 *Fisheries Jurisdiction* case (Great Britain v. Iceland), I.C.J. Reports 1974, p. 33.
123 The same would arguably hold true for equity *praeter legem*, i.e. the extension of the law by filling gaps.
124 *India-Pakistan Western Boundary Arbitration*, (India v. Pakistan, 1968), *supra* note 62.
125 *Ibid.*, p. 530.
126 *North Atlantic Coast Fisheries Arbitration* (Great Britain v. United States), 11 R.I.I.A., p. 173.
127 *Free Zones of Upper Savoy and the District of Gex: Free Zones* (France v. Switzerland, 1933), 10 P.C.I.J. Ann. R. (Ser. E), p. 106.

G. The Arbitral Award

The activity of the tribunal will typically result in the rendering of an arbitral award although there is no lack of cases where tribunals failed to carry out their duties.[128] Just as a judgement by a court is binding, so does an arbitral award require compliance on the part of the parties. This is unequivocally spelled out in Article 15 of the 1899 Hague Convention and Article 37 of the 1907 Hague Convention which state that:

> *"Recourse to arbitration implies an engagement to submit in good faith to the award."*

It is again observed that the issuance of a binding arbitral award distinguishes most distinctively arbitration from diplomatic dispute settlement. However, the binding effect neither entails that the arbitral award is *final* nor that it is *enforceable*.

As a general rule, there is no appellate stage in international law proceedings because international public law lacks a hierarchical system of courts and tribunals.[129] That being said, if provisions have been made to this effect, each party may invoke the right of appeal. However, States are reluctant to allow for appeals procedures which is due not least to the fact that it runs counter to some of the very reasons for having recourse to arbitration, most importantly, to settle a dispute in a short period of time with limited procedural costs. Moreover, States have the opportunity to determine the composition of the tribunal according to their own preferences. They can ensure that the tribunal consists of jurists of the highest repute and competence that will give due considerations to the legal viewpoints of the parties. They thus deserve less protection than in court proceedings where the influence on the composition of the bench of judges is much more restricted.[130] If an appeals procedure is permissible, the States may either choose to refer the case to a newly established tribunal or even the ICJ or allow the case to be reheard by the arbitral tribunal that rendered the original decision.

Revision may be sought in the form of requesting the interpretation of the decision, calling for the admission of new evidence, or pleading the nullity of the arbitral award.

When a dispute arises over the meaning of an arbitral award, and subject to an express reservation in the *compromis*, the parties may ask the court to provide clarification on

---

128 See Advisory Opinion of the Court on the Interpretation of Peace Treaties with Bulgaria, Hungary and Romania, (1950), *supra* note 91.
129 See K. OELLERS-FRAHM, Judicial and Arbitral Decisions, Validity and Nullity, in R. Wolfrum (Ed.), *The Max Planck Encyclopedia of Public International Law*, (2008), online edition, [www.mpepil.com], para. 2, visited on 18 April 2009.
130 Although, there are also court proceedings where parties retain considerable influence on the appointment of the judges, see *supra* note 10.

the points at issue. In the *Continental Shelf Delimitation* arbitration it was thus agreed that:

> "Either party may, within three months of the rendering of the decision, refer to the Court any dispute between the Parties as to the meaning and scope of the decision".[131]

The revision of the arbitral award on the ground of the discovery of new evidence requires, in addition to an express authorization of the tribunal to reopen proceedings, that the new facts are of such a nature as to lead in all probability to a modification of the award. Furthermore, the evidence relied on must not have been previously known either to the party or to the tribunal.[132]

As mentioned above, a State is not bound by an arbitral award that constitutes a nullity. Nullity can be defined as the legal non-existence of an international act or as the denial of a specific legal status of an act sought by its author.[133] Widely recognized grounds for nullity are (a) the existence of a void or invalid *compromis*, (b) the excess of power/lack of jurisdiction, (c) a serious departure from fundamental rules of procedure, (d) corruption of a tribunal member, (e) the failure to state the reasons for the award, and, most contentiously, (f) an essential or manifest error (of fact or law).[134]

The invalidity of a *compromis* may generally be established by reference to the *Vienna Convention on the Law of Treaties* which is considered to reflect to a large extent customary international law.[135] A party may plead invalidity where the *compromis* was obtained, inter alia, by error (Article 48), fraud (Article 49), corruption (Article 50), coercion (Article 50, 51), or where the *compromis* violated a norm of *ius cogens* at the time it was concluded (Article 53). If the parties were aware of the facts that result in the nullity of the *compromis* without objecting to it, they are precluded from advancing nullity at a later stage of the proceedings.[136]

---

131 Article 10 (2) of the Arbitration Agreement of 10 July 1975, *U.K.T.S.* No. 137 (1975), Cmnd. 2680; The text of the 1975 arbitration agreement is also given in full in the introduction to the 1977 decision, See *supra* note 63.
132 C. H. BROWER, Arbitration, in R. Wolfrum (Ed.), *The Max Planck Encyclopedia of Public International Law*, (2008), online edition, [www.mpepil.com], para. 82, visited on 19 April 2009.
133 See M. REISMAN, Nullity in International Law, in R. Wolfrum (Ed.), *The Max Planck Encyclopedia of Public International Law*, (2008), online edition, [www.mpepil.com], para. 1, visited on 18 April 2009.
134 These grounds reflect to a large extent the grounds for seeking annulment of an arbitral award according to Article 35 of the ILC Model Rules on Arbitral Procedure.
135 G. WILLIAMS, H. CHARLESWORTH, *The Fluid State: International Law and National Legal Systems*, (2005), p. 131.
136 Some writers no longer consider this ground acceptable, arguing that where it is put forward in due time it will prevent the rendering of any arbitral award. See K. OELLERS-FRAHM, Judicial and Arbitral Decisions, Validity and Nullity, in R. Wolfrum (Ed.), *The Max Planck Encyclopedia of Public International Law*, (2008), online edition, [www.mpepil.com], para. 13, visited on 19 April 2009.

Probably the most relevant ground for nullity is the excess of power.[137] The claim is typically based on the argument that, in rendering its decision, a tribunal has transgressed the boundaries of the *compromis* by either deciding on questions not submitted to it or applying rules it was not authorised to apply.[138] In order to establish a serious departure from fundamental rules of procedure the party must show that the rule from which the tribunal departed was fundamental and that the departure was serious. In this connection, the principles of fairness, impartiality, equal treatment, and respect for the right to be heard can be considered fundamental. The seriousness requirement is satisfied where a party is completely or substantially deprived of the benefit which the fundamental rule was designed to provide.[139]

Both, the corruption of a tribunal member and the failure to state the reasons for the award, can be classified as a subcategory of the serious departure from fundamental rules of procedure. However, they are ususaly depicted as independent grounds for nullity. Corruption of a tribunal member is to be presumed where there is evidence for actions which have or are likely to have impaired impartiality. One of the most obvious cases would be the acceptance of money in connection with the arbitration proceedings. The contention that the tribunal has failed to state reasons brings up the question what form and degree of reasoning the tribunal is required to give. It has been established that the arbitral award must only indicate the reasons on which it is based in a general manner. It is not necessary that every particular plea of the parties be meticulously addressed with reasons for upholding or rejecting it.[140]

The most controversial of all claims is the essential or manifest error. The rather cool reception this ground is accorded by many international law experts results from the perceived lack of clarity and the indeterminable new disputes to which it would thus open the door.[141] Examples of an essential error of law which are being discussed in academia are a mistake as to the appropriate law to be applied or not taking into account a relevant treaty.[142] In any event, the plea does not allow a party to request the merits of the decision to be reconsidered or the evidence relied on by the tribunal to be re-evaluated.

If the parties have provided for an appeals procedure, it is to be used to assert nullity claims. Where no appeals procedure is available or where the arbitral award has

---

137 Please note that in the present context "excess of power" and "lack of jurisdiction" are considered as carrying the same meaning.
138 M. N. SHAW, *International Law*, (2008), p. 1053; See *Palena Arbitration, supra* note 97.
139 L. REED, J. PAULSSON, N. BLACKABY, *Guide to ICSID Arbitration*, (2004), p. 97.
140 Application for Review of Judgment No. 158 of the United Nations Administrative Tribunal (*Fasla Case*, 1973), Advisory Opinion, 1973 I.C.J. Report 166, p. 210, (para. 95).
141 J. H. W. VERZIJL, *Interstate Disputes and Their Settlement*, (1976), p. 578; It is thus not surprising that this ground was not included in Article 35 of the *ILC Model Rules on Arbitral Procedure*.
142 M. N. SHAW, *International Law, supra* note 137.

been upheld on appeal, the parties must find agreement through diplomatic or political means.[143]

As indicated above, although the arbitral award is binding on the parties there are considerable limitations on its enforcement. Simply put, it is uncertain whether the unsuccessful party will honour the arbitral award. If a State does not comply with the arbitral award, there is little the other party can do other than answer this violation of international law with a retorsion or a reprisal.[144] The most promising avenue for resolving any controversy regarding the validity of nullity claims is therefore recourse to diplomatic or political means.

That being said, it has to be stressed that arbitral awards are in the majority of cases recognised by the parties. Since the negative consequences of non-compliance would be considerable, States are ill-advised to incur them lightly. A State could not expect other States to submit future disputes to arbitration or, what is more, that awards in its own favour would be implemented by the opposite party. In consequence, a State would lose an important tool in solving potentially crippling disputes in its international relations. Moreover, non-compliance could generally harm the State's repute in the international community and frustrate efforts to engage in successful political and economical cooperation.

The Parties can adopt different approaches to ensure that arbitral awards are followed by the parties. A very effective way was devised in the *Iran-U.S. Claims Tribunal* where a fund was established by the original agreement out of which the arbitral awards were to be paid. The arbitral awards were thus enforced "in advance" and consequently immunized from subsequent uncooperative behaviour by the parties. The parties may also undertake to frame the *compromis* narrowly with regard to the grounds for nullity in order to discourage later pleas from the unsuccessful party. Finally, the tribunal can try to balance the conflicting interests and find a decision that takes account of the wishes of both parties to the greatest possible extent. However, as arbitration is based on the rule of law there are obvious limitations to this approach.

Despite these possibilities, the fact remains that the enforceability of an award is generally subject to acceptance by the aggrieved party. Nevertheless, by and large, great pessimism concerning enforceability seems unwarranted as the parties, by submitting to arbitration, have already given a clear indication of their willingness to comply with the future award.

---

143 C. H. BROWER, Arbitration, in R. Wolfrum (Ed.), *The Max Planck Encyclopedia of Public International Law*, (2008), online edition, [www.mpepil.com], para. 86, visited on 19 April 2009.
144 Enforcement by the Security Council would only be conceivable in the unlikely event that the violation of the tribunal award constitutes a threat to the peace according to Article 39 of the U.N. Charter.

H. Conclusion

To render an objective assessment of the merits of arbitration and its future prospects on the international law plane, it has to be put into perspective with its main alternatives, diplomacy and court-administered dispute settlement.[145]

Many international conflicts have been resolved by diplomacy and often quite successfully in a way that would have not been possible through judicial settlement, be it in the form of arbitration or adjudication by courts. However, diplomatic negotiations between States can end in deadlock. In particular, when negotiations have been protracted and claims bitterly contested, States often find it impossible to make any concessions. To give up their own position is perceived as damaging to credibility and reputation. Nevertheless, to settle a conflict, even when it requires painful concessions, is often more beneficial to the interests of States than leaving the dispute unresolved. Submitting to the jurisdiction of an independent judicial body is a way of potentially relinquishing a State's claim without losing the face. Importantly, the losing party can still protest the validity of its own legal position when the decision is unfavourable, something a State would find harder to do when the compromise is of its own doing. In addition, when both parties are convinced of the validity of their legal standpoint, diplomatic negotiations would force at least one of them, typically both, to make concessions which are legally unjustified from their perspective. In the event of legal settlement, both parties preserve the chance to fully succeed with their respective claims. This outlook can outweigh the fact that the involved parties stand to lose more than they would by negotiating a deal. It is also important to point out that diplomatic negotiations can only bring about non-binding agreements. Arbitration, on the other hand, will result in binding arbitral awards, non-compliance with which would amount to a violation of international law. There is thus a distinctively higher likelihood that the parties will adhere to the arbitral award than to the negotiated agreement.

States are notoriously suspicious of compulsory judicial settlement because it is considered an intrusion upon national sovereignty. If a dispute has arisen that falls under the jurisdiction of a court, there is little States can do to stop the instigation of proceedings. Even the refusal to engage in court procedures will not bar the court from finding a decision. In contrast, it is only upon the parties' own agreement that a dispute will be brought before an arbitral tribunal. In each individual case, it is for the parties to decide whether they would like to make it the subject of legal proceedings. From the State perspective, arbitration therefore offers a very attractive compromise between the advantages of submitting to legally binding adjudication and preserving national sovereignty. Not surprisingly, the attempt to introduce a world court with compulsory jurisdiction has, until now, been resisted by many States and remained rather unsuccessful. Despite Article 36 (2) of the Statute of the ICJ, providing that State parties to

---

145 It is noted that despite Article 33 of the UN Charter it is still for States to decide whether or not to settle a dispute. States thus may also decide to leave a conflict completely unresolved.

the Statute of the Court may at any time declare that they recognize the compulsory jurisdiction of the Court, only a minority of 66 States has deposited the respective declarations and, importantly, often accompanied them with many and far-reaching reservations. In view of the limited jurisdiction of the ICJ and other international courts, arbitration has consequently remained an important mechanism in international dispute settlement.

From the perspective of the parties, there are some important institutional advantages that arbitration enjoys over judicial settlement, some of which have been discussed in this article. Arbitration enables States to obtain a decision from a judicial body of their own choice. By exerting considerable control over the composition of the arbitral tribunal, the involved States have great influence on later decisions. Judicial activism, an accusation frequently leveled against international courts and identified by many politicians as one of the main imperfections of the current system of international dispute settlement, can thus be effectively prevented. In addition, the parties alone determine the jurisdiction of the arbitral tribunal and lay down the procedural rules. From an institutional point of view, arbitration is a way of dispute settlement that, next to diplomacy, respects to the greatest possible extent the autonomy of States.

In contrast to many courts, arbitral tribunals normally do not suffer from a backlog of cases so that the proceedings can be opened immediately. The promptness of dispute settlement is further assisted by flexible procedural rules on which the parties frequently agree. The confidentiality of the proceedings is a further attractive feature of arbitration. The publication of the proceedings and of the award is entirely a matter to be decided by the parties. States may be much more prone to settle conflicts that are highly sensitive or likely to cause reputational harm when brought before an international court. A potential reduction of cost may be another factor in favour of arbitration. While the establishment of a permanent court will result in fixed costs irrespective of the case-load, the costs of arbitral tribunals will only be incurred during the periods of their existence. However, if States have to go to arbitration repeatedly, the costs of setting up these tribunals are likely to off-set considerably the aforementioned costs savings as the process of examining and hiring arbitrators, drafting instructions or establishing rules of procedure are also cost-intensive.

Despite the many advantages of arbitration, it must be recognised that arbitration has its inherent weaknesses, too. Leaving it to the States to submit to arbitration in each individual case will likely induce them to "err on the side of caution" more often than not, i.e. with the protection of their national interests, and decide against arbitration. Another often lamented disadvantage is their rather episodic nature. In the past, arbitral tribunals have generally been established on an *ad hoc* basis. Due to their intermittent character, they have been less capable of contributing to the development of international law principles than international courts, most notably the ICJ. This problem is intensified by the lack of appellate bodies which has the effect of encouraging tribunals to render decisions that are not fully based on law. Further limitations arise from the fact that the parties tend to prefer narrowly framed instructions in order to limit the jurisdiction of the tribunal. Even where parties agree to submit a dispute to arbitration they may decide to exclude the legally most controversial questions from the tribunal's jurisdiction. A particular impediment to the development of international law can also be seen in the discretion of the parties to agree on secrecy. In this case, the reasoning of the tribunal will not enter into the public sphere and cannot be relied on by other legal bodies. Finally, what was conducive to State sovereignty, the influence of States on the set-up of the tribunals, has the potential to harm the quality of the decisions. Whether the arbitral awards rendered by tribunals are always arrived at on objective and impartial considerations of law is much more open to question than is the case with court proceedings. This is all the more so as arbitrators have to be concerned that handing down a decision which is unsatisfactory for the parties will disqualify them from future proceedings. It follows that the advantages of arbitration also constitute in many instances its very shortcomings.

To sum up, States are traditionally keen to preserve their sovereignty and are therefore reluctant to make a general commitment to judicial settlement. As a result, they avail themselves in many cases of diplomacy in order to retain full control of the decision-making process. However, in many situations, they are interested in a final and binding decision by judicial procedure, in particular when diplomatic means are unsuitable or have failed to solve a dispute. Interstate arbitration as a combination of both diplomatic and judicial elements represents a welcome instrument for reconciling these conflicting interests of States. The very essence of arbitration and its cornerstone is the confidence of each party that its side of the case will be properly represented and fairly protected. Regardless of the fact that its heyday lies undoubtedly in the past and that a renaissance, in all likelihood, is not to be expected, it will retain some importance for the settlement of disputes of minor importance and, in particular, of such "fringe disputes" which because of their particularities do not lend themselves to adjudication by courts. Historically, it has maintained and stimulated the legal dialogue between States and in doing so has, despite its intrinsic weaknesses, proven itself not only as a meritorious factor but as the nucleus of the judicialization of international law and it is in this process in which it will live on.

The WTO Dispute Settlement System: From Arbitration to a World Court System

THOMAS COTTIER [1]

The GATT dispute settlement was exclusively based upon the conciliatory procedures of Article XXIII of the 1947 General Agreement. Since the 1950s, it developed on a case by case basis into a customary law system of judicial arbitration. Panels, instead of working parties, were appointed to analyze complaints in a process of claims and responses. It is only since the 1980s that panels were supported by legal advice and staff in the GATT Secretariat. 1979 saw the first legal description and codification of the panel system. It served as a basis for negotiations in the Uruguay Round. These negotiations tackled the problem of endemic non-compliance due to veto powers. They resulted – in terms of international law – in a revolutionary two-tier system, complementing panels with the Appellate Body of seven jurists retained for the job of reviewing panel decisions upon appeal. It abolished consensus and veto powers and obliged losing defendants to implement findings, pay compensation or face stiff multilaterally approved sanctions (withdrawal of concessions).

The system has worked well since 1995. The case load dispatched is impressive. Many of the more than 350 disputes notified are settled by negotiations and consultations in the first place. As to adjudication in some 130 cases, the overall record of compliance with adopted panel and Appellate Body reports is high. Except for some highly politicized cases, almost all of the disputes adjudicated have been implemented at home. WTO dispute settlement emerged as the procedural stronghold of the Organization. In particular, the panel system was able to bring about much progress in interfacing different areas of international law, such as trade and environment. That relationship has been mainly advanced by case law, rather than international negotiations. The same will be true for other interlinkages. Nevertheless, a number of important systemic issues exist and need to be addressed. They are rooted in the nature of arbitration.

The appointment of panelists and arbitrators is not sufficiently transparent. While based upon a roster, people are chosen randomly, often from outside the roster, and the selection process is often used to bring about time delays in setting up the panel.

---

1 Professor at the University of Berne, Panelist in various dispute settlements in WTO/GATT, Director of the Institute of European and International Economic Law, Director of the World Trade Institute and of the MILE programme (Master of International Law and Economics), Dean of the Faculty of Law of the University of Berne.

The powers of the Appellate Body are limited to questions of law. Panels are solely responsible for the factual assessment of a case. The division leads to practical problems if the legal approach taken by the panel is challenged and dismissed while the factual analysis for an alternate approach is missing. The Appellate Body cannot send the case back, but needs to find a solution within the bounds of a given and perhaps complemented factual analysis undertaken by the panel.

This problem has been particularly strong in the second Hormones case.[2] Instead of limiting itself to jurisdictional issues before it, the panel anticipated a full examination of the measures at stake under the SPS Agreement.[3] It did so in order to provide the Appellate Body with necessary factual determination for a potential ruling on the merits. A lot of time and energy was spent and lost.

The case again shows that the introduction of a remand power would make sense. The Appellate Body should be in a position to return a finding for further review and to instruct panels how to proceed. This would apply both to questions of law and fact. Remand power, in return, requires a departure from the traditional system of ad hoc panels and thus from arbitration, since in arbitration remand powers risk that ad hoc panelists – busy with other issues – will not be prepared to serve on what risk to become protracted procedures. It was therefore suggested by the EU to establish a body of professional panelists. Alternatively, I suggested to appoint professional chairpersons and to select panelists randomly from a college of some 25 panelists which are retained to serve on panels.[4]

The point I wish to make is that the two-tier system of the WTO – which is unique in international law apart from UN staff litigation – inherently moves the system from ad hoc arbitration towards a system of partly permanent structures of panels and towards an overall two-tier world court system in matters of trade regulation. On the global level, it would seem that dispute settlement will further legalize, rather than returning to the old days of political conciliation.

The main weaknesses are the imbalances created by the consensus-based political process.[5] Main efforts at reform today therefore rather deal with the political process, than with dispute settlement. The advances of WTO dispute settlement – in particular the turn to majority ruling and departure from blocking powers by consensus – created an imbalance to the political branch of decision making in WTO, i.e. the negotiating process. Consensus policies still rule the day. There are many advantages to it. But

---

2   WTO Dispute DS 320: *United States – Continued Suspension of Obligations in the EC – Hormones Dispute*, see http://www.wto.org/english/tratop_e/dispu_e/cases_e/ds320_e.htm.
3   Appellate Body Report, *United States – Continued Suspension of Obligations in the EC – Hormones Dispute*, WT/DS320/AB/R 16. October 2008 para. 282.
4   T. Cottier, "The WTO Permanent Panel Body: A Bridge Too Far?" (2003) 6 *Journal of International Economic Law* 187-202.
5   T. Cottier, "Preparing for Structural Reform in the WTO" (2007) 10 *Journal of International Economic Law* 497-508.

there are serious shortcomings, too. It is questionable whether it may continue to bring about process in what has become a multipolar world. The days where in fact substantive decisions could be taken by the United States unilaterally, and later on jointly with the European Union (such as the Blair House Agreement in the Uruguay Round) are days of the past. We need to come to grips with a more complex world and we thus need more complex rules on decision-making in the political process. Parallel to dispute settlement structures, we may see the advent of weighted voting as a fallback to back up consensus based trade policy. The powers of the dispute settlement mechanism in WTO need to be balanced by efficient and workable tools of legislative response. Immobility and the practical impossibility to correct dispute settlement findings based upon the interpretation of the existing agreements by amending these agreements on an ad hoc basis and within the decade which a trade round usually takes, will be detrimental to the proud achievements in dispute settlement.

In conclusion: while reform of dispute settlement is in need of specific points, in particular remand and staffing of panels, the emphasis in coming years should be placed on the reform of the political process. Dispute settlement and political process find themselves in a dialectical process. They need moving forward in tandem in the process of constitutionalising international economic law.

Discussion

GABRIELLE KAUFMANN-KOHLER
Thank you very much for these explanations on interstate arbitration. That really completes the picture. Now we have a very broad picture of arbitration starting from private arbitration and going over mixed arbitration to truly public arbitration. We have enough time for the discussion now. Who has the first question?

SVEN NORBERG
I have a question for Professor Rau. I found your presentation extremely interesting. My question concerns the *Eco Swiss v. Benetton* judgment[1] by the ECJ in which the question arose, to what extent an arbitration tribunal should apply Articles 81 and 82 EC of its own motion without the parties invoking the said Articles. The ECJ concluded – referring to a particular provision of the New York Convention regarding public policy – that this action by the arbitrational tribunal constitutes a breach of the public policy principle. Would you like to comment on that?

ALAN RAU
Well, that is a very important point and it reminds me of the discussion earlier today in a different context about the margin of appreciation. Everything is a question of what kinds of deference a court will give to arbitrators who issue an award which may or may not be in violation of Community antitrust law or may or may not be very different of what a court itself would do if it had the case. If an arbitrator were to say: *"Yes, we have considered the Treaty of Rome, but we do not much care for it, we are going to issue an award without regard to the Treaty of Rome"*, he would probably never be an arbitrator again and obviously that award would not be enforced.

I wish I had the exact quote, as Justice Holmes said in some connection, an obligation without any possibility of enforcement is like a ghost that walks in the night. You can sort of hear it but it does not affect your life in any serious way and in my opinion that is true in antitrust law.

CARL BAUDENBACHER
In my opinion, the position of the Cour d'Appele is absolutely untenable. This almost amounts to conspiracy. The Commission should go after them because they

---

1 Case C-126/97 – *Eco Swiss China Time Ltd v. Benetton International NV*, ECR-1999, I-03055.

make themselves a part of the cartel by acting in this way. Unfortunately, the Federal Supreme Court of Switzerland, a couple of years ago, has given a ruling along the same lines, holding that the competition rules of the European Community are not part of the *ordre public* in Switzerland.

I know a couple of arbitrators in Zurich, who – at least in their writings – take the view that in certain cases, if the parties do not plead the nullity issue under Article 81 EC themselves, they would ask them out of their own motion.

SVEN NORBERG

If I may add a comment to that. The reason I asked that question is that in my home country, Sweden, it was revealed some years ago, that a majority of the Supreme Court judges earn more from arbitration work than they do as "regular" judges. Of course I have to add, that judges in Sweden are poorly paid. The fact that so many of them deal so much with arbitration, might, however, explain why they are extremely afraid to apply Community Law out of their own spontaneous volition, without the parties evoking it by themselves.

ALAN RAU

The imaginary horrible is that the arbitrators will be the cat's paw of a cartel. That the parties will, as part of their conspiracy, enlist this third party called an arbitrator to ratify their cartel for them. That is a legitimate fear except that it is not likely to be the case. And I do not think that is what is happening in these cases and it is not what is happening in *Thalès*. In my opinion, to step back and say, *"let's look at this agreement, let's look at this award and see whether in fact there appears to be a violation of Community law"*, is a reasonable position to take, unless one is prone to conspiracy theories.

CARL BAUDENBACHER

But when we get to the enforcement stage, one party still could plead for the nullity of the award, which would send the case to a state court, which would probably have to make a reference to the European Court of Justice.

GABRIELLE KAUFMANN-KOHLER

I would like to make two practical comments and one theoretical one. As a practical matter, I really think an arbitrator today would not act responsibly if he or she were not to raise these issues. I did it in one case even though the parties had not raised the problem. I asked them if a certain clause of a distribution agreement was in conformity with Article 81 EC. The parties presented then their submissions and I could make a decision. That, in my opinion, is the responsibility of the arbitrator.

There is a difficulty, of course, namely that the arbitrator has no investigation powers at all. So how does he/she determine a market share for instance? Well, if the parties come forward with credible evidence, then there is no problem. However, if they do not, the arbitrator is in a difficult position. That is the practical barrier.

It seems to me that the more the scope of arbitration disputes expands into areas that have a strong public policy element, the more the arbitrators must apply the law that governs these areas. Otherwise this expansion would be inconsistent.

The practice and the theory have moved a lot. Twenty years ago, there were a number of contract clauses for arbitration in Switzerland under Swiss law on contracts that affected the European market where the parties clearly had the intention of avoiding European competition law by setting their arbitration in Switzerland. Today, this does not work anymore. Admittedly, the Federal Supreme Court of Switzerland held not long ago that European competition law was not part of international public policy, a decision that seems contrary to the general tendency everywhere else.

Let us now move to the next question.

HANSPETER TSCHÄNI
I have a question to Professor Schreuer and also to Professor Kaufmann-Kohler as a practitioner. Professor Schreuer, you alluded to an issue that has become extremely relevant, namely investment arbitration. One can argue that investment arbitration has moved from the purely commercial side over to the more public domain and as a result of it, there are cases in which issues are at stake that really pertain to the public interest. In that regard we have seen certain changes in the ICSID Convention as well as in the amendment of the UNCITAL Convention. It has been decided to split off the more investor state part from the normal UNCITAL rules. How does one experience this development and how far do you think it can go, considering that you still have to achieve the results for which you are on the panel?

CHRISTOPH SCHREUER
I think the problem stems from the fact that investment arbitration essentially uses the established tool of commercial arbitration for something that is not exactly commercial arbitration. Traditional arbitration takes place behind closed doors under the direction of the parties and the public is essentially locked out. Now in the beginning, people seemed to assume that this was also an ideal tool for investment arbitration. The investor and the host state would withdraw behind closed doors and settle their dispute there and then hopefully implement it. Nowadays, we have more and more public interest groups banging at the doors. They want to participate since what is being decided are not just commercial issues, but very important issues of public interest. In fact, the issues came to the fore mostly in cases regarding water supplies. And the compromise that was reached in the meantime was to allow *amicus curiae* participation in a limited way. Now, the problem with opening the doors to third party participation is, of course, where do you draw the line? How do you establish the legitimacy of these third parties, the *amici*? At worst, the *amici* would be hired guns for one of the parties. And there are some indications that sometimes one or the other party will rent an NGO. Things like that do happen. On the other hand, you do have very legitimate causes of concern for the public who wants to be let in. The other extreme would be

a bunch of corrupt politicians settling their disputes with greedy foreign investors. I'm exaggerating for effect. Of course, this is not my genuine perspective.

So you have to draw a proper balance. The practice so far has been to take a very careful look at these third party participants, to ask them for their credentials, to second guess their claims and finally, to only admit them once it is clear that they are really acting in the public interest and to limit their participation to written submissions of no more than a certain number of pages, so the tribunal does not get flooded with hundreds or thousands of pages.

These are all very difficult practical problems that so far have been resolved on an ad hoc basis. The ICSID rules have been adjusted to a certain extent. The experience so far is still very limited and I do not think there are simple black or white solutions here. Neither total exclusion of public interest groups nor their unlimited admission will be the solution to the problem.

GABRIELLE KAUFMANN-KOHLER

The right balance between including and excluding the public from the arbitration is difficult to achieve. I have participated in the first decision that opened ICSID proceedings to NGOs as *amici curiae* before the ICSID rules were changed to expressly permit it. We looked at the practice of the WTO and NAFTA – a form of judicial dialogue – and set up a number of requirements that NGOs must satisfy before the tribunal decides on their admissibility.

PATRICIA HANSEN

My question is more general. What are your views on the appropriateness of having ad hoc arbitrators resolve these issues? I know Professor Alan Rau believes there is no real reason to think that a national court would resolve a particular case better or more correctly than an arbitrator. But, as you have pointed out, investorstate arbitrators are involved in the development of general rules of law. They are defining basic legal concepts such as due process and fair and equitable treatment. Professor Kaufmann-Kohler pointed out that there is a split between arbitrators who believe they should fly like condors, and those who believe they are part of a larger project of developing the law. But even if an arbitrator does seek to develop the law, she is not devoted full time to this project, unlike a court. Moreover, in light of the today's spirited discussion of the problem of judicial independence, it seems to me there may be even greater concerns about the independence of arbitrators who are engaged in so many competing professional activities. Do any of you view any of these issues as problematic for investorstate arbitration?

GABRIELLE KAUFMANN-KOHLER

The ad hoc nature of the panels and the decisions is indeed a problem when it comes to ensuring consistency in the development of the law, a problem that Christoph Schreuer addressed when he spoke of precedent.

Another problem is the fact that contradictory results are emerging from decisions and there is uncertainty about the evolution. Some people are convinced that unless you have an appeals mechanism, unless you have a permanent court, you will not get consistent results. I am not certain about this. Time will show.

One last question.

NIKOLAOS LAVRANOS
Should not common rules be implemented for arbitrators and judges, clarifying how and when they should approach issues of jurisdiction? Especially, when it comes to the applicable tools of interpretation? Would that not ensure that judges and arbitrators go in the same direction regarding the way they approach identical or similar issues?

CHRISTOPH SCHREUER
Much of this actually exists I believe. If you look at ICSID practice, you will find a lot of commonalities. I would say on 90% there is fairly consistent case law. There are of course a few areas where that is not the case. But the problem is that all of these decisions are made by human beings and human beings tend to disagree on some points. And it is very difficult to tell arbitrator B to follow arbitrator A because arbitrator A has come first especially when arbitrator B feels that arbitrator A was wrong. That is an oversimplification, but I would say, most of the time this is exactly what is happening and there is a large area of agreement but there are certain islands of disagreement. I do not think there is a simple method to simply eradicate these islands of disagreement. You cannot tell arbitrators that they have to decide in a particular way.

A system of precedent, as in the common law sense, is out of the question, but there is a practice of *de facto* reference and deference. So, I think the area of improvement is limited unless you adopt one of the institutional approaches. But the institutional approaches typically take some formal step by governments. I do not think you absolutely need an amendment of treaties, which is extremely difficult, but at least a decision, say, within the Administrative Council ICSID would be necessary.

ALAN RAU
We all know that the law is always evolving and certainty in the law is an illusion. And if we know what the result will be 80% of the time and 20% of the time we do not know the result, there is a certain fruitful messiness where the law evolves. But the search for consistency and predictable results 100% of the time is something we should avoid.

GABRIELLE KAUFMANN-KOHLER
That was a very realistic observation. Closing upon the "fruitful messiness of all this", I would like to thank the speakers very much for their contributions and everyone for interesting questions.

Keynote

The World Trade Organization Dispute Settlement System: Embedded In Public International Law?

JACQUES BOURGEOIS[1]
RAVI SOOPRAMANIEN[2]

A. Introduction to WTO Dispute Settlement

I. Background

1. Historical Development

World Trade Organization (WTO) dispute settlement is regulated by the Understanding on Rules and Procedures Governing the Settlement of Disputes (DSU). Prior to the DSU, and under the General Agreement on Tariffs and Trade (GATT) 1947 system, Article XXIII (on Nullification and Impairment) made no reference to "Panels." Rather, Article XXIII referred only to the "Contracting Parties" – an indication that disputes could only be heard at a plenary meeting of all signatory States. Contracting Parties collectively realized at an early stage of the GATT 1947's existence that plenary meetings were not a practical venue for the settlement of disputes. Contracting Parties first delegated dispute settlement duties to the Chairman of the Contracting Parties. When this proved impractical, Contracting Parties delegated the dispute settlement duties to smaller groups (termed "working parties") before ultimately delegating them to a body referred to in the Seventh Session of the Contracting Parties as a "Panel on Complaints" in 1952.[3] Towards the end of the GATT's existence, Contracting Parties had greater ability to "forum-shop," even within the WTO framework through the choice of arbitration contained in GATT Article XXIII (on Nullification or Impairment) and specialized procedures established pursuant to the Tokyo Multilateral Round of negotiations.[4] Following the GATT's absorption into the WTO framework, however, the DSU has dramatically altered the face of WTO dispute settlement.

---

1 Advocaat, Wilmer, Cutler, Pickering, Hale & Dorr LLP (Brussels), Professor at the College of Europe (Bruges). This paper is based on a presentation given at the INTERNATIONAL DISPUTE SETTLEMENT CONFERENCE 2008, organized by the University of St. Gallen (St. Gallen, October 3, 2008).
2 Barrister, LLB, King's College London (Hons); LLM, London School of Economics (with Distinction); M.I.L.E., World Trade Institute (Summa Cum Laude).
3 For a discussion of the Panel's evolution, see Robert E. Hudec, The Role of the GATT Secretariat in the Evolution of the WTO Dispute Settlement Procedure in Jagdish Bhagwati & Mathias Hirsch (Eds.), The Uruguay Round and Beyond: Essays in Honour of Arthur Dunkel 101-120 (Springer-Verlag; New York; 1998).
4 For a discussion of these alternate GATT dispute forums, see Ernst-Ulrich Petersmann, The Transformation of the World Trading System through the 1994 Agreement establishing the World Trade Organization, 6(2) European Journal of International Law 161-221 (1995).

2. Statistics

No less than 240 dispute settlement reports (for all intents and purposes "judgments") were circulated to the Dispute Settlement Body (DSB) between 1995 and 2008.[5] Disputing parties appealed 88 of these reports to a standing Appellate Body. Twenty five of these 240 reports involved recourse (compliance) proceedings. Disputing parties appealed 17 of these recourse panel reports to the Appellate Body. The Appellate Body received a total of 97 notices of appeal during this period, of which 80 arose from original proceedings.[6] The DSU featured in 74 of these notices; the GATT in 58 notices; and the Agreement on Implementation of Article VI of the General Agreement on Tariffs and Trade 1994 ("ADA Agreement") and Agreement on Subsidies and Countervailing Measures (SCM Agreement) each featured in 24 notices. The Safeguards Agreement, in contrast to the ADA and SCM Agreements, has featured in only 7 notices.[7] This latter statistic lends itself to the suggestion that WTO Member trade authorities actively engage comparatively more in trade remedies arising from dumping and subsidy investigations, than safeguard investigations. It is also noted that the Agreement on Trade-Related Investment Measures is the only WTO Agreement not to be featured in any notice of appeals during this period.

As of January 19, 2009, Members have requested consultations a total of 390 times.[8] The US ranks as the most active litigant, featuring as complainant in 92 of these disputes, and as respondent on 105 occasions. The EU ranks second, appearing as complainant in 79 of these disputes, and as respondent on 64 occasions. Canada ranks distant third, appearing as complainant in 31 disputes, and as respondent on 15 occasions. Brazil and India both rank fourth. Brazil appeared as complainant in 24 disputes, and as respondent on 14 occasions. India appeared as complainant in 18 disputes, and as respondent on 20 occasions. Not to be outdone by its NAFTA partners, Mexico ranks as the sixth most active litigant, appearing as complainant in 20 disputes, and as respondent on 14 occasions.

A study based on World Bank income classifications illustrates that: (i) high income Members registered 245 complaints, and featured as respondent 234 times; (ii) upper middle income Members registered 90 complaints, and featured as respondent 79 times; (iii) lower middle income Members registered 46 complaints, and featured as respondents 53 times; and (iv) low income Members registered 25 complaints, and

---

5   Appellate Body Annual Report for 2008, WT/AB/11 (February 9, 2009), at Annex 4. See Annex I of this paper.
6   Ibid, at Annex 3. See Annex II of this paper.
7   Id, at Annex 5. See Annex III of this paper.
8   See http://www.wto.org/english/tratop_e/dispu_e/dispu_status_e.htm (chronological list) and http://www.wto.org/english/tratop_e/dispu_e/dispu_by_country_e.htm (country-specific list).

featured as respondent 25 times.[9] The study reveals a close correlation between the number of complaints launched and received across all 4 income groups.

Empirical studies of WTO adjudicative outcomes suggest that a Member's success before a WTO tribunal may turn upon that Member's status as a complainant or respondent. A recent study published in March 2009, for example, concludes that WTO complainants fare "with win rates ranging from 83% to 91% across case-types."[10] One must always exercise caution in drawing sweeping conclusions from these figures. It is nonetheless interesting to note that the complainant success rate put forward by Robert Hudec with respect to the GATT 1947, of 88% for "valid complaints,"[11] falls squarely within the 83–93% range put forward in the 2009 study.

3. Introduction to the DSU

WTO dispute settlement remains contentious under the DSU. Rulings are now "quasi-automatic" by operation of a negative consensus rule (reversing the GATT 1947's positive consensus rule).[12] Members may appeal a panel's findings to the Appellate Body. DSU Article 17.6 limits the mandate of the Appellate Body to "issues of law covered in the panel report and legal interpretations developed by the panel."

DSU Article 23.1 states that whenever "Members seek the redress of a violation of obligations or other nullification or impairment of benefits under the covered [WTO] agreements, they shall have recourse to, and abide by, the rules and procedures of this Understanding." The "nullification or impairment" threshold contained in DSU Article 23.1 is a low adjudicative trigger, which applies effectively to "non-violation" measures. A Panel considered in *Japan-Film*[13] that DSU Article 23.1 serves "to protect the balance of concessions under GATT by providing a means to redress government actions not otherwise regulated by GATT rules that nonetheless nullify or impair a Member's legitimate expectations of benefits from tariff negotiations."[14]

---

9   See http://www.worldtradelaw.net/dsc/database/classificationcount.asp. The study qualifies that "a number of complaints have been filed by multiple Members acting jointly. In some of these complaints, the Members filing the complaint fall into different income categories. Where this is the case, we have counted the complaint in each income category in which at least one complainant falls. Therefore, the number of the complaints in these tables will add up to more than the total number of complaints under the DSU." See Annex IV of this paper.

10 Juscelino Colares, *A Theory of WTO Adjudication: From Empirical Analysis to Biased Rule Development*, 42(2)
    Vanderbilt Journal of Transnational Law 383-439 (2009), at p. 439.

11 Robert E. Hudec, *Enforcing International Trade Law: The Evolution of the Modern GATT Legal System* 353 (Butterworths Legal Publishers; Salem, 1993).

12 Gabrielle Marceau, *Conflicts of Norms and Conflicts of Jurisdictions*, 35(6) Journal of World Trade 1081-1131 (2001), at p. 1117. Under the GATT 1947's positive consensus rule, any country could veto the adoption of a Panel report. Such a situation typically arose with respect to the losing contracting Party.

13 Panel Report, *Japan – Measures Affecting Consumer Photographic Film and Paper*, WT/DS44/R, adopted April 22, 1998.

14 Ibid, at para. 10.50.

The WTO dispute settlement system is compulsory. Any Member seeking recourse to the WTO dispute settlement mechanism must first request consultations with the prospective respondent pursuant to DSU Article 4.4. DSU Article 4.4 requires all requests for consultations to be "submitted in writing and ... give the reasons for the request, including identification of the measures at issue and an indication of the legal basis for the complaint." Once a complaining Member submits a request for consultations, the responding Member must enter into negotiations with the complainant. DSU Article 4.3 addresses the consequences of a responding Member's failure to engage in negotiations with the complaining Member: "if the Member does not respond within 10 days after the date of receipt of the request, or does not enter into consultations within a period of no more than 30 days, or a period otherwise mutually agreed, after the date of receipt of the request, then the Member that requested the holding of consultations may proceed directly to request the establishment of a panel."

The WTO website's "Dispute Settlement Gateway" states that "although much of the [DSU] procedure does resemble a court or tribunal, the preferred solution is for the countries concerned to discuss their problems and settle the dispute by themselves."[15] A majority of WTO disputes settle before reaching panel proceedings.[16] The compulsory nature of WTO dispute settlement stands in contradistinction to the optional jurisdiction of the International Court of Justice (ICJ).[17]

In EC – Commercial Vessels,[18] the EC argued that Article 23.1 was an "exclusive jurisdiction clause" whose main purpose was to "ensure the exclusivity of WTO jurisdiction over WTO law and the suspension of concessions."[19] The Panel disagreed with this interpretation, and was of the view that "we consider that the requirement 'to have recourse to' the DSU when Members seek the redress of a violation[...] is broader in scope than suggested by the expression 'exclusive jurisdiction clause' used by the EC. This requirement is violated not only when Members submit a dispute concerning rights and obligations under the WTO Agreement to an international dispute settlement body outside the WTO framework but also when Members act unilaterally to seek to obtain the results that can be achieved through the remedies of the DSU."[20]

The Panel's findings in EC – Commercial Vessels confirm the broad jurisdictional reach of DSU Article 23.1. DSU Article 23.1 effectively prevents Members from resorting to

---

15 See http://www.wto.org/english/thewto_e/whatis_e/tif_e/disp1_e.htm.
16 Ibid. The website states that "by July 2005, only about 130 of the nearly 332 cases had reached the full panel process. Most of the rest have either been notified as settled "out of court" or remain in a prolonged consultation phase — some since 1995."
17 See Article 36(2) of the Statute of the International Court of Justice, signed on June 26, 1945, 59 Stat. 1055, 33 U.N.T.S. 993. On October 7, 1985, US Secretary of State George Schultz notified then-UN Secretary General Javier Pérez de Cuéllar that the US was withdrawing from the compulsory jurisdiction of the ICJ.
18 Panel Report, *European Communities – Measures Affecting Trade in Commercial Vessels*, WT/DS301/R, adopted 20 June 2005.
19 Ibid, at para. 7.179.
20 Id, at para. 7.195.

unilateral remedies. This sets the DSU aside from the "default" position in customary international law, where States may unilaterally resort to countermeasures to redress an international tort committed against them.[21]

WTO dispute settlement is thus contentious, compulsory and exclusive.

4. The Role of Precedent

Despite the lack of formal *stare decisis* in the DSU, WTO tribunals have attributed the role of precedent to the requirement in DSU Article 3.2 that WTO dispute settlement "is a central element in providing security and predictability to the multilateral trading system." The Appellate Body took the position in US – Stainless Steel[22] that "dispute settlement practice demonstrates that WTO Members attach significance to reasoning provided in previous panels and Appellate Body reports. Adopted panel and Appellate Body reports are often cited by parties in support of legal arguments in dispute settlement proceedings, and are relied upon by panels and the Appellate Body in subsequent disputes. In addition, when enacting or modifying laws and national regulations pertaining to international trade matters, WTO Members take into account the legal interpretation of the covered agreements developed in adopted panel and Appellate Body reports. Thus, the legal interpretation embodied in adopted panel and Appellate Body reports becomes part and parcel of the *acquis* of the WTO dispute settlement system. Ensuring 'security and predictability' in the dispute settlement system, as contemplated in Article 3.2 of the DSU, implies that, absent cogent reasons, an adjudicatory body will resolve the same legal question in the same way in a subsequent case."[23] The Panel had "respectfully disagree[d] with the line of reasoning developed by the Appellate Body"[24] in an earlier report on dumping margin calculations in that dispute.

US – Stainless Steel marked the first time in which a panel expressly registered its disagreement with Appellate Body jurisprudence. The Appellate Body's reaction to the panel confirms not only the extent to which Appellate Body jurisprudence should be followed by subsequent panels "absent cogent reasons," but also indicates that the Appellate Body sees its role as extending beyond the mere settlement of disputes between the parties. This sets the WTO dispute mechanism aside from other international economic dispute bodies such as tribunals convened under the International Center for

---

21 Gaetano Arangio-Ruiz refers to this as the "time immemorial" method of redressing international torts, which he criticizes as not forming "the best way to make justice and promote the rule of law." See Gaetano Arangio-Ruiz, *Counter-Measures and Amicable Dispute Settlement Means in the Implementation of State Responsibility: A Crucial Issue before the International Law Commission*, 5(1) European Journal of International Law 20-53 (1994), at pp. 21–22. James Crawford writes that "at present there are few established legal constraints on non-forcible counter-measures, apart from the criterion of proportionality and the prohibition of counter-measures violating individual human rights or rights of protected persons under international humanitarian law." See James Crawford, *Counter-Measures as Interim Measures*, 5(1) European Journal of International Law 65-76 (1994), at p. 65.
22 Appellate Body Report, *United States – Final Anti-dumping Measures on Stainless Steel from Mexico*, WT/DS344/AB/R, adopted May 20, 2008.
23 Ibid, at para. 160 (Appellate Body Report).
24 Ibid, at para. 7.106.

the Settlement of Investment Disputes (ICSID), whose findings, in the words of the *AES Corporation v. Argentina* ICSID tribunal,[25] "in one case in consideration [...] of the terms of a determined Bilateral Investment Treaty, are not necessarily relevant for other ICSID tribunals, which were constituted for other cases."[26]

It becomes difficult to escape the impression that the Appellate Body is of the view that is has a role to play in the creation and development of a WTO legal system. Previous Appellate Body reports, either in their reasoning or interpretations, reflect concerns or solutions that are justified from a systemic point of view, as opposed to mere dispute settlement. This is partly reflected in Gabrielle Marceau's statement that "from its inception, the Appellate Body has also been concerned with the 'internal coherence' of the [WTO agreements]."[27]

Joseph Weiler is more critical of the Appellate Body, writing that "both in its decisions (sometimes gratuitously scathing of panel decisions) and in its organization of its work and self-understanding, it has not grasped that one of its tasks is to be the custodian of the entire judicial element of dispute settlement and that it has an institutional responsibility towards its 'first instance' – the panels." Weiler contrasts the Appellate Body with the European Court of Justice (ECJ), the latter of which he credits with understanding "early on how critical it was to develop a productive relationship with national courts."[28]

Weiler and Marceau both agree that the Appellate Body is concerned with ensuring the internal coherence of the WTO agreements,[29] but Weiler would have the Appellate Body adopt a more conciliatory dialogue with panels – in part to avoid open disagreements of the type manifested in *US – Stainless Steel*.

5. Comparison with European Courts

Weiler is not alone in drawing analogies between the WTO and the EC. Given that both systems possess judicial bodies with strong adherence records, commentators

---

25 AES Corporation v. The Argentine Republic, ICSID Case No. ARB/02/17, Decision on Jurisdiction, April 26, 2005.
26 Ibid, at para. 26. For a contrary view, see Ole Kristian Fauchald, *The Legal Reasoning of ICSID Tribunals – An Empirical Analysis*, 19(2) European Journal of International Law 301-364 (2008).
27 See Gabrielle Marceau, *Balance and Coherence by the WTO Appellate Body: Who could do Better?* in Giorgio Sacerdoti, Alan Yanovich and Jan Bohanes (Eds.), *The WTO at Ten: The Contribution of the Dispute Settlement System* 326-347 (Cambridge University Press; Cambridge; 2006), at p. 326. Marceau describes the Appellate Body's use of the principle of effectiveness and a teleological interpretive approach to ensure that the WTO Agreements are respected by Members as a "single undertaking."
28 Joseph H.H. Weiler, *The Rule of Lawyers and the Ethos of Diplomats: Reflections on the Internal and External Legitimacy of WTO Dispute Settlement*, Harvard Jean Monnet Working Paper 9/00 (2000), at pp. 16-17.
29 Ibid, at p. 16. Weiler writes that "the legitimation strategy practiced by the Appellate Body (whether express or implicit) has been one of hermeneutic prudence and institutional modesty with a keen eye on balancing internal and external legitimacy."

often compare the two systems.³⁰ However, as Jose Alvarez previously warned, "this Euro-fixation ignores the fact that the ECJ (along with the European Court of Human Rights at Strasbourg) have been built on commonalities of economic interest, politics and culture that are distinctly absent from the multilateral trade regime." Practically speaking, "what might be feasible today for the ECJ or the Strasbourg Court is not indicative of what is possible for WTO panelists."³¹ The EC legal framework, while unquestionably supranational, is perhaps better viewed as quasi-international.³² Other commentators too have suggested that the European courts are "more like domestic courts than like international courts."³³ For the time being at least, the EC model is a "bridge too far" from the WTO's trajectory.

II. Membership Composition

As of July 23, 2008, the WTO has a membership of 153 countries and customs territories.³⁴ There are currently 30 observer territories to the WTO.³⁵ Private parties have no standing under the DSU. The DSU refers only to the obligations of "Members." Accordingly, WTO obligations accrue only to its signatory Member States.

III. Private Parties

1. No Right of Access to Dispute Settlement Proceedings

While private parties exercise no formal access rights to WTO dispute settlement proceedings, the grievances of private parties are at the root of many cases brought by Members.

---

30 See for example,Thomas Opperman and Jose Christian Cascante, *Dispute Settlement in the EC: Lessons for the GATT/WTO Dispute Settlement System?* In Ernst-Ulrich Petersmann (Ed.) *Studies in Transnational Economic Law Vol. 11 International Trade Law and the GATT/WTO Dispute Settlement System* 467-486 (Kluwer Law International; the Hague, 1997); Ernst-Ulrich Petersmann, *Time for Integrating Human Rights into the Law of Worldwide Organizations: Lessons from European Integration Law for Global Integration Law*, Jean Monnet Working Paper 7/01 (2001); and Meinhard Hilf and Sebastian Puth, *The Principle of Proportionality on its Way into WTO/GATT Law*, in Armin von Bogdandy, Petros Mavroidis and Yves Meny, *European Integration and International Co-ordination: Studies in Transnational Economic Law in Honor of Claus-Dieter Ehlermann* 199-218 (Kluwer Law International; the Hague, 2002).
31 Jose Alvarez, *How Not to Link: Institutional Conundrums of an Expanded Trade Regime*, 7(1) Widener Law Symposium Journal 1-19 (2001), at p. 15.
32 It should be noted in this regard that some commentators have identified the US Supreme Court as a quasi-international tribunal. See Thomas Lee, *The U.S. Supreme Court as Quasi-International Tribunal: Reclaiming the Court's Original and Exclusive Jurisdiction Over Treaty-Based Suits By Foreign States Against States*, 104(7) Columbia Law Review 1765-1885 (2004).
33 Eric Posner and John Yoo, *A Theory of International Adjudication*, The Law School of The University of Chicago John M. Olin Law and Economics Research Paper Series Working Paper No. 206 (February 2004), at p. 48. For a contrary view, see Laurence Helfer and Anne-Marie Slaughter, *Why States Create International Tribunals: A Response to Professors Posner and Yoo*, Princeton Law and Public Affairs Working Paper No. 05-005 (2005), at pp. 21–25.
34 See http://www.wto.org/english/thewto_e/whatis_e/tif_e/org6_e.htm.
35 Ibid.

Some countries have adopted procedures to enable private parties to lodge complaints and seek redress for alleged WTO violations via their relevant trade authorities.[36] However, none of these countries allows the "direct application" of WTO law in their domestic legal systems.[37] A comparative study on the applicability of WTO law in national legal systems reveals that "Members refusing direct effect of the WTO Agreements include the US, the EC, the Commonwealth members and most probably, Japan, while the Members recognizing the direct effect are mainly those with a civil-law tradition."[38]

The Panel observed in US – Section 301[39] that "it would be entirely wrong to consider that the position of individuals is of no relevance to the GATT/WTO legal matrix. Many of the benefits to Members which are meant to flow as a result of the acceptance of various disciplines under the GATT/WTO depend on the activity of individual economic operators in the national and global market places. The purpose of many of these disciplines [...] is to produce certain market conditions which would allow this individual activity to flourish."[40] Despite the lack of formal private party representation in WTO proceedings, WTO tribunals are nonetheless aware of the intricate private "dimensions" of WTO law.

WTO tribunals have also exercised caution in delineating what constitutes "Member action" (as opposed to unregulated private party action) for the purposes of assessing relevant Member "measures" under GATT Article XXIII.1.b and the DSU.

2. Impact of Private Party Actions

A Panel dealt with the issue of what constitutes "Member action"[41] for the purposes of the DSU in *Japan-Film* (more popularly known as the "Kodak/Fuji" case, reflecting the private sector origins of the dispute). In *Japan-Film*, the Panel addressed the WTO-consistency of the Japanese Fair Competition Code. Approximately 6600 business

---

36 These exist in the US with the Section 301 procedure (19 USC 2411-2420), in the EC with the Trade Barriers Regulation (Regulation (EC) 3286/94, OJ 1994, L349/71), and in China with the MOFCOM Foreign Trade Barriers Investigation Rules (see http://www.chinadaily.com.cn/bizchina/2006-04/18/content_570345.htm). For a discussion of these laws, along with other ways that private parties may currently participate in WTO proceedings, see Marco Bronckers, *Private Appeals to WTO Law: an Update*, 42(2) Journal of World Trade 245-260 (2008).
37 See John H. Jackson, *Direct Effect of Treaties in the US and EU, the Case of the WTO: Some Perceptions and Proposals* in Anthony Arnull, Piet Eeckhout & Takis Tridimas (eds.), *Continuity and Change in EU Law: Essays in Honour of Sir Francis Jacobs* 361-382 (Oxford University Press; Oxford, 2007).
38 Zin Zhang, *Direct Effect of the WTO Agreements: National Survey*, 9(2) International Trade Law Review 35-46 (2003), at p. 44. At pp. 41–43, the author identifies the Republic of Korea, Mali, Mexico, Switzerland, Bahrain and Egypt as countries that either allow or *should* allow for the direct application of treaty law (including GATT 1947 and the WTO) in their domestic legal systems.
39 Panel Report, *United States – Sections 301–310 of the Trade Act of 1974*, WT/DS152/R, adopted January 27, 2000.
40 Ibid, at para. 7.73.
41 For a comprehensive account of relevant GATT and WTO jurisprudence on what constitutes actions of "Members" for the purposes of the DSU, see Rex J. Zedalis, *When do the Activities of Private Parties Trigger WTO Rules?* 10(2) Journal of International Economic Law 335-362 (2007).

entities in 47-perfecture-wide retailers' association collaborated on the Fair Competition Code. The Japan Fair Trade Commission (JFTC) approved the Fair Competition Code on March 31, 1987. Article 13 of the Fair Competition Code vested oversight authority to a Retailers' Council. The US alleged that actions of the Retailers' Council resulted in the discriminatory treatment of US film products. Japan argued that the Fair Competition Code constituted "self-regulation among business entities approved by the JFTC in accordance with the [relevant laws], and that the Retailers' Council is a voluntary organ established by the code to implement this self-regulation."[42]

The Panel stated that "the WTO Agreement, refers only to policies or actions of governments, not those of private parties. But while this 'truth' may not be open to question, there have been a number of trade disputes in relation to which panels have been faced with making sometimes difficult judgments as to the extent to which what appear on their face to be private actions may nonetheless be attributable to a government because of some governmental connection to or endorsement of those actions."[43] The Panel clarified that "the issue here is not whether the JFTC's approval of the Retailers' Fair Competition Code and its enforcement body, the Retailers' Council, in and of itself should be viewed as a governmental measure. Clearly, the act of approval by a governmental body – the JFTC – is a government measure. Rather, the issue is whether such approval by the JFTC means that actions taken by the Retailers Council under the code and the provisions embodied in the code may be assimilated to government measures."[44] The Panel concludes that the term "measure" for purposes of GATT Article XXIII.1.b should be interpreted so as to prevent actions by entities with governmental-like powers from nullifying or impairing expected benefits.[45]

3. The Contentious Issue of Amicus Briefs, and an Insight into the "Schizophrenic" Attitude of WTO Members

The furthest WTO Panels and the Appellate Body have ventured to directly accommodate private parties is arguably in accepting amicus curiae briefs from parties other than WTO Members in specified circumstances.[46] This initiative provoked a heated Special Session of the General Council on November 22, 2000.[47]

---

42 See Panel Report, DS44, supra note 11, at para. 10.326.
43 Ibid, at para. 10.52.
44 Ibid, at para. 10.324.
45 Ibid, at para. 10.328.
46 Panel Report, *United States – Import Prohibition of Certain Shrimp and Shrimp Products*, WT/DS58/R and Corr.1, adopted 6 November 1998, modified by Appellate Body Report, WT/DS58/AB/R, at para. 7.7 for an example of the Panel ruling that it may accept amicus briefs pursuant to DSU Article 13, and Appellate Body Report, *European Communities – Measures Affecting Asbestos and Asbestos-Containing Products*, WT/DS135/AB/R, adopted April 5, 2001, at para. 51 for an example of the Appellate Body ruling that it may set forth procedures to accept amicus briefs pursuant to Rule 16.1 of the Working Procedures for Appellate Review. For a comprehensive discussion featuring these two disputes, see Petros Mavroidis, *Amicus Curiae Briefs Before the WTO: Much Ado About Nothing*, in Armin Von Bogdandy, Petros Mavroidis and Yves Meny (Eds.), *European Integration and International Co-ordination: Studies in Transnational Economic Law in Honour of Claus-Dieter Ehlermann* 317-330 (Kluwer Law International; London, 2002).
47 See Minutes of Meeting, WT/GC/M/60 (January 21, 2001).

The Uruguayan representative stated in the session that "the practical effect [of setting procedures for the acceptance of amicus briefs] had been to grant individuals and institutions outside of the WTO a right that Members themselves did not possess."[48] The representative from Singapore indicated that "the WTO was a Member-driven organization and only Members could decide on the merits of proposals in order to determine what was acceptable to the membership."[49] The representative of Hong Kong and China expressed the view that "Members should send the strongest signal to the Appellate Body [...] that submission of amicus briefs was a substantive matter. It was a matter for Members, and Members only," before emphatically projecting that "a lesson had been learned and that history should not repeat itself."[50] Only the US representative expressed the view that "the Appellate Body had acted appropriately in adopting its additional procedures in the asbestos appeal."[51]

The Chairman of the Special Session summarized that the issue of private party participation via amicus briefs raised more than "a transparency issue, but rather a legal issue and concerned the question of who should participate in the legal system." The Chairman concluded that "in light of the views expressed and in the absence of clear rules [...] the Appellate Body should exercise extreme caution in future cases until Members had considered what rules were needed."[52]

Whether or not events that transpired can be seen as the Appellate Body reacting to the General Council warning can be left aside. The fact is that subsequently, the Appellate Body rejected all of the requests received for leave to file amicus briefs in EC – Asbestos[53] for "failure to comply sufficiently with all the requirements" set out in the Appellate Body procedures.[54] The Appellate Body's apparent adherence to the wishes of Members by curtailing its amicus initiative douses to some extent commentaries on the "unconstrained" powers of WTO tribunals.[55]

The sentiments expressed in that General Council session indicate that WTO Members are not ready to embrace an enhanced role for private parties in WTO litigation. Tellingly, the representative from Singapore justified its stance on amicus briefs on the

---

48   Ibid, at para. 7.
49   Ibid, at para. 61.
50   Ibid, at para. 28.
51   Ibid, at para. 74. Argentina, Australia, Bolivia, Brazil, Canada, Chile, Colombia, Costa Rica, Cuba, the EC, Egypt, Hungary, India, Jamaica, Japan, Korea, Mexico, New Zealand, Norway, Pakistan, Panama, Switzerland, Tanzania, Turkey, and Zimbabwe also expressed their opposition to the Appellate Body's amicus curiae initiative.
52 IbidId, at paras. 118-120.
53   See Appellate Body Report, DS135, supra note 44.
54   Duncan B. Hollis, *Private Actors in Public International Law: Amicus Curiae and the Case for the Retention of State Sovereignty*, 25 Boston College International & Comparative Law Review 235-256 (2002), at p. 253.
55   See for example Karen J. Alter, *Resolving or Exacerbating Disputes? The WTO's New Dispute Resolution System*, 79(4) International Affairs, 783-800 (2003).

need to "safeguard the integrity of the WTO as an intergovernmental organization."[56] Yet, intergovernmental organizations such as the United Nations (UN), the World Bank and the International Monetary Fund (IMF) actively engage with international civil society. The World Bank and IMF sometimes collaborate operationally with civil society organizations.[57] Article 71 of the UN Charter, further, specifically contemplates that the UN Economic and Social Council may "make suitable arrangements for consultation with non-governmental organizations which are concerned with matters within its competence."[58]

To the extent that the integrity of the WTO as an intergovernmental organisation rests on its refusal to engage productively with civil society, the argument must suppose that the UN, World Bank and IMF have adversely affected their respective legitimacies by openly engaging with civil society organizations. This argument is not only counter-intuitive (not least of which because most WTO Members are also members of these three intergovernmental organizations); it also seems to substantively contradict the thrust of WTO Director-General Pascal Lamy's October 2007 speech to civil society members, in which he stated "let me be clear – the WTO is looking for your contribution, it needs you to help shape its agenda."[59]

How then can one rationalize WTO Members' collective aversion to the limited form of private participation afforded by amicus briefs?[60] We would submit that there is at best a functional justification – one has only to look as far back as the Doha Development round of negotiations, which stalled on subjects perfectly familiar to WTO Members, to predict how the political branch will manage "new" institutional issues. But this functional justification featured nowhere in Members' deliberations on amicus briefs – rather, the argument put forward by the dissenting majority sought to frame amicus briefs as a substantive – and not procedural – matter. The polemic nature of such an argument bears reflection upon the schizophrenic attitude of Members towards international legal obligations.

---

56 See Minutes of Meeting, supra note 45, at para. 59.
57 A 2002-2004 review of the World Bank's activities reveals that civil society organizations were involved in 67% of 2002 products; 71% of 2003 projects; and 74% of 2004 projects. See Civil Society Team, *World Bank Civil Society Engagement: Review of Fiscal Years 2002-2004* (2005), at p. 15. Available at http://siteresources.worldbank.org/CSO/Resources/World_Bank_Civil_Society_Progress_Report_2002-2004.pdf. A 2003 IMF Guide for Staff Relations with Civil Society Organizations (CSOs) contemplates that "CSOs can highlight important issues for the formulation, implementation, and review of Fund and Fund-supported policies and programs." See http://www.imf.org/external/np/cso/eng/2003/101003.htm#III.
58 Charter of the United Nations, signed on June 26, 1945, 59 Stat. 1031, T.S. 993 (entered into force October 24, 1945).
59 Pascal Lamy, *Civil Society is Influencing the WTO Agenda*, keynote address to the WTO Public Forum on October 4, 2007. Transcript available at http://www.wto.org/english/news_e/sppl_e/sppl73_e.htm.
60 A study by Joseph Kearney and Thomas Merrill on the impact of amicus briefs submitted to the Supreme Court reveals that such briefs have an average "petitioner win" success rate of less than 1% when filed for the petitioner, and –7% when filed for the respondent, which the authors seem not statistically significant after a regression analysis. See Joseph Kearney and Thomas Miller, *The Influence of Amicus Curiae Briefs on the Supreme Court*, 148 University of Pennsylvania Law Review 743-855 (2000), at p. 812.

The absence of formal private party participation in WTO panels or the Appellate Body is more pronounced than in other international tribunals. The North American Free Trade Agreement (NAFTA), for example, authorizes panels to seek counsel from any "person or body that it deems appropriate," provided that the immediate parties to the dispute consent.[61] In restricting the scope for objection to the immediate parties to the dispute, NAFTA is more accommodating towards amicus briefs than the WTO which, according to the Chair of the General Council, requires all Members to agree upon amicus disciplines prior to allowing panels and the Appellate Body to formulate procedural rules for the submission of such amicus briefs.

The International Court of Justice, further, is empowered at Article 50 of its Statute to seek counsel from "any individual, body, bureau, commission or other organization" it chooses. However, the Court has restricted itself to seeking such counsel from "public international organizations," under another provision of its statute.[62] Investment treaties, in contrast to most public international law tribunals, contemplate direct private party access to judicial proceedings.

4. Contrast with International Investment Law

Nicholas DiMascio and Joost Pauwelyn trace the historical development of international trade and investment treaties, to summarize that "the trade regime is about overall welfare, efficiency, liberalization, state-to-state exchanges of market access, and trade opportunities – not individual rights."[63] The authors note *a contrario* that investment treaties are "about fairness grounded in customary rules on treatment of aliens, not efficiency."[64]

DiMascio and Pauwelyn offer an interesting analysis of the contrasts between international trade and investment treaties. However, the notion that the WTO is efficiency-driven *contra* investment treaties is not universally shared by trade commentators.[65]

A better (albeit less technical) explanation is that Member governments continue to exercise a monopoly over decisions to initiate WTO dispute settlement proceedings

---

61   See Article 2014 of the North American Free Trade Agreement, signed on December 17, 1992, 107 Stat. 2066 32 I.L.M 296 (1993).
62   See Article 34.2 of the Statute of the International Court of Justice, signed on June 26, 1945, 59 Stat. 1031, T.S. 993 (entered into force October 24, 1945). See also Josh Robbins, *False Friends: Amicus Curiae and Procedural Discretion in WTO Appeals under the Hot-Rolled Lead/Asbestos Doctrine*, 44(1) Harvard International Law Journal 317-329 (2003), at p. 325.
63   Nicholas DiMascio & Joost Pauwelyn, *Nondiscrimination in Trade and Investment Treaties: Worlds Apart or Two Sides of the Same Coin?* 102 American Journal of International Law 48-89 (2008), at p. 54.
64   Ibid, at p. 56.
65   See for example Jeffrey Dunoff, *Death of the Trade Regime*, 10(4) European Journal of International Law 733-762 (1999). At p. 9 (LexisNexis printout), Dunoff argues that the impact of "trade and [non-WTO]" issues in WTO litigation has altered the efficiency-driven characteristics of international trade as "these issues cannot be satisfactorily resolved by the argument that, from within the efficiency perspective, the environmental or labor rules [two examples of "trade and" issues] are simply another form of welfare-reducing trade restriction, for this response presupposes precisely the assumption that the challenged rule calls into question."

due to the diplomatic implications that necessarily arise from such initiatives. Joseph Weiler notes that this government monopoly is a "relic" of the GATT 1947: "disputes, and their resolution [...] were perceived as being between – "belonging to" – and pertaining to governments. The implications of GATT rules generally and the outcome of dispute resolution specifically to non-governmental constituencies were only dimly perceived."[66] Weiler critically assesses this arrangement, noting that it remains premised on two considerations: (i) a "government-is-the-State fallacy;" and (ii) the failure by GATT practitioners to "understand the deep social and political domestic consequences of the regime and disciplines of which they were custodians and their implications for constituencies beyond governments in general and trade ministries in particular."[67]

B. Is WTO Law "Embedded" into Public International Law?

Before engaging with the role played by substantive and procedural public international law within the WTO dispute settlement mechanism, it is instructive to "debunk" the three common arguments raised against the WTO's standing as a public international legal institution. These arguments consider, firstly, that the WTO exacerbates the problem of public international "fragmentation," secondly, that the WTO's alleged trade proclivity conflicts with Members' competing international obligations and, thirdly, that the WTO operates as a "self-contained regime." We will address each in turn.

I. Fragmentation

The debate on whether the WTO is "embedded" into public international law is partly linked to the notion that the international legal order is "fragmented" into uncoordinated chunks of international obligations. It should be noted that the fragmentation argument runs more as a criticism of public international law in general, rather than as a specific criticism of any sub-category of international law.

One commentator attributes the cause of fragmentation to "the specialization of [international law's] different branches and the functionalist theory of international organizations that underpins the United Nations."[68] Another commentator writes that "the multiplication of international courts and tribunals as such is not a problem [...] the main reason for the [...] problems is the fact that there is no hierarchical legally binding relationship between all these courts and tribunals. In other words, there is

---

66 See Weiler, supra note 26, at p. 6.
67 Ibid.
68 Caroline Henckels, *Overcoming Jurisdictional Isolationism at the WTO-FTA Nexus: A Potential Approach for the WTO*, 19(3) European Journal of International Law 571-599 (2008), at p. 571.

no hierarchy between the various courts and tribunals, so they are not bound by each other's jurisprudence. Hence they can act – formally and legally speaking – in 'clinical isolation'."[69] The latter argument is a variation of the classic Austinian challenge to international law – that absent the coercive commands of an ascertainable sovereign, international "law" is at best a body of custom.[70]

The abstract problem of fragmentation takes concrete manifestation in two recent WTO disputes: *Mexico – Soft Drink*[71] and *Brazil – Tyres*.[72] *Mexico – Soft Drink* formed part of a larger "sugar war" between the US and Mexico that encompassed a prior WTO dispute and several NAFTA arbitral tribunal decisions.[73] Mexico raised a preliminary objection to the Panel's jurisdiction on the ground that a NAFTA Chapter 20 Arbitral Panel was better placed to "address both Mexico's concern with respect to market access for Mexican cane sugar in the US under the NAFTA and the US's concern with respect to Mexico's tax measures."[74] The Panel rejected Mexico's request in a preliminary ruling, and clarified that "under the DSU, [it] had no discretion to decide whether or not to exercise its jurisdiction in a case properly before it."[75] On appeal, the Appellate Body upheld the Panel's preliminary ruling on this point.

In *Brazil – Tyres*, Brazil sought to justify an inconsistency in its application of an import ban on retreaded tyres by arguing that it was bound by a MERCOSUR arbitral tribunal to exempt MERCOSUR partners from its import ban. The Appellate Body was of the view that notwithstanding the possibility of a genuine conflict in obligations between MERCOSUR and WTO, "discrimination can result from a rational decision or behaviour, and still be 'arbitrary or unjustifiable', because it is explained by a rationale that bears no relationship to the objective of a measure provisionally justified under one of the paragraphs of Article XX, or goes against that objective".[76] Ultimately, the Appellate Body reasoned that "we observe [...] that, before the arbitral tribunal established

---

69 Nikolaos Lavranos, *The Solange-Method as a Tool for Regulating Competing Jurisdictions Among International Courts and Tribunals*, Loyola of Los Angeles International & Comparative Law Review (2008) (Forthcoming; on file with the authors).
70 For a view of how Austin's challenge has lost its normative sting against WTO law, see Raj Bhala and Lucienne Attard, *Austin's Ghost and DSU Reform*, 37 International Lawyer 651-676 (2003).
71 Appellate Body Report, *Mexico – Tax Measures on Soft Drinks and Other Beverages*, WT/DS308/AB/R, adopted March 24, 2006.
72 Appellate Body Report, *Brazil – Measures Affecting Imports of Retreaded Tyres*, WT/DS332/AB/R, adopted December 17, 2007.
73 For a comprehensive discussion, see Alice Vacek-Aranda, *Sugar Wars: Dispute Settlement under NAFTA and the WTO as seen through the Lens of the HFCS Case and its Effects on US-Mexican Relations*, 12 Texas Hispanic Journal of Law & Policy 121-160 (2006).
74 See Panel Report, Panel Report, *Mexico – Tax Measures on Soft Drinks and Other Beverages*, WT/DS308/R, adopted 24 March 2006, modified by Appellate Body Report, WT/DS308/AB/R, at para. 3.2. On appeal, the US argued at para. 20 that "the Panel's own terms of reference in this dispute instructed the Panel to examine the matter referred to the DSB by the United States and to make such findings as will assist the DSB in making the recommendations and rulings provided for under the DSU."
75 Ibid, at para. 7.1.
76 See Appellate Body Report, DS332, supra note 70, at para. 232.

under MERCOSUR, Brazil could have sought to justify the challenged import ban on the grounds of human, animal, and plant health under Article 50.d of the Treaty of Montevideo. Brazil, however, decided not to do so [...] Article 50.d of the Treaty of Montevideo, as well as the fact that Brazil might have raised this defence in the MERCOSUR arbitral proceedings, show, in our view, that the discrimination associated with the MERCOSUR exemption does not necessarily result from a conflict between provisions under MERCOSUR and the GATT 1994."[77]

The Appellate Body's approach to the MERCOSUR arbitral tribunal award can be summarized as follows: (i) MERCOSUR obligations cannot excuse the performance of WTO obligations; but (ii) in any event, Brazil did not properly conduct its defense before the arbitral tribunal. It is arguable that the Appellate Body selectively applied MERCOSUR law to justify its conclusions. Such an approach risks the distortion of non-WTO obligations.

How can the WTO better "co-exist" in this fragmented international legal order? Suggested remedies vary. One commentator advocates recourse to the dispute avoidance tool of *res judicata*.[78] A second commentator suggests the use of *forum non conveniens* on the basis of comity.[79] A third commentator suggests that WTO tribunals issue declarations *non liquet*, or borrow from the US Supreme Court's "Political Question Doctrine" to avoid pronouncing in "corrosive conflicts."[80] A fourth commentator proposes that international courts emulate the approach of the German Constitutional Court towards the ECJ by reserving ultimate jurisdiction "so long as" the ECJ does not contravene specified German "fundamental rights."[81]

A common assumption to these suggested remedies is that the power to redress the problem of fragmentation lies within international tribunals. This is a debatable assumption: to the extent that DSU Article 23 renders WTO dispute settlement compulsory (and exclusive) once a Panel is seized of a dispute it is obliged to adjudicate on it. Failure to do so will violate the Panel's obligations under the DSU. Arguably the only dispute avoidance technique a Panel may exercise is to declare a WTO *non-liquet* but it is difficult to imagine WTO tribunals doing so as these tribunals are meant only to "clarify the existing provisions of the [WTO] agreements" under DSU Article 3.2. Further, any *non-liquet* declarations would presumably arise at the preliminary stage of the dispute, following appropriate objection by the other disputing party.

---

77 Ibid, at para. 234.
78 See Joost Pauwelyn, *Adding Sweeteners to Softwood Lumber: The WTO-NAFTA "Spaghetti Bowl" is Cooking*, 9(1) Journal of International Economic Law 197-206 (2006), at p. 205.
79 See Caroline Henckels, *Overcoming Jurisdictional Isolationism at the WTO-FTA Nexus: A Potential Approach for the WTO*, 19(3) European Journal of International Law 571-599 (2006), at p. 584.
80 See Claude E. Barfield, *Should the WTO Determine US Tax Policy?* Testimony to the House Committee on Small Business (July 7, 2004). Available at http://useu.usmission.gov/Article.asp?ID=E39669CB-0BB1-4CC9-9072-D5F1A6A05482.
81 See Lavranos, supra note 67, at p. 40.

A better solution to the fragmentation *problématique* can be found in DSU Article 3.7, which obliges Members to exercise judgment as to whether recourse to a panel "would be fruitful." The WTO is not greater than the sum of its parts: it is a Member-driven organization. To the extent that neither Panels nor the Appellate Body have prosecutorial powers under the WTO agreements, these tribunals are not willingly exacerbating the "spaghetti bowl" of conflicting international obligations.

Before leaving our discussion of fragmentation, it should be noted that the WTO is itself a victim of fragmentation: the proliferation of regional trade agreements notified under GATT Article XXIV, and the alternate dispute settlement mechanisms contained in some have led Pascal Lamy to warn Members against the "distraction" from multilateralism "not least because of the resources required to negotiate and implement such agreements."[82] One commentator notes that RTAs may "establish the exclusive jurisdiction of the regional dispute settlement system but more often a choice of forum clause will be inserted. This means that parties to the [RTA] who are also WTO Members can choose where to bring their dispute but once the choice is made, the chosen system enjoys exclusive jurisdiction."[83] This analysis overlooks the Panel's preliminary findings in *Mexico – Soft Drink* that the DSU does not accommodate competing exclusive jurisdiction clauses. Fragmentation may thus occur within the WTO/RTA framework. We will turn next to conflicts in public international law.

II. Conflicts in Public International Law

The WTO is sometimes faulted for demonstrating a trade proclivity, particularly in the legal reasoning of panels and the Appellate Body. Commentators sometimes postulate that this trade proclivity leads to conflicts with other international legal obligations, particularly those related to human rights and the environment. As Donald McRae phrased it: "At the theoretical level, international trade law and international law are in important respects based on different assumptions. The organizing principle for the international trading regime is the economic theory underlying a liberal trade order, that is the principle of comparative advantage; the organizing principle for international law, by comparison, is the concept of the sovereignty of states [...] International law is built on the fundamental construct of a community of sovereign States whose relations with each other is the substance of the discipline – international trade law runs counter to that construct and in significant ways acts to undermine it."[84]

---

82 Pascal Lamy, *Trade Expansion is Insurance against Financial Turbulences*, Geneva Lectures on Global Economic Governance (February 6, 2008). Available at http://www.wto.org/english/news_e/sppl_e/sppl85_e.htm.

83 Isabelle Van Damme, *Seventh Annual WTO Conference: An Overview*, 11(1) Journal of International Economic Law 155-165 (2008), at p. 161.

84 Donald McRae, *The WTO in International Law: Tradition Continued or New Frontier?* 3(1) Journal of International Economic Law 27-41 (2003), at p. 29.

McRae's argument downplays the "simple truth" that the WTO agreements do not prevent Members from adopting human rights or environmental measures with incidental trade-distorting effects, provided that such measures do not arbitrarily discriminate between Members where the same conditions prevail, or operate as disguised restrictions to trade. GATT Article XX, for example, states that "nothing in this agreement shall be construed to prevent" Members from adopting or enforcing measures necessary or related to the protection of *inter alia* public morals, human, animal or plant health, and the conservation of exhaustible natural resources. As we will explain below, provisions such as GATT Article XX militate against the risk of legal conflicts between WTO and non-WTO obligations.

The 1969 Vienna Convention on the Law of Treaties (1969 VCLT)[85] sets forth the rules and procedures for the interpretation of treaty provisions, and the reconciliation of conflicts in international legal obligations. Wilfred Jenks formulated the classic test for ascertaining a conflict in public international law in 1953: a "conflict in the strict sense of direct incompatibility arises only where simultaneous compliance with the obligations of different instruments is impossible."[86] Pauwelyn suggests that this definition of conflicts in international law is too narrow, and should be expanded to include situations where a State frustrates the performance of WTO obligations by entering into competing international agreements that conflict in principle with WTO commitments.[87] This view is refuted by Marceau, who suggests that this expanded approach would "lead to providing a third party (an adjudication body or an interpreter) with the power to set aside provisions that have been voluntarily negotiated by States."[88] The Appellate Body in *Guatemala – Cement I*[89] articulated a narrow definition of conflicts in relation to competing WTO Agreement provisions: "It is only where the provisions of the DSU and the special or additional rules and procedures of a covered agreement cannot be read as complementing each other that the special or additional provisions are to prevail."[90]

1969 VCLT Article 30 regulates conflicts between successive treaties addressing the same subject matter. Article 30 codifies the principles that *lex posterior derogat priori* – later law trumps earlier law, and *lex posterior generalis non derogat legi priori speciali* – later general law does not trump earlier specialized law. Pauwelyn argues that the WTO agreements are exempt from Article 30 as they collectively form a "continuing treaty,"

---

85 Vienna Convention on the Law of Treaties, 1155 U.N.T.S. 331, 8 I.L.M. 679, entered into force on January 27, 1980.
86 Wilfred Jenks, *The Conflict of Law-Making Treaties*, British Yearbook of International Law 401-453 (1953), at p. 425.
87 See Joost Pauwelyn, *The Role of Public International Law in the WTO: How Far can we Go?* 95(3) American Journal of International Law 535-578 (2001), at p. 551.
88 See Gabrielle Marceau, *WTO Dispute Settlement and Human Rights*, 13(4) European Journal of International Law 753-814 (2002), at p. 792.
89 Appellate Body Report, *Guatemala – Anti-Dumping Investigation Regarding Portland Cement from Mexico*, WT/DS60/AB/R, adopted November 25, 1998.
90 Ibid, at para. 65.

unsuitable for the "guillotine" approach of "time of conclusion," which "may not make sense and could lead to arbitrary solutions."[91] It is debatable whether the 1969 VCLT supports the notion of a "continuing treaty," but it is unlikely that States will create a new international trade regime in the near future. It should be noted that RTAs do not clash with the WTO agreements by operation of GATT Article XXIV. GATT Article XXIV essentially exempts WTO disciplines between Member States forming a customs union or free-trade area, provided that the regional trading bloc created satisfies formative threshold requirements, and the "duties and other regulations of commerce" imposed by the entity are not "on the whole [...] higher or more restrictive" than prior to its creation.

1969 VCLT Articles 31 and 32 regulate conflicts between treaties addressing diverse subject-matter. Articles 31 and 32 set a hierarchy of interpretive approaches to treaty interpretation. Article 31 stipulates that treaty provisions must be read: (i) within their ordinary meaning; (ii) by reference to their object and purpose (as a whole); and (iii) if relevant, with the conduct of the parties subsequent to the completion of the treaty. Article 32 then states that recourse may be had to "supplementary means of interpretation," such as the "preparatory work of the treaty and the circumstances of its conclusion" where sole recourse to the Article 31 interpretive methods would otherwise: (i) leave the meaning of the treaty provisions ambiguous or obscure; or (ii) lead to a result which is manifestly absurd or unreasonable.

To the extent that the performance of WTO obligations "conflicts" with other international obligations within the meaning of the 1969 VCLT, the Preamble to the WTO agreements links the "object and purpose" of these agreements to a range of socio-developmental objectives. Further, there are provisions within the WTO agreements that allow Members to pursue a wide range of policy matters that may adversely impact trade. These provisions, such as GATT Article XX, require Members seeking to pursue such policy matters to do so in a way that curbs any such adverse impacts beyond what is strictly necessary.

The Preamble to the Agreement Establishing the World Trade Organization states that WTO Members recognize that international trade should be conducted "with a view to raising standards of living [...] while allowing for the optimal use of the world's resources in accordance with the objective of sustainable development, seeking both to protect and preserve the environment and to enhance the means for doing so in a manner consistent with their respective needs and concerns at different levels of economic development." The Preamble thus contemplates that the pursuit of trade liberalization is not antithetical to the pursuit of such socio-developmental objectives. To the contrary, the Preamble confirms that the WTO agreements seek to complement such objectives.

---

91   See Pauwelyn, supra note 85, at p. 546.

GATT Article XX, sometimes referred to as the "trade and" clause, contemplates that "subject to the requirement that such measures are not applied in a manner which would constitute a means of arbitrary or unjustifiable discrimination between countries where the same conditions prevail, or a disguised restriction on international trade," Members are free to adopt measures necessary or related to: (i) the protection of public morals; (ii) the protection of human, animal or plant health; (iii) trade in gold or silver; (iv) compliance with domestic laws or regulations not otherwise inconsistent with the GATT 1994; (v) prison labor products; (vi) the protection of "national treasures;" (vii) the conservation of exhaustible natural resources; (viii) performance of obligations under specified intergovernmental commodity agreements; (ix) export controls on "essential quantities" of domestic materials for "domestic processing industr[ies];" and (x) transactions involving products in "general or short local supply."

GATT Article XX restricts the ability of Members to pursue these 10 objectives in two ways. Firstly, measures adopted in the pursuit of such objectives must satisfy the requirement of being either "necessary" or "related to" the relevant objective. Secondly, the "Chapeau" to GATT Article XX prohibits such measures from arbitrarily or unjustifiably discriminating between Members, or from operating as "disguised restriction[s] on international trade." GATT Article XX essentially articulates a good faith requirement upon Members seeking to deviate from WTO obligations. Provided these Members ensure that trade is not adversely affected beyond what is necessary to achieve the relevant objective, there is nothing in GATT Article XX that prevents a Member from pursuing a wide range of non-trade objectives that have a negative impact on trade.

Language similar to GATT Article XX can be found in General Agreement on Trade in Services (GATS) Article XIV, Article 27 of the Agreement on Trade-Related Aspects of Intellectual Property Rights (TRIPS), TBT Article 2.2 and, to some extent, SPS Article 2.2. The existence of these provisions reduces the possibility of "legal" conflicts between the WTO agreements and other international legal instruments, as recourse to 1969 VCLT Articles 31 and 32 should allow for consistent interpretations of WTO and non-WTO obligations.

Where a conflict in treaty obligations does arise, 1969 VCLT Article 59 states that the conflicting provisions of the earlier treaty shall be terminated. However, if the contracting parties manifested a desire not to have the earlier conflicting provisions terminated, Article 59 directs that these provisions should be suspended instead.

III. Embedded into Public International Law or a Self-Contained System?

Commentators sometimes express the view that the WTO operates as a "self-contained regime."[92] Bruno Simma, a proponent of "self-contained regimes," defines this term as "a subsystem which is intended to exclude more or less totally the application of the general legal consequences of wrongful acts, in particular the application of the countermeasures normally at the disposal of an injured party."[93] Resort to public international law and principles within self-contained regimes is mostly voluntary (and at times motivated by legitimacy-building concerns).[94]

Commentators such as James Crawford express doubts that any regime can "genuinely" be "self-contained" to the extent that all regimes are subordinate to peremptory norms of international law. Crawford writes instead that "a genuinely self-contained regime would be a special *lex specialis*, a *lex specialis* to the nth degree."[95]

In more recent writing, Simma concedes that the notion of self-contained regimes has itself been called into question: tracing the International Law Commission's (ILC's) differing approach to self-contained regimes by Special Rapporteur, he writes that "the ILC first appeared to embrace the concept of self-contained subsystems [via Special Rapporteur Willam Riphagen], then became highly critical of the systematic feasibility of such isolation from state responsibility [via Special Rapporteur Gaetano Arangio-Ruiz], and finally adopted the position of a pragmatic maybe [via Special Rapporteur James Crawford]."[96] Simma attributes the waning interest in "self-contained regimes" to a misconception of the term "in favor of entirely autonomous legal subsystems." He writes that "no treaty, however special its subject-matter or limited the number of its parties, applies in a normative vacuum but refers back to a number of general, often unwritten principles of customary law concerning its entry into force and its interpretation and application."[97]

To the extent that: (i) the existence of self-contained regimes is contested in international law; and (ii) proponents of the term concede that self-contained regimes do not operate in isolation from general international law, the question of whether or not an international legal regime is "embedded" cannot simply be answered in the affirmative or negative. The more appropriate question probably is: to what degree is WTO law

---

92 See for example Pieter Jan Kuijper, *The Law of GATT as a Special Field of International Law*, 25 Netherlands Year Book of International Law 227-257 (1995), at p. 227.
93 Bruno Simma, *Self-Contained Regimes*, 16 Netherlands Yearbook of International Law 111-136 (1985), at p. 117.
94 See text above infra notes 149-151.
95 James Crawford, *The ILC's Articles on Responsibility of States for Internationally Wrongful Acts: A Retrospect*, 96(4) American Journal of International Law 874-890 (2002), at p. 880.
96 Bruno Simma & Dirk Polkowski, *Of Planets and the Universe: Self-Contained Regimes in International Law*, 17(3) European Journal of International Law 483-529 (2006), at p. 493.
97 Ibid, at p. 6.

embedded in public international law? The answer given by WTO tribunals lies in the DSU as interpreted so far by them. To date, these tribunals have drawn a sharp distinction between substantive and procedural public international law.

C. Substantive Public International Law

The starting point for an analysis of the depth of public international legal values within the WTO is the DSU. DSU Article 3.2 states that the dispute settlement system of the WTO serves "to preserve the rights and obligations of Members under the covered agreements, and to clarify the existing provisions of those agreements in accordance with customary rules of interpretation of public international law." As we will illustrate below, the Appellate Body confirmed that these "customary rules of interpretation" refer to, *inter alia*, the 1969 VCLT Articles 31 and 32.

Former Appellate Body Chair Claus-Dieter Ehlermann writes that the Appellate Body's interpretation of DSU Article 3.2 has served as "the starting point and general justification for frequent references to public international law rules and principles in many Appellate Body Reports." Ehlermann observed that early references to public international law in WTO disputes have been more procedural than substantive in nature, and predicted that "the true importance of the interrelationship between the WTO Agreements and public international law will become apparent only when more of these latter problems of substance have to be addressed."[98]

It should be noted that, to the extent that panels and the Appellate Body have drawn upon 1969 VCLT Articles 31 and 32 to remedy procedural gaps in the DSU, these two provisions aim to regulate substantive conflicts of norms in public international law.[99] We will show that panels and the Appellate Body have adopted three competing approaches towards interpreting substantive public international law: (i) an isolationist approach, typified by the refusal of WTO tribunals to engage with substantive non-WTO law; (ii) an integrated approach, whereby WTO tribunals actively engage with non-WTO law; and (iii) a hybrid or mixed approach, where WTO tribunals engage to some extent, or *obiter* with non-WTO law.

A distinction should be drawn between interpreting non-WTO law, which WTO tribunals have done on occasion, and giving effect to non-WTO law. Regarding the latter, there are [currently] no disputes in which a WTO tribunal allowed non-WTO law to "trump" WTO obligations.

---

98 Claus-Dieter Ehlermann, *Six Years on the Bench of the "World Trade Court,"* 36(4) Journal of World Trade 605-639 (2002), at p. 618.
99 See Campbell McLachlan, *The Principle of Systemic Integration and Article 31(3)(c) of the Vienna Convention*, 54(2) International & Comparative Law Quarterly 279-320 (2005).

We will first canvass the relevant provisions of the DSU, before posing the open question of whether WTO tribunals may give effect to non-WTO norms of *ius cogens* or obligations *erga omnes*. We will then outline some inconsistencies in the approach of WTO tribunals towards interpreting non-WTO law.

I. The DSU and the 1969 VCLT

As touched upon above, DSU Article 3.2 refers to the "customary rules of interpretation of public international law." The Appellate Body clarified in *US – Reformulated Gasoline*[100] that "the general rule of interpretation (set out in 1969 VCLT Article 31.1) has attained the status of customary or general international law. As such, it forms part of the 'customary rules of interpretation of public international law' which the Appellate Body has been directed [...] to apply."[101] In *Japan – Alcohol*,[102] the AB added that "there can be no doubt that Article 32 of the Vienna Convention, dealing with the role of supplementary means of interpretation, has also attained the same status [as Article 31.1 of the Vienna Convention of the Law of Treaties]."[103] Reference to the 1969 VCLT by the Appellate Body, and implicitly in the DSU confirms that the WTO does not operate as a "self contained regime." The Appellate Body confirmed this in *US – Reformulated Gasoline*, when it stated that DSU Article 3.2 illustrated that "the General Agreement is not to be read in clinical isolation from public international law."[104] The WTO agreements are thus to be interpreted according to the "customary rules of interpretation" contained in the 1969 VCLT.

It should be noted that while the "customary rules of interpretation" referred to in DSU Article 3.2 necessarily includes the general and supplemental rules of interpretation codified at 1969 VCLT Articles 31 and 32, respectively, WTO tribunals have expressly cited other provisions of the 1969 VCLT. These include: (i) Article 26 (on *Pacta Sunt*

---

100 Appellate Body Report, *United States – Standards for Reformulated and Conventional Gasoline*, WT/DS2/AB/R, adopted May 20, 1996.
101 Ibid, at Part III.
102 Appellate Body Report, *Japan – Taxes on Alcoholic Beverages*, WT/DS8/AB/R, WT/DS10/AB/R, WT/DS11/AB/R, adopted November 1, 1996.
103 Ibid, at Part D.
104 See Appellate Body Report, DS2, supra note 98, at Part. III.

Servanda);[105] (ii) Article 28 (on the Non-Retroactivity of Treaties);[106] and (iii) Article 33 (on the Interpretation of Treaties Authenticated in Two or More Languages).[107] This indicates that the 1969 VCLT applies to WTO law in greater depth than the two provisions on interpretation.

Treaties of course are not the only source of international law. Article 38.1 of the Statute of the International Court of Justice lists three other categories of sources, the most important of which is customary international law. The International Court of Justice (ICJ) has previously ruled in *Nicaragua v. US*[108] that customary international law shares primacy with treaty law as the most determinative source of public international law. The Preamble to the 1969 VCLT affirms that "the rules of customary international law will continue to govern questions not regulated by the provisions of the [1969 VCLT]." 1969 VCLT Article 38 stipulates as a general rule that treaty provisions between two States cannot bind a non-party State. However, Article 38 states that none of the 1969 VCLT provisions on treaties and third States "precludes a rule set forth in a treaty from becoming binding upon a third State as a customary rule of international law, recognized as such." Customary international law is thus accommodated within the framework of the 1969 VCLT.

In *Korea – Government Procurement*,[109] a Panel stated that "customary international law applies generally to the economic relations between the WTO Members. Such international law applies to the extent that the WTO treaty agreements do not 'contract out' from it."[110] The Panel's findings on this point are instructive: Marceau writes that the DSU identifies the WTO as a "subsystem of international law which contains its specific rights and obligations (the covered agreements), specific causes of action, specific remedies and specific countermeasures. Specific rights and obligations, specific remedies and a specific dispute settlement mechanism are mandatory, and counter-

---

105 See Appellate Body Report, *United States – Continued Dumping and Subsidy Offset Act of 2000*, WT/DS217/AB/R, WT/DS234/AB/R, adopted January 27, 2003. At para. 296, the AB observed that "Article 26 of the Vienna Convention, entitled Pacta Sunt Servanda, to which several appellees referred in their submissions, provides that "[e]very treaty in force is binding upon the parties to it and must be performed by them in good faith." The United States itself affirmed 'that WTO Members must uphold their obligations under the covered agreements in good faith.'" See also Appellate Body Report, *European Communities – Trade Description of Sardines*, WT/DS231/AB/R, adopted October 23, 2002. At para. 258, the AB considered that "we must assume that Members of the WTO will abide by their treaty obligations in good faith, as required by the principle of pacta sunt servanda articulated in Article 26 of the Vienna Convention. And, always in dispute settlement, every Member of the WTO must assume the good faith of every other Member."
106 See Appellate Body Report, *Brazil – Measures Affecting Desiccated Coconut*, WT/DS22/AB/R, adopted March 20, 1997, at p. 15. See also Appellate Body Report, *Canada – Term of Patent Protection*, WT/DS170/AB/R, adopted October 12, 2000, at para. 72.
107 See Appellate Body Report, *United States – Final Countervailing Duty Determination with Respect to Certain Softwood Lumber from Canada*, WT/DS257/AB/R, adopted February 17, 2004, At fn. 50 to para. 59. See also Appellate Body Report, *United States – Subsidies on Upland Cotton*, WT/DS267/AB/R, adopted March 21, 2005, at fn. 510 to para. 424.
108 Military Activities in and Against Nicaragua [1986] I.C.J. Rep. 14.
109 Panel Report, *Korea – Measures Affecting Government Procurement*, WT/DS163/R, adopted June 19, 2000.
110 Ibid, at para. 7.96.

measures have been regulated."[111] The Official Commentary to the 2001 Draft Articles on State Responsibility cites the WTO dispute settlement system as an example of a regulatory scheme where "States may agree between themselves on other rules of international law which may not be the subject of countermeasures, whether or not they are regarded as peremptory norms under general international law."[112] Customary international law thus applies to the extent that the WTO agreements have not "contracted out" of them.

Beyond this general statement, however, it remains difficult to ascertain the role of customary international law in the WTO. In EC – *Hormones*,[113] for example, the EC argued that the precautionary principle formed a "general customary rule of international law, or at least a general principle of law."[114] The Appellate Body started its analysis by stating that "the status of the precautionary principle in international law continues to be the subject of debate among academics, law practitioners, regulators and judges. The precautionary principle is regarded by some as having crystallized into a general principle of customary international environmental law. Whether it has been widely accepted by Members as a principle of general or customary international law appears less than clear." The Appellate Body backtracked further by concluding that "it is unnecessary, and probably imprudent, for the Appellate Body in this appeal to take a position on this important, but abstract, question."[115] The Appellate Body's reluctance to engage or clarify upon the WTO's interaction with non-WTO public international law in EC – *Hormones* is unfortunate. However, as we will set out below, WTO tribunals are operationally barred by the DSU from adjudicating on public international law.

II. Limiting Provisions of the DSU?

1. DSU Article 3.2

Article 3.2, last sentence stipulates in no uncertain terms that "recommendations and rulings of the DSB cannot add to or diminish the rights and obligations provided in the covered agreements." In *Mexico – Soft Drink*, the Appellate Body rejected an argument by Mexico that the Panel erred in failing to decline jurisdiction in favor of a NAFTA Arbitral Panel. The Appellate Body was of the view that "we see no basis in the DSU for panels and the Appellate Body to adjudicate non-WTO disputes. Article 3.2 of the DSU states that the WTO dispute settlement system serves to preserve the rights and obligations of Members under the covered agreements, and to clarify the existing provisions of those agreements. Accepting Mexico's interpretation would imply that

---

111 See Marceau, supra note 86, at p. 767.
112 Draft Articles on Responsibility of States for Internationally Wrongful Acts, in Report of the International Law Commission on the Work of Its Fifty-third Session [hereinafter ILC 53d Report], UN GAOR, 56th Sess., Supp. No.10, at 43, UN Doc. A/56/10 (2001), at p. 133 (Official Commentary Version).
113 Appellate Body Report, *EC Measures Concerning Meat and Meat Products (Hormones)*, WT/DS26/AB/R, WT/DS48/AB/R, adopted February 13, 1998.
114 Ibid, at para. 121.
115 Ibid, at para. 123.

the WTO dispute settlement system could be used to determine rights and obligations outside the covered agreements."[116]

DSU Articles 7.2 and 11 further restrict the ability of WTO tribunals from adjudicating upon non-WTO public international law: Article 7.2 obliges panels to address only "the relevant provisions in any covered agreement or agreements cited by the parties," while Article 11 places panels under an obligation to "make an objective assessment of the matter before it."

2. DSU Article 7.2

Article 7.2 restricts panels to addressing only those aspects of the covered agreements cited by the disputing Members in their terms of references. This provision would seem to preclude panels from positively pronouncing on non-WTO law, as the Appellate Body indicated in Mexico – Soft Drink. However, the Panel in an earlier decision, Korea – Government Procurement,[117] expressed doubt about the exclusionary nature of Article 7 when it stated that "the purpose of the terms of reference is to properly identify the claims of the party and therefore the scope of a panel's review. We do not see any basis for arguing that the terms of reference are meant to exclude reference to the broader rules of customary international law in interpreting a claim properly before the Panel."[118] The Appellate Body in Mexico – Soft Drink did not address Korea – Government Procurement.

Joel Trachman writes that "the mandate to WTO dispute resolution panels, to the Appellate Body and to the DSB is clear: apply (directly) only WTO law."[119] He lists two limited instances where panels may directly apply non-WTO: "First, as specifically authorized by article 3.2 of the DSU, they refer to customary rules of interpretation of international law. This reference does not appear to include substantive non-WTO international law. While Article 31.3.c of the Vienna Convention, which is taken as reflective of customary rules of interpretation, refers to applicable international law, it does so only to indicate what materials should be taken into account in interpreting treaty texts [. . .] second, substantive non-WTO international law may be incorporated by reference in WTO law, either by treaty language such as the references in TRIPS to intellectual property treaties or by a waiver such as the Lome waiver." Trachman considers that "substantive non-WTO law may indirectly be incorporated by reference in provisions such as article XX(b) of GATT."[120]

Pauwelyn offers a competing analysis to Trachman, arguing that even if Article 7 precludes panels from positively pronouncing on non-WTO law, this non-WTO law may

---

116 See Appellate Body Report, DS308, supra note 69, at para. 56.
117 Panel Report, *Korea – Measures Affecting Government Procurement*, WT/DS163/R, adopted June 19, 2000.
118 Ibid, at para. 7.101, fn. 755.
119 Joel Trachman, *The Domain of WTO Dispute Resolution*, 40 Harvard International Law Journal 333-377 (1999), at p. 342.
120 Ibid.

still be raised as a "fact" relevant to a defense. Such a fact would exert influence "not as a legal right or obligation, but as proof of an alleged fact."[121] Pauwelyn suggests that Members may wish to invoke non-WTO law as facts when raising sub-provisions of GATT Article XX as a defense. This view is accommodated by DSU Article 13.1, which allows panels "to seek information and technical advice from any individual or body which it deems appropriate," subject only to the precondition that the panel inform the disputing parties before seeking such information.

Pauwelyn further suggests that non-WTO law may only be raised as applicable law by recourse to 1969 VCLT Article 31.3.c, which refers to "any relevant rules of international law applicable between the parties." Critically, he argues that WTO tribunals should understand reference to the "parties" to mean the "common intention of the WTO Members."[122] Pauwelyn cites a passage by the Appellate Body in EC – *Computer Equipment*[123] to support his contention; the Appellate Body in EC – *Computer Equipment* indicated that reference to "common intentions of the parties" in the 1969 VCLT could not be ascertained "on the basis of the subjective and unilaterally determined 'expectations' of one of the parties to a treaty."[124] It is difficult to draw support for a "common intention of the WTO Members" standard from the Appellate Body's findings in EC – *Computer Equipment*. Reference to "parties" in the plural form in the 1969 VCLT renders the non-unilateral nature of 1969 VCLT Article 31.3.c evident. What is less clear is whether "parties" refers to State entities beyond the parties involved in the matter giving rise to recourse to the 1969 VCLT (typically a dispute). It should be noted that Pauwelyn acknowledges as uncontroverted that panels may apply non-WTO treaties "to the extent [...] that both disputing parties are legally bound by them and it is done in the examination of WTO claims."[125]

The Panel in EC – *Biotech*[126] opted for a more restrictive interpretation of "parties," and interpreted the term to apply to law applicable to all WTO Members: "in considering this issue, we note that Article 31.3.c does not refer to "one or more parties." Nor does it refer to "the parties to a dispute." We further note that Article 2.1.g of the Vienna Convention defines the meaning of the term "party" for the purposes of the Vienna Convention. Thus, "party" means "a State which has consented to be bound by the treaty and for which the treaty is in force." It may be inferred from these elements that the rules of international law applicable in the relations between "the parties" are the rules of international law applicable in the relations between the States which have consented to be bound by the treaty which is being interpreted, and for which that

---

121 See Pauwelyn, supra note 85, at p. 567.
122 Ibid, at p. 575.
123 Appellate Body Report, *European Communities – Customs Classification of Certain Computer Equipment*, WT/DS62/AB/R, WT/DS67/AB/R, WT/DS68/AB/R, adopted June 22, 1998.
124 Ibid, at para. 84.
125 See Pauwelyn, supra note 85, at p. 563.
126 Panel Report, *European Communities – Measures Affecting the Approval and Marketing of Biotech Products*, WT/DS291/R, WT/DS292/R, WT/DS293/R, Corr. 1 and Add. 1, 2, 3, 4, 5, 6, 7, 8 and 9, adopted November 21, 2006.

treaty is in force. This understanding of the term 'the parties' leads logically to the view that the rules of international law to be taken into account in interpreting the WTO agreements at issue in this dispute are those which are applicable in the relations between the WTO Members."[127] The Panel's restrictive interpretation of "the parties" renders recourse to applicable non-WTO law narrow, to the extent that it is difficult to identify international legal obligations common to all 153 WTO Members.

Commentators and WTO tribunals have differed on the scope of Article 7.2. Brazil invoked non-WTO law as a defense to GATT obligations in *Brazil – Tyres* with mixed results. The Appellate Body acknowledged Brazil's lack of bad faith in complying with MERCOSUR obligations, but engaged in an analysis of Brazil's pleadings before the MERCOSUR arbitral tribunal to find a violation of GATT Article III. Nonetheless, *Brazil – Tyres* confirms that Members may invoke non-WTO law as a defense.

It is also settled that reference to "the parties" at 1969 VCLT 31.3.c cannot apply to the law of a single party. Beyond this, the Panel in EC – *Biotech* has adopted a restrictive interpretation of "the parties," in which only the law applicable to all 153 Members may be taken into account. This surely militates against the possibility of invoking treaty obligations in WTO dispute settlement proceedings (as there are few treaties that all 153 Members are bound to aside from the WTO agreements). Ironically, such an interpretation may prove counterintuitive: to the extent that all Members are bound by customary law and peremptory norms of international law, WTO tribunals may be asked to deal with customary international legal obligations more amorphous than their treaty equivalent.

3. DSU Article 11

Article 11 obliges panels to make "an objective assessment of the facts of the case and the applicability of and conformity with the relevant covered agreements, and make such other findings as will assist the DSB in making the recommendations or in giving the rulings provided for in the covered agreements." Thomas Schoenbaum controversially argues that panels may adopt an expansive interpretation of Article 11. He refers to Article 11 as an "implied powers" clause, that "should be interpreted broadly so that the Panels and Appellate Body can decide all aspects of a dispute."[128] Schoenbaum's perspective is not, however, widely endorsed.[129]

Article 11 jurisprudence suggests that panels are given a wide margin of discretion to determine the objectivity of their assessments: in EC – *Hormones*, the Appellate Body

---

127 Ibid, at para. 7.68
128 See Thomas Schoenbaum, *WTO Dispute Settlement: Praise and Suggestions for Reform*, 47(3) International & Comparative Law Quarterly 647-658 (1998), at p. 653.
129 See for example Marceau, supra note 86, at p. 764. The author argues that "many international and national legal instruments will need to be examined and interpreted to the extent necessary to interpret and apply the WTO provision. But these considerations will be performed only to the extent necessary to interpret and apply WTO law, not to decide 'all aspects of a dispute'."

took the view that it would not infer violations of Article 11 in cases involving "an error of judgment in the appreciation of evidence," but rather for cases involving an "egregious error that calls into question the good faith of a panel."[130] When a party appeals to the Appellate Body claiming a violation of Article 11, the Appellate Body will closely scrutinize the Panel's factual determinations: in EC – *Hormones*, the Appellate Body confirmed that "the consistency or inconsistency of a given fact or set of facts with the requirements of a given treaty provision is, however, a legal characterization issue. It is a legal question. Whether or not a panel has made an objective assessment of the facts before it, as required by Article 11 of the DSU, is also a legal question which, if properly raised on appeal, would fall within the scope of appellate review."[131]

Panels have previously interpreted their combined duties under DSU Articles 7 and 11 to exercise judicial economy over certain matters raised by the parties, as exemplified by the Appellate Body's refusal to adjudicate upon the place of the precautionary principle in public international law in EC – *Hormones*.[132] However, it would seem that short of exhibiting "bad faith," nothing in Article 11 explicitly prevents panels from adjudicating upon non-WTO law. Indeed, it is possible to interpret the Appellate Body's findings in EC – *Hormones* to support the contention that a panel's failure to address non-WTO law may in some circumstances lead to a failure to make an "objective assessment" of facts relevant to a case, particularly where a party invokes non-WTO law as a fact to a defense of GATT obligations.

Yet, the hesitation exhibited by some WTO tribunals towards non-WTO law calls into question not only the role of various sources of public international law, particularly peremptory norms of international law within the WTO legal framework, but also whether WTO tribunals will ever be prepared to give effect to non-WTO law generally.

III. The Open Question of Ius Cogens and Erga Omnes Obligations

The dispute-avoidance techniques exercised by WTO tribunals faced with non-WTO public international law indicate that WTO tribunals will not likely clarify the role of *ius cogens* or *erga omnes* obligations within the WTO in the near future. Yet, 1969 VCLT Articles 53 and 64 indicate that where a treaty conflicts with a *ius cogens* norm, the treaty is voided. As touched upon above, the Appellate Body has referred to 1969 VCLT provisions beyond Articles 31 and 32.

---

130 See Appellate Body Report, DS26, supra note 111, at para. 133.
131 Ibid, at para. 132.
132 See supra note 113.

The 1969 VCLT does not directly address obligations *erga omnes*. The ICJ first expounded upon obligations *erga omnes* in *Barcelona Traction*.[133] According to the ICJ, an "essential distinction should be drawn between the obligations of a State towards the international community as a whole, and those arising vis-à-vis another State in the field of diplomatic protection. By their very nature the former are the concerns of all States. In view of the importance of the rights involved, all States can be held to have a legal interest in their protection; they are obligations *erga omnes*."[134] The Official Commentary to the 2001 International Law Commission (ILC) Draft Articles on State Responsibility makes no less than 14 references to obligations *erga omnes*, notably towards the interpretation of Draft Article 48 on the Invocation of Responsibility by a State other than an Injured State.[135] It should be noted that the ICJ indicated in *Gabcikovo-Nagymaros Project*[136] that the Draft Articles reflect customary international law.[137] Furthermore, WTO tribunals have often referred to the Draft Articles.[138] Obligations *erga omnes* are thus as potentially applicable to WTO law as *ius cogens* norms. Indeed, it would seem from a WTO arbitrator decision in *US – FSC*[139] that they apply with respect to export subsidies.

In *US – FSC*, the EC successfully secured authorization to retaliate against the global value of a US export subsidy, in the amount of USD 4,043 million. The US had argued before the arbitrator that the EC's share of the global trade effects of the subsidy stood at 26.8%. In rejecting the US argument, the arbitrator held that: "The United States' breach of obligation is not objectively dismissed because some of the products benefiting from the subsidy are, e.g., exported to another trading partner. It is an *erga omnes* obligation owed in its entirety to each and every Member. It cannot be considered to be 'allocatable' across the Membership. Otherwise, the Member concerned would be only partially obliged in respect of each and every Member, which is manifestly inconsistent with an *erga omnes* per se obligation. Thus, the United States has breached

---

133 Barcelona Traction, Light and Power Company, Limited, Second Phase, Judgment, I.C.J. Reports 1970.
134 Ibid, at para. 33.
135 See Draft Articles, supra note 110.
136 Gabcikovo-Nagymaros Project (Hungary/Slovakia) I.L.M. 37 [1998], at p. 162.
137 Ibid, at para. 52.
138 See Decision by the Arbitrators, *European Communities – Regime for the Importation, Sale and Distribution of Bananas – Recourse to Arbitration by the European Communities under Article 22.6 of the DSU*, WT/DS27/ARB/ECU, March 24, 2000, at para. 6.16; Decision by the Arbitrators, *Brazil – Export Financing Programme for Aircraft – Recourse to Arbitration by Brazil under Article 22.6 of the DSU and Article 4.11 of the SCM Agreement*, WT/DS46/ARB, August 28, 2000, at para. 3.44; Decision by the Arbitrator, *United States – Tax Treatment for "Foreign Sales Corporations" – Recourse to Arbitration by the United States under Article 22.6 of the DSU and Article 4.11 of the SCM Agreement*, WT/DS108/ARB, August 30, 2002, at para. 5.58; Appellate Body Report, *United States – Transitional Safeguard Measure on Combed Cotton Yarn from Pakistan*, WT/DS192/AB/R, adopted November 5, 2001, at para. 120; Appellate Body Report, *United States – Definitive Safeguard Measures on Imports of Circular Welded Carbon Quality Line Pipe from Korea*, WT/DS202/AB/R, adopted March 8, 2002, at para. 259; and Appellate Body Report, United States – Countervailing Duty Investigation on Dynamic Random Access Memory Semiconductors (DRAMS) from Korea, WT/DS296/AB/R, adopted July 20, 2005, at fn. 188 to para. 116.
139 Decision by the Arbitrator, *United States – Tax Treatment for "Foreign Sales Corporations" – Recourse to Arbitration by the United States under Article 22.6 of the DSU and Article 4.11 of the SCM Agreement*, WT/DS108/ARB, August 30, 2002.

its obligation to the European Communities in respect of all the money that it has expended, because such expenditure in breach – the expense incurred – is the very essence of the wrongful act."[140]

At the DSB meeting of March 7, 2003, the US stated that the arbitrator "incorrectly and inappropriately purport[ed] to import into WTO jurisprudence the concept of *erga omnes* [...] the concept of *erga omnes* is squarely at odds with the fundamentally bilateral nature of WTO and GATT dispute settlement and with the notion that WTO disputes concern nullification and impairment of negotiated benefits to a particular Member. WTO adjudicators are tasked with resolving disputes between specific complaining and defending parties. Adjudicators may not, through improper importation of the concept of *erga omnes*, enforce WTO obligations on behalf of non-parties to a dispute."[141] The US comments were noted in the minutes to the meeting of March 7, 2003, but nothing more arose from them.

One commentator has expressed skepticism about the strength of the US argument against the use of obligations *erga omnes* in WTO law, as it overlooks the systemic nature of WTO disputes.[142] Further, export subsidies stand aside from other measures in occupying a *per se* notorious position within WTO law, as clarified by SCM Article 3.

Marceau submits that conflicts between *ius cogens* and the WTO agreements are unlikely to arise as "many WTO provisions are drafted in terms of a general prohibition, giving Members flexibility in the implementation of their WTO obligations."[143] At a more fundamental level, she questions the ability of WTO tribunals to adjudicate on *ius cogens* norms, given the effect of 1969 VCLT Articles 53 and 64, by asking a series of rhetorical questions: "Can a WTO panel or the Appellate Body identify a norm as having reached a *ius cogens* status? Can WTO adjudicating bodies determine the consequences of a *ius cogens* violation by a WTO provision or a member's specific application of a WTO norm? Can WTO adjudicating bodies violate *ius cogens*?"[144]

The rhetorical questions posed by Marceau on whether WTO tribunals *can* give effect to *ius cogens* norms apply to the larger question of whether WTO tribunals can give effect to non-WTO law generally. The Appellate Body's equivocal evaluation of the precautionary principle in EC – *Hormones* may serve as indication that WTO tribunals will not be shedding light on any of these questions anytime soon.

---

140 Ibid, at para. 6.10.
141 See Minutes of Meeting, WT/DSB/M/149 (July 8, 2003), at Item 2. United States – Tax Treatment for "foreign Sales Corporations."
142 See Tarcisio Gazzini, *The Legal Nature of WTO Obligations and the Consequences of their Violation*, 17(4) European Journal of International Law, 723-742 (2006), at p. 740. Gazzini continues to consider that "nevertheless, there is nothing intrinsically wrong with extending some features of indivisible obligations to international economic law."
143 See Marceau, supra note 86, at p. 799.
144 Ibid, at p. 798.

IV. Interpreting Non-WTO Law

WTO tribunals have shown that they are more comfortable interpreting non-WTO law than giving effect to such law. As we will illustrate below, the interpretative approaches adopted by these tribunals have not been uniform.

In EC – Poultry,[145] for example, the Appellate Body reviewed the Panel's determination that the Oilseeds Agreement concluded bilaterally between the EC and Brazil could be used to interpret the relevant EC Schedule of Commitments. The Appellate Body considered that "the Oilseeds Agreement is not a 'covered agreement' within the meaning of Articles 1 and 2 of the DSU. Nor is the Oilseeds Agreement part of the multilateral obligations accepted by Brazil and the European Communities pursuant to the WTO Agreement, which came into effect on January 1, 1995. The Oilseeds Agreement is not cited in any Annex to the WTO Agreement. Although the provisions of certain legal instruments that entered into force under the GATT 1947 were made part of the GATT 1994 pursuant to the language in Annex 1A incorporating the GATT 1994 into the WTO Agreement, the Oilseeds Agreement is not one of those legal instruments."[146] The Appellate Body nonetheless upheld the Panel's findings and allowed the interpretation to stand.

The Appellate Body pushed the interpretive envelope in US – Reformulated Gasoline and US – Shrimp. In US – Reformulated Gasoline,[147] the Appellate Body allowed "clean air" to constitute an "exhaustible natural resource" for the purposes of GATT Article XX.g. In US – Shrimp,[148] the Appellate Body cited no less than 4 environmental agreements to support its contention that reference to "exhaustible natural resources" in Article XX.g could apply to sea turtles.[149]

WTO tribunals have not employed interpretative tools consistently. Sometimes panels have touched upon non-WTO law only to reinforce the normative superiority of WTO rules: in Argentina – Footwear,[150] for example, the Appellate Body approved the Panel's

---

145 Appellate Body Report, *European Communities – Measures Affecting the Importation of Certain Poultry Products*, WT/DS69/AB/R, adopted July 23, 1998.
146 Ibid, at para. 79.
147 See Appellate Body Report, DS2, supra note 98, at p. 14.
148 Appellate Body Report, *United States – Import Prohibition of Certain Shrimp and Shrimp Products*, WT/DS58/AB/R, adopted November 6, 1998.
149 Ibid, at paras. 129-131. These agreements included: (i) the United Nations Convention on the Law of the Sea (signed at Montego Bay on December 10, 1982, UN Doc. A/CONF.62/122; 21 International Legal Materials 1261)(entered into force on November 16, 1994); (ii) the Convention on Biological Diversity (signed at Rio de Janeiro on June 5, 1992, UNEP/Bio.Div./N7-INC5/4; 31 International Legal Materials 818)(entered into force on December 29, 1993); (iii) Agenda 21 (adopted by the United Nations Conference on Environment and Development in Rio de Janeiro on June 14, 1992, UN Doc. A/CONF. 151/26/Rev.1); and (iv) the Final Act of the Conference to Conclude a Convention on the Conservation of Migratory Species of Wild Animals (signed at Bonn on June 23, 1979, 19 International Legal Materials 11)(entered into force on November 1, 1983).
150 Appellate Body Report, Argentina – Measures Affecting Imports of Footwear, Textiles, Apparel and Other Items, WT/DS56/AB/R and Corr.1, adopted April 22, 1998.

findings that "there is nothing in the Agreement between the IMF and the WTO, the Declaration on the Relationship of the WTO with the IMF or the Declaration on Coherence which justifies a conclusion that a Member's commitments to the IMF shall prevail over its obligations under Article VIII of the GATT 1994."[151] The Appellate Body in *Brazil – Tyres* adopted a similar approach as in *Argentina – Footwear* towards Brazil's MERCOSUR obligations. Why has the approach of WTO tribunals varied dramatically with respect to the interpretation of non-WTO legal obligations?

Simma suggests that the WTO refers to non-WTO public international law to boost its legitimacy. He writes that panels generally refrain from "unnecessarily cross-linking WTO provisions with other rules of the 'universe'," thus adopting an isolationist discursive strategy. However, "once the legitimacy of the decision comes under fire, the invocation of 'unity' rather than 'particularity' becomes an interesting discursive option."[152] Simma cites *US – Shrimp* as an example of the Appellate Body referring to "international environmental instruments outside the WTO to counter the image of the WTO as a cold-hearted trade-over-everything institution." He further notes that "adopting such a unitary discourse did not even require the Appellate Body to reverse the recommendations of the Panel in substance."[153]

Simma's argument is partly correct – while unitary discourse is certainly reflected in the sheer number of environmental treaties discussed by the Appellate Body in *US – Shrimp* (4 in total), the manner in which the Appellate Body found against the US measure at issue – an extraterritorial sea turtle conservation law – allowed the US to succeed in the recourse proceedings that followed. While this may not have impacted the substance of the Panel's recommendations, it certainly shifted the outcome of the dispute.

The Appellate Body essentially condemned the US for failing to engage in "serious, across-the-board negotiations with the objective of concluding bilateral or multilateral agreements for the protection and conservation of sea turtles."[154] In coming to this conclusion, the Appellate Body (rightly) drew applicable context from the Preamble to the Agreement Establishing the World Trade Organization, which seeks in part to "protect and preserve the environment and to enhance the means for doing so *in a manner consistent with their respective needs and concerns at different levels of economic development* (emphasis added)." The Appellate Body noted that this text "must add color, texture and shading to our interpretation to the agreements annexed to the WTO Agreement, in this case, the GATT 1994,"[155] and construed an obligation to engage in

---

151 Ibid, at para. 70. The Appellate Body analyzed the relationship between the IMF Agreements with the WTO Agreements in a detailed manner, and came to the correct conclusion. However, the statement on the superiority of WTO law to IMF commitments is strongly-worded.
152 See Simma and Polkowski, supra note 94, at p. 511.
153 Ibid.
154 See Appellate Body Report, DS58, at para. 166.
155 Ibid, at para. 153.

multilateral negotiations prior to adopting or enforcing measures justified under GATT Article XX. g. Such multilateralism would mitigate against the risk that such measures arbitrarily or unjustifiably discriminate between Members. In coming to this conclusion, the Appellate Body did not, as some suggest, "impute to the chapeau of Article XX concepts that were not intended."[156] Rather, the Appellate Body was emphasizing the requirement of good faith that underpins the WTO agreements. As touched upon above, the text of Article XX itself seeks to articulate this good faith requirement into binding legal obligations.

Following the DSB's adoption of the Appellate Body report, the US made minor alterations to the measures, and participated in 4 international conferences on the preservation of sea turtles. The US did not conclude any agreements pursuant to these conferences, nor did the US meaningfully alter its measures thereafter. Malaysia initiated recourse proceedings against the US, alleging that the US had failed to bring its measures into conformity with the DSB's rulings and recommendations *contra* DSU Article 21.5. The Recourse Panel, citing the US participation in the 4 conferences, deemed the "revised" US measure WTO-consistent as the US had engaged in "serious good faith efforts to conclude an international agreement on the protection and conservation of sea turtles"[157].

Malaysia argued before the Recourse Appellate Body that the Recourse Panel had "erred in considering the obligation of the United States as an obligation to *negotiate*, as opposed to an obligation to *conclude* an international agreement."[158] The Recourse Appellate Body dismissed Malaysia's argument, and opined that "it is one thing to *prefer* a multilateral approach in the application of a measure that is provisionally justified under one of the subparagraphs of GATT Article XX; it is another to require the *conclusion* of a multilateral agreement as a condition of avoiding 'arbitrary or unjustifiably discrimination' under the chapeau of Article XX. We see, in this case, no such requirement."[159]

It may be true that the Appellate Body was conscious of an institutional need to deflect criticism of a trade proclivity within the WTO in its deliberations. This does, however, call into question the correctness of the Appellate Body's findings. In underpinning the requirement of good faith in international relations between WTO Members by emphasizing a need to engage in multilateral discussions before imposing measures provisionally justified under GATT Article XX. g, the Appellate Body sought to defer to the WTO membership. When Malaysia put forward the argument that the Chapeau

---

156 See Colares, supra note 8, at p. 434.
157 See Panel Report, *United States – Import Prohibition of Certain Shrimp and Shrimp Products – Recourse to Article 21.5 of the DSU by Malaysia*, WT/DS58/RW, adopted November 21, 2001, upheld by Appellate Body Report, WT/DS58/AB/RW, notably at para. 5.87.
158 See Appellate Body Report, *United States – Import Prohibition of Certain Shrimp and Shrimp Products – Recourse to Article 21.5 of the DSU by Malaysia*, WT/DS58/AB/RW, adopted November 21, 2001, at para. 16.
159 Ibid, at para. 124.

to GATT Article XX required Members to conclude international agreements, the Appellate Body unequivocally disagreed.

It is worth noting that the concerns of WTO Members on the potential for spill-over trade effects in environmental measures seeking to promote sustainable development predates the WTO agreements. Pursuant to the 1994 Marrakesh Ministerial Decision on Trade and Environment, Members had established a WTO Committee on Trade and Environment (CTE) to, *inter alia*, "identify the relationship between trade measures and environmental measures, in order to promote sustainable development,"[160] and suggest rules to improve this relationship. In 1996, the CTE recommended that "in the event a dispute arises between WTO Members who are each Parties to a [Multilateral Environmental Agreement] over the use of trade measures they are applying among themselves pursuant to the MEA, they should consider in the first instance trying to resolve it through the dispute mechanisms available under the MEA."[161] In deferring at the first instance to a possible multilateral solution, it is more likely that the Appellate Body sought to adopt an approach commensurate with the 1996 recommendations of the CTE, rather than engage in the legitimacy-seeking exercise that Simma suggests. In other words, the Appellate Body recognized that the body of WTO rules formulating the *lex specialis* of international trade law did not accommodate the *lex specialis* of international environmental law, and deferred at first instance to the latter. This is hardly "smoking gun" evidence of a self-contained regime.

In sum, it is difficult to find a clear or uniform approach by WTO tribunals towards substantive public international law. WTO tribunals readily concede that they do not operate in clinical isolation from the wider corpus of public international law, but beyond this panels and the Appellate Body have adopted three competing approaches to substantive public international law:

a. An isolationist approach, typified by the Panel's refusal to engage with the NAFTA obligations of the US and Mexico in *Mexico – Soft Drink*.

b. An integrated approach, typified by the Appellate Body's reference to, and emphasis upon multilateralism in *US – Shrimp*.

c. A hybrid approach, exemplified by the Appellate Body's selective assessment of Brazil's substantive pleadings before a MERCOSUR tribunal in *Brazil – Tyres*, and the Appellate Body's exercise of dispute avoidance techniques in relation to the status of the precautionary principle in *EC – Hormones*.

---

160 See http://www.wto.org/english/docs_e/legal_e/56-dtenv_e.htm.
161 Report (1996) of the Committee on Trade and Environment, WT/CTE/W/40 (November 12, 1996), at Annex 1C.

It is easier to ascertain a reason for why WTO tribunals have approached public international law inconsistently: despite a "deficit in international governance,"[162] it seems that one matter the WTO Membership can agree upon is that they do not want panels or the Appellate Body straying too far into public international legal principles. One commentator writes that the GATT 1947 was "a self-contained regime of international law only in aspiration but not in reality."[163] To the extent that some Members held the same aspirations towards the WTO, they can hardly be excited by the prospect of a second "World Court" forming in Geneva. This sentiment manifested itself in the Special Session warning to the Appellate Body with respect to its amicus curiae brief initiative in EC – Asbestos.

Weiler makes the interesting point that nomenclature "can be, and often [is], a mask over a discomforting reality and equally often a slide into self-deception." He cites reference to "'dispute settlement' (rather than judicial process) or 'Appellate Body' (rather than High Trade Court or something similar)"[164] as examples of this. Until the WTO Membership exhibits a greater willingness to accept that the WTO lives symbiotically with public international law, WTO tribunals will be slow to "forge ahead" by engaging in a process of judicial legislation. Rather, they will continue to operate within their presently delineated adjudicative boundaries.[165]

D. Procedural Public International Law

WTO tribunals have shown a greater willingness to adopt procedural public international law principles than substantive public international law principles. Marceau suggests that WTO tribunals draw authority to adopt procedural public international law principles from DSU Article 11, which can be read "as providing panels with the necessary power and even the obligation to adopt practices and follow judicial principles to ensure that the application of the covered agreements and the administration of the dispute settlement process are done objectively."[166] Examples of the Appellate Body applying procedural public international law include:[167]

---

162 For a discussion on this theme, see Jacques Bourgeois, *On the Internal Morality of WTO Law*, in Armin Von Bogdandy, Petros Mavroidis and Yves Meny (Eds.), *European Integration and International Coordination: Studies in Transnational Economic Law in Honour of Claus-Dieter Ehlermann* 39-54 (Kluwer Law International; London, 2002).
163 See Kuijper, supra note 90, at 252. However, the author continues to write that the WTO has "moved decisively in the direction of such a self-contained regime." We disagree with this statement, in light of the AB's confirmation in US – Reformulated Gasoline that "the General Agreement is not to be read in clinical isolation from public international law." See supra note 102.
164 See Weiler, supra note 26, at pp. 10–11.
165 For a discussion on the "constrained independence" of international tribunals, see Slaughter and Helfer, supra note 31.
166 See Marceau, supra note 86, at p. 765.
167 From Jacques Bourgeois, *The Umpire Needs Better Rules of the Game*, in Giorgio Sacerdoti, Alan Yanovich and Jan Bohanes (Eds.) *The WTO at Ten: The Contribution of the Dispute Settlement System* 235-245 (Cambridge University Press; Cambridge; 2006), at p. 236.

a. Due Process: in *Brazil – Desiccated Coconuts*,[168] the Appellate Body stated that "terms of reference fulfil an important due process objective – they give the parties and third parties sufficient information concerning the claims at issue in the dispute in order to allow them an opportunity to respond to the complainant's case."[169]

b. Standing: in *EC – Bananas III*,[170] the Appellate Body evaluated ICJ and Permanent Court of International Justice precedent cited by the disputing parties to conclude that "we do not read any of these judgments as establishing a general rule that in all international litigation, a complaining party must have a 'legal interest' in order to bring a case."[171] The Appellate Body considered that DSU Article 3.7, which states that "before bringing a case, a Member shall exercise its judgment as to whether action under these procedures would be fruitful," sets the principal WTO standing requirement.[172]

c. Right to private counsel: in *EC – Bananas III*, the US objected to the EC's use of private counsel in dispute settlement proceedings. The Panel did not allow the presence of private counsel at the first substantive meeting of the parties.[173] On appeal, however, the Appellate Body held that "we can find nothing in the Marrakesh Agreement Establishing the World Trade Organization (the "WTO Agreement"), the DSU or the Working Procedures, nor in customary international law or the prevailing practice of international tribunals, which prevents a WTO Member from determining the composition of its delegation in Appellate Body proceedings [...] we rule that it is for a WTO Member to decide who should represent it as members of its delegation in an oral hearing of the Appellate Body."[174]

d. *Tantum devolutum quantum appellatum*: in *India – Patents*,[175] the Appellate Body overruled the Panel's determination that the Panel could exercise its discretion to consider legal arguments other than by reviewing the terms of reference to the dispute. The Appellate Body opined that "a panel may consider only those claims that it has the authority to consider under its terms of reference. A panel cannot assume jurisdiction that it does not have."[176]

---

168 See Appellate Body Report, DS22, supra note 104.
169 Ibid, at p. 22.
170 Appellate Body Report, *European Communities – Regime for the Importation, Sale and Distribution of Bananas*, WT/DS27/AB/R, adopted September 25, 1997.
171 Ibid, at para. 133.
172 Ibid, at para. 135.
173 Ibid, at para. 7.10–7.12 (Panel Report).
174 Ibid, at para. 10 (Appellate Body Report).
175 Appellate Body Report, *India – Patent Protection for Pharmaceutical and Agricultural Chemical Products*, WT/DS50/AB/R, adopted January 16, 1998.
176 Ibid, at para. 92.

e. *Ultra petita*: in EC – Hormones, the Appellate Body upheld the Panel's decision not to abide by the rules and procedures of Appendix 4 of the DSU when it consulted individual experts. Panels are required to follow Appendix 4 when they convene an "expert review group." The Appellate Body stated that if the Panel had convened an expert review group, the rules and procedures of Appendix 4 of the DSU would have been applicable. Since the Panel did not convene such a group, the Panel's decision not to follow the rules and procedures of Appendix 4 was completely consistent with the DSU and was within the discretion accorded to panels in their procedural decisions.[177]

f. The distinction between claims and arguments: in EC – Bananas III, the Appellate Body modified the Panel's findings that defective terms of reference could be cured by written submissions. The Appellate Body considered that "Article 6.2 of the DSU requires that the claims, but not the arguments, must all be specified sufficiently in the request for the establishment of a Panel in order to allow the defending party and any third parties to know the legal basis of the complaint."[178]

g. *Actori incumbit onus probatio*: in US – Wool Shirts and Blouses,[179] the Appellate Body reluctantly endorsed the Panel's findings on the shifting burden of proof in international disputes. The Appellate Body noted that "although the Panel's findings [...] are not a model of clarity, we do not believe the Panel erred in law."[180] The Appellate Body considered that "it is, thus, hardly surprising that various international tribunals, including the ICJ, have generally and consistently accepted and applied the rule that the party who asserts a fact, whether the claimant or the respondent, is responsible for providing proof thereof".[181]

h. The discretion to draw negative inferences in appropriate circumstances: in Canada – Aircraft,[182] the Appellate Body upheld the Panel's refusal to draw a strong negative inference from Canada's failure to provide documentation. Brazil argued that the Panel erred in law by not finding that the undisclosed documentation conferred an unauthorized "benefit" for the purposes of the SCM Agreement. The Panel instead considered the conferment of the benefit as "not proven." The Appellate Body considered that "a panel should be willing expressly to remind parties – during the course of dispute settlement proceedings – that a refusal to provide information requested by the panel may lead to inferences being drawn about the inculpatory character of the information withheld."[183]

---

177 See DS26, supra note 111, at para. 56.
178 See DS27, supra note 168, at para. 143.
179 Appellate Body Report, *United States – Measure Affecting Imports of Woven Wool Shirts and Blouses from India*, WT/DS33/AB/R and Corr.1, adopted May 23, 1997.
180 Ibid, at p. 13.
181 Ibid, at p. 14.
182 Appellate Body Report, *Canada – Measures Affecting the Export of Civilian Aircraft*, WT/DS70/AB/R, adopted August 20, 1999.
183 Ibid, at para. 204.

i. The distinction between questions of fact and questions of law: in *Canada – Periodicals*,[184] the Appellate Body dismissed an argument by Canada that the Appellate Body could not properly examine a claim under the second sentence of GATT Article III.2 as "no party has appealed the findings of the Panel on this provision." The Appellate Body was of the view that "as the legal obligations in the first and second sentences are two closely-linked steps in determining the consistency of an internal tax measure with the national treatment obligations of Article III.2, the Appellate Body would be remiss in not completing the analysis of Article III.2."[185]

E. Conclusion

There is no question that the WTO is "embedded" into public international law. DSU Article 3.2's reference to the "customary rules of interpretation" has enabled WTO tribunals to engage with the 1969 VCLT and non-WTO law in ways that GATT 1947 Panels could not. The Panel's findings in *Korea – Government Procurement* that "customary international law applies [...] to the extent that the WTO treaty agreements do not 'contract out' from it" lends itself to the proposition that the WTO agreements form *lex specialis*.

Regardless of whether this *lex specialis* system rises to the level of operating as a "self-contained regime," public international law can play an important role in WTO dispute settlement. Procedurally, public international legal principles have assisted panels to "close the gaps" left by a procedurally-bare DSU. Substantively, however, the role of public international law is less clear. In *US – Shrimp*, the Appellate Body's emphasis on multilateralism enabled a US sea turtle conservation law to ultimately bypass the WTO's "non-discrimination" pillar.[186] In *EC – Hormones*, on the other hand, the Appellate Body deemed discussion of the precautionary principle "imprudent." It is difficult to conceptually reconcile these two environmental disputes. Would codification of the precautionary principle into treaty form have enabled the Appellate Body to engage in a fuller discussion of the precautionary principle? It is doubtful.

The inconsistent approach by WTO tribunals towards substantive public international law leaves many questions unanswered, not least of which on whether these tribunals will give effect to non-WTO public international law where appropriate. To compound matters, it is unclear whether WTO tribunals are even authorized to positively an-

---

184 Appellate Body Report, *Canada – Certain Measures Concerning Periodicals*, WT/DS31/AB/R, adopted July 30, 1997.
185 Ibid, at p. 24.
186 The WTO's bifurcated non-discrimination pillar amalgamates two principles: (i) the Most-Favored Nation (MFN) principle, which obliges Members to treat all WTO Members equally; and (ii) the National Treatment (NT) principle, which obliges Members to treat imported and domestic goods equally.

swer such questions: DSU Articles 3.2, 7.2 and 11 arguably restrict panels to positively pronouncing exclusively on WTO obligations. What is far less unclear is that WTO Members have no desire for these panels to answer such questions.

A pragmatic "way forward" is to reform the DSU – but this has already been attempted without success. A 1994 WTO Ministerial Decision invited Members to attempt a "full review of dispute settlement rules and procedures" by January 1, 1999. Following deadlock, Members agreed to extend the deadline to July 31, 1999. This deadline proved too soon. Members agreed at the Doha Ministerial Conference of November 20, 2001 to "agree to negotiations on improvements and clarifications of the Dispute Settlement Understanding" by no later than May 31, 2003.[187] Members have yet to agree to DSU revisions in DSB Special Sessions. Until (if ever) Members reach consensus on alterations to the DSU, WTO tribunals will continue to struggle to apply substantive public international law in a coherent manner.

---

187 See Ministerial Declaration, WT.MIN(01)/DEC/1 (November 20, 2001).

Annex I PERCENTAGE OF PANEL REPORTS APPEALED BY YEAR OF ADOPTION: 1995–2008 [a]

Year of adoption	All panel reports			Panel reports other than Article 21.5 reports [b]			Article 21.5 panel reports		
	Panel reports adopted [c]	Panel reports appealed [d]	Percentage appealed [e]	Panel reports adopted	Panel reports appealed	Percentage appealed	Panel reports adopted	Panel reports appealed	Percentage appealed
1996	2	2	100%	2	2	100%	0	0	–
1997	5	5	100%	5	5	100%	0	0	–
1998	12	9	75%	12	9	75%	0	0	–
1999	10	7	70%	9	7	78%	1	0	0%
2000	19	11	58%	15	9	60%	4	2	50%
2001	17	12	71%	13	9	69%	4	3	75%
2002	12	6	50%	11	5	45%	1	1	100%
2003	10	7	70%	8	5	63%	2	2	100%
2004	8	6	75%	8	6	75%	0	0	–
2005	20	12	60%	17	11	65%	3	1	33%
2006	7	6	86%	4	3	75%	3	3	100%
2007	10	5	50%	6	3	50%	4	2	50%
2008	11	9	82%	8	6	75%	3	3	100%
Total	143	97	68%	118	80	68%	25	17	68%

a   No panel reports were adopted in 1995.

b   Under Article 21.5 of the DSU, a panel may be established to hear a "disagreement as to the existence or consistency with a covered agreement of measures taken to comply with the recommendations and rulings" of the DSB upon the adoption of a previous panel or Appellate Body report.

c   The Panel Reports in EC – *Bananas III (Ecuador)*, EC – *Bananas III (Guatemala and Honduras)*, EC – *Bananas III (Mexico)*, and EC – *Bananas III (US)* are counted as a single panel report. The Panel Reports in US – *Steel Safeguards*, in EC – *Export Subsidies on Sugar*, and in EC – *Chicken Cuts*, are also counted as single panel reports in each of those disputes.

d   Panel reports are counted as having been appealed where they are adopted as upheld, modified, or reversed by an Appellate Body report. The number of panel reports appealed may differ from the number of Appellate Body reports because some Appellate Body reports address more than one panel report.

e   Percentages are rounded to the nearest whole number.

Source: Appellate Body Annual Report for 2008, WT/AB/11 (February 9, 2009), at Annex 4.

Annex II   APPEALS FILED: 1995–2008

Year	Notices of Appeal filed	Appeals in original proceedings	Appeals in Article 21.5 proceedings
1995	0	0	0
1996	4	4	0
1997	6[a]	6	0
1998	8	8	0
1999	9[b]	9	0
2000	13[c]	11	2
2001	9[d]	5	4
2002	7[e]	6	1
2003	6[f]	5	1
2004	5	5	0
2005	10	8	2
2006	5	3	2
2007	4	2	2
2008	13	10	3
Total	**97**	**80**	**17**

a   This number includes two Notices of Appeal that were filed at the same time in related matters, counted separately: EC – Hormones (Canada) and EC – Hormones (US). A single Appellate Body report was circulated in relation to those appeals.

b   This number excludes one Notice of Appeal that was withdrawn by the United States, which subsequently filed another Notice of Appeal in relation to the same panel report: US – FSC.

c   This number includes two Notices of Appeal that were filed at the same time in related matters, counted separately: US – 1916 Act (EC) and US – 1916 Act (Japan). A single Appellate Body report was circulated in relation to those appeals.

d   This number excludes one Notice of Appeal that was withdrawn by the United States, which subsequently filed another Notice of Appeal in relation to the same panel report: US – Line Pipe.

e   This number includes one Notice of Appeal that was subsequently withdrawn: India – Autos; and excludes one Notice of Appeal that was withdrawn by the European Communities, which subsequently filed another Notice of Appeal in relation to the same panel report: EC – Sardines.

f   This number excludes one Notice of Appeal that was withdrawn by the United States, which subsequently filed another Notice of Appeal in relation to the same panel report: US – Softwood Lumber IV.

Source: Appellate Body Annual Report for 2008, WT/AB/11 (February 9, 2009), at Annex 3.

Annex III WTO AGREEMENTS ADDRESSED IN APPELLATE BODY REPORTS CIRCULATED THROUGH 2008 [a]

Year of circulation	DSU	WTO Agmt	GATT 1994	Agriculture	SPS	ATC	TBT	TRIMs	Anti-Dumping	Import Licensing	SCM	Safeguards	GATS	TRIPS
1996	0	0	2	0	0	0	0	0	0	0	0	0	0	0
1997	4	1	5	1	0	2	0	0	0	1	1	0	1	1
1998	7	1	4	1	2	0	0	0	1	0	0	0	0	0
1999	7	1	6	1	1	0	0	0	0	0	2	1	0	0
2000	8	1	7	2	0	0	0	0	2	0	5	2	1	1
2001	7	1	3	1	0	1	1	0	4	0	1	2	0	0
2002	8	2	4	3	0	0	0	0	1	0	3	1	0	1
2003	4	2	3	0	1	0	0	0	4	0	1	1	0	0
2004	2	0	5	0	0	0	0	0	2	0	1	0	0	0
2005	9	0	5	2	0	0	0	0	2	0	4	0	1	0
2006	5	0	3	0	0	0	0	0	3	0	2	0	0	0
2007	5	0	2	1	0	0	0	0	2	0	1	0	0	0
2008	8	1	9	1	2	0	0	0	3	0	3	0	0	0
Total	74	10	58	13	6	3	2	0	24	2	24	7	4	3

[a] No appeals were filed in 1995.

Source: Appellate Body Annual Report for 2007, WT/AB/9 (January 30, 2008), at Annex 5

Annex IV. A Total Number of Complainants and Respondents, by income classification

Complainants

*A number of complaints have been filed by multiple Members acting jointly. In some of these complaints, the Members filing the complaint fall into different income categories. Where this is the case, we have counted the complaint in each income category in which at least one complainant falls. Therefore, the number of the complaints in these tables will add up to more than the total number of complaints under the DSU.

High Income	Upper Middle Income	Lower Middle Income	Low Income
Number of Complaints	Number of Complaints	Number of Complaints	Number of Complaints
245	90	46	25

Respondents

High Income	Upper Middle Income	Lower Middle Income	Low Income
Number of Complaints	Number of Complaints	Number of Complaints	Number of Complaints
234	79	53	24

Copyright © 2002–2003 WorldTradeLaw.net LLC

Source: http://www.worldtradelaw.net/dsc/database/classificationcount.asp

Annex IV. B Opponents in WTO Disputes, grouped by income classification

Complaints by High Income Members Against:			
High Income	Upper Middle Income	Lower Middle Income	Low Income
Number of Complaints	Number of Complaints	Number of Complaints	Number of Complaints
159	42	23	21
Complaints by Upper Middle Income Members Against:			
High Income	Upper Middle Income	Lower Middle Income	Low Income
Number of Complaints	Number of Complaints	Number of Complaints	Number of Complaints
48	24	18	0
Complaints by Lower Middle Income Members Against:			
High Income	Upper Middle Income	Lower Middle Income	Low Income
Number of Complaints	Number of Complaints	Number of Complaints	Number of Complaints
25	9	10	2
Complaints by Low Income Members Against:			
High Income	Upper Middle Income	Lower Middle Income	Low Income
Number of Complaints	Number of Complaints	Number of Complaints	Number of Complaints
16	6	2	1

Copyright © 2002–2003 WorldTradeLaw.net LLC

Source: http://www.worldtradelaw.net/dsc/database/classificationcount.asp

Discussion

CARL BAUDENBACHER
Thank you very much, Jacques, for this beautiful final speech here at this conference.

If I may, I would like to ask the first question. You spoke about many interesting issues. One that struck me particularly, was your consideration on whether there is a system of precedent in the practice of the WTO Appellate Body. And I could easily follow on what you based this assessment. I may just add that in the case of a new international court, a system of precedent is a crucial feature. And I can tell from my own experience at the EFTA Court, that was a matter of dispute among the judges. Because there were those, probably political appointees, who opposed the idea of establishing a system of precedent, because they realised that by doing that, they would make the institution more powerful. It becomes – in the case of the WTO Appellate Body and in the case of the EFTA Court – more like the ECJ and it is fascinating to see that in the WTO the development is going along the same lines.

JACQUES BOURGEOIS
You are perfectly right and it gives an adjudicative body of panels and the Appellate Body self-confidence as well.

GABRIELLE KAUFMANN-KOHLER
I would like to make a side remark about this. Dr. Bourgeois, you referred to the WTO Appellate Body. For the first time the WTO Appellate Body referred to an ICSID award. ICSID awards do regularly refer to WTO cases for instance on national treatment or like circumstances. The reverse was not the case until a decision referred to an ICSID award precisely on the issue of precedent. In the context of judicial dialogue this is a noteworthy point.

JACQUES BOURGEOIS
Thank you, I will take that on board.

PHILIPPE VLAEMMINCK

It is an interesting perspective on these rules of precedence, but how do you see it regarding the development of diverging opinions, which are also emerging? Indeed, we saw it recently referring to a gambling case under the 226 panel. One of the panellists disagreed with another one and his opinion was published, therefore becoming part of the panel report.

JACQUES BOURGEOIS

I know how difficult it is for adjudicators in international settings to issue diverging opinions. I know how negative that can work out for the institution itself. But on the other hand, I am convinced that it is rather healthy, since the diverging opinion of today may become the majority opinion of tomorrow. And you know, precedent is very nice, but the law cannot stand still either. There must be development and, frankly, I am not shocked by that. I think it is probably a good development. I have been chairing panels and I know how it is; you try to come to some consensus and by doing that, you paper over differences. And the report becomes less clear. Whereas when you have a dissenting opinion, you know you have a majority and that says clearly what it thinks and a dissenting says *"I do not agree for that and that and that reason."* I do not think it is unhealthy.

CARL BAUDENBACHER

Now, forgive my ignorance. According to my state of knowledge under the WTO rules a panellist may dissent but the dissent remains secret. Is it not like that?

JACQUES BOURGEOIS

No.

CARL BAUDENBACHER

They openly dissent? In many cases?

JACQUES BOURGEOIS

In fact, in quite a few cases the dissent is buried because the panel tries to come to an unanimous view. But when that is not possible, which has not happend very often, you have the possibility for a member of the panel to say: *"I don't agree on that!"* Even in the Appellate Body you have the famous *Asbestos* case, which was a dissenting opinion.

CARL BAUDENBACHER

In the Luxembourg Courts, the only way to dissent is to give a speech or to write an article. I am not distancing myself from the court.

Any other questions?

Well obviously we are all a little bit exhausted. It does not have to do with the subject or your speech but it is Friday night and if there are no more questions it is just for me to say a few final words here.

I think we had two good days here in St. Gallen with four panels and four keynote speeches. I would like to thank from the bottom of my heart the speakers and the moderators who have come here and shared these two days with us. I would like to thank my team here, Philipp Speitler, Christian Mayer, Felipe Pérez Pose, Benjamin Rhyner, Frank Bremer and, in particular, I would like to mention Simon Planzer, who was in charge of preparing this conference, not only with regard to organisation, he was also heavily involved in the substance of the conference. He contacted the moderators and the speakers in order to make sure that there is a red line going through the panels and I think he has managed extremely well. I thank him very much for this. He will in the near future move to the United States in order to finalise his doctoral thesis but he will remain in contact with the University here.

I would also like to thank the participants who have come, in particular, obviously, Professor Kaufmann-Kohler, who was kind enough to bring her whole class, her post graduate programme class to St. Gallen.

During these two days, I have mentioned a few times, that the University of St. Gallen is planning to set up some kind of centre for international dispute resolution, first on the international level and eventually also on a national level.

I am confident that we will see each other again in the future, here in St. Gallen and with this I wish you all a safe trip home and a nice weekend.

JACQUES BOURGEOIS
Abusing the dominant position I am in, sitting at this table, in the name of all participants let me thank you and the people around you for having organised this. We were very impressed by the quality of the organisation, chapeau. And secondly, I want to take the opportunity to wish you luck and success with that new venture you are embarking on. Thank you very much, Carl.